D0783060

Administrative Law

Administrative Law

Rethinking Judicial Control of Bureaucracy

CHRISTOPHER F. EDLEY, JR.

YALE UNIVERSITY PRESS
NEW HAVEN AND LONDON

Published with assistance from the Mary Cady Tew Memorial Fund.

Designed by James J. Johnson and set in Baskerville type by The Composing Room of Michigan, Inc. Printed in the United States of America by BookCrafters, Inc. Chelsea, Michigan.

Library of Congress Cataloging-in-Publication Data
Edley, Christopher F., 1953–
    Administrative law : rethinking judicial control of bureaucracy/
    Christopher F. Edley, Jr.
        p. cm.
    Includes bibliographical references.
    ISBN 0-300-04079-2 (cloth)
            0-300-05253-7 (pbk.)
    1. Judicial review of administrative acts—United States.
    2. Administrative law—United States.   3. Political questions and judicial power—United States.   I. Title.
    KF5425.E35 1990
    342.73'06—dc20
    [347.3026]   89-22610
                                                                            CIP

A catalogue record for this book is available from the British Library.

The paper in this book meets the guidelines for permanence and durability of the Committee on Production Guidelines for Book Longevity of the Council on Library Resources.

10 9 8 7 6 5 4 3 2

For Tana

Contents

Preface

This is a critical exposition of how administrative law shapes governance, especially through judicial review of actions taken by executive branch agencies and departments. I examine the structure of the legal model for the administrative process and the structure of the doctrinal analysis of whether an outcome is "good."

My premise is that the quality of governance matters because private activity cannot by itself resolve our most vital problems. Today, important fashions in political ideology—not to mention the views of some rather successful politicians—emphasize private sector autonomy and nongovernmental or market solutions to difficulties of every description. This book rests on a broad rejection of that view. We have a modern administrative state that cannot be dismantled or denied. And it is not merely a minimalist state, with proportions irreducible in light of modern life's countless opportunities for savagery. It is, rather, the ambitious state constructed as an instrument for common purposes. (Flexible doctrines of constitutional and administrative law have served as midwives in the evolution.) Ex ante principled constraints on what may fall within the public domain have been replaced almost entirely by the constraints of practical concern for consensus, resources, and efficiency. We are pragmatists, not political philosophers.

All this suggests broad enterprise and governmental ambition, which I welcome, provided our wisdom is sufficient to sustain it. That, in turn, demands that we constantly repair and renovate the public sphere. Therein lies the motivation for my work.

Another premise of this book is that the law influences the process of policymaking and implementation and therefore partially determines whether we have good institutions, decent processes, and just outcomes—in short, sound governance. It may be that this claim is simply the vain wish of a lawyer to be "relevant" to the challenges of the day. My experiences, however, tell me otherwise.

All of this should be of cross-cultural if not practical interest to students of government who are unfamiliar with law, because the legal environment is hugely important to policymaking. Litigation is the most obvious context. But as schools of public policy and management now recognize in their curricula, public policymaking and advocacy must take account of the legal dimension in addition to economic, political, operational, and ethical concerns.

My second goal in this book is more professional. The underlying structure of doctrine suggested in chapters 1 through 4 explains how advocates and judges can *craft arguments* in an administrative law controversy. I do not attempt to eliminate confusion in the law. (It can't be done.) Instead, I try to clarify the *sources* of conceptual confusion. The same play of ideas that generates confusion also generates the terms of argument. Anyone, except perhaps a litigator, appreciates that the availability of many arguments is the hallmark of confusion.

I am not suggesting that my instruction on how to sow confusion will help salvage a losing cause. This is, rather, a demonstration of the old truth that a skillful attorney can search out the best argument on *either* side of a proposition. I want to demonstrate how, for better or worse, that can be done in administrative law.

I began this work almost as soon as I started teaching in 1981. I had served three years in the Carter administration, working on domestic policy issues in both the White House and the Department of Health, Education, and Welfare (now Health and Human Services). That experience gave me an unshakeable belief in the capacity of government—and of the individual bureaucrat—to make an important difference in the lives of thousands and even millions of people. Of course, while I may believe that expanding a child nutrition program or adding a safety requirement for nuclear reactors is important, others will dismiss these as trivial pursuits. Priests and philosophers, cynics and pollsters argue about what truly matters in life. I am content with muddling so long as it matters to the intended beneficiaries. And as we will see, administrative law is about nothing if not muddling.

My experience also left me supremely confident that those who inveigh against the federal government because it is more likely to do harm than good are woefully ill-informed at best and perhaps deceitfully furthering an unspoken agenda contrary to the public interest.

My enthusiasm about the capacity and potential net benefits of government was tempered by a keen sense that a great deal depends not just on personnel but on the processes by which ends and means are selected. I saw that the procedural and substantive discretion of executive decision makers is often vast and thinly constrained. Good results often seem more fortuitous than foreordained. Yet, I had also a determined optimism that we can do better. The quality and dedication of federal public servants holds enormous promise. The problem is how best to design our institutions to see that we keep that promise.

I chose administrative law as my principal field because I am interested in whether law does all it can and should to promote sound governance—by preventing mistakes and by increasing the likelihood that officials will pursue the commonweal efficiently and effectively. I was in for a rude surprise. The administrative law revealed in the cases and literature is far removed from a concern with improving the chances that government will make a positive difference. Bloodless abstractions of process abound. Even "fairness" is reduced to the elaboration of jousting rules for armed attorneys before hearing officers. Inasmuch as administrative law is about government, it seemed to me that the evident determination to divorce doctrine from the *ends* of government is an unlikely strategy for success, however defined. (I felt a little like a '60s liberal again—we came to law school and were dismayed that the curriculum had so little that was "relevant" to social justice.)

Law has not been nearly so imperialistic as its critics imagine. Administrative law has only an indirect and ambivalent relation to the quality of program outcomes. The primary focus is on procedure—*how* the officials made their decision rather than *what* they decided. Somewhere in the middle falls the examination of *why* they decided as they did, and courts are ambivalent about applying too tough a quality test here. There is, after all, no explicit constitutional, statutory, or common law mandate for courts to ensure that agencies make "good" policy. Indeed, many people assume erroneously that defining good policy is even more difficult than defining good art. Typically, judicial review of policy choices involves a loose inquiry into whether the official action is "arbitrary or capricious," which is a far cry from "wise." Imagine a museum curator accepting all proferred work that would not be generally regarded as ugly.

Just as law and policy analysis are not coextensive, so too is there considerable distance between law and public management. The legally permissible ways to organize a bureau or a decision making exercise are countless, whereas there will only be a few mechanisms that can reasonably claim to be the best known to administrative science and experience.

Thus, while the goal of producing sound governance is the right one, law is only a necessary but not sufficient component of the means. This book is a piece of broader analysis that must consider reform of the organization, personnel, and processes of both the executive and legislative branches. Ultimately, we must consider restructuring the fundamental public processes that shape government and perceptions of the public agenda, including election campaigns and the media. And the rise of ever stronger private centers of power will challenge our assumptions about the relation between government and business.

Having spent as long as I have on this work, I have too many people to thank. I will mention only a few. I feel especially entitled to record a tribute to my wife, Tana Pesso. This project has taken many more years, and many more weekends, than even the most loving relationship should have to bear. No mere words can express my gratitude, or the importance of her support.

Stephen Breyer made administrative law come alive for me as a student and continues to illuminate doctrine for all of us from the bench. Abram Chayes and Charles Nesson read the first, crude two hundred pages five years ago and persuaded me to throw it all away and start again. But for them, I'd be dead. Several colleagues, among them Philip Areeda, Richard Fallon, Terry Fisher, Louis Kaplow, Duncan Kennedy, Arthur von Mehren, David L. Shapiro, Richard Stewart, and Don Trautman, invested many hours carefully reading drafts and probing for weaknesses and worse. Responding to them made the work stronger and generated much of the conceptual filigree in the footnotes. Jerry Mashaw, William Pedersen, and Peter Strauss were especially helpful among colleagues elsewhere.

I am most deeply indebted, however, to Gerald Frug and Clark Byse. One helped stiffen my resolve to be bold; the other helped me be careful, lawyerly, and, I hope, persuasive. These words can only trivialize their contributions to my growth.

I have had many student assistants, but David Zensky, Richard Udell, and Michael Gillespie have been especially important. Kathleen Maloney has been my secretary throughout most of the project and could not possibly have been more helpful. I have periodic nightmares in which she leaves me because she doesn't like administrative law.

With all of these helpers, I should be able to blame someone else for the many errors that surely remain. Alas, I have no one to blame but myself.

I took a leave of absence for almost two years to serve as national issues director in the Dukakis campaign. The delay in readying this book for press means that a few recent cases receive briefer mention than I might like, but without injury to the analysis. More important, the campaign provided some confirmation of my thoughts on governance.

America faces great challenges: from budget and trade deficits to drugs, from secondary education to ozone depletion, from Pentagon waste to racial justice. I retired from the campaign seriously questioning whether our institutions and processes of governance are up to the tasks. The breadth and gravity of the challenges means that we must demand higher standards and higher quality from all of our institutions, including law, and particularly administrative law.

PART I

The Structure of Administrative Law

CHAPTER 1

---◆—●——

Introduction: The Discretion Problem and the Continuing Importance of Separation of Powers Theory

Even after decades of experience, we are only resigned to life with big government, not comfortable with it. The attempts through administrative law to ease this discomfort have a certain a dog-chasing-its-tail quality—courts use various legal doctrines to control bureaucratic discretion, but these doctrines afford judges themselves largely unconstrained discretion in displacing agency decisions. In this fundamental respect, administrative law embodies a strategy for dizzyingly limited success. How and why this is so, with speculation about more promising strategies, is my subject.

My method involves analysis of paradigms. I argue that many areas of doctrine attempt to scale judicial deference to agency action by appraising that action in terms of three paradigmatic methods of decision making, which I term the trichotomy: *adjudicatory fairness, politics,* and *"scientific" expertise.* Each paradigm is a rich picture of a mode of reasoning or problem solving. Doctrinal analysis can be understood largely as a process of distinguishing these paradigms and matching particular elements of an agency decision with an appropriate paradigm. A court then determines the appropriate degree of deference based on its assessment of (1) whether the agency employed the right method of decision making ("This is a question for scientific expertise; don't decide it by applying partisan ideology or interest group accommodation") and (2) whether the method was properly executed ("Do the expert's numbers add up; was the agency adjudicator neutral?").

Since neither courts nor commentators refer to this so-called trichotomy, my expositional burden is to show that both the overt categories and doctrinal reasoning rely implicitly and fundamentally on the dis-

3

tinctions of the trichotomy. That dependence is largely unstated, so the only possible demonstration is that the trichotomy accounts for observable patterns of doctrine and analysis. I believe it does.

What has this to do with the limited success of administrative law? To rely on the trichotomy of decision making methods is to reincarnate separation of powers formalism, which was interred in the 1930s as an unworkable means of controlling arbitrariness in modern governance. Similarly, a series of practical and conceptual failings make the trichotomy unworkable as a foundation for doctrine.

My argument is not an attack on the straw man propositions that separation of powers orthodoxy is feasible or that any given public policy question can be answered by one of three distinct decision making paradigms. My concern is that the *foundation* of doctrine does not reflect these old and obvious lessons and that serious problems result. A great deal of what is written by courts and commentators implicitly proceeds as if technical expertise, adjudicatory fairness, and politics can be usefully disentangled to determine institutional roles. Notwithstanding its complex subtlety, this method of legal reasoning belies the claim that we are modern, post-New Deal pragmatists, eschewing wooden separation of powers formalism.

1.1 The Project of Administrative Law

Historically, the separation of powers bulwarks were intended to minimize the risk of arbitrary government.[1] Beginning in the late nineteenth century, however, and culminating with the Supreme Court's acquiescence in the New Deal's suggestion of administrative hegemony, courts and commentators increasingly recognized that a less rigid design was necessary to accommodate modern exigencies. In response, a variety of modern judicial doctrines and attitudes developed. The elements of this new approach to constraining bureaucratic discretion were the regularization of administrative processes, the presumptive availability of judicial review, and judicial deference to administrative expertise—expertise being itself a rational and professional constraint against arbitrariness. These elements were eventually reflected in the Administrative Procedure Act of 1946 (APA).[2]

---

1. *See generally* M. Vile, Constitutionalism and the Separation of Powers (1967); W. Gwynn, The Meaning of Separation of Powers (1965); D. Epstein, The Political Theory of the Federalist (1984) (*see also* ch. 5).

2. The somewhat open-textured character of that statute leaves significant room for continuing judicial innovation. For "open-textured" terminology, *see, e.g.,* Ely, Democracy and Distrust chs. 1, 2 (1980) (discussion of interpretivism); Brest, *The Miscon-*

It is too late in the day to protest the interment of separation of powers formalism, at least in the context of multifunction administrative agencies.[3] But the underlying concern with arbitrary government remains with us, and the occasions for that concern multiply as unelected bureaucrats accumulate enormous policy and law-making discretion. The "administrative" state is now inevitable because of the ever-lengthening agenda of complex public policy problems and the institutional limitations of legislatures. The broad delegations of power to these agencies—make the workplace "reasonably" safe,[4] assist the disabled who cannot engage in "substantial gainful activity,"[5] award licenses and allocate scarce resources in accordance with the "public interest, convenience and necessity,"[6] and similar formulas—create administrative discretion far more sweeping in scope and pervasiveness than the familiar and inherent ministerial discretion of the executive.[7]

---

ceived Quest for the Original Understanding, 60 B.U.L. Rev. 204, 222–24 (1980). On judicial innovation, examples include "hard-look" review, the paper hearing requirement, principles of consistency, and much of the structure of scope of review doctrine. *See, e.g.,* Garland, *Deregulation and Judicial Review,* 98 Harv. L. Rev. 505, 525–37 (1985); Stewart, *Regulation, Innovation, and Administrative Law,* 69 Cal. L. Rev. 1259, 1275 (1981). While there have been great figures in the development of administrative law, no small crew of architects is as identifiable as for, say, the Uniform Commercial Code. The proper sense is evolution rather than invention. Administrative law's process of development, and its relative buoyancy with respect to statutory texts, make it much like constitutional law.

3. I say this despite the dissonant and anachronistic themes in such recent cases as INS v. Chadha, 462 U.S. 919 (1983) (unconstitutionality of one-house legislative veto); Bowsher v. Synar, 106 S. Ct. 3181 (1986) (balanced budget statute, Gramm-Rudman-Hollings, includes unconstitutional assignment of executive functions to the comptroller general, an agent of Congress); and Morrison v. Olson, 108 S. Ct. 2597 (1988) (Ethics in Government Act upheld despite role of judges in appointing independent counsel). *See also* Northern Pipeline Construction Co. v. Marathon Pipe Line Co., 458 U.S. 50 (1982) (Bankruptcy Act impermissibly granted essential article III powers to article I judges); Buckley v. Valeo, 424 U.S. 1 (1976) (Federal Election Commission had executive functions and thus could not include members appointed by Congress). It seems highly doubtful that these cases portend a reconsideration of the half-century consensus regarding legislative delegations to the executive, since they are concerned with overreaching or article III encroachment rather than abdication by the legislature.

4. Occupational Safety and Health Act, 29 U.S.C. § 651 *et seq.* (1985). *See also* Civil Aeronautics Act, 49 U.S.C. § 1301 *et seq.*; Federal Water Pollution Control Act, 33 U.S.C. § 1251 *et seq.*; Federal Insecticide, Fungicide and Rodenticide Act, 7 U.S.C. § 135 *et seq.*

5. Social Security Act (Disability Insurance), 42 U.S.C. §§ 423, 1382. *See also* 33 U.S.C. § 908 (Longshore and Harbor Workers' Compensation Act gradation of disability).

6. Federal Communications Act, 47 U.S.C. § 151 *et seq. See also* various Interstate Commerce Commission statutes, codified at 49 U.S.C. § 10101 *et seq.*

7. Indeed, mandamus doctrine contrasts "ministerial" responsibilities with the discretionary functions of the modern administrator. Thus mandamus will usually issue

6   THE STRUCTURE OF ADMINISTRATIVE LAW

As if to codify sweeping discretion, many statutes include a catchall delegation of substantive rule making authority to the agency, instructing the administrator to make any rules "necessary" or "appropriate" to accomplish the purposes of the statute.[8] The sense that this discretion must be controlled continues to animate administrative law.[9] As the bureaucracy's role has grown, so have the risks and benefits associated with official action. The stakes involved in judicial intervention to check malfeasance and misfeasance have also grown, so that familiar postures of judicial review now assume unfamiliar dimensions. In a way, discontent with judicial activism and the powerful social role of unelected judges is only a derivative problem, the principal one being awesome agency power.

The Rule of Law[10] approach to constraining discretion, which

---

only where a claimant has established "that he has a clear and certain right and that the duties of the respondent are ministerial, plainly defined and peremptory." Martins Ferry Hosp. Ass'n v. NLRB, 654 F.2d 455, 456 (6th Cir. 1981) (citations omitted). *See also* Marbury v. Madison, 1 Cranch 137, 16 (1803); Dunlap v. Black, 128 U.S. 40, 48 (1888); Carpet, Linoleum, and Resilient Tile Layers, Local Union 419 v. Brown, 656 F.2d 564, 566 (10th Cir. 1981). Given its emphasis on "ministerial duties," mandamus becomes a near-useless tool to police the discretion delegated to agency decision makers. *See generally* K. Davis, 4 Administrative Law Treatise §§ 23.8–14 at 156–82 (2d ed., 1979) [hereinafter, Treatise]. "*Mandamus does not fit modern needs.*" *Id.* at 156 (emphasis in original). Of course the "ministerial discretion" test is itself an artifact of trichotomy-based separation of powers reasoning. Since I am ultimately skeptical of such efforts to identify inherently "expert," "judicial," or "political" questions, I also doubt that a category of "ministerial discretion" can be given a definition robust enough to withstand the critique in chs. 3 and 4.

8. *See, e.g.,* 47 U.S.C. § 154(i) ("The Commission may perform any and all acts, make such rules and regulations, and issue such orders not inconsistent with this chapter, as may be necessary in the execution of its functions") (FCC); 49 U.S.C. § 1324(a) ("The Board is empowered to make . . . such general or special rules, regulations, and procedure . . . as it shall deem necessary to carry out the provisions of, and to exercise and perform its powers and duties under, this chapter") (CAB).

9. *See generally* Stewart, *The Reformation of American Administrative Law,* 88 Harv. L. Rev. 1667, 1669–1711 (1975); Garland, *supra* n. 2 at 586–91; Davis, 2 Treatise §§ 8:1–12 at 157–213 (1979). One might argue that the objective of administrative law is to improve the quality of public sector decision making in some broader fashion, not limited to checking arbitrariness. This has been the thrust behind the work of Professor Colin Diver. *See* Diver, *Statutory Interpretation in the Administrative State,* 133 U. Pa. L. Rev. 54a, 568–73 (1985) (use of utilitarian calculus to analyze the problem of scope of review of agency statutory interpretations); Diver, *Policymaking Paradigms in Administrative Law,* 95 Harv. L. Rev. 393, 428–34 (1981) (choice between incremental and synoptic/comprehensive rationality modes of policymaking); Diver, *The Optimal Precision of Administrative Rules,* 93 Yale L.J. 65, 71–79 (1983) (utilitarian analysis to ascertain the proper mix of transparency, accessibility, and congruence in formulating regulations).

10. I use this term, with reservations, to capture the cluster of attributes and norms familiar to lawyers; I do not mean to implicate the broader literature in political theory. See sec. 2.1.

achieved maturity with the enactment of the APA, entails a strong role for subconstitutional judicial review. Such oversight by the unelected branch, however, is itself problematic in terms of those same values that cause us to fear official abuses in the first place. Thus, the continuing dilemma for administrative law has been that the effort to impose Rule of Law constraints on agencies must contend with the critique that judicial review simply replaces the *objectionable discretion of the administrator* with the *objectionable discretion of the judge.*

There is a hopeful response to that critique. We have a continuing project of constructing and reforming a matrix of legal doctrines and attitudes intended to discipline the judges. That project reflects our powerful commitment to legal formality.[11] If it is successful, the discipline judges themselves impose on administrators will not be simply another form of arbitrariness. But that is a rather large "if."

1.2 The Plan of This Work

In chapter 2, I describe the trichotomy of decision making paradigms—adjudicatory fairness, scientific expertise, and politics. The content and interrelationship of these paradigms is suggested in figure 1 and discussed in detail in sections 2.1 and 2.2. I provide several examples of how doctrines attempt to scale judicial deference through implicit reliance on asserted distinctions between the paradigms. In particular, sections 2.3 and 2.4 examine the two most pervasive doctrinal themes in the field, the fact-law-policy distinction and the rule making–adjudication comparison.

In chapters 2 and 3, I argue that judicial reliance on this separation of powers-based trichotomy has two crucial failings. As a *descriptive* matter, it propagates seriously inaccurate visions of political and bureaucratic processes—the realists' critique of separation of powers formalism applies to the reincarnation as well. As a *conceptual* matter, doctrines are confused because they depend on the trichotomy's unworkable effort to define and distinguish decision making paradigms as though separable when they are necessarily interrelated. Justice Holmes observed that "[t]he great ordinances of the constitution do not establish and divide fields of black and white . . . . [H]owever we may disguise it by veiling words, we do not and can not carry out the distinction between legislative and executive action with mathematical precision, and divide the branches into watertight compartments."[12]

---

11. *See* Kennedy, *Legal Formality,* 2 J. Leg. Stud. 351 (1973).
12. Springer v. Philippine Is., 277 U.S. 189, 209–11 (1928) (Holmes, J., dissenting). *See also* FTC v. Rubberoid Co., 343 U.S. 470, 487–88 (1952) (Jackson, J., dissenting)

Moreover, each paradigm, or method, has associated with it both positive and negative attributes, which can be selectively emphasized in judicial decisions in rather unpredictable ways. Chapter 4 contains my central example of these failings: doctrines shaping the scope of judicial review of administrative action depend explicitly on the touchstone distinctions between law, fact, and policy—reflecting perfectly an underlying reliance on the trichotomy's unsustainable distinctions between adjudicatory fairness, expertise, and politics.

If the trichotomy has these flaws, why have I bothered with it, especially at such length? First, because it seems to have subtle and pervasive influence on the law notwithstanding the problems. Second, these descriptive and conceptual failings of the trichotomy account for our ability to make plausibly persuasive yet contradictory arguments when deciding how deferential a court should be toward any particular agency choice—making the fundamental judicial task in administrative law controversies rather indeterminate. These difficulties are not limited to some small, peripheral set of "hard cases." Indeed, in only a few cases do the trichotomy's distinctions seem logically compelling as a definitive means of scaling judicial deference. Beyond a familiar criticism of failed legal science, however, my purpose is to explain the mechanism of the failure. Along the way, I suggest that reliance on the trichotomy may cause mistaken diagnoses of, and poor doctrinal responses to, such "deep" problems of governance as incompetence, systemic agency delay or inaction, and political bias.

The point is not that the trichotomy is *the* way to understand doctrine. That claim would be fatuous. But as an analytical construct implicit in the cases and, as I demonstrate in chapter 5, in the commentary, it does account for some serious problems of clarity and consistency, and for their intractability. From a professional perspective, the trichotomy and its failings offer both an accounting of and a formula for generating varieties of legal arguments in any particular context.

This analysis also offers clues about observable fashions in doctrine. Paramount among them is today's general impoverishing of judicial review. As if in cynical frustration with an unsuccessful matrix of fine doctrinal categories, courts seem increasingly attracted to either of two extremes in scope of review: unstructured "reasonableness" or flat nonreviewability. In sum, the traditional administrative law approach,

---

("Administrative agencies have been called quasi-legislative, quasi-executive, and quasi-judicial, as the occasion required, in order to validate their functions within the separation of powers scheme of the Constitution. The mere retreat to the qualifying quasi is implicit with the confession that all recognized classifications have broken down, and 'quasi' is a smooth cover which we draw over our confusion").

suffused with a separation of powers ethos, seems destined to fail as an effective discipliner of agency and judicial discretion.

I do not gainsay "[t]he possibility . . . of much good being brought out of an ill-designed and limping machinery of measures," as Llewellyn put it.[13] The questions before us, however, are whether we delude ourselves concerning the effectiveness of present instruments and whether better ones can be fashioned. I therefore end with a tentative effort to be constructive. Chapter 6 presents some marginal reforms under the rubric of "harder-look review" intended to address deficiencies of trichotomy-based approaches to the project of constraining discretion. My central example is the ineffectual ambivalence of present doctrine toward politics. To what extent may political preferences enter into agency decision making, and with what consequences for the scope of judicial review? Case law is a muddle with respect to when political forces are acknowledged, and whether they are treated as legitimate or as danger signals. I also briefly sketch harder-look approaches to scientific uncertainty and to the design of procedures.

These tentative proposals accept the conventional project and its conceptual apparatus: the objective of controlling discretion, the underlying reliance of doctrine on the trichotomy of decision making paradigms, and the implicit trichotomy-based approach to shaping and distinguishing institutional roles. It follows, from the failings detailed in chapters 3 and 4, that these marginal reforms cannot fully escape the problems of obscure judicial discretion and doctrinal uncertainty.

In chapter 7, therefore, I sketch a more speculative approach to judicial review of administrative action that does not scale judicial deference by relying on the trichotomy to categorize problems and roles. That approach takes as its point of departure the familiar partnership metaphor for the agency-court relationship[14] but adds a distinctly hierarchical dimension. Rather than the traditional antidiscretion project, *a reconceived administrative law* could stress judicial review to ensure the integration of all three paradigms of decision making and to correct *directly* departures from an evolving set of norms for effective political and bureaucratic processes. This contrasts with the very indirect and often doubtful link between the antidiscretion project and the promo-

13. K. Llewellyn, The Bramble Bush 9 (2d ed. 1951).

14. *See* United States v. Morgan, 307 U.S. 183, 191 (1939); Greater Boston Television Corp. v. FCC, 444 F.2d 841, 851 (D.C. Cir. 1970), *cert. denied*, 403 U.S. 923 (1971); Gardner, *Federal Courts and Agencies: An Audit of the Partnership Books*, 75 Colum. L. Rev. 800 (1975).

tion of sound governance—sound governance somehow, if at all, defined.[15] With judicial oversight no longer focused on control, the measure of administrative law's shortcomings would be unnecessarily bad public sector performance rather than unchanneled discretion. The evolution of legal doctrine would be a search for norms or principles of sound governance rather than norms about institutional roles. I do not deny, in chapter 7, the difficulty of constructing such norms. But I suggest that re-formed administrative law and redefined courts might play substantial, complementary roles in that construction.

1.3 Alternative Projects for Administrative Law

Because much of my analysis emphasizes the attempt to control discretion, it is worth pausing to sketch two competing characterizations of the project of administrative law. First, there is the Vulgar-Realist perspective. Perhaps, argue frustrated cynics, the project is to devise practiced forms of incantation which masquerade as legal analysis but in truth merely rationalize the desired result. In this image of judicial review, the judge forms a subjective and intuitive judgment about whether the agency's choice was sound and then writes an elaborate opinion that only ends up where the judge started. This charge of result-oriented legal analysis is a special favorite of students who are understandably troubled by the great variations in judicial deference and interventionism in the cases and by the plethora of verbal formulas for the scope of judicial review. This naive cynicism is encouraged by the frankness (if not defeatism) of some prominent commentators and judges, who confess that judges are poorly cabined by administrative law doctrines. But the deeper question is this: *Where does the reviewing judge get that preliminary intuitive judgment about the soundness of the agency's choice?*

To some fraction of cases the judge may bring a substantive predisposition, such as trade union animus, so strong and unshakeable that nothing more can usefully be said. This is bad and, we hope, rare. But if the lay judge is susceptible to persuasion, then we are left to wonder how she will form a view about substantive and procedural

15. My argument entails an attack on the implicit assumption that a remedial order directed at political or governmental processes is more intrusive, hence less desirable, than a narrow order apparently tailored to correct an individual policy result. I am thus led to criticize not only the emerging pattern of broader judicial deference to agency conclusions of law and policy but also the central teaching of the Supreme Court's problematic decision in Vermont Yankee Nuclear Power Corp. v. NRDC, 435 U.S. 519 (1978). *See* sec. 7.2.3.

soundness. Doctrine—such as general deference to policy choices or the requirement of "adequate consideration" for significant regulatory alternatives—plays an important role if it plausibly captures in general terms those qualities of an agency choice or decision making process that tend to persuade a lay reviewer that the result is sound.

We can therefore restate the Vulgar-Realist project in less pejorative terms: administrative law is the search for heuristic codifications of intuitive judging. This is plausible only if the doctrines either accurately describe the reviewer's intuition or powerfully shape it. The latter occurs when judges accept the doctrines as a compelling normative model of how agency and judicial decision making ought to occur. In sum, we can reconcile the Rule of Law machinations with the result-oriented characterization *if* doctrine is a fair heuristic for sound results. Then legal analysis is not for *rationalizing* a poor intuition but is instead an indirect means of reasoning (or persuading) about sound governance.

This suggests the third characterization of administrative law's project: the pursuit of sound governance. I will explore this theme, including the problem of definition, at length in chapter 7. I must stress from the beginning, however, that the content of present doctrine and the processes of judicial review are hugely influenced by (1) our conventional presumption that the unobjectionable end of sound governance is very well served *indirectly* by the effort to constrain discretion and (2) our pervasive use of separation-of-powers based distinctions among law, science, and politics to conceive and accomplish those constraints. As will become clear in part I, whatever interest judges may have in promoting sound governance, the structure of administrative law regularly gets in the way of clear thinking and forthright explanation. The sound governance project of administrative law is at present inchoate and aspirational. It must be ill served, I will argue, by our unchallenged emphasis on traditional assumptions regarding discretion and institutional roles.

In essence, my closing argument will be that our preoccupation with the discretion-focused conception of administrative law neither serves us well in practice nor is a fruitful focus for theory. Making the break with separation of powers formalism, attempted but not fully achieved fifty years ago, would free us to use law and legal institutions as tools for the direct promotion of sound governance.

Limitations of scope in this work are indicated at various points along the way. Two deserve immediate mention. First, although there is no logically essential connection between separation of powers and my critique of the trichotomy, I offer the connection both as a plausible genealogical explanation for the content of the trichotomy's paradigms and because I see the implicit use of the trichotomy as a device for distinguishing institutional roles, as required by the separation of powers principle. Nevertheless, I do not explore what implications my critique might have for the broader range of separation of powers issues in, for example, constitutional law, federal jurisdiction, or equitable remedies in public law litigation.

A second, more important limitation is my omission (because I have not done it) of empirical work concerning the interaction of doctrine and bureaucratic decision making. I have strong instincts concerning these issues based on my own service in government and my years as a student of public administration and policy, but rigorous study would be useful. For example, the literature contains no thorough description of the varieties of ex parte communications engaged in by agencies and their significance. Nor are there rich descriptions of the means by which uninformed agency heads do and should endeavor to evaluate the recommendations and actions of "expert" subordinates. Nor are there detailed explorations of the interaction of political ideology and scientific expertise in program administration. As to these and many other issues, though I have been content to proceed in this work on the basis of limited experience, empirical study would give the reader and me more confidence in the prescriptions of chapters 6 and 7.

CHAPTER 2

An Expository Essay: The Trichotomy of Politics, Science, and Adjudicatory Fairness

In this chapter, I describe a trichotomy of paradigmatic decision making methods and demonstrate that, in a variety of doctrines, the paradigms and their interrelationships are the underlying framework both for calibrating the degree of judicial deference to be accorded agency action and for normative prescriptions about administrative procedure. Of course, administrative law is largely about institutional roles. The wrinkle added here is that the framework for analyzing roles in particular cases emphasizes three separable models of cognition or problem solving, together with a rich set of positive and negative normative associations; the obvious correspondence between these models and the three branches of government reflects the continuing potency of the separation of powers ethos.

An Organizational Note: At the risk of some diffuseness and multiplication of themes, I will use many examples to demonstrate the trichotomy's pervasiveness in doctrinal analysis. Readers may forgo some of this by reviewing my description of the paradigms in section 2.1 and then turning to chapters 3 and 4, on difficulties arising from reliance on the trichotomy.

2.1 Distinctive, Separated Methods of Decision Making

At their core, the three paradigms are inspired by crude images of the judge, the faceless technocratic expert, and the pol, whose reasoning processes and domains are considered distinguishable:

The *adjudicatory fairness* paradigm is constructed of several principles or techniques that, though naturally associated with the judiciary, are also familiar in other settings. Elements of the paradigm include: consistency over time (stare decisis), consistency across situations (treating like cases alike), reasoned elaboration, neutrality of the decision maker, and rich notions of hearing and confrontation.[1] An important facet of this methodology—logically entailed by the emphasis on consistency—is the discerning of any extant rules (statutory, constitutional, common law) thought to control a particular dispute. Decision making by an appellate court is close to a prototype; a bench trial is also close, although the fact-finding process, as distinguished from the law-applying process, implicates a second paradigm, expertise.

The paradigm of *science*, or expertise, is in my terms a generalization of the familiar images of a scientist bent over laboratory bench, an accountant dissecting a balance sheet, or a mechanic servicing a helicopter. The methods of reasoning and choice I group here are characterized by claims of rationality, objectivity, deductive reasoning, and specialized knowledge. The "process values" emphasized are the scientific method and managerial efficiency rather than broad participation or public disclosure. Facts and perhaps investigation are often critical. The decision maker is depersonalized—we learn and remember the author of an important court opinion and perhaps even the principal sponsors of noteworthy legislation, but we rarely note or remember the author of a regulation, even important and controversial ones. I also include within this paradigm the putatively nondiscretionary rationality of routine bureaucratic administration, such as the seizure of banned varieties of imported produce by Department of Agriculture border inspectors. Examples of actions that are more conventionally scientific in character include the Federal Aviation Administration's certification that the engineering of a new airplane is airworthy or the identification of hazardous substances for environmental or occupational health regulation.

Finally, the *politics* paradigm encompasses interest accommodation or balancing but also the extreme or limiting case in which dissenting interests are underweighted to permit a straightforward application of

1. Hearing and confrontation are important to the fairness methodology because they communicate and create respect for the affected party or interest; to the extent that fairness is the exclusive concern (it never is), hearing and confrontation rights would be important even if they promised no instrumental improvement in the accuracy of the outcome. *See* Michelman, *Formal and Associational Aims in Procedural Due Process,* 18 Nomos 126–28 (1977); L. Tribe, American Constitutional Law §§ 10.7–9, 10–19 at 501–22, 559, 563 (1978) (hereinafter Tribe, Treatise). Hearing and confrontation may be important for instrumental reasons if one focuses on the importance of assuring that there be an informed decision whether or not the decision maker is an appropriately expert or scientific agent, as I discuss immediately below.

the decision maker's personal values, partisan preferences, or ideology. I explore these several senses of politics in chapter 6 (especially 6.2) and argue that they are strongly married conceptually by the method of reasoning employed by the decision maker. However, our perception of political decision making, more than the other methodologies, is influenced by the level of aggregation under analysis. In a collective or institutional setting, politics looks like pluralism, democracy, or electoral competition. As practiced by an individual, operation of the same forces can appear to be the dispensing of favors, log-rolling, or allegiance to constituents' interests. (There is, as we shall see, good and bad in both characterizations.) It is usually appropriate to include discretionary or policy choices within this paradigm, because the factor distinguishing such actions from instances of science-like expertness and adjudicatory fairness is the central importance of highly subjective social values and the balancing of various interest group concerns.

These asserted differences between paradigms, summarized in figure 1 (chapter 2, below), serve three broad functions: doctrinal, sociological, and normative.

First, courts use the trichotomy to define and police differences in institutional role and domain, usually in the context of determining what mix of deference and intervention is called for in judicial review of agency action. Two striking instances of this doctrinal function of the trichotomy are the fact-law-policy distinction, which is the basis for scope of review doctrine, and the rule making–adjudication distinction, which makes countless appearances throughout the field. I consider these areas in brief examples in sections 2.3 and 2.4 below and in more detail throughout chapters 3 and 4.

This distinguishing and policing of institutional roles by reference to modes of decision making is possible because each corner of the trichotomy—each ideal type—is often explicated *as though* sharply differentiable from, or even incompatible with, the others; examples follow soon.[2] Even when a court acknowledges the connectedness of the paradigms (or the murkiness of doctrinal categories), that candor is irrelevant to the logic of the opinion. The bite in the legal analysis, pushing a fuzzy case toward one resolution rather than another, is provided by the paradigmatic distinctions and normative attributes of the trichotomy. Aspects of an agency's action that are appropriately resolved by political or expert methods of decision are owed deference by the courts because those decision making methods are presump-

2. As to why these paradigms assume such importance, *see* ch. 7. *See* Michelman, *Traces of Self-Government*, 100 Harv. L. Rev. 4 (1986).

tively alien to courts.[3] On the other hand, matters a court deems appropriate for adjudicatory fairness methods are likelier game for intervention.[4] Thus, for example, the standard for disqualifying an administrator for impermissible bias is more lenient in quasi-legislative action than in quasi-adjudication. Relatedly, the court will police the agency's choice of decision making method (whether or not it involves adjudicatory fairness) in order to enforce the court's sense of appropriate match between problems and methods.[5] This matching and polic-

3. For example, dissenting in Industrial Union Dep't v. American Petroleum Inst. *(Benzene)*, Justice Marshall, joined by Justices Brennan, White, and Blackmun, thought the Court should defer to the judgment of the secretary of labor in promulgating an Occupational Safety and Health Administration (OSHA) standard on both counts: "[T]he issues often reach a high level of complexity. In such circumstances, the courts are required to immerse themselves in matters to which they are unaccustomed by work of experience . . . . [And] when the question involves determination of the acceptable level of risk, the ultimate decision must necessarily be based on considerations of policy as well as empirically verifiable facts." 448 U.S. 607, 705–6 (1980). The D.C. Circuit had reached a similar conclusion six years earlier in Industrial Union Dep't v. Hodgson (asbestos), 499 F.2d 467, 474–76 (D.C. Cir. 1974) (court must defer to legislative policy judgments that "cannot be anchored secretly and solely in demonstrable fact"). *See also* Mourning v. Family Publications Serv., Inc., 411 U.S. 356, 369–75 (1973) (court should defer to Federal Reserve Board when reviewing regulations promulgated under Truth and Lending Act due to board's broad authority to employ expertise in preventing evasion of the act's purposes); NLRB v. Hearst Publications, Inc., 322 U.S. 111, 130–31 (1944) (board's knowledge and experience as to varying circumstances of employment relations in different industries calls for limited judicial review when such expertise is brought to bear in applying broad statutory terms to specific proceedings); Center for Auto Safety v. Peck, 751 F.2d 1336, 1342 (D.C. Cir. 1985) (extreme deference called for when agency engages in cost-benefit analysis since it "epitomize[s] the types of decisions that are most appropriately entrusted to the expertise of an agency"); United Steelworkers of Am. v. Marshall, 647 F.2d 1189, 12–6–07 (D.C. Cir. 1980) (courts do not have the "competence of jurisdiction to resolve technical controversies in the record, or, where the rule requires setting a numerical standard, to second-guess an agency decision that falls within a zone of reasonableness") (citations omitted).

4. *Compare* Association of Nat'l Advertisers, Inc. v. FTC, 627 F.2d 1151 (D.C. Cir. 1979), *cert. denied*, 447 U.S. 921 (1980) (disqualification in hybrid rule making only for "irrevocably closed mind"), *with* Gilligan, Will & Co. v. SEC, 267 F.2d 461, 469 (2d Cir.), *cert. denied*, 361 U.S. 896 (1959) (test in formal adjudication is whether "a disinterested observer may conclude that [the administrator] has in some measure adjudged the facts as well as the law of a particular case in advance of hearing it."); Cinderella Career and Finishing Schools, Inc. v. FTC, 425 F.2d 583 (D.C. Cir. 1970). *Compare also* United States v. Florida E. Coast Ry., 410 U.S. 224 (1973) (courts should be very reluctant to interpret the APA to require rule making on a formal record when precise "hearing on the record" verbal requirement of the APA is not met by the organic statute), *with* Seacoast Anti-Pollution League v. Costle, 572 F.2d 872 (1st Cir.), *cert. denied*, 439 U.S. 824 (1978) (courts should readily require formal record in adjudications even when the organic statute refers only to "public hearing" rather than hearing "on the record"; Florida E. Coast Ry. distinguished). *See* sec. 2.2.

5. *See, e.g.*, Hornsby v. Allen, 326 F.2d 605 (5th Cir. 1964) (Tuttle, C.J.) (awarding of liquor licenses inappropriate for political decision making; due process requires ad-

ing rests on propositions about comparative institutional competence, about desirable institutional roles, and about the problem-solving qualities called for by the tasks of government.

Although this matching is rooted in separation of powers formalism, there is today little orthodoxy about what an agency can or cannot be empowered to do. That, after all, is what the New Deal victory in structural constitutional theory was all about.[6] Instead, our formalism emerges subtly (but no less unsatisfactorily) by conceiving of administrative acts as things to be parsed into subproblems we can match naturally with distinct decision making methods, in light of some particulars about the circumstances, such as statutory context. The modern subtlety is that the resulting pigeonhole does not determine some rigid assignment to an institution (this kind of subproblem must be decided over there, and that type decided here). Instead, the categories correspond to the applicable verbal formula for the balance of judicial deference and intervention—in many contexts termed the scope of judicial review. All this reformulates the role-definition game, so that it is now played using considerable indirection and a seeming fineness of context-specific calculation. Such sorting processes are central to almost every aspect of administrative law.

Second, the trichotomy legitimates the power of countermajoritarian judicial review.[7] I can take only brief note of the layers upon layers of complexity in the concept and processes of legitimation. For

---

judicatory fairness paradigm); D.C. Fed'n of Civic Ass'ns v. Volpe, 459 F.2d 1231 (D.C. Cir. 1971), *cert. denied*, 405 U.S. 1030 (1972) (informal agency process to fund bridge construction is appropriate for bureaucratic expertise but not for the political paradigm—apparent role of congressman's pressure was impermissible); Heckler v. Campbell, 461 U.S. 458 (1983) (existence of suitable jobs for any given combination of age, education, experience, and residual functional capacity is appropriate for expert resolution through general rule making rather than determination through individual disability adjudications—hearing rights displaced by application of expertise).

6. *See generally* Stewart, *The Reformation of American Law*, 88 Harv. L. Rev. 1667 (1975) (hereinafter cited as *Reformation*) (discussion of New Deal); S. Breyer & R. Stewart, Administrative Law 29–32 (1985); Tribe, Treatise § 5.7 at 284–91. We continue to be held, however, in the loose grip of a separation of powers-based orthodoxy concerning the judicial role. For example: "[P]olicy arguments are more properly addressed to legislators or administrators, not to judges . . . . The responsibilities for assessing the wisdom of such policy choices and resolving the struggle between competing views of the public interest are not judicial ones." Chevron USA, Inc. v. NRDC, 467 U.S. 837, 864, 866 (1984).

7. On legitimation, *see generally* E. Genovese, Roll Jordan, Roll 585–665 (1974); M. Weber, Economy and Society (1978); *and* J. Habermas, Legitimation Crisis (1975), *and* Problems in Communication and the Evolution of Society (1979). *See also* Hyde, *The Concept of Legitimation in the Sociology of Law*, 1983 Wis. L. Rev. 379; Jackson Lears, *The Concept of Cultural Hegemony: Problems and Possibilities*, 90 Am. Hist. Rev. 567 (1985).

my purposes, I am concerned with the general public's regard for the institutions of government, and particularly the assertions of power and the perceived bases for its exercise. But I am also concerned with the perceptions and attitudes of politico-legal elites, both because they are the principal players in the daily drama of governance and because the roles and actions of public institutions are understood by the general public largely through the filter of portrayals and assessments by elites.

The separation of powers-based faith that government can be controlled through compartmentalization gives the trichotomy tremendous derivative legitimacy, because applying its paradigmatic distinctions means reinforcing the assigned, safe roles. The courts' explications of these roles often have a certain self-denying quality, in that the analyses typically emphasize (at least rhetorically) the limited realm appropriate for judgelike decision methods, even as they assertively cabin agency discretion within some judicially fashioned role conception. The self-denying method seems to me more than a means of making judges feel comfortable in some personal sense. The judge's comfort may flow from satisfying a genuinely felt need to reconcile judicial actions with a role conception that emphasizes restraint, or the comfort may be a more cynical one of having "packaged" actions to satisfy an elite audience concerned with such restraint. The crucial point is that such self-denying postures need not result in failure to exercise judicial power (even putting aside the point that either inaction or action can amount to a decision for all practical purposes). The all-time best example is *Marbury v. Madison,* asserting the power to declare acts of Congress unconstitutional in order to find itself without jurisdiction to provide controversial relief.[8]

A good example of self-denying, agency-rewarding judicial rhetoric can be found in *Chenery I:*

> [In remanding] we do not intend to enter the province that belongs to the [commission] . . . . All we ask of the [commission] is to give clear indication that it has exercised the discretion with which Congress has empowered it. This is to affirm most em-

---

8. 5 U.S. (1 Cranch) 137 (1803). Judge Posner has recently offered an elaborate argument for a brand of activist judicial "self-restraint" that would take the form of an active program to reduce the power of the judiciary vis-à-vis state and local governments. R. Posner, The Federal Courts: Crisis and Reform ch. 7 (1985). Professor Bickel praised the "passive virtues" of certain modes of constitutional adjudication precisely because they were at once powerfully effective and nonthreatening to the Court's legitimacy. A. Bickel, The Least Dangerous Branch ch. 5 (1962).

phatically the authority of the [commission] . . . . In finding
that the Commission's order cannot be sustained, we are not
imposing any trammels on its powers . . . we are not suggesting
that the commission must justify its exercise of administrative
discretion in any particular manner . . . we merely hold that an
administrative order cannot be upheld unless the grounds upon
which the agency acted . . . where those upon which its action
can be sustained.[9]

In sum, the distinctions flowing from the trichotomy are used vari-
ously to explain why it is safe or desirable for courts to have countermajoritarian powers, why those powers must be exercised with delicacy,
but also why certain decisions by another branch deserve a deference
that limits or trumps such antidemocratic judicial power altogether.[10]
    Third, the trichotomy offers a perspective with which to develop
normative principles about good government, in both procedural and
substantive senses. We tend to portray and analyze the successes and
failures of government in terms of the quality of adjudicatory fairness,
expertise, and political decision making. Indeed, to a considerable extent the prescriptions generated by theories of public management and
policy analysis share with legal doctrine an implicit reliance on separation of powers formalism. To the extent that this shared framework is
conceptually flawed, instability and confusion will be generated in both
doctrine and prescriptive commentary (see sections 5.3 and 6.2).

9. SEC v. Chenery Corp., 318 U.S. 80, 94–95 (1943). Over 40 years later, the
principle remains the same. In vacating and remanding the FAA's denial of certain
exemption petitions for failure to apply consistent criteria, the court refused either to
enter a final order or to prescribe the correct decisional criteria: "It is for the FAA,
however, and not this court to determine the circumstances in which exemptions should
be granted or denied . . . we will not prescribe particular criteria for the FAA to apply;
the FAA retains broad discretion to determine whether the public interest will be best
served by granting or denying petitions. We must insist, however, that the FAA act upon
the petition in a consistent manner and that any deviation from prior rulings be carefully
reasoned and fully explained." Airmark Corp. v. FAA, 758 F.2d 685, 695 (D.C. Cir.
1985).
10. *See, e.g.,* Bickel, *supra* n. 8 (contrasting the character of political decision making in the legislature and the executive with the decision making methods appropriate
for unelected judges and emphasizing the risk to judicial legitimacy created by certain
forms of judicial activism); D. Horowitz, The Courts and Social Policy (1977) (contrasting
the expertise of agencies and political institutions with the limited expertise of courts).
These and many other writings assume implicitly that politics and expertise are distinguishable from what judges can or should do. This is a compound proposition involving
the distinctiveness of decision making methods and the natural assignment of those
methodologies to particular institutions. I question both.

2.2 The Normative Foundation of the Trichotomy

There is more to this than simply an abstract preference for a set of familiar institutional roles. Invoking the attributes associated with each paradigm helps justify and reinforce reliance on the trichotomy. These attributes have normative content; they are why the trichotomy seems sensible and useful. (A technical point: I use "norms" and "attributes" almost interchangeably. More precisely, each paradigm is associated with certain attributes, and we evaluate each attribute as positive or negative in a normative or prescriptive sense. In appraising a putative instance of a paradigm, we often want to insist on the presence of a certain attribute—a positive attribute if we are making a good point about the paradigm and a negative attribute if we are not. In this sense, the list of attributes is also a normative prescription for what the paradigm should be. Again, one may cite the prescription with approval or regret. See figure 1.)

Thus, *politics* is associated negatively with subjective, willful decision making[11] and tyranny of the majority.[12] In this image, politics is dangerous because it is unfettered by concern for the positive norms of adjudicatory fairness (especially consistency and neutrality) and rationality (especially objectivity, empiricism, and depersonalization)[13] characteristic of the trichotomy's two alternative modes of decision making—politics simply does not strive to reflect those values. So, trial-type agency action can be challenged because the intrusion of politics damages at least the appearance of adjudicatory fairness, and informal

11. *See* ILGWU v. Donovan, 722 F.2d 795 (D.C. Cir. 1984) (the Home Knitters Case) (Edwards, J.) (the electorate may have endorsed a new administration, but the executive branch must nevertheless convince Congress to relegislate in accord with such philosophy). *See also* Weeks, *Legislative Power versus Delegated Legislative Power*, 25 Geo. L.J. 314, 316 (1937) (the legislature exercises "will" in lawmaking, whereas the bureaucracy exercises "intelligence"); H. Laski, Democracy in Crisis 81 (1933) ("It is not a paradox to argue that a legislative assembly is unfitted by its very nature directly to legislate," *cited* in Jaffe, Treatise at 36; Parker, *The Past of Constitutional Theory—and Its Future*, 42 Ohio St. L.J. 223, 225 (1981) [early process theorists saw constitutional order "as transcending—disembodied from—the clash of wills and movement of passions that characterize day-to-day political life. It may then be enforced *on* political life, to discipline those wills and passions"]).

12. Parker, *supra* n. 11 at 227 (noting that the post-1930s process theorists recognized "the constant danger that majorities might oppress minorities and ride over fundamental rights of individuals"). Indeed, Parker associates politics in America today most often with tyranny by a *minority*. *Id.* at 240–57. *See also* J. Choper, Judicial Review and the National Political Process 65 (1980).

13. By depersonalization I mean that the scientific method is supposed to produce results independent of who the scientist is, while exactly the opposite is true of political choice.

FIGURE 1. Trichotomy of Decision Making Methods, Institutions, and Norms

Method	adjudicatory fairness; reasoned elaboration	science and technical expertise	politics; interest accommodation
Positive Norms	Rule of Law; consistency; precedent; neutrality; reasoned elaboration	objective; rational; verifiable; efficient	democratic; responsive; participatory; accountable
Negative Norms	politically unaccountable; proceduralistic; stylized and arcane; conservative and past-focused	impersonal; alienating; inaccessible to laymen; mechanical	subjective; willful; tyranny by the majority; non-scientific
Primary Situs	judiciary	executive	legislature

agency action can be challenged because the intrusion of politics calls into question the dominance of expertise. For example, from a case concerning political interference, by senators at a committee hearing, with a formal Federal Trade Commission (FTC) adjudication:

> To subject an administrator to a searching examination as to how and why he reached his decision in a case still pending before him, and to criticize him for reaching the "wrong" decision, as the Senate subcommittee did in this case, sacrifices the appearance of impartiality—the sine qua non of American judicial justice—in favor of some short-run notions regarding the Congressional intent underlying [implementation of a statute], unfettered administration of which was committed by Congress to the Federal Trade Commission. It may be argued that such officials as members of the [FTC] are sufficiently aware of the realities of governmental, not to say "political," life as to be able to withstand such questioning as we have outlined here. However, this court is not so "sophisticated" that it can shrug off such a procedural due process claim merely because the officials involved should be able to discount what is said and to disregard the force of intrusion into adjudicatory process.[14]

14. Pillsbury Co. v. FTC, 354 F.2d 952 (5th Cir. 1966) (Tuttle, C.J.).

And from a case concerning political pressure to approve a bridge project: "Taken as a whole, the defects in the Secretary's determinations . . . lend color to the plaintiffs' contention that the repeated public threats by a few Congressional voices did have an impact on the Secretary's decisions. . . . We hold only that the Secretary must reach his decision strictly on the merits and in the manner prescribed by statute, without reference to irrelevant or extraneous considerations."[15]

The politics paradigm is also associated, however, with the normatively positive attributes of democratic or representative choice and electoral accountability—curatives for deficiencies in the other decisional methods. Thus, judges and commentators frequently urge agencies to use the public notice and democratic interaction of rule making to develop broad policy rather than the narrowly participatory procedures of formal adjudication, because participation by outsiders leavens agency expertise, prevents insularity, and even promotes expertness. For example, in a dissenting opinion, Justice Douglas protested the reliance by the National Labor Relations Board (NLRB) on formal adjudication to formulate general policy.

> The rule-making procedure performs important functions. It gives notice to an entire segment of society of those controls or regimentation that is forthcoming. It gives an opportunity for persons affected to be heard. . . . This is a healthy process that helps make a society viable. The multiplication of agencies and their growing power make them more and more remote from the people affected by what they do and make more likely the arbitrary exercise of their powers. . . . Agencies discover that they are not always the repositories of ultimate wisdom; they learn from the suggestions of outsiders and often benefit from that advice.[16]

Bureaucratic expertise is associated with the positive attributes of science and rationality,[17] but it is also criticized as alienated, lacking in

15. D.C. Fed'n of Civic Ass'ns v. Volpe, 459 F.2d 1231, 1245, 1248 (D.C. Cir. 1971). *See also* the opinion in the lower court by Judge Sirica, 316 F. Supp. 754, 762–68 (D.D.C. 1970).

16. NLRB v. Wyman-Gordon, 394 U.S. 759, 777–78 (1969) (Douglas, J., dissenting) (citing H. Friendly, The Federal Administrative Agencies 45 [1962], and Shapiro, *The Choice of Rulemaking or Adjudication in the Development of Administrative Policy*, 78 Harv. L. Rev. 921, 946–47 [1965]). I return to the rule making–adjudication distinction in detail in sec. 2.4.

17. The following passage by a leading commentator reveals the interplay of positive and negative attributes of politics and expertise: "Under the original understanding of rulemaking, there was no prohibition of *ex parte* contacts, and public disclosure was not

compassion, and self-absorbed[18]—as in some harsh caricature of automatons in a welfare office or the Internal Revenue Service. As Judge Wyzanski put it, "One of the dangers of extraordinary expertise is that those who have it may fall into the grooves created by their own expertness."[19] Similarly, Justice White has written that "[e]xpert discretion is the lifeblood of the administration process, but unless we make the requirements for administrative action strict and demanding, *expertise,* the strength of modern government, can become a monster which rules with no practical limits on its discretion."[20]

Finally, we can fill out this sketch of how the trichotomy's normative associations are deployed by considering the adjudicatory fairness paradigm in a bit more detail. The key positive associations with that paradigm are Rule of Law themes: neutrality, adherence to existing rules or precedent, reasoned elaboration, and dignitary rights of participation and confrontation. The nature of the matter may lead a court to require that the agency stress these attributes rather than those associated with politics or science.[21] And, even if the agency has identified the appropriate methodological pigeonhole, misexecution will in-

---

required. This result was a natural outgrowth of the legislative model of administration. Legislators are not discouraged from communicating informally with affected citizens about proposed measures. On the contrary, informal communications are affirmatively encouraged because they facilitate the process of obtaining information about the nature and extent of constituent desires. Similarly, administrators deciding on proposed rules were not to be precluded from consulting informally with all interested parties. [*Citing* Scalia, *Vermont Yankee: The APA, the D.C. Circuit, and the Supreme Court,* 1979 Sup. Ct. Rev. 345.] Such consultation would hardly impair the legitimacy of the administrative process; indeed it would promote it.

"Recent judicial efforts to require disclosure of *ex parte* contacts stem from an altogether different conception of administration. That conception departs from the original legislative understanding based on constituent pressure in favor of a more deliberative role for administrators. The new conception reflects a belief that the pluralist understanding of administration threatens to subvert statutory goals by reflecting private whim."

18. *See* Frug, *The Ideology of Bureaucracy in American Law,* 97 Harv. L. Rev. 1276 (1984); Sunstein, *Interest Groups in American Public Law,* 38 Stan. L. Rev. 29, 63 (1985).

19. United States v. United Shoe Machine Corp., 110 F. Supp. 295, 346 (D. Mass. 1953).

20. Burlington Truck Lines, Inc. v. United States, 371 U.S. 156, 167 (1962) (emphasis in original).

21. In Hornsby v. Allen, 326 F.2d 605 (5th Cir. 1964), the court interpreted due process to require that liquor licensing decisions by the Atlanta aldermanic council be made pursuant to standards rather than through a system of political "courtesy" between members. That system, however, would seem to be a rational way of allowing District Nine representatives to implement the wishes of their constituents concerning the number, placement, and character of licensees. In addition to holding that license applicants must know the standards and the basis for decision, the court was insisting that the dominant decision making methodology be adjudicatory fairness rather than politics.

vite court intervention measured by reference to attributes and norms of the fairness paradigm. An example of norm-based pigeonholing is the judicial use of fairness attributes to justify constraining ex parte contacts in some informal rule making, although the business at hand is quasi-legislative and presumably suitable for expert and political decision making methods. A touchstone in these cases has been the characterization of the agency's task as the resolution of "conflicting private claims to a valuable privilege,"[22] with the largely unargued assumption that such controversies have a special claim to adjudicatory fairness decision making. An example of norm-based intervention to correct agency misexecution is the reasoning in cases requiring disclosure in the record of otherwise secret agency science or the otherwise inaccessible substantiation for officially noticed facts. For example: "To allow an agency to play hunt the peanut with technical information, hiding or disguising the information that it employs, is to condone a practice in which the agency treats what should be a genuine interchange as mere bureaucratic sport. An agency commits serious procedural error when it fails to reveal portions of the technical basis for a proposed rule in time to allow for meaningful commentary."[23]

Those "secret science" and related opinions refer to the instrumental value of disclosure as a means of testing the correctness of scientific conclusions.[24] Two aspects of this reasoning are noteworthy. First, we

22. Sangamon Valley Television Corp. v. United States, 269 F.2d 221, 224 (D.C. Cir. 1959). *See also* Home Box Office, Inc. v. FCC, 567 F.2d 9, 51–59 (D.C. Cir. 1977), *cert. denied*, 434 U.S. 829, *rehearing denied*, 434 U.S. 988 (1977); Action for Children's Television v. FCC, 564 F.2d 458, 474–78 (D.C. Cir. 1977); Sierra Club v. Costle, 657 F.2d 298, 396–404 (D.C. Cir. 1981). *See generally* Note, *Ex Parte Communication during Informal Rulemaking*, 14 Colum. J.L. & Soc. Prob. 269 (1979).

23. Connecticut Light and Power Co. v. Nuclear Reg. Comm'n, 673 F.2d 525, 530–31 (D.C. Cir. 1982). *See also* United States v. Nova Scotia Food Prod., 568 F.2d 240, 251–52 (2d Cir. 1977); Portland Cement Ass'n v. Ruckelshaus, 486 F.2d 375, 392–95 (D.C. Cir. 1973); Sierra Club v. Costle, *supra* n. 22 at 397 n. 484.

A similar rationale underlies cases in which agency action is invalidated for violating the exclusivity of the record by use of staff reports that contain new information. *See generally* United Steelworkers of America v. Marshall, 647 F.2d 1189, 1216–20 (D.C. Cir. 1980); Seacoast Anti-Pollution League v. Costle, 572 F.2d 872, 880–82 (1st Cir. 1978).

On official notice, *see, e.g.*, Ohio Bell Tel. Co. v. Public Util. Comm'n, 301 U.S. 292 (1937); United States v. Abilene & S. Ry., 265 U.S. 274, 288–90 (1924); Air Prod. and Chem., Inc. v. FERC, 650 F.2d 687, 695–700 (5th Cir. 1981); Wiscope S.A. v. CFTC, 604 F.2d 764, 768 (2d Cir. 1979); United States Lines, Inc. v. FMC, 584 F.2d 519, 533–36 (D.C. Cir. 1978). Pre-APA holdings were based on procedural due process or general principles of administrative common law. Ohio Bell, 301 U.S. at 300–306. The problem in federal law is now addressed by the disclosure requirement in § 556(e) of the APA, and by those strictures of hard-look review applicable to informal agency action.

24. *See, e.g., Abilene & S. Ry., supra* n. 23 at 290 ("The course pursued denied to the Commission the benefit of that full presentation of the contentions of the parties which is often essential to the exercise of sound judgment").

believe that disclosure and adversarial testing have such instrumental value only because we believe that *adjudicatory fairness* methods (especially adversarial confrontation) are valuable for discovering truth. Yet, neither science nor politics customarily proceeds through adversarial hearings as such; disclosure is a distinctly ancillary and—in many political contexts—often destructive theme. So the peculiar forms of revelation and testing imposed by courts and procedural statutes are, conceptually, the imposition of the adjudicatory fairness paradigm on other methods of decision making. The impositions may, of course, be helpful. (Indeed, melding the paradigms is a promising alternative to the implicit emphasis in much doctrine on *separating* and *distinguishing* the paradigms [see section 7.2.1].) The conceptual difficulty arises in disciplining judicial choices of when to make such impositions, as I explore in chapter 4. Second, opinions in disclosure cases invoke adjudicatory fairness concerns wholly *apart* from instrumental arguments, including the importance of simply letting the affected parties know what is going on and of facilitating judicial review designed to hold the agency within the bounds of (1) its delegation and (2) the evidence.[25]

For example, in *United States Lines,* the court stated that reliance on extra-record facts "precludes effective judicial review." The court wrote:

> [W]e simply cannot determine whether the final agency decision reflects the rational outcome of the agency's consideration of all relevant factors when we have no idea what factors or what data were in fact considered . . . . Even where the reviewing court is informed of the specific information upon which reliance was placed, a barrier to effective judicial review remains: the absence of any adversarial comment among the parties . . . . [Disclosure requirements] provide a means by which a reviewing court, called upon to determine whether agency action is arbitrary capricious, can secure needed guidance in the performance of this function from both the parties and the agency.[26]

In the conceptually related area of agency reliance on facts received via ex parte contacts, the court in *Home Box Office* argued that "agency

25. *See, e.g., Air Prod. and Chem., Inc., supra* n. 23 at 699 ("We believe that § 556(e) of the APA, as well as our sense of fair play, requires the FERC to afford the producers here an opportunity to respond to the evidence relied upon"); *Ohio Bell, supra* n. 23 at 303 (Justice Cardozo asking, "[h]ow was it possible for the appellate court to review the law and the facts and intelligently decide that the findings of the Commission were supported by the evidence when the evidence that it approved was unknown and unknowable?").

26. *Supra* n. 23 at 533–34.

secrecy stands between us and fulfillment of our obligation . . . to test the actions of the Commission for arbitrariness or *inconsistency with delegated authority*" (emphasis added).[27]

In addition to doctrines controlling ex parte communications and secret agency science, other good examples of judicial appeal to positive adjudicatory fairness attributes when faced with unsatisfactory use of the other paradigms include: requirements of agency consistency (especially when expertise or politics may have produced problematic results);[28] the *Arizona Grocery* principle that "an agency must follow its own rules," notwithstanding its expert or political inclination otherwise;[29] and requirements that agencies formulate prospective standards limiting their discretion, notwithstanding the bureaucracy's claims for expert or political flexibility.[30]

But adjudication and formality also have negative associations which often lead courts to avoid imposing such decision making meth-

---

27. *Supra* n. 22 at 54.

28. *See* Airmark Corp. v. FAA, 758 F.2d 685, 691–92 (D.C. Cir. 1985) (agency cannot "treat like cases differently" and "must provide a reasoned explanation for any failure to adhere to its own precedents" [citations omitted]); United States v. Diapulse Corp. of Am., 748 F.2d 56, 62 (2d Cir. 1984) (permanent injunction disallowing manufacture and sale of device was properly modified by district court where FDA had approved sale of similar device; FDA must "apply its scientific conclusions evenhandedly and it [may] not grant to one person the right to do that which it denies to another similarly situated" [citation omitted]); Local 777, Democratic Organizing Comm. v. NLRB, 608 F.2d 862, 872 (D.C. Cir. 1978) ("The Board cannot, despite its broad discretion, arbitrarily treat similar situations dissimilarly").

29. Arizona Grocery Co. v. Atchison, T. & S. F. Ry., 284 U.S. 370 (1932) (during adjudication agency may not ignore former pronouncement promulgated through "quasi-legislative" proceedings). *See also* Kelly v. Railroad Retirement Bd., 625 F.2d 486, 491–92 (3d Cir. 1980) ("It is a well established proposition that an agency is bound by its regulations . . . . Failure to comply with regulations is a fatal flaw to administrative action"); Nader v. Bork, 366 F. Supp. 104, 107–8 (D.D.C. 1973) (attorney general bound by self-imposed regulations restricting power to fire Watergate special prosecutor). *See generally* Gellhorn, Byse, & Strauss, Administrative Law 395–98 (7th ed. 1979). *But see* American Farm Lines v. Black Ball Freight Serv., 397 U.S. 532, 539 (1970) (noting general principle that agencies and courts alike have discretion to modify procedural rules when justice so requires).

30. Morton v. Ruiz, 415 U.S. 199, 232 (1974) ("No matter how rational or consistent with congressional intent a particular decision might be, the determination of eligibility [in a general relief program for Indians] cannot be made on an ad hoc basis by the dispenser of the funds"); United States v. Markgraf, 736 F.2d 1179 (1984) (secretary must develop standards for administration of discretionary farm debt relief program); Matzke v. Block, 732 F.2d 799 (1984) (secretary must develop standards for administration of discretionary farm debt relief program, and standards must be developed through rule making rather than adjudication); Holmes v. New York City Hous. Auth., 398 F.2d 262 (2d Cir. 1968) (selection among applicants for public housing must be made in accordance with ascertainable standards).

ods. Although the principal drawback is usually cost, courts have also cited lack of accountability and the danger of stultifying, dehumanizing proceduralism.[31] Thus, pretermination hearings in public employment have sometimes been denied in part because the due process balancing[32] must consider the interference with flow of relationships in the workplace.[33] Chief Justice Burger dissented in *Goldberg v. Kelly* in part because he saw the potential for adjudicatory formality to become a costly and disruptive interference with the operation of the welfare system.[34] And in *United States v. Florida East Coast Railway,* the Supreme

31. The Supreme Court has acknowledged that proceduralism can carry with it non-cost adverse consequences. In Goldberg v. Kelly, the Court would not impose "any procedural requirements beyond those demanded by rudimentary due process," partly in recognition that welfare officials and recipients are "used to dealing with one another informally." 397 U.S. 254, 267 (1970). In Mathews v. Eldridge, the Court held that in the Social Security disability context pretermination evidentiary hearings were not required: "The ultimate balance involves a determination as to when, under our constitutional system, judicial type procedures must be imposed upon administrative action to assure fairness . . . . The judicial model of an evidentiary hearing is neither a required, *nor even the most effective* method of decisionmaking in all circumstances . . . . [T]he procedures [must] be tailored, in light of the decision to be made, to "the capacities and circumstances of those to be heard" . . . . In assessing what process is due in this case, substantial weight must be given to the good-faith judgments of the individuals charged by Congress with the administration of social welfare programs that the procedures they have provided assure fair consideration of the entitlement claims of individuals" (emphasis supplied) 424 U.S. 319, 348–49 (1976). Such respect for administrators is in marked contrast to the distrust implicit in the *Goldberg* decision and is a general endorsement of informality for most circumstances. *See also,* in that regard, *Florida E. Coast Ry., supra* n. 4.

32. *See, e.g.,* Cleveland Bd. of Educ. v. Loudermill, 470 U.S. 532, 542–47 (1985); Board of Regents v. Roth, 408 U.S. 564 (1972). *See generally* Tribe, Treatise at §§ 10.9–13, 514–39 (1978); Gellhorn, Byse, & Strauss, *supra* n. 29 at 420–515 (7th ed. 1979).

33. This consideration is reflected in two of the five opinions in Arnett v. Kennedy, 416 U.S. 134 (1974). Five justices agreed, under different theories, that a nonprobationary federal employee was not constitutionally entitled to a pretermination trial-type hearing. For example, Justice Powell, concurring in part, argued that "[p]rolonged retention of a disruptive or otherwise unsatisfactory employee can adversely affect discipline and morale in the workplace, foster disharmony and ultimately impair the efficiency of an office or agency." *Id.* at 168. And Justice White, concurring in part and dissenting in part, was short and to the point: mandating that the government retain employees pending a pretermination hearing could lead to "an uproar at the workplace." *Id.* at 194. Although in Loudermill, *supra* n. 32, the Court held that oral or written notice and some opportunity to present the employee's side of the case were required, it did make clear that anything more "would intrude to an unwarranted extent on the government's interest in quickly removing an unsatisfactory employee."

34. 397 U.S. 254, 283–84 (1970) (Burger, C.J., dissenting) ("[W]e ought to hold the heavy hand of constitutional adjudication and allow evolutionary processes at various administrative levels to develop, given their flexibility to make adjustments in procedure . . . . [N]ew layers of procedural protection may become an intolerable drain on the very funds earmarked for food, clothing, and other living essentials."). Mathews v.

Court established that courts will be reluctant to impose formal hearing requirements on agency rule makings, even in a proceeding that results in imposition of a fee or charge; Justice Rehnquist's majority opinion emphasized the negative associations with formality, which he portrayed as conflicting with the positive norms associated with the expert and political decision making employed in quasi-legislative agency action.[35]

These contrasting associations are often more than mere negations of each other. Their disjointness gives us a considerable richness in the matrix of normatively negative and positive attributes. For example, we like politics for reasons beyond the fact that it avoids some problems of the competing alternatives—such as the unaccountable, nonparticipatory character of science and adjudication. Even for a given paradigm and particular setting, moreover, its negative associations are not simply denials of the positive. If they were, a net assessment of positive and negative would at least be simple to frame as an empirical question (for example, "Were the 'key' groups involved or weren't they?"). But the dangers of politics are not merely that the interest accommodation may fail to be adequately participatory but also the independent problems that careful weighing of competing public concerns may fail to withstand the temptations of willfulness and majority tyranny.

As I will explore later, this duality of disjoint negative and positive associations promotes confusion and ambiguity in the application of doctrines, because the advocate and the judge may plausibly choose to

---

Eldridge later added as a governmental interest to be weighed in the calculation of what process is due, "the fiscal and administrative burdens that the additional or substitute procedural requirement would entail." 424 U.S. at 335. In a related context, Schweiker v. Gray Panthers sustained a regulation authorizing the deeming-as-"available" of spousal income for purposes of medicaid eligibility in part by noting that "[t]o require individual determinations . . . would mandate costly factfinding procedures that would dissipate resources that could have been spent on the needy." 453 U.S. 34, 48 (1981).

35. 410 U.S. 224, 240–46 (1973). See also Vermont Yankee Nuclear Power Corp. v. NRDC, 435 U.S. 519 (1978) (reviewing courts may not impose procedures in informal rule making beyond those specified in § 553 of the APA or the organic statute); United Airlines, Inc. v. CAB, 766 F.2d 1107 (7th Cir. 1985) (sustaining agency's refusal to provide evidentiary hearing in an informal antitrust rule making, even though the resulting rule was based on adjudicative facts); National Classification Comm. v. United States, 765 F.2d 1146 (D.C. Cir. 1985) (sustaining agency's refusal to address reply comments and provide a hearing in informal rule making used to simplify classifications in advance of rate making); Wisconsin Gas Co. v. FERC, 770 F.2d 1144, 1167 (D.C. Cir. 1985) (expressly rejecting its earlier decision in Mobil Oil Co. v. FPC, 483 F.2d 1238 [1973], which held that "some sort of adversary, adjudicative-type procedures" might be required in ratemaking if informed rule making proved insufficient and holding that the commission need not provide a hearing in a rule making which invalidated certain minimum billing practices).

focus on either side of the duality, and doctrine, as discussed in section 4.2, does a very poor job of instructing how we should choose.

My purpose in this chapter thus far has been to reveal the implicit role of three decision making paradigms, including their associated norms, in the structure of doctrinal categories and reasoning. I now offer a more detailed demonstration by focusing on what seem to me the two most pervasive doctrinal themes in the entire field: the effort to distinguish law, fact, and policy and the contrast between rule making and adjudication.

2.3 Distinguishing Law, Fact, and Policy

Like "reasonableness" in tort law and "intent" in criminal law, no doctrinal device is more pervasive in administrative law than line drawing based on distinctions between conclusions of law, findings of fact, and discretionary choices of policy. This is the framework for choosing the scope for judicial review of administrative action. Indeed, since scope of review is the principal vehicle for scaling judicial deference, the fact-law-policy categories are a force, implicitly or explicitly, almost everywhere one turns. With respect to scope of review, this line drawing both reflects and is accomplished through the separation-of-powers-based trichotomy. A description and critique of the trichotomy, therefore, must have wide-ranging significance.

I defer until chapter 4 (sections 4.3–4) an analysis of the difficulties in distinguishing fact, law, and policy and of calibrating the corresponding verbal formulas that specify degrees of judicial deference.[36]

The general contours of doctrine provide for increasingly deferential scope of review as one moves from questions of law, to questions of fact, to questions of policy as to which there are express statutory delegations of discretion to the agency. As the following paragraphs suggest, a justification for this scaling of deference flows neatly from the trichotomy: courts generally view conclusions of law, factual findings, and discretionary policy choices as the products, respectively, of adjudicatory fairness, scientific (expert), and political methods. For

36. To all of the following "explanations" for the scope of judicial review one can add that the statute and/or the precedents in a given circumstance require it. This positivist observation begs the question in at least two respects. First, it is worth examining why the law is what it is, both to understand it more deeply and to judge whether it should be changed. Second, it is simply not true that the various commands of statute and precedent are unambiguous: were it so, treatises and casebooks would devote a dozen pages to judicial review rather than hundreds.

each area of case law I present the central principle, together with its important qualification.

Questions of Law: It is often stated that courts should decide questions of law independently or with only modest weight accorded the view of the implementing agency: "[S]ince the only or principal dispute relates to the meaning of [a] statutory term, the controversy must ultimately be resolved, not on the basis of matters within the special competence of the [agency], but by judicial application of the canons of statutory construction."[37]

The scope of review is relatively independent because courts are the ultimate authority on what the law is, per *Marbury v. Madison,* and that is in turn because law finding is (by definition) more appropriate for the characteristically court-centered adjudicatory fairness methods than it is for expert or political decision making. As James Landis put it: "I return thus to the issue of 'law' as being the dividing line of judicial review—as bounding the province of that 'supremacy of law' that is still our boast. Its content, insofar as it relates to judicial review of administrative action, reaches back to the issue of expertness. *Our desire to have courts determine questions of law is related to a belief in their possession of expertness with regard to such questions. It is from that very desire that the nature of questions of law emerges. For, in the last analysis, they seem to me to be those questions that lawyers are equipped to decide.*[38] The common law development of this principle was codified in the APA's command that "the reviewing court shall decide all relevant questions of law."[39]

37. Barlow v. Collins, 297 U.S. 159, 166 (1970). *See also* Volkswagenwerk v. FMC, 390 U.S. 261, 272 (1968) (though the agency's interpretation is entitled to some deference, "[t]he courts are the final authorities on issues of statutory construction"); Petrov Fisheries, Inc. v. ICC, 727 F.2d 542, 545 (5th Cir. 1984) ("[W]hen the court is presented with issues of pure statutory construction, we accord little deference to the agency's decision, since the agency possesses no special skill in statutory interpretation"). The qualification to this rule—it might indeed be considered a conflicting line of authority—concerns the occasions when the statute arguably delegates lawmaking powers to the agency, in which case an indeterminately more deferential scope of review is applicable. *See* Chevron USA, Inc. v. NRDC, 467 U.S. 837, 844 (1984) ("Considerable weight should be accorded to an executive department's construction of a statutory scheme it is entrusted to administer").

38. J. Landis, The Administrative Process 152, 153 (1938) (emphasis in original). In a sense, therefore, the classic allocation of roles uses a metaprinciple of expertness: to each branch according to its form of expertness. My "science" label helps to distinguish the paradigmatic decision making method from this more general sense of expertness as specialization.

39. APA § 706. *See* K. Davis, 5 Administrative Law Treatise § 29.1 (1984) (hereinafter Davis, Treatise) (§ 706 "basically a codification of law created by courts"); Stern, *Review of Findings of Administrators, Judges and Juries: A Comparative Analysis,* 58 Harv. L. Rev. 70 (1944); Brown, *Fact and Law in Judicial Review,* 56 Harv. L. Rev. 899 (1943); St.

Codification, however, has by no means led either to stability in scope of review doctrine over time or to certainty in application. An *important qualification* is that where Congress has delegated lawmaking powers to the agency, the court must defer if the agency's conclusion of law is reasonable and within the scope of the delegation. But this qualification poses further questions of law concerning the scope of the delegation, and so the nature of the court's more independent posture is again key.[40] As Landis indicated, the principle that questions of law are ultimately for the courts flows directly from our sense that the decision making called for entails precisely that adjudicatory fairness methodology at which we consider courts and lawyers expert.[41] Indeed, the general principle and its qualification are superficially reconcilable insofar as one can distinguish law finding from lawmaking and can view the statutory delegation of lawmaking powers as the legislature's judgment that *the question is less appropriate for the court's decision making paradigm.* Thus, both the rule scaling judicial deference in questions of law *and* the rule's qualification directly reflect asserted distinctions in decision making paradigms.

Questions of Fact: Agency findings of fact are to receive somewhat more deference, and they will be accepted by the reviewing court if not "arbitrary or capricious" and, in on-the-record formal proceedings, if supported by "substantial evidence in the record as a whole."[42] Such judicial deference on questions of fact is consistent with the most natural reading of the statutory instructions on scope of review,[43] although there is ample room for interpretation. The more general rationale,

---

Joseph Stock Yards Co. v. United States, 298 U.S. 38, 84 (1936) (Brandeis, J., concurring) ("Supremacy of law demands that there be opportunity to have some court decide whether an erroneous rule of law was applied . . . . But supremacy of law does not demand that the correctness of every finding of fact to which the rule of law is to be applied shall be subject to review by a court").

40. *See, e.g.,* Chevron USA, Inc. v. NRDC, 467 U.S. 837, 843–44 (1984) (holding that Congress had left a gap in the statute and, absent legislative expression to the contrary, that the gap was for the agency to fill); Schweiker v. Gray Panthers, 453 U.S. 34, 43–44 (1981) (same, with express congressional delegation of rule making powers).

41. Landis, *supra* n. 38; *see also* H. Hart & A. Sacks, Materials on the Legal Process 1345–47 (tent. ed. 1958).

42. APA § 706(2)(A),(E). *See* Universal Camera Corp. v. NLRB, 340 U.S. 474 (1944) (attempt by Frankfurter, J., to define substantial evidence standard); Citizens to Preserve Overton Park, Inc. v. Volpe, 401 U.S. 402 (1971) (attempt by Marshall, J., to define arbitrary and capricious standard); Abbott Laboratories, Inc. v. Gardner, 387 U.S. 136, 143 (1967) (substantial evidence test is less deferential). As for the problematic character of fine distinctions in scope of review, see sec. 4.4.

43. The APA provisions are largely a jumble of verbal formulas taken from early judicial opinions. As students quickly discover, the overlapping and vague clauses defy tidy application. See section 4.3.1, below.

however, is that such determinations are the product either of scientific or expert inquiry and judgment or of an assimilation of detailed and varied evidence or experience, for which the agency is particularly well qualified by virtue of its bureaucratic organization of resources.[44] As four judges put it in their dissent in the D.C. Circuit's en banc *Ethyl* case, a technically complex review of the Environmental Protection Agency's (EPA) auto lead emissions rule: "Properly understood, our role is not to review directly the evidence, but to review the agency's treatment and analysis of the evidence. Of course, in so doing we will defer to the agency's expertise and experience in the subject matter of the decision."[45]

The *important qualification* to the general rule of deference to expert factual determinations is, in a sense, the whole rule: the agency's finding is "conclusive," as the statutes often say, only if it passes muster under the "arbitrary or capricious" test and, for formal proceedings, the "substantial evidence" test.[46] Thus the flat statement of deference, respectful of the agency's distinctive decision making paradigm of expertise, is limited by a conventional task of adjudicatory fairness: the assaying of evidence for sufficiency using an abstract criterion framed by law rather than expertise. (An expert would ask whether the agency fact-finder actually got it right.) The court reviewing an agency fact-finding is often analogized to an appellate court's review of trial court findings, where deference is appropriate because of the appellate tribunal's distance from the testimonial process.[47] The analogy has important deficiencies, and the case for deference to administration is

44. Landis, *supra* n. 38, 23–28 (expertness is both the critical characteristic *of* administrative agencies *and* the pressing need that engendered them); C. Koch, 1 Administrative Law and Practice § 1.26 (1985) [hereinafter cited as Koch, Treatise] ("When searching for government solutions to specific problems it is often found that *a specialized information gatherer* and expert decisionmaker is necessary. Often this condition leads to the decision to constitute an agency" [emphasis added]).

45. Ethyl Corp. v. EPA, 541 F.2d 1, 100 (D.C. Cir. 1976) (en banc) (Wilkie, J., dissenting). Following this mild statement of the applicable standard, however, the dissent conducted a probing review of the agency action, concluding, "We find no plausible showing that lead in the air makes a 'significant contribution to elevated blood lead levels' in either the general population or among children. . . . We judges may be, as we are sometimes reminded, without scientific background or access to expertise, but we think this brand of administrative agency action [in the present case] should be readily apparent—and equally abhorrent—to any appellate judge. To detect and set aside agency action based on such shoddy foundations, not to engage in rival scientific calculations or substitute judgment, is the function of a reviewing court." *Id.* at 111.

46. Absent specific scope of review provisions in the organic statute, the scope of review is specified by the APA, § 706. See sec. 4.4.

47. *See also* Hart & Sacks, *supra* n. 41 at 373–85 (relation of fact-law dichotomy to judge and jury roles). I do not believe, however, that lay judgment is an accepted basis for deference to administrative fact-finding. At a stretch, of course, even lay judgment is a form of expertise, if one defines the problem so that common experience and popular

somewhat different because the reasoning and fact-finding process employed by the agency is apt to be less familiar to the reviewing court than are the processes of judicial trials, especially when (as is usual) the agency proceeding was other than a trial-type hearing. My bottom line, however, is that both the general doctrine of deference to agency fact-finding and the qualification of that deference in terms of a test of sufficiency of evidence can be understood to express an underlying sense that fact determinations by the agency entail a reasoning method distinct from the comparative advantage of the generalist judiciary, especially in its appellate mode.

There are, of course, other reasons why the legislature and court might adopt judicial deference to agency fact-finding: efficiency, the substantive orientation of the agency toward the issues or program constituents, and legislators' general distrust of courts. The argument that agency fact-finding is more economical or efficient is an appeal to managerial efficiency, which I include within the paradigm of expertise and science. The other arguments—and several I have not mentioned—are not so much responses to the specific problem of allocating fact-finding as they are general considerations bearing on the court-agency relationship. On close inspection, the driving concerns are well accounted for by the trichotomy of politics, science, and adjudicatory fairness. Thus, preference for an agency with a "tilt" reflects a judgment that the political paradigm is an appropriate method of decision making; distrust of judges may reflect misgivings about either their expertise or their accountability to popular will.

Discretion and Policy: Within the traditional formulation, agency policy choices (including so-called mixed questions applying law to facts, discussed next) are accorded still more deference and, whether made through rule making or adjudication, are approved if they have a "reasonable basis in the law."[48] Policy choices are entitled to even more

---

preferences are germane. *Compare* the Jacksonian argument for generalist judges at sec. 7.3.3.(c).

48. *See, e.g.,* Gray v. Powell, 314 U.S. 402, 412–13 (1941) (where an expert determination "has been left to an administrative body, this delegation will be respected and the administrative conclusion left untouched"); NLRB v. Hearst Publications, Inc. 322 U.S. 111, 131 (1941) ("[T]he board's determination . . . is to be accepted if it has 'warrant in the record' and a reasonable basis in law"); *see also* FCC v. WNCN Listeners Guild, 450 U.S. 582, 594 (1981) (Commission's general rule making authority permits it to implement its view of public interest standard if based on permissible factors and reasonable); Ford Motor Credit Co. v. Milhollin, 444 U.S. 555, 565–69 (1980) (staff opinions of Federal Reserve Board interpreting the "highly technical" Truth in Lending Act should be dispositive "unless demonstrably irrational"); Industrial Union Dep't v. Hodgson, 499 F.2d 467, 474–76 (D.C. Cir. 1974) (review of facts and review of legislative policy judgments are conceptually distinct tasks; court must be flexible and sensitive in reviewing latter); *see generally* Jaffe, Treatise 575–88; Davis, 5 Treatise §§ 29:10–13 (1984).

deference than findings of fact because they reflect political choices—
accommodation of competing interests, application of value choices,
and responsiveness to the electorate—methods of decision making
thought to be sharply distinguishable from the chief business of the
courts, and hence owed great deference. A good statement of this
approach is *SEC v. Chenery (Chenery II)*, which involved judicial review
of the commission's retroactive application of a new policy concerning
fair dealing by officers during reorganization of a holding company:
"The Commission's conclusion here rests squarely in that area where
administrative judgments are entitled to the greatest amount of weight
by appellate courts. It is the product of administrative experience,
appreciation of the complexities of the problem, realization of the
statutory policies, and responsible treatment of the uncontested facts.
It is the type of judgment which administrative agencies are best
equipped to make and which justifies the use of the administrative
process. . . . Whether we agree or disagree with the result reached, it is
an allowable judgment which we cannot disturb."[49] The reasoning is
that the decision making methods and skills called for are foreign to the
court and, thus distinguished, are due some deference.[50]

Again, there is an *important qualification*. The policy discretion must
be exercised within the limits of the statutory delegation. This limit
reflects the trichotomy-based prescription that where there is a statutory constraint on the agency, discerning those constraints is appropriate for conventional adjudicatory methods rather than the methods of
politics or scientific expertise.

Mixed Questions: Finally, the common situation in which the agency
is required to apply a broad statutory term to undisputed circumstances contains elements of law, fact, and policy—the so-called mixed

49. 332 U.S. 194, 207–9 (1947). *See also Chevron*, 467 U.S. 834, 837 (1984) ("[T]he
principle of deference to administrative interpretations 'has been consistently followed
by this Court whenever decision as to the meaning or reach of a statute has involved
reconciling conflicting policies, and a full understanding of the force of the statutory
policy in the given situation has depended upon more than ordinary knowledge respecting the matters subjected to agency regulations'" (citations omitted)). *But see* Hi-Craft
Clothing Co. v. NLRB, 660 F.2d 910, 915 (3d Cir. 1981) ("[Agencies are] not the exclusive repository of technical expertise. . . . Even if the question does involve interpretation of a statute, which is considered within the specialized knowledge of an administrative agency, the courts are still not free to relinquish their responsibility of judicial
review. . . . [W]hen the agency diet is food for the court on a regular basis, there is little
reason for judges to subordinate their own competence to administrative 'expertness'").

50. Courts do engage in interest balancing and the like. But the more prominent
such methods are in judicial reasoning, and the more such methods are framed as overt
value choices or interest group accommodation, the more likely the judge is to be concerned about breach of role constraints.

questions. As to these, the judicial gloss most closely fits the mold of deference to policy, as in the following passage from *NLRB v. Hearst Publications,* involving the question of whether newsboys whose wages and other employment conditions were undisputed were employees covered by the Labor Act rather than independent contractors:

> It is not necessary in this case to make a completely definitive delimitation around the term "employee." That task has been assigned primarily to the agency created by Congress to administer the Act. Determination of "where all the conditions of the relation require protection" involves inquiries for the Board charged with this duty. Everyday experience in the administration of the statute gives it familiarity with circumstances and backgrounds of employment relationships in various industries, with the abilities and needs of the workers for self-organization and collective action, and with the adaptability of collective bargaining for the peaceful settlement of their disputes with their employers. The experience thus acquired must be brought frequently to bear on the question who is an employee under the Act. Resolving that question, like determining whether unfair labor practices have been committed, "belongs to the usual administrative routine" of the Board.[51]

Thus, the majority ruled that deference was appropriate on the specific content of the statutory term *employee* because the nature of the determinations called for the fact-finding and policy-making expertise of the bureaucratic agency rather than the decision making skills most familiar to courts.

The *important qualification* to this rule of deference for "mixed" questions is no more than a reinforcement of the importance of these distinctions in decision making paradigms: the mix may often be disaggregated into constitutive questions of law, fact, and policy, thereby providing opportunity for less deferential review, discussed in section 4.1.1. In *Hearst,* for example, the Court used an independent scope of review to conclude that Congress did not intend to import into the Labor Act the assorted complexities of master-servant and independent contractor doctrine from tort law in forty-eight state jurisdictions.[52] On the other hand, had there been a genuine dispute as to the

---

51. 322 U.S. 111, 130 (1944), quoting Gray v. Powell, 314 U.S. at 411.

52. 322 U.S. at 120. A more recent example of "Hearst parsing" is FTC v. Indiana Fed'n of Dentists, 476 U.S. 447, 454–55 (1986) (applying highly deferential substantial evidence standard to the FTC's findings of fact but an independent scope of review with only "some deference" to the agency's review of legal questions). *See* Nathanson, *Admin-*

wages, hours, or supervision of newsboys, these matters would have received substantial evidence review.

Are some principles larger than the trichotomy? For example, a flatly unambiguous statutory command (if constitutional) trumps judicial or administrative discretion, period; likewise, no principle of deference suspends the laws of arithmetic, period. With specific reference to the institutional relationship between court and agency, or between appellate and trial court, the cost-effective use of resources seems at least superficially independent of the trichotomy. But how so? The general efficiency principle must be carefully separated from unproven, trichotomy-based presumptions about comparative institutional competence. Hence, the claim that interventionist judicial review is wasteful usually depends on a judgment that the appellate forum is not (in the run of cases) going to handle the task as well as the primary forum.

I will explore the practical difficulty of distinguishing law, fact, and policy in sections 3.1 and 4.1. For now my only aim has been to offer a first demonstration that the politics-fairness-expertise trichotomy shapes even areas of doctrine not so obviously related to structural problems of separation of powers.

2.4 The Rule Making–Adjudication Distinction

Another pervasive theme in administrative law is the distinction between rule making and adjudication. Not uncommonly an agency faces a choice between conducting its business through rule making, which results in a regulation, or through adjudication, which results in an

---

istrative Discretion in the Interpretation of Statutes, 3 Vand. L. Rev. 470, 470–76 (1950) (suggesting how apparent deference in mixed questions contains a core of independent review regarding the most general issues of statutory construction).

This is not, however, another way of saying that on many questions of application of law to fact the courts give agencies little latitude, although the effect is the same. This is the one area that seems clear after *Cardoza-Fonseca.* In *Cardoza-Fonseca,* Justice Stevens, who also wrote *Chevron,* indicated that, though statutory interpretation is the province of the courts even when the provision admits of some ambiguity, deference would still be appropriate in cases where the challenges to agency action involved application of a legal standard to a particular set of facts. *See also* International Union, United Auto., Aerospace and Agricultural Implement Workers of Am. v. Brock, 816 F.2d 761, 764–67 (D.C. Cir. 1985); Union of Concerned Scientists v. NRC, 824 F.2d 108, 133–14 (D.C. Cir. 1987). *But see* NLRB v. United Food and Commercial Workers Union, 108 S. Ct. 413, 426 (1987) (Scalia, J., concurring) (casting doubt on the interpretation of *Chevron* in *U.C.S.*). To be sure, the court in *Hearst* was explicit about the need for deference as to mixed questions (*see supra* n. 51), but there are no reliable boundaries to that category of questions. *See* sec. 4.3.1.

order.[53] An adjudication is individualized in the sense that the resulting order has an addressee. Its general applicability, if any, to future situations and other parties is accomplished indirectly through the modified principle of administrative stare decisis. In contrast, a regulation or rule is usually addressed more generally, though this is not required as a matter of definition, the chief counterexample being a rate setting that affects one company.[54]

In any event, the agency's choice between rule making and adjudication may be challenged on any of four general grounds—due process, abuse of discretion, consistency with statute, and consistency with APA procedural requirements:

- First, the choice may be unconstitutional. Rule making may be impermissible if the nature of the problem is thought to require an individualized hearing as a matter of procedural due process.[55] On the flip side, courts have occasionally held that

53. The APA definitions are in 5 U.S.C. § 554(4)–(7), (9). An order is defined as "the whole or a part of a final disposition, whether affirmative, negative, injunctive, or declaratory in form, of an agency in a matter other than rule making, but including licensing," whereas a rule is "the whole or part of an agency statement of general or particular applicability and future effect designed to implement, interpret, or prescribe law or policy describing the organization, procedure or practice requirements of an agency and includes the approval or prescription for the future of rates, wages, corporate or financial structures or reorganizations thereof, prices, facilities, appliances, services or allowances therefore or of valuations, costs, or accounting, or practices bearing on and of the foregoing."

54. In APA terminology, rates are set by "rule," even though agencies typically refer to them as rate orders. The anomaly is that such rules are often directed at one firm. In a sense, though, even a narrow rate regulation is general in that it also determines the interests of the company's several customers. (Adjudications often have this quality of general effect, too.) In setting a railroad rate between two points served by only one company, for example, the agency must consider a variety of competing interests, comparing the circumstances of many categories of shippers among whom must be apportioned the burden of supporting the revenue and profit requirements of the owners. Described in this way, what seemed a very individualized determination appears quasi-legislative. Moreover, although the power to adjudge common carrier rates "unreasonable" and hence "unjust" was familiar to courts at common law, the power to set rates prospectively was consistently characterized by courts as a function of the legislature. The legislature's delegation of the task to an agency would not convert it to adjudication merely by virtue of the addition of formal trappings to prevent abuses. *But see* Shapiro, *The Choice of Rulemaking or Adjudication in the Development of Administrative Policy*, 78 Harv. L. Rev. 921, 924, 954 n. 128 (setting rate for individual railroad should be considered adjudication).

55. *Compare* Londoner v. Denver, 210 U.S. 373 (1908) (individualized hearing required before assessments could be finally affixed for street improvements apportioned among benefited property owners), *with* Bi-Metallic Investment Co. v. Colorado State Bd. of Equalization, 239 U.S. 441 (1915) (individualized hearings not required for agency's across-the-board 40 percent increase in assessed values).

due process requires that the agency write regulations to provide standards to guide case-by-case adjudications under a broad statutory delegation.[56]

- Second, the choice may be an *abuse of discretion*, the principal case authority being *Chenery II*.[57] The deferential scope of review makes these challenges generally unsuccessful, but doctrinal considerations in the analysis include problems of retroactivity, surprise, inconsistency, and participation.[58]

- Third, the agency's choice of rule making or adjudication may be in conflict with the organic statute, that is, ultra vires.[59] The dispute may concern whether Congress has actually delegated the asserted substantive rule making power, but this is rare. The growing popularity of rule making as an administrative device has made this argument uncommon, because Congress routinely grants rule making authority, and in a doubtful case, courts seem ready to imply a delegation of regulatory powers.[60] Several cases have challenged agency regulations (usually informal) that effectively deprive the petitioner of an adjudicatory hearing (usually formal) provided by statute—by, for example, settling the critically dispositive issue with a rule so as to preempt controversy in subsequent adjudications.[61]

56. *See* Holmes v. New York City Hous. Auth., 398 F.2d 262 (2d Cir. 1968); Soglin v. Kaufman, 418 F.2d 163 (7th Cir. 1969); Historic Green Springs, Inc. v. Bergland, 497 F. Supp. 839, 851–57 (E.D. Va. 1980).

57. "[T]he choice made between proceeding by general rule or by individual, *ad hoc* litigation is one that lies primarily in the informed discretion of the administrative agency." SEC v. Chenery Corp. (II), 332 U.S. 194, 203 (1947). *See also* Columbia Broadcasting Sys. v. United States, 316 U.S. 407, 421 (1942); NLRB v. Bell Aerospace Co., 416 U.S. 267 (1974); NLRB v. Wyman-Gordon Co., 394 U.S. 759 (1969); *cf.* Ford Motor Co. v. FTC, 673 F.2d 1008 (9th Cir. 1981), *cert. denied*, 459 U.S. 999 (1982) (abuse of discretion for the FTC to impose novel restrictions on secured creditor practices through adjudication rather than regulation); Jean v. Nelson, 711 F.2d 1455 (11th Cir. 1983) (rule making required to effect change in Immigration and Naturalization Service [INS] policy of routinely granting parole to refugees pending normal adjudication).

58. *See supra* n. 30 and cases cited therein.

59. APA, 5 U.S.C. §§ 706(2)(A), (C) (reviewing court to set aside agency action "not in accordance with law" or "in excess of statutory jurisdiction, authority, or limitations").

60. *See* Nat'l Petroleum Refiners Ass'n v. FTC, 482 F.2d 672 (D.C. Cir. 1973) (reversing lower court ruling that commission lacked substantive rule making authority and was therefore required to proceed through adjudications).

61. *See, e.g.*, United States v. Storer Broadcasting Co., 351 U.S. 192 (1956); FPC v. Texaco, 377 U.S. 33 (1964); Heckler v. Campbell, 461 U.S. 458 (1983); American Airlines, Inc. v. CAB, 359 F.2d 624 (D.C. Cir.) (en banc), *cert. denied*, 385 U.S. 843 (1966); Air Line Pilots Ass'n v. Quesada, 276 F.2d 892 (2d Cir. 1960).

- Fourth, the agency may be challenged on procedural grounds. For example, agencies have erroneously promulgated rulelike statements of real consequence without following rule making procedures required by statute.[62]

All four means of policing the agency's choice between rule making and adjudication entail distinctions that depend on the trichotomy. I will consider only the first two here, sketching the essential doctrine and then the relevance of the trichotomy.

2.4.1 Example: The Classic Distinction—*Londoner* and *Bi-Metallic*

In *Londoner v. Denver,* decided in 1908, plaintiffs challenged assessments against them for improvements to public streets on which their properties fronted. The statutes prescribed the following procedures: (1) on petition of a majority of affected owners, and (2) after notice and public hearing, (3) the board of public works could order paving of a street; the order (4) has to be confirmed by a city council ordinance. After reviewing the completed work, (5) the board was to propose an apportionment of the costs among benefited owners. The apportionment was then forwarded to the city council, where, (6) after published notice and opportunity to file written objections, (7) the council could impose the assessments through adoption of another ordinance. The council's determinations reflected in the two ordinances were made "conclusive and binding" on the state courts. The Supreme Court held, inter alia, that due process required the council to provide more elaborate hearing rights to the property owners before finally imposing the tax.[63]

---

62. APA notice and comment procedures are not required for an interpretative rule, general statements of nonbinding policy, and matters of internal procedure or organization. 5 U.S.C. § 553(b)(A). A party may, however, challenge the nonlegislative character of the rule—arguing, for example, that what claims to be a nonbinding policy pronouncement will in practice be controlling and uncontestable in subsequent adjudications—and demand that the agency's policy view be subject to the notice and comment or other procedural requirements applicable to legislative rules. *See, e.g.,* Pacific Gas & Elec. Co. v. FPC, 506 F.2d 33 (D.C. Cir. 1974); Batterton v. Marshall, 648 F.2d 694 (D.C. Cir. 1980); American Mining Congress v. Marshall, 671 F.2d 1251 (10th Cir. 1982). In a related vein, six justices concluded in NLRB v. Wyman-Gordon Co., 394 U.S. 759 (1969), that the board violated the APA's notice-and-comment rule making requirements by adopting a new "election list" obligation for employers in the course of adjudication. The board applied the new obligation prospectively only, arguably causing its action to fall within the APA definition of "rule" rather than adjudicatory "order."

63. 210 U.S. 373 (1908). Several claims made by the property owners doubtless aided their cause. They alleged that the petition by a majority of owners had never been filed, that the work was incomplete, and that the assessments were disproportionate to

In *Bi-Metallic v. Colorado State Board of Equalization*,[64] decided in 1915, plaintiffs sought to enjoin a state agency's across-the-board, 40 percent increase in property tax valuations in the city of Denver, arguing that they were entitled to individual hearings on the correctness of their assessments before any increase. The Supreme Court concluded that "[t]here must be a limit to individual argument in such matters if government is to go on," distinguished *Londoner* (see below), and ruled in favor of the state.

The key distinction usually developed between the cases is that adjudication is required for facts peculiar to the affected individual, whereas facts of a general sort can be developed through quasi-legislative processes—the model being a legislative hearing.[65] The underlying relationship to the trichotomy of decision making methods is evident in Kenneth Culp Davis's succinct explanation: "[R]ulemaking is the part of the administrative process that resembles a legislature's enactment of a statute. An order is the product of adjudication, and adjudication is the part of the administrative process that resembles a court's decision of a case."[66]

---

the distribution of benefits. The Court did not consider that hearing rights were necessary before authorizing the paving, so long as a hearing was provided before the actual assessing of a tax.

64. 239 U.S. 441 (1915) (Holmes, J.).

65. All of this is only applicable in the case of deprivations cognizable under the due process clause. The modern proliferation of such protected interests (*see* Tribe, Treatise at 514 *et seq.*) puts considerable pressure on such a sharp distinction between adjudicatory and quasi-legislative hearings. Two modern developments ease the pressure. First, the informal rule making and judicial review provisions of the federal APA and state law counterparts provide some structure for otherwise amorphous quasi-legislative processes, making it now less problematic to use those processes to determine cognizable property and liberty interests. Second, the notion of an adjudicatory hearing has itself become flexible, so that a complex balancing inquiry is used to determine the detailed nature of the hearing, i.e., "what process is due."

66. Davis, 2 Treatise § 7.2 (2d ed. 1979). Also: "Adjudicative facts are the facts about the parties and their activities, businesses, and properties. Adjudicative facts usually answer the questions of who did what, where, when, how, why, with, what motive or intent; adjudicative facts are roughly the kind of facts that go to a jury in a jury case. Legislative facts do not usually concern the immediate parties but are general facts which help the tribunal decide questions of law and policy and discretion. [Adjudicative facts] are intrinsically the kind of facts that ordinarily ought not to be determined without giving the parties a chance to know and to meet any evidence that may be unfavorable to them, that is, without providing an opportunity for trial. The reason is that the parties know more about the facts concerning themselves and their activities than anyone else is likely to know, and the parties are therefore in an especially good position to rebut or explain evidence that bears upon adjudicative facts. Yet people who are not necessarily parties, frequently the agencies and their staffs, may often be the masters of legislative facts. Because the parties may often have little or nothing to contribute to the development of legislative facts, the method of trial is not required for the determination of disputed issues about legislative facts." Davis, 1 Treatise § 7.02 (1958).

More specifically, the following interrelated factors tend to make the problem appropriate for adjudication: the contested matters relate to particular individuals; the individual(s) can offer evidence of a sort not generally accessible to the decision maker; participation by the individual will decrease the risk of agency mistake; and the number of people affected is small. Factors tending to make the problem one for rule making include: the contested matters are of a general rather than particular nature, so that any individual has no special or personal contribution to make in resolving of the issue; the action will have only prospective effect; and the number of people affected is large.[67] The analysis contributed in more modern cases adds little to what can be gleaned from *Londoner* and *Bi-Metallic*.

These factors reflect the methodological and normative distinctions of the trichotomy. First, generality and numerosity are relevant inasmuch as they suggest the appropriateness of interest accommodation methods; a general problem affecting many people might in theory be the subject of political action, whereas any individual's particular and peculiar problem is far less likely to be addressed through political processes.[68] Justice Holmes suggested this in his opinion for the Court in *Bi-Metallic*, where the state board's general hike in tax assessments could very well have become a political cause, and the ballot remedy was, in principle, available. In contrast, an individual might complain in the circumstances of *Londoner* that an apportionment of costs for street improvements was based on an incorrect measurement of street frontage. This claim would be an unlikely political cause. Second, the notion that agency staff either knows more than the affected individual or would be no more accurate with individual participation is a claim that the methods of expertise are more essential to the problem than are the methods of adjudicatory fairness, with their greater attention to confrontation and explanation. Third, to the extent that such participatory rights as "knowing the case against you" are grounded on noninstrumental concerns, that grounding implicitly invokes fairness and rule of law values.

Thus, the trichotomy provides the persuasive force to the sorting of problems into those appropriate for rule making rather than adjudication. The conceptual and descriptive shortcomings of the trichotomy,

---

67. *See generally* Davis, 2 Treatise §§ 12.3, 12.4. *See also* Cramton, *A Comment on Trial-Type Hearings in Nuclear Power Plant Siting,* 58 Va. L. Rev. 585, 587–91 (1972).

68. Note that it is not enough to say that generality and numerosity would make rule making more "efficient," because this leaves unspecified how efficiency is to be measured and *what it is about the rule making methods* that would lead to these supposed efficiency advantages. I made a similar point above, concerning the relation between efficient institutional design and the trichotomy.

detailed in chapters 3 and 4, provide one explanation for our uncertainty in prescribing rule making versus adjudication in many situations. But when we *are* certain about the choice between rule making and adjudication, it is rarely because of any proof that one procedure will better advance purely instrumental concerns, such as accuracy.[69]

Accuracy may be considered an end in itself, but in view of the trade-offs between accuracy and other desirable qualities, such as efficiency and equity, (see note 69, above), accuracy is best understood as being merely instrumental to the ultimate objective of sound governance or maximum social welfare. It does not get us very far in the analysis.

More often than not, the rule making–adjudication choice is a matter of custom, and the conformity with custom just seems correct, in a conclusory sort of way. Davis's often cited differentiation between legislative and adjudicative facts is reasoning of this sort: "*this* thing" is a matter for adjudication because it is the sort of problem we usually handle through adjudication; "*that* thing" is a matter for quasi-legislative rule making because it is the sort of thing a legislature might well decide if it had the time.[70] But this is hardly a persuasive form of argument to the complaining party who is out of step with general assumptions about how problems ought to be sorted among institutions. Such a person might well claim that conventions must be reconsidered and tested: "You're wrong—I *deserve* a fancier hearing."

2.4.2 Example: The Abuse of Discretion Inquiry

According to *Chenery II*, "The choice made between proceeding by general rule or by individual, ad hoc litigation is one that lies primarily in the informed discretion of the administrative agency."[71] The rationale for this highly deferential "abuse of discretion" test, and the guide-

69. *See* Cramton, *supra* n. 67 at 590 (evaluative criteria for procedural choices include efficiency, accuracy, and acceptability). Breyer & Stewart, *supra* n. 6 at 842, offers a laundry list of purposes for hearings, which includes: accuracy, consistency, individual responsiveness, efficiency, conduciveness to an atmosphere of cooperation, promotion of dignitary and participation values, agency effectiveness, and accountability. These purposes also track the trichotomy. The point is not that the trichotomy provides a superior framework for analyzing procedural due process claims or discretionary design of administrative processes. My argument, instead, is that tha same underlying conceptual apparatus is at work in a great many areas of law.
70. See *supra* n. 66.
71. SEC v. Chenery Corp., 332 U.S. 194 (1947). *See also* Columbia Broadcasting Sys. v. United States, 316 U.S. 407, 421 (1942); NLRB v. Bell Aerospace, 416 U.S. 267 (1974); Shapiro, *supra* n. 54.

lines for its practical application, reflect the separation of powers ethos of the trichotomy.

Chenery II involved a Securities and Exchange Commission (SEC) adjudicatory order that announced and applied a new policy concerning requirements of fair dealing. The petitioners were thereby deprived of profits they expected from certain transactions undertaken while reorganizing a holding company of which they were officers. The policy was developed through adjudication, although it was the sort of matter seemingly amenable to the commission's prospective rule making powers. Justice Murphy, writing for the Court, upheld the agency's choice of procedure and retroactive application of the new policy to the Chenerys.[72]

Justice Murphy may have meant that the agency first chooses rule making or adjudication and, if adjudication, then chooses by a balancing of factors whether circumstances require an exception to the usual rule that adjudicated orders apply to the immediate parties. This approach, however, was rejected by a majority of the Court some twenty years later, after the APA was adopted. In *NLRB v. Wyman-Gordon Co.*, six justices took the position that a purely prospective policy is a "rule" rather than an "order," and thus invalid unless promulgated using the broader participation requirements of rule making.[73] But since Article III of the Constitution permits courts discretion in retroactive application of new principles, why should the rule for agencies differ?

The answer is suggested by the trichotomy of decision making methods. Agencies often have the option of proceeding through quasi-legislative, prospective rule making, but courts have only the adjudicatory process at their disposal.[74] If the problem at hand is appropriate to

72. Justices Black, Reed, and Rutledge joined; Justice Burton concurred in the result; Chief Justice Vinson and Justice Douglas took no part; Justice Jackson wrote a stinging dissent, concurred in by Justice Frankfurter. The Court held that the agency had discretion to choose between rule making and adjudication, that no principle of law prohibited all retroactivity, that any adjudication of a case of first impression entails some retroactivity; the ills of retroactivity must be balanced against the ills of foregoing retroactive application and allowing the past admittedly undesirable behavior (i.e., that of the Chenerys) to go unaddressed, in violation of the statutory design and purpose. 332 U.S. at 202–3.

73. 395 U.S. 759 (1969). The number and variety of opinions casts at least a cloud over the proposition that an agency is free to choose adjudication as a means of formulating new policy, and then free to "balance" whether or not to apply the new policy retroactively. *But see* Retail Union v. NLRB (Coca-Cola Bottling Works, Inc.) 466 F.2d 380 (D.C. Cir. 1972) (arguing that *Wyman-Gordon* should not be read to prevent an agency from choosing during an adjudication to apply a new principle prospectively only). In any case, my purpose is to characterize the nature of judicial analyses rather than to state definitively what the dominant view is or should be.

74. Hart & Sacks, *supra* n. 41 at ch. 7.

legislative methods of interest accommodation (politics), and less obviously appropriate for familiar adjudicatory fairness methods, then the agency should be nudged into using the appropriate rule making procedures rather than legislating through adjudication. (One would emphasize the normatively positive attributes of the politics paradigm.) Moreover, purely prospective orders undermine the adversarial check afforded by adjudication—the losing party is less likely to appeal or seek judicial review because, after all, they were let off the hook. Analogous reasoning led the Supreme Court to apply its prospective-only holding in *Stovall v. Denno* to the parties in the case, since nonapplication of new principles could decrease "the incentive of counsel to advance contentions requiring a change in the law." Also analogous is the rule that before a litigating party can properly invoke the doctrine of offensive collateral estoppel, they must show that the issue was litigated, decided adversely to the other party in the earlier lawsuit, and essential to the judgment.[75] Prospective-only orders also undermine the inherent discipline that case-by-case adjudication imposes through testing the holding against the flesh-and-blood facts at hand rather than hypothetical or unspecified circumstances. Nor has the prospectively applied principle been subject to the alternative safeguards afforded by rule making procedures, particularly general public notice and comment. These objections to prospective adjudication seem to reflect concern for the careful application of the trichotomy's decision making methods. Thus, without retroactivity: (1) the adjudicatory fairness paradigm is compromised because adversariness has been undermined, and (2) the political interest accommodation paradigm is compromised because the agency has avoided the broader participation frequently triggered in rule making by notice-and-comment requirements and in controversial judicial appeals by publicity, intervention, and *amici*. In casting doubt on purely prospective adjudicatory orders, the justices in *Wyman-Gordon* were responsive to the separation of powers ethos and procedural norms that *are* the trichotomy's distinctions in decision making methods.

This is even more apparent in assessing the basic rule making-adjudication choice, the central issue in *Chenery II*. Case law indicates that unfair surprise is only one of several factors to be considered in the agency's choice of procedures (and reconsidered by the court in its review for abuse of discretion). In *Chenery II* itself, Justice Murphy approved the commission's choice of adjudication after noting the

75. 388 U.S. 293, 301 (1967).

problems of (1) unforeseeable policy questions and circumstances, (2) agency inexperience, and (3) decisional matters so varying in specific nature as to defy general rules.[76] On their face, these considerations seem unrelated to the trichotomy. But they are not. Suppose Murphy's three criteria are satisfied. Then decision about a future-effect principle on fair dealing would be inappropriate for the methods of interest accommodation, because prediction and uncertainty would make it impossible to identify the interests at stake and balance them in general, prospective terms. And the methods of science or technical expertise would be inappropriate because the variability of fact patterns, unpredictable due to the posited agency inexperience, would preclude the application of empirical and deductive skills characteristic of that paradigm. The decision making paradigm appropriate in such circumstances is the one familiar to courts faced with individual, immediate controversies: case-by-case adjudicatory fairness. The commission is therefore correct (not abusing its discretion) to mimic a court rather than a legislature.

Justice Murphy's posited obstacles to rule making could not lead to case-by-case application of a paradigm other than adjudicatory fairness. The science paradigm is inappropriate for resolving a case of this sort because, without prior experience as a benchmark, the fair dealing standard has no content that technical expertise could apply to the facts at hand. The politics paradigm is inappropriate because we have a strong normative view that interest group accommodation is appropriate for formulating general rules but not for deciding individual cases. This resonates with the constitutional ban on bills of attainder. Of course, rules (laws) can be formulated in the process of adjudication. As suggested by the trichotomy's normative elements (and discussed in section 2.2), however, the positive attributes of adjudicatory fairness (for example, neutrality) make this individualized lawmaking more acceptable than the political alternative, with its negative associations (for example, subjectivity, willfulness, and majority tyranny).

This deep correspondence with the trichotomy is also evident in David Shapiro's oft-cited article elaborating on the considerations that bear on the choice of policy-making procedures.[77] Here is how his arguments, from the standpoint of advocating greater use of rule mak-

---

76. *Chenery II*, 32 U.S. at 202–3. *See also* Stewart, *supra* n. 6 at 1700–1701 (echoing these cautions in arguing that courts are ill prepared to make the judgments necessary to impose requirements of rules to constrain agency discretion).

77. Shapiro, *supra* n. 54 at 929–42.

ing procedures, relate to the paradigmatic themes of science, politics, and adjudicatory fairness:

- Notice and opportunity for comment are provided by rule making—these yield advantages of participation and accountability, presumed to aid expertise and interest accommodation. (Invoking the paradigms of science and politics)

- Advance planning and forseeability are enhanced by rule making, although Murphy in *Chenery II* urged that planning could be overly burdensome. (The expertness and managerial efficiency aspects of the science paradigm)

- Undesired retroactivity is minimized through rule making (Fairness), although when there is a public policy imperative to undo bad acts, a prospective rule can often be shaped accordingly. Thus, Shapiro argues, carefully crafted rules can advance the retroactivity demands of quasi-legislative policy while balancing the interests of those being regulated in avoiding surprise. (Politics)

- Uniformity of the standards developed and applied through rule making promotes both fairness and accountability. (Fairness and Politics)

- Flexible procedures in rule making create less risk of the distortions that sometimes occur when the agency decides to formulate broad policy via adjudication. This argument is a claim about managerial efficiency, a species of expertise; note the contrast to the adjudication's negative attribute of proceduralism. (Science)

- Clarity and accessibility of rules is greater than that of adjudicatory opinion-orders. Shapiro seems to mean this more for the political values of accountability than for the fairness values of confrontation and disclosure. (Politics and Fairness)

- Judicial review before imposition of a burden or sanction is facilitated by rule making, thereby promoting fidelity to statutory standards.[78] One might add that political actors, such as the Congress, may also take advantage of greater opportunity to become involved, thus enhancing accountability.(Fairness and Politics)

78. Interestingly, this argument was far more persuasive two years after Shapiro presciently made it, once the Supreme Court gave qualified general approval to preenforcement review of regulations in Abbott Laboratories v. Gardner, 387 U.S. 136 (1967), despite earlier misgivings on grounds of ripeness.

My purpose here is not to evaluate the correctness of the Shapiro and Murphy positions,[79] for much undeniably turns on particular circumstances.[80] My point is that the approach of courts and commentators is infused with separation-of-powers ethos on two levels: (1) the considerations material to the choice of procedures, and (2) the assessment of the relative institutional competence of agency and court to evaluate those considerations. The general result is reflected in Justice Murphy's *Chenery II* reasoning: expert considerations, evaluated by the expert, are deferred to by the non-expert; political judgments, made by a political branch, are deferred to by the unelected judge.

The lesson from this examination of the rule making–adjudication choice is that our customary way of thinking about the issue is keyed to the trichotomy in a subtle way. The distinctions and normative associations of the trichotomy are an engine for generating the arguments we use to assess procedural choices and assign responsibility for them. A second lesson, to be developed in the following two chapters, is that this reliance on the choice—so common in administrative law—generates arguments on both sides in concrete settings.

This, then, is the basic structure of the trichotomy and a suggestion of how diverse areas of doctrine rely on its distinctions and its normative associations to calibrate the degree of judicial deference to agency

---

Ripeness and exhaustion can also be appreciated in terms of the trichotomy. Earlier objections to preenforcement review of rule making stressed the concrete focus provided by an enforcement action, making the dispute more amenable to the court's familiar Rule of Law decisional methods. Indeed, the enforcement action often begins as an administrative adjudication, which the courts may feel quite comfortable overseeing because of its familiar qualities. In contrast, review of quasi-legislative action poses the risk that courts will be thrust into assessments of the agency's expert and political decisionmaking methods. Ripeness and exhaustion are in this sense particular species of trichotomy-based deference to the agency.

79. *See, e.g.,* Robinson, *The Making of Administrative Policy: Another Look at Rulemaking and Adjudication and Administrative Procedure Reform,* 118 U. Pa. L. Rev. 485, 535 (1970) ("Rulemaking procedures are inherently no more productive of effective policy-making than are adjudicatory proceedings").

80. For example, although Shapiro argues that rule making will generally promote more uniformity, much depends on the method of measurement. All requests to the attorney general for suspension of deportation may be denied pursuant to a flat rule, and in this sense everyone is treated alike. But if there are "important" differences in the equities and circumstances, then there is a strong argument that differently situated individuals have *not* been accorded degrees of consideration proportionate to the equities of their situations. Thus, Shapiro's many cautions are well taken. Moreover, as I argue in chs. 4 and 5, courts and commentators are handicapped in their analyses by implicit reliance on the trichotomy, because the trichotomy's categories are unstable and the norms are not readily amenable to empirical testing.

action. In the next two chapters I explore the resulting descriptive and conceptual failings. Before that, however, I pause to consider a closely related problem: the gap between the realities of agency decision making and the picture painted by doctrine and courts.

2.5 Presumptions versus Experience: The Trichotomy's Descriptive Failings

Do judges and hearing officers actually make decisions in accordance with adjudicatory fairness methods? Is administrative decision making genuinely infused with expertness and scientific method, ably executed? What does experience teach us about the extent to which processes denominated political do in fact have the attributes assumed (for better or worse) in the trichotomy, including choice based on electoral calculations or accommodation of interest group preferences?

It is unfortunate enough that legal analyses regularly seem to err when considering (or avoiding) these questions. But beyond this, several ancillary doctrines prevent or impede judicial efforts to discern the realities of agency decision making.[81] (The reader will by now find no surprise in the theoretical underpinnings of those doctrines.) The bottom line is that misperception and misunderstanding of what goes on in agency decision making leads to poor judgments about the deference or intervention appropriate in specific controversies.

For example, In spite of common observations by commentators that agencies may not be so expert and that expertise is oversold,[82] courts commonly rule that deference is due the agency's action *because of* expertise:[83] The modest realist point is naturally ignored on judicial

81. *See, e.g.,* United States v. Morgan, 313 U.S. 409 (1941) *(Morgan IV)*; Camp v. Pitts, 411 U.S. 138 (1973); Bethlehem Steel v. NLRB, 120 F.2d 641 (D.C. Cir. 1941); Association of Nat'l Advertisers v. FTC, 627 F.2d 1151 (D.C. Cir. 1979), *cert. denied,* 447 U.S. 921 (1980).

82. *See, e.g.,* Freedman, *Expertise and the Administrative Process,* 28 Admin. L. Rev. 363, 371–74 (1976); Schwartz, *Legal Restriction of Competition in the Regulated Industries: An Abdication of Judicial Responsibility,* 67 Harv. L. Rev. 436, 471–75 (1954); McGraw, *Courts Must Look behind the Myth of Expertise,* Legal Times of Washington, Apr. 6, 1981, 12:1.

83. *See, e.g.,* FCC v. WNCN Listeners Guild, 450 U.S. 582, 593–96 (1981) (deference to rule based on policy and predictive facts); Ethyl Corp. v. EPA, 541 F.2d 1, 36, *cert. denied,* 426 U.S. 941 (1976) (deference to complex findings of fact); Chevron USA, Inc. v. NRDC, *supra* n. 49, at 843–44 (1984) (deference to statutory interpretation in rule making); Ford Motor Credit Co. v. Milhollin, 444 U.S. 555, 556 (1980) (deference to nonbinding statutory interpretation of agency staff). *See generally* Diver, *Statutory Interpretation in the Administrative State,* 133 U. Pa. L. Rev. 549, 574–92 (1985); Woodward and Levin, *In Defense of Deference: Judicial Review of Agency Action,* 31 Ad. L. Rev. 329, 337–41 (1979).

review. The same can be said of deference to agency execution of rule-of-law, fairness-based decision making.[84]

True, it is often assumed that judges form a general assessment of an agency's reputation and that this influences the scaling of deference. But both the appraisal and the decisional significance of reputation are unconfessed, unpoliced, and undisciplined through doctrine or effective empirical scrutiny. Thus, the SEC's general reputation as a well-staffed, professional agency is said to predispose courts toward greater deference; the same is generally true of the Internal Revenue Service. The National Labor Relations Board (NLRB) and the Social Security Administration (SSA) are at the other extreme and are far more frequently reversed.[85] The difficulties are that an agency's general reputation may be presently unfounded or totally irrelevant to the case at hand, and the degree of influence such a reputation should have on the scaling of deference should be articulated and refined in doctrine rather than *sub silentio*.

So, in reality the agency may have tried to apply expertise but did not do the science correctly; or perhaps it tried to accommodate competing interests but forgot to listen to some important voices; or it tried to imitate adjudicatory fairness but prejudged the facts or failed to

---

84. *See* Shapiro, *The Choice of Rulemaking or Adjudication in the Development of Administrative Policy,* 78 Harv. L. Rev. 921, 947–52 (1965) (adjudication allows for inconsistent and unexplained application of contradictory policies and decisions); Bierman, *Judge Posner and the NLRB: Implications for Labor Law Reform,* 69 Minn. L. Rev. 881, 900–901 (1985) (adjudication allows for NLRB bias); Mashaw, *Conflict and Compromise among Models of Administrative Justice,* 1981 Duke L.J. 181–82 (1981) (noting substantial criticism of social security administration's adjudicatory procedures and inconsistent results); Davis, 4 Treatise 20.9–11 (1983).

85. *Compare* Werner, *The SEC as Market Regulator,* 70 Va. L. Rev. 755, 762 (1984) (the SEC has a "high reputation" and "has been remarkably free of the criticism heaped on other economic regulators"); *and The SEC after Fifty Years: An Assessment of Its Past and Future,* 83 Colum. L. Rev. 1593, 1608 (1983) (book review) (acknowledging the SEC's "solidly based reputation for regulatory vigor and excellence in regulation"), *with* Estreicher, *Policy Oscillation at the Labor Board: A Plea for Rulemaking,* 37 Admin. L. Rev. 163, 170–75 (1985) (discussing how perception of board as unstable agency "shows disrespect" such that "courts are reluctant to pay little more than lip service to the doctrine of deference to agency policymaking"); *and* Irving, *The Crisis at the NLRB: A Call For Reordering Priorities,* 7 Emp. Rel. L.J. 47, 63–65 (1981) (board faces a "crisis of legitimacy in the courts" and "invites litigation because of the quality of its decision making"); Mashaw, *supra* n. 181 at 181–83 (noting substantial criticism of SSA for its failure to use adequate adjudicatory procedures and to produce predictable and consistent results, as well as its failure to provide adequate service to claimants). With respect to the SSA, however, high reversal rates may be substantially explainable by the fact that the record remains open throughout administrative and judicial appeals, so that new medical evidence, for example, may present the court with a very different claim than that originally considered by the SSA.

develop and consistently apply principles of decision. Of these, judicial review is most likely to catch *and act on* a failing of expertise, particularly if the court for some reason is using one or another version of heightened scrutiny, such as "hard-look" or "adequate consideration" review. But these cases (see section 6.1) are in the minority, and the far more common judicial stance is to presume expertise rather than probe to test its genuineness. And it is rarer still to see aggressive judicial inquiry into questions of political representativeness[86] or adjudicatory neutrality.[87]

For example, Justice Jackson, dissenting in *Chenery II,* summed up the problem of fictional expertise quite well. The majority approved the SEC's choice of adjudication rather than rule making to announce and apply retroactively a new prohibition on certain securities transactions by management in the midst of a holding company reorganization. By Justice Jackson's count, the majority invoked deference to experience five times. He protested:

> What are we to make of this reiterated deference to "administrative experience" when in another context the Court says, "Hence, we refuse to say that the Commission, *which had not previously been confronted with the problem of management trading during reorganization,* was forbidden from utilizing this particular proceeding for announcing and applying *a new standard of conduct.*"? . . . .
>
> The Court's reasoning adds up to this: The Commission must be sustained because of its accumulated experience in solving a problem with which it had never before been confronted![88]

---

86. This is true even when the court acknowledges that the interest-accommodation paradigm is appropriate for the matter at hand. This is analogous to the problem posed by qualification of name plaintiffs in class action suits or by proposals to move the law of standing to a self-conscious focus on plaintiff's representational capacity. *See* Chayes, *Foreword: Public Law Litigation and the Burger Court,* 96 Harv. L. Rev. 4 (1982). These entail judgments about representativeness, participation, diversity, and voice.

87. *Compare* Association of Nat'l Advertisers, Inc. v. FTC, 627 F.2d 1151 (D.C. Cir. 1979) ("clear and convincing showing that the agency member has an unalterably closed mind on matters critical to the disposition of the proceeding" is required "to rebut the presumption of agency regularity"), *cert. denied,* 447 U.S. 921 (1980) *with* the decision it overruled, 460 F. Supp. 996 (D.D.C. 1978) (Gesell, J.); United States v. Morgan, 313 U.S. 409, 422 (1941) *(Morgan IV).*

88. SEC v. Chenery Corp., 332 U.S. 194, 213 (Jackson, J., dissenting) (citations omitted) (emphasis in original). *See also* Pittston Stevedoring Corp. v. Dellaventura, 544 F.2d 35 (2d Cir. 1976) (Friendly, J.) (persuasive value of agency's consistent interpretation of the statute is weakened because its initial view was formed when it had little experience administering the statute, and subsequent decisions simply followed precedent).

The majority wrapped the agency's action in a cloak of presumed expertise so heavy that it could not be lifted to address sensibly the degree of deference appropriate to the agency's action in a case of first impression.

The newness of the problem, however, is not really the fundamental difficulty. Every new situation is in some respects novel or mysterious and in some respects familiar. The question is whether its capital stock of past experience, professional skills, and accumulated insights gives the agency a special competence, so that any given problem is less novel and mysterious to the agency than it would be to someone else, especially a court. But Justice Jackson's basic point remains: What assurance is given by administrative law, including judicial review, that the agency has in fact acquired and deployed the capital stock of experience, professional skills, and insights (or judgment) that justify the delegations and deference the agencies receive?

The National Labor Relations Board is an especially easy target for skeptics of agency expertise, consistency and neutrality. From its inception, the controversial nature of the NLRB's business has subjected it to attack, and not without reason. With respect to expertise, it has been observed that courts routinely incant that the board is expert in industrial relations, so that it can evaluate the effects of suspect management actions on workers; yet the board does no empirical work, nor does its staff include experts in social science, industrial relations, or business administration who might ably address such questions.[89]

In a sense, the NLRB myth is functional because it allows the court to narrow its scope of review rather than independently address the complex factual and policy matters about which it knows even less than the board. So, sometimes courts acknowledge doubts about the reality of board expertise but then defer anyway.[90] But the veil of fictional

89. Getman & Goldberg, *The Myth of Labor Board Expertise*, 39 U. Chi. L. Rev. 681 (1972); Samoff, *NLRB Elections: Uncertainty and Certainty*, 117 U. Pa. L. Rev. 228 (1968); J. Freedman, Crisis and Legitimacy: The Administrative Process and American Government 44–57 (1978); Bok, *The Regulation of Campaign Tactics in Representation Elections under the National Labor Relations Act*, 78 Harv. L. Rev. 38, 82–92 (1964). *See also* Hedstrom Co. v. NLRB, 629 F.2d at 324 (dissent) (board's "claimed expertise . . . is more mythical than real"); United Oil Mfg. Co., Inc. v. NLRB, 672 F.2d 1208 (3d Cir. 1982) (dissent) (objecting to reliance on nebulous concept of board expertise in displacing evidentiary findings of hearing officer).

90. *See, e.g.*, Hedstrom Co. v. NLRB, 629 F.2d 305 (3d Cir. 1980); Peerless of Am., Inc. v. NLRB, 576 F.2d 119, 122 n. 3 (7th Cir. 1978); Walgreen Co. v. NLRB, 509 F.2d 1014 (7th Cir. 1975); Harlan #4 Coal Co. v. NLRB, 490 F.2d 119 (6th Cir. 1974). On the absence of standards with which courts can appraise expert decision making, see secs. 2.5.2 and 6.3.

expertise also obscures the continuing costs of possibly unsound decisions. Rigorous judicial scrutiny might prod the agency to develop
genuine and useful expertise, if only to resist encroachment.

This area deserves empirical study. Some literature supports the
view that over time agencies adjust the form and rigor of their decision
making processes to anticipate a pattern of concerns established by judicial review. No substantial work exists on the record of, or possibilities
for, a direct effect of judicial review on the character and extent of
scientific investigation by the agency. For example, have courts played
an important role in advancing the quality of testing regimes for new
drugs or environmental chemicals? Has administrative law aided the
evolution of cost-benefit analysis, or policy science generally? In section 6.5, I will argue that the possibilities are considerable.

2.5.1 Fairness and Rule of Law

What about deference to agency adjudication? The charge that
judges (and, *a fortiori*, agency adjudicators) are "result-oriented" or
otherwise willful is familiar and popular, but not particularly persuasive. But why *not* persuasive? Are the charges so plainly false? The
usual response to such allegations is to marginalize them—either by
isolating the critics or by suggesting that the criticisms are valid in only
exceptional or peripheral situations.

In legal thinking a recurring pattern distinguishes the core and the
periphery, or the primary proposition and its qualification or supplement. This analysis is generally offered to distinguish rule and exception or to add complexity and sophistication to a doctrine. One must
often ask, however, whether the periphery or supplement does not in
fact undermine the basic validity of the core proposition. If it does, the
core-periphery analysis amounts to a delusive protection of the core.[91]
Judge Irving R. Kaufman has written, for example, that "the bona
fides of the party are a factor, perhaps a compelling factor, in the
appellate court's decision *in a very close case*."[92] But there are other,
implicitly more critical views. Professor Bernard Schwartz has written:
"Judges continue to repeat that they may not substitute their discretion
for that of administrators, and will reverse only when administrative
discretion has been clearly abused. . . . [But] when counsel is able to

---

91. *See* Frug, *The Ideology of Bureaucracy in American Law*, 97 Harv. L. Rev. 1276,
1288–89 ("dangerous supplement," after Jacques Derrida).

92. 45 N.Y.U.L. Rev. 201, 209 (1970) (emphasis added) *quoted in* W. Gellhorn, C.
Byse, & P. Strauss, Administrative Law 317 (1978).

. . . convince the judges that his client was dealt with unfairly—even if, theoretically speaking, the administrative decision was a reasonable one—he will obtain reversal."[93]

It is important to note that "result-oriented" has different senses, deserving different reactions. Thus, a judge may use political or policy reasoning to conclude what seems best. I treat politics and policy together, because the distinguishing feature of policy judgments is that they so clearly implicate value choices and consideration of interest group preferences or stakes. In this respect they are exceedingly similar to the ordinary understanding of "politics." Electoral calculations may not be *overtly* present in policy choices, but weighing interest group claims is almost that (see section 6.2).

Then, too, much of what we understand to be the grist of political decision making on the bench is only tenuously connected to poll-watching; rather it involves a more general sensitivity to public or interest group sentiment and translation of the reasoning and result into doctrinal language. This translation is not the same as willful and arbitrary decision making masquerading as principled adjudication. After all, the judge's political decision is methodologically and substantively sound rather than arbitrary. But our description (perhaps caricature?) of the Rule of Law method by which we suppose the decision was reached belies the workings of the court as an institution peopled with, well—people.

Our objection to a judge using political and policy methods is an obvious manifestation of separation-of-powers ethos: such behavior does not square with the trichotomy's assignment of methods to institutions. The same method employed by an unelected administrator might well be considered both sound and legitimate.

Relatedly, there are some practical considerations that might explain judicial reluctance to pierce the veil of fictions concerning the neutrality and consistency of agency decision making, including administrative quasi-adjudication. Once such an analytical engine were fired up, it might break loose and turn on judges. The same point applies in other areas where it is only natural for judges to analogize between the administrator and themselves regarding the privileged and unquestionable confidences between personal staff and decision maker.[94] A less ignoble reason, however, is that there is a poverty of

93. Schwartz, *Administrative Law*, in 1970/71 Annual Survey of Administrative Law 57, 69 (1971).

94. *See* Mazza v. Cavicchia, 15 N.J. 498, 527–30, 105 A.2d 545, 561–63 (1954) (dissenting opinion) ("[The board's] administrator has the same capacity for wholesome administration of justice in his lawful sphere as judges have in theirs. . . . [T]he director's

standards or norms with which to assess neutrality and consistency. Faced with a suggestion of prejudgment or inconsistency, one is hard put to state and apply defensible boundary lines. *So why look?*

I would not object to this state of things were it not that the basis for judicial deference to the agency is often the agency's presumed use of adjudicatory fairness methods, with its normatively positive attributes of Rule of Law and so on. Why *defer* if we will not look to ensure that deference is really due? There are other grounds for deference (all understandable by reference to the trichotomy) to which I now turn.

2.5.2 Expertise and Science in Bureaucratic Life

The administrator's decision would probably be considered legitimate even if the administrator lacked all expertise and just happened to stumble on an "objectively" reasonable decision or rubber stamp the recommendation of a subordinate. (I myself disagree that such serendipitous reasonableness should satisfy legal standards of sound governance.)[95] This reality of agency expertise is quite unlike the descriptions in judicial opinions. When presidential and subcabinet appointees are selected, extensive experience in the subject matter too often weighs far less than considerations of party loyalty, campaign contributions (financial and otherwise), general intelligence, and reputation in the extended circle of advisers to the president or relevant cabinet officer. The median tenure for subcabinet presidential appointees has been estimated at only eighteen to twenty months. Then, too, any mere mortal in such a job would be unable to master the variety and number of issues presented, no matter how long the tenure. So, it is said that agency expertise must be understood as an institutional rather than personal attribute.[96] But what does that really mean?

There may be scores of experienced civil servants and politically

procedure did not materially differ from that followed by appellate judges, whose law clerks prepare preliminary memoranda often embodying analyses of the testimony and their views").

95. I would argue that a substantively sound agency choice made by happenstance should not survive review under the "arbitrary and capricious" standard in the APA. It is not enough that the decision be reasonable and within the statutorily submitted range of discretion; ratiocination should be required, rather than a coin flip, unless the statutory design plausibly suggests otherwise. *See* Citizens to Preserve Overton Park, Inc. v. Volpe, 401 U.S. 402, 416 (1971) (obscure passage which arguably supports this interpretation).

96. Nathanson, *Probing the Mind of the Administrator,* 75 Colum. L. Rev. 721 (1975); Peck, *Regulation and Control of Ex Parte Communications with Administrative Agencies,* 76 Harv. L. Rev. 233 (1962).

appointed aides[97] working on a difficult issue and preparing it for the administrator's final decision. But they know that she will have the time to focus on only a handful of the most crucial issues, and for each of these, on only a handful of competing considerations. The subtleties of the problems must be distilled, clarified, and distilled again. That nuance of analysis or interpretation of data may occupy the agency experts in heated debate with one another and with their counterparts employed by interested private parties or in other levels of government. But the administrator will rarely be educated in those nuances and thus cannot consider them in assessing the distilled recommendations of subordinates. Moreover, individual staff experts may be just that—individuals working on their small pieces of the greater whole, with few professional checks and balances operating to ensure the soundness of these judgments. As the judgments are passed up the line, distilled and summarized at each level, the possibilities for probing review and deep comprehension of the problem as a whole diminish. Ultimately, even the best administrator may spend less than an hour reviewing a brief cover memorandum on a regulatory package that took tens of thousands of hours to prepare.

The ultimate institutional response of the agency will therefore be an amalgam of rational and nonrational factors, reflecting an interplay of science, interpersonal dynamics, bureaucratic routines, internal and external political currents and pressures, and so forth. And the result may be importantly shaped by aspects of organizational structure or the personal style of agency leaders.

The agency's decision on whether to formulate policy through rule making or through adjudication, for example, undoubtedly reflects far more than an expert evaluation about the appropriateness of generality as compared with particularity. What will the public, industry, and political response be to a general rule making initiative? What is the relative likelihood of successful policy development in a carefully shaped adjudication as compared with quasi-legislation? Is the leadership style of agency officials more consistently with the informality of a legislative process or with the detached and measured tone of formal adjudication? What are the comparative costs in time and agency resources? These and related concerns do not appear in Justice Murphy's

---

97. In general, presidential appointees throughout the executive branch have some personal aides and advisers who, rather than being career civil servants, are political appointees: they can be dismissed or reassigned at will, and there is no rigorous civil service system for screening their competence, as there is in the competitive senior executive civil service.

majority opinion in *Chenery II*. (*See* section 2.4.2.) In fundamental and immutable respects, science and bureaucracy are incompatible. This is true not only of laboratory science but also of any expert knowledge one might attempt to bring to bear on the problem. Familiar examples of frustrated expertise include the experience of medical professionals in the Indian Health Service, air traffic controllers in the Federal Aviation Administration (FAA), engineers and astronauts in the National Aeronautics and Space Administration (NASA), and career officers in the State Department. To be sure, the attractive claim of bureaucracy is that it permits the mobilization of appropriate and specialized experts to whatever task is at hand. This suggests the image of an automobile assembly line or well-organized warehouse of automotive parts: the organization provides just the right gizmo at just the right moment for every task within its mission. But, of course, the subtle problems of modern policymaking are more akin to automobile *design* or composition of a symphony. The artistry is in the complete vision and in the integration of subsidiary skills. No natural law assures us that a collection of skilled musicians will produce beautiful music, and no natural law of management assures us that a collection of experts will produce worthy administration. The whole is neither more nor less than the sum of its parts. It is an altogether different phenomenon.

What, then, is the fair way to characterize the decision making process of the agency? Even when the dominant paradigm appears to be science, expertise is certainly a misnomer, and hence a poor basis on which to calibrate the balance of judicial deference and intervention.

There is as yet no clearly articulated and distinct paradigm of "bureaucratic" decision making incorporated into the doctrinal image of administration. Whereas administrative law is constantly looking over its shoulder at structural issues of constitutional law and political theory, some important contributions in the public management literature instead take as their point of departure the fields of private sector business management, group psychology, sociology, political science, and economics. This perspective permits a break with separation of powers ethos and the possibility of constructing an altogether different paradigm of decision making.[98] Legal doctrine does not reflect this possibility in its descriptions and assessments of agency processes.[99]

98. *See, e.g.,* G. Allison, Essence of Decision (1971); J. Steinbrunner, The Cybernetic Theory of Decision (1974). Interestingly, even as these theorists search for a model of bureaucratic rationality by, for example, importing interest-maximizing paradigms from economics, the result differs greatly from the familiar model of a unitary actor rationally pursuing public ends. Anthony Downs, for example, grounds his theories in individual rationality, but the inevitability of complex personal objectives, together with

In the end, however, the possibility of effective judicial scrutiny of decisions within the paradigm of expertise is circumscribed by the willingness and competence of courts and judicial bureaucracies to make the necessary judgments and implicit prescriptions. A broader role could be facilitated by the mildly utopian changes discussed in section 7.3.3. The evolution of the hard-look and adequate consideration brands of review, with their heightened scrutiny of the agency's reasoning and explanations, demonstrates that adversarial methods of quasi-procedural judicial review can in principle do much to assure sound science (see section 6.5). Nevertheless, the reluctance of courts to embrace fully the possibility of such searching analysis is amply demonstrated by the continuing and perhaps resurgent strain of highly deferential judicial review. Certainly, such deference is generally attributable to the grip of separation of powers ethos through the trichotomy. But this problem of judicial oversight of science and expertise is comparable to the problem of effectively policing the adjudicatory fairness paradigm: the poverty of norms presently available to most generalist judges as measures of agency behavior. I admit that it does little good to decry, as I do, the unwillingness of courts to probe for shoddy policy science if the court cannot tell it when it sees it.

2.5.3 Politics and Interest Accommodation

The trichotomy's paradigm of politics, often the basis on which deferential review is claimed, is also flawed by descriptive inaccuracy. Just as most critiques of judges give rise to parallel critiques of agency adjudicators, the obvious concerns about the genuine representativeness of legislators are valid, *a fortiori,* for agency quasi-legislators. I include within the trichotomy's paradigm of politics a range of methods encompassing both election-driven choice and the subtler process of identifying and weighing competing group claims or interests. The

---

plausible principles for interpersonal interactions, leads to patterns of bureaucratic behavior quite unrelated to the atomistic premises. A. Downs, Inside Bureaucracy (1967).

    99. Colin Diver's work addresses this deficiency somewhat, but it focuses more on the proper substantive content of the regulatory state than on the relationship between courts and agencies. *See* Diver, *The Optimal Precision of Rules* 93 Yale L.J. 65 (1983); Diver, *Policymaking Paradigms in Administrative Law,* 95 Harv. L. Rev. 393 (1981). Jerry Mashaw's work on Social Security Disability Insurance, by contrast, while developing useful themes concerning the relation between traditional due process concerns and bureaucratic rationality, in substantial respects embraces and exalts an ideal of expert administration in place of judicial review, or rule of law, constraints on discretion. Mashaw, Bureaucratic Justice: Managing Social Security Disability Claims (1983); Mashaw, *The Management Side of Due Process,* 59 Cornell L. Rev. 772 (1974). *See* secs. 5.3–4.

latter is involved in the familiar portrait of public policy choice—economists would put it in terms of specifying the social welfare function against which the decision maker evaluates policy alternatives—but the inevitably subjective or partisan quality of the judgment makes the policymaking bureaucrat a very close relative of the policymaking legislator.

The functioning of Congress falls far short of the ideal for many reasons, including low voter participation, incumbency biases, the campaign finance system, shortcomings of the media, countermajoritarian internal procedures of the legislative branch, and inequalities in the lobbying system by which constituents and interest groups communicate with and influence elected officials. Many of the same factors seriously flaw the process of political interest accommodation that drives the agency's decision making: accountability is attenuated, access and influence are skewed in often undesirable ways, and many bureaucratic factors impede the free flow of ideas and reactions between affected interests and agency decision makers. For example, a group may be relegated to meeting with subordinate officials to express concerns about a pending policy initiative, but features of bureaucratic life may prevent clear transmission of those concerns to the actual decision maker. Indeed, agencies commonly organize their public liaison operations to accomplish just that—to filter, screen, and insulate. Though all parties probably understand thoroughly all general viewpoints in most agency proceedings, the same can also be said of legislative and court proceedings. And yet most administrative participants acknowledge the importance of access and advocacy in several respects, such as communicating intensity of preferences or providing specific data.

Assume that a reviewing court understands the issue faced by the agency to be appropriate (at least in large part) for the politics paradigm. If we believe that a president has an electoral mandate to pursue a specific course of regulatory action, then judicial deference to politics could be understood as a principle to minimize conservative intervention in political shifts. The losers in the regulatory policy battles—for example, workers faced with nonenforcement or outright rescission of occupational safety rules—would find a nearly deaf ear in court, because the political majority has already been heard. Consider the following expression of this view by then-Justice Rehnquist in a case involving the rescission of auto safety rules: "A change in administration brought about by the people casting their votes is a perfectly reasonable basis for an executive agency's reappraisal of the costs and benefits of its programs and regulations. As long as the agency remains within the bounds established by Congress, it is entitled to assess administrative records and evaluate priorities in light of the philosophy of the administration."[100] Alternatively, we could refuse to interpolate a general electoral mandate to the specifics of a particular regulation, in which case effective agency politics would require broad participation, and genuine rather than dismissive confrontation with opponents. A goal of judicial review would be to promote such a process and to press the agency to reach conclusions that, as in the electoral and legislative arenas, demonstrate an accommodating responsiveness to the range of competing voices. (See chapter 6 on the possibilities for giving content to these tests.)

Either basis for politics-based deference—mandate or participation—invites descriptive inaccuracy. Courts err either (1) in discerning the existence and specificity of an electoral mandate supposedly transmitted through the presidential power of appointment[101] or (2) in assuming that processes of agency participation have pseudo-electoral qualities that make the agency democratically responsive.

A broader obstacle to descriptive accuracy, however, is in determining whether politics is being employed at all. Although courts often defer to an agency decision because it is political (including policy-based), they also may intervene because they suspect a political method was used when the expert or adjudicatory methods should have been. So it is not unusual for an agency to decide based substantially on political calculations but to explain the conclusion in apolitical terms in hopes of securing what under the circumstances appears to be a form of legitimacy more resistant to judicial intervention. But here's the rub: If the agency hides the political nature of its method, a reviewing court cannot very well evaluate the existence or quality of that method.[102]

100. *See* Motor Vehicle Mfrs. Ass'n v. State Farm Mut. Auto. Ins. Co., 403 U.S. 29, 59 (1983) (Rehnquist, J., concurring in part and dissenting in part). *See also* Chevron USA, Inc. v. NRDC, 467 U.S. 837, 865–66 (1984): "Judges are not experts in the field, and are not part of either political branch of the Government. . . . In contrast, an agency to which Congress has delegated the policymaking responsibility, may, within the limits of that delegation, properly rely upon the incumbent administration's views of wise policy to inform its judgment. While agencies are not directly accountable to the people, the Chief Executive is, and it is entirely appropriate for this political branch of the Government to make such policy choices. . . .

"[F]ederal judges—who have no constituency—have a duty to respect legitimate policy choices by those who do."

101. *State Farm* and *Chevron* have received mixed reviews from the courts of appeal. *Compare* National Black Media Coalition v. FCC, 775 F.2d 342, 356n.17 (D.C. Cir. 1985) (attempting to limit proposition) *with* Lugo v. Schweiker, 776 F.2d 1143, 1150 (3d Cir. 1985) (accepting proposition). Scholarly commentary has likewise differed. *See, e.g.,* Garland, *Deregulation and Judicial Review,* 98 Harv. L. Rev. 507, 523, 585–86, 590n.487 (1984); *The Supreme Court,* 1983 Term, 98 Harv. L. Rev. 247, 254 (1984); Merrill, *The Common Law Powers of Federal Courts,* 52 U. Chi. L. Rev. 1, 24–27 (1985).

102. There is more to say on why agencies reasonably hesitate to disclose political

But this cuts both ways, reducing opportunities for anti-politics intervention by courts, as well as pro-politics deference. Courts frequently undertake judicial review of agency actions that seem on their face to be largely political in motivation, meaning they are motivated by ideology, social vision, and interest group calculations rather than science or fairness. Much of the deregulatory zeal of the Reagan administration seems fairly subject to this characterization, including, for example, the decision by the Federal Energy Regulatory Commission to dismantle the rate setting machinery for oil pipelines in favor of market forces; the National Highway Transportation Safety Administration's decision to rescind the passive restraints (airbags) rule; and the decision of the Wage and Hour Administrator to exempt "home knitters" from the homework prohibition of the Fair Labor Standards Act.[103] It is descriptively inaccurate for courts to defer to such choices on the basis of *expertise* if the "true" basis for the action is *politics*. And deference based on politics-as-mandate is inappropriate except in those rare cases when a problem has had campaign visibility. Finally, it is descriptively inaccurate to defer to politics-as-participation if the agency has not confessed politics and opened up the process of interest group participation and accommodation to scrutiny structured to test the quality of the political decision making process.[104]

These descriptive failings are widespread and of varying significance. Current doctrines encourage judicial deference to agency decision making thought to be *appropriately* within the politics paradigm—that is, within the range of policy judgment. The premise of such deference is that participation and political accountability are respon-

considerations. Judicial reactions to an agency's disclosure of political considerations are difficult to predict because the scaling of deference depends not only on (1) the perceived choice of agency method but also on (2) whether the court thinks the problem or circumstance was appropriate for that method and (3) whether the court chooses to focus on the positive or the negative norms associated with attributes of politics. These judgments in turn depend on the court's characterization of the circumstances, primarily with respect to the fact-law-policy distinction, which I criticize in sec. 4.1 as conceptually undisciplined, hence unpredictable. Furthermore, the problem of unpredictably selective emphasis on norms results from the conceptual problem of attributive duality (see sec. 3.2).

103. Farmers Union Cent. Exch., Inc. v. FERC, 734 F.2d 1486 (D.C. Cir. 1984). Motor Vehicle Manufacturers Ass'n v. State Farm Mutual Auto. Ins. Co., 463 U.S. 29 (1983), affirming 680 F.2d 206 (D.C. Cir. 1982) (Mikva, J.) (criticizing apparent reliance on political ideology); ILGWU v. Donovan, 722 F.2d 795 (D.C. Cir. 1983) (Edwards, J.) (reversing Department of Labor, with dicta criticizing apparent reliance on political ideology). *See also* Action on Smoking and Health v. CAB, 699 F.2d 1209 (D.C. Cir.), *supplemented,* 713 F.2d 795 (D.C. Cir. 1983).

104. *See* sec. 6.3 (recommending doctrinal reform to require disclosure of political factors in decision making).

sive to the central concern of administrative law—the disciplining of discretion. More broadly, the premises of a fully articulated interest group representation theory of administrative law would include normative judgments that (1) political process within the agency can, with appropriate controls on its character, be a valuable check on agency discretion and that (2) the quality of agency politics can be improved (at least marginally) through (among other things) careful judicial interventions.

But for the present at least, there is no sign of doctrine having brought about the political reform of government bureaucracies to redress the imperfections evident in the model of participatory control of discretion. In particular, there is the difficulty of evaluating whether politics is or is not working well in a given instance of agency decision making. Here, the problem of assessing bureaucratic performance is even more difficult than judging the quality with which the fairness or science paradigms have been executed by the agency; the poverty of norms is profound.

2.5.4 Example: Agency Policy Shifts

Chapters 3 and 4 concern major conceptual difficulties with doctrinal analyses based on the trichotomy of decision making paradigms, including the difficulty of sharply distinguishing the paradigms in the actual world of complex policy choice. One symptom of these conceptual failings is that it is difficult to tell whether a problematic decision is the result of the agency using the "wrong" paradigm or the agency using the "right" paradigm ineptly.

For example, when agency actions evidence questionable expertise, the paradigm of politics may well be at work. By one estimate, as of mid-1984, the Reagan NLRB had overturned thirty-one policies of the previous board majority.[105] Louis B. Schwartz put it well some thirty years ago:

> Think of the recent political debate over the addition of one Republican member to the bipartisan Tariff Commission. Was his presence desired because he would bring new expertise to the Tariff Commission's decisions or because he would bring a

105. Estreicher, *supra* n. 85 at 163–66 (citing 31 cases reversing or altering past board policies and decisions). *See also* Bernstein and Gold, *Mid-Life Crisis: The NLRB at Fifty*, BNA Daily Labor Report, June 3, 1985, No. 106, p. E-1; (cite oversight hearings by Rep. Clay of House Labor and Education subcommittee, "Has Labor Law Failed?"; report indicting NLRB for politicization, backlogs, and "debasement" of the NLRB).

new point of view; and if the latter, why defer to his "expert-ness"? Consider the reversal of policy achieved by the FTC by a single new appointment, and reconcile this, if possible, with the notion that the resolution of large policy issues stems from data rather than dogma. What is left of the administrative expertise basis for the American Trucking decision when it is recalled that the expert commissioners were closely divided among them-selves and ultimately retreated from the position which they had persuaded the Supreme Court to endorse?[106]

In particular, courts often invoke deference to expertise when re-viewing agency policy shifts: "The fact that the agency has from time to time changed its interpretation of [a statutory term] does not, as re-spondents argue, lead us to conclude that no deference should be accorded the agency's interpretation of the statute. An initial agency interpretation is not instantly carved in stone. On the contrary, the agency, to engage in informed rulemaking, must consider varying in-terpretations and the wisdom of its policy on a continuing basis."[107]

It is certainly an error to evaluate the agency's action as born of expertness to the exclusion of politics. It compounds the error to ac-cept general or conclusory agency explanations of its actions swathed in claims of agency expertise.[108] An important example is provided by

106. Schwartz, *supra* n. 82 at 472–73 (footnotes omitted) (referring to American Trucking Ass'n v. United States, 344 U.S. 298 [1953], which involved controversial restrictions of truck trip-leasing that arguably circumvented International Commerce Commission [ICC] entry and rate regulation).

107. Chevron USA, Inc. v. NRDC, 467 U.S. 837, 867 (1984) (approving the En-vironmental Protection Agency's [EPA] relaxation of air quality regulations in nonattain-ment areas accomplished through redefinition of "point source" to implement "bubble" concept of plantwide tradeoffs in pollution reduction), overruling 685 F.2d 718 (D.C. Cir. 1982). Also: "[W]e fully recognize that 'regulatory agencies do not establish rules of conduct to last forever,' . . . and that an agency must be given ample latitude to 'adapt their rules and policies to the demands of changing circumstances.'" Motor Vehicle Mfrs. Ass'n v. State Farm Mut. Auto. Ins. Co., 463 U.S. 29, 42 (1983), quoting American Trucking Ass'n v. Atchison, T. & S. F. Ry. Co., 387 U.S. 397, 416 (1967), and Permian Basin Area Rate Cases, 390 U.S. 747, 784 (1968).

108. "In the thousands of federal court decisions annually reviewing federal admin-istrative action, only a few invalidate agency action [using the arbitrary and capricious standard]. Litigants attempting to persuade a reviewing court that the balance struck by an agency among relevant factors is 'arbitrary and capricious' must be prepared to persuade the court that the agency's decision has no rational basis whatsoever. Given the artfulness of agency opinion writers, the skills of government lawyers, and the plau-sibility of agency claims of 'expertise,' this is a difficult burden to carry." Breyer & Stewart, *supra* n. 6 at 336–37 (1985). This seems overstated, since many agency decisions, or parts of them, are remanded on the ground that the court is left with significant unanswered questions. Nevertheless, for cases supporting the quoted proposition, *see,*

recent court decisions concerning administrative deregulation in the wake of the 1980 presidential election, which brought Ronald Reagan and his appointees into office on a platform that included substantial relaxation of regulatory burdens on industry. The platform stated: "Where possible, we favor deregulation, especially in the energy, transportation, and communications industries. We believe that the market place, rather than the bureaucrats, should regulate management decisions."[109]

In the leading case *Motor Vehicle Manufacturers Association v. State Farm Mutual Automobile Insurance Co.,*[110] the Supreme Court reviewed a decision by the National Highway Transportation Safety Administration (NHTSA) rescinding a rule that would have required automobile manufacturers to include airbags or automatic seatbelts in new cars.[111] This passive restraints regulation had a tortured history over a decade of some sixty notices, proposals, revisions, promulgations, and reconsiderations.[112] Finally promulgated in 1977, applying to new cars in phases beginning August 1982, it was nevertheless rescinded in 1981 by the newly elected administration. NHTSA cited as reasons for this action changes in the economic conditions faced by the automobile industry, indications that manufacturers intended to use a detachable belt design, which the agency believed would substantially undercut the belt usage otherwise expected from automatic belts, and the agency's general expectation of consumer resistance to *any* passive restraint system.

The Supreme Court analyzed NHTSA's action strictly in terms of the paradigm of expertise, applying a fairly rigorous, "adequate consideration" brand of arbitrary and capricious review. The majority

---

e.g., Texas v. United States, 756 F.2d 419 (5th Cir. 1985); World Communications, Inc. v. FCC, 735 F.2d 1465 (D.C. Cir. 1984); National Ass'n of Broadcasters v. FCC, 740 F.2d 1190 (D.C. Cir. 1984); National Tour Brokers Ass'n v. ICC, 671 F.2d 528 (D.C. Cir. 1982) (policy reversal can be supported by agency experience instead of factual support).

109. 1980 Republican Platform, 36 Cong. Q. 58-B, 71-B (1980). *See also* 1984 Republican Platform, 40 Cong. Q. 41-B, 42-B (1984). *See generally* G. Eads & M. Fix, eds., Relief or Reform? Reagan's Regulatory Dilemma (1984) (Urban Inst. Press).

110. 463 U.S. 29 (1983).

111. Automatic seatbelts consist of a strap extending from the top of the door frame to the center of the front seat, so that the occupant moves into the seat by sliding under the strap; with the door closed, the slack is automatically taken up, so that the seatbelt is effective without requiring any active measure. The belt connection to the front seat can be either detachable or permanent. *See generally* Warner, *Bags, Buckles, and Belts: The Debate over Mandatory Passive Restraints in Automobiles,* 8 J. Health, Pol. Pol'y L. 44 (1983).

112. 463 U.S. at 34. For a more complete account, *see* Milstone, *Automatic Occupant Restraints and Judicial Review: How a Federal Agency Can Violate Congressional Will and Get Away With It,* 19 U. Va. L. Rev. 693, 696–705 (1985).

concluded that NHTSA erred by failing to analyze obvious and important alternatives to total rescission of the rule, including a requirement that manufacturers use nondetachable automatic seatbelts rather than detachable ones, or that they use airbags. Thus, science and implicit norms about good science were the Court's touchstones for evaluating the adequacy of the agency's decision making process as described in NHTSA's statement of basis and purpose in the rule making record.

In contrast, Justice Rehnquist, joined by three others in partial dissent,[113] noted the undeniable role of politics in the decision: NHTSA's action was most easily understandable as the result of the 1980 election and a consequent change in regulatory philosophy, and such shifts are entitled to deference:

> The agency's changed view of the standard seems to be related to the election of a new President of a different political party. It is readily apparent that the responsible members of one administration may consider public resistance and uncertainties to be more important than do their counterparts in a previous administration. A change in administration brought about by the people casting their votes is a perfectly reasonable basis for an executive agency's reappraisal of the costs and benefits of its programs and regulations. As long as the agency remains within the bounds established by Congress, it is entitled to assess administrative records and evaluate priorities in light of the philosophy of the administration.[114]

By contrast, nowhere does the majority refer to an election, to regulatory philosophy, or to the possibility that politics might have played any role, positive or negative, in NHTSA's decision.

If politics means anything short of crass interest group giveaways, then politics was plainly involved in the rescission of the passive restraints regulation. Not only had candidate Reagan spoken out about deregulation generally, he had specifically discussed the auto industry and even the passive restraints regulation.[115] Presidential appointees

113. Justice Rehnquist, joined by Chief Justice Burger and Justices Powell and O'Connor, disagreed with that part of the majority opinion, holding that it was arbitrary and capricious for NHTSA to conclude that the potential benefits of detachable seatbelts were too doubtful to support the 1977 regulation.

114. Despite this sympathetic tone, the four dissenters joined key portions of the majority opinion, including the disposition. Their more deferential posture made a difference only in assessing NHTSA's rejection of detachable seatbelts.

115. See Lawyers as Lobbyists: Auto Safety Regulation, Harvard Law School Program on the Legal Profession (1983) (discussing Reagan campaign speech of May 19, 1980, and labeling it "a scathing indictment . . . of the Carter Administration's auto safety regulations and their effect on the health of the auto industry").

throughout the government were thoroughly committed to wholesale deregulation. It is totally implausible to suggest that NHTSA's evaluation of the scientific evidence and consideration of the regulatory alternatives were pursued within the trichotomy's paradigm of neutral, objective expertise. The regulatory result was all but ordained by the election results. The misidentification of the paradigm as science rather than politics gives the Court's decision an odd quality. If the strong role I posit for politics *was* permissible and indeed cause for deference (emphasizing the positive attributes of that paradigm), as Rehnquist suggested in *State Farm*, then failure of the agency and the Court to identify the political element in the agency's action may have resulted in too little judicial deference. If instead the strong role of politics was *not* permissible (emphasizing the negative), then perhaps an even more interventionist posture would have been appropriate, whether through the doctrinal content of the Court's reasoning or through the specificity of the remand order.[116]

Similarly, the court of appeals in *NRDC v. Gorsuch*[117] did not mention the obviously critical role of the 1980 election in explaining the EPA's change in regulatory direction concerning the "bubble" concept

---

116. *See, e.g.*, ILGWU v. Donovan, 722 F.2d 795 (D.C. Cir. 1983) (relaxation of wage and hour regulation of home knitwear industry rejected under heightened scrutiny within expertise paradigm; dicta on role of politics suggest that the court's awareness of the political context may have influenced it in striking an interventionist posture). As it is, even though the rescission was struck down, the agency on remand issued a rule suspending the effective date of the passive restraint requirement to allow states to enact mandatory seatbelt laws; if enough states enact such laws, NHTSA will not impose a passive restraints requirement. Thus, despite the Supreme Court loss, the administration was able to table the regulation for at least several years. Another sharp example is Public Citizen v. Steed, 733 F.2d 93 (D.C. Cir. 1984), in which the court of appeals struck down NHTSA's rescission of a consumer information regulation on grading of tire tread wear. The agency argued that information provided by the mandated testing and disclosure was too variable to be of good use to consumers was thus not justified by the costs to manufacturers and was misleading. The court reversed, noting that the agency had in the past evaluated the same evidence differently, and NHTSA now offered no new evidence sufficient to justify a change in policy. *Id.* at 101. As in *State Farm*, the court proceeded as though the agency action fell within the expertise paradigm, focusing on the variability of the industry's grade-assignment practices, and the asserted statistical unreliability of test procedures. The court concluded simply that as a matter of science or expertise "the data relied upon by NHTSA provided an insufficient basis for eliminating the tread wear grading requirements," and it evaluated the adequacy of the explanation as though the 1980 election and change in regulatory philosophy were wholly irrelevant to the administrator's judgment about the balancing of uncertain and disputable benefits and costs. *Id.* at 100. *See* R. Pierce, S. Schwartz, & P. Verkuil, Administrative Law and Process 366–68, 400–401 (1985) (arguing that greater deference is necessary in such areas of empirical uncertainty).

117. 685 F.2d 718 (D.C. Cir. 1982), *rev'd sub nom.*, Chevron USA, Inc. v. NRDC, 467 U.S. 837 (1984).

of air emissions tradeoffs among "point sources" under the Clean Air Act. It reversed the agency using a fairly independent scope of review, casting the problem of enforcement strategy as a matter of statutory interpretation rather than discretionary agency policy choice. The court of appeals thus never confronted the possible relevance of a new administration's regulatory philosophy, either because it assumed politics was irrelevant (an unlikely bit of navet) or because it implicitly ruled politics inadmissible (without revealing any reasoning, cogent or otherwise). In overruling, the Supreme Court in *Chevron USA, Inc. v. NRDC* acknowledged the political shift, and this may in part account for that court's willingness to view the bubble concept as a matter for reasonable agency discretion entitled to deference.

Several other recent cases involving administrative deregulation show a similar pattern of judicial misidentification of the decision making paradigm. Nor is the phenomenon limited to instances of rule making.[118] Moreover, the misidentification of decision making paradigms in this field of policy reversals is not new.[119] The result of it all is a structure of doctrine in which untested, easy assumptions about agency methods form a basis for consequently unreliable judgments about judicial deference.

2.5.5 Misspecifying the Attributes of the Decision Making Paradigms

A final descriptive difficulty concerns the weakness of the correlations between each decision making method and various positive and negative normative qualities. By way of brief review, recall: *politics* is associated positively with representative and democratic choice and negatively with subjectivity and willfulness; *science* and *expertise* are associated positively with rationality, objectivity, and efficiency and negatively with alienated, dehumanizing, and unresponsive (or anti-democratic) decision making; and *adjudicatory fairness* is associated pos-

118. Thus far courts have tended to uphold agency deregulatory policies announced through adjudication. Nevertheless, the proposition stands up: review is for fidelity not to *politics* but to the science-expertise paradigm. *See* RTC Transp. v. ICC, 731 F.2d 1502 (11th Cir. 1984) (sustaining award of motor carrier certificate based on new policy deregulating restrictions in new certificates of convenience and necessity). *Compare* Texas v. United States, 756 F.2d 419 (5th Cir. 1985) (new ICC construction of statute deregulating controls over bus lines sustained via straightforward *Chevron* statutory construction analysis rather than endorsing simple deference to political decision making).

119. Brennan v. Giles & Cotting, Inc., 504 F.2d 1255 (4th Cir. 1974) (court insisted on Occupational Safety and Health Revenue Commission [OSHRC] explanation of decisional inconsistency, although shift was probably associated with change in OSHRC membership and enforcement philosophy oddly unacknowledged by the court); Atchison, T. & S. F. Ry. Co. v. Wichita Bd. of Trade, 412 U.S. 800, 806 (1973).

itively with justice, neutrality, and consistency and negatively with stultifying proceduralism and unaccountability (see section 2.2 and fig. 1). These associations give the trichotomy's distinctions salience, but they also go far to account for the dynamics of legal and political discourse concerning administration, discretion, and judicial review.

Adjudicatory Fairness: We expect reasoned elaboration, consistency (as in stare decisis), and neutrality on the positive side of the scale and wooden proceduralism and unaccountability on the other. Does reality typically fit the model? One is struck with a flood of contrary examples and considerations: the ill-explained or even unexplained judgment, with selective use of precedents and legislative history, by both advocates and judges;[120] the litigator's practiced skill of predicting the votes of an appellate bench before the brief is even drafted; the judicial management of complex trials to assure efficiency rather than procedural gridlock; the evolution of small claims courts, housing courts, and alternative methods of dispute resolution.

Politics and Interest Accommodation: Again, the attributes correlate only loosely with reality. As regards Congress, there are several reasons to question the association with the positive norm of democratic representativeness. That is, even when the paradigm appears to be properly executed, with broad and balanced participation, critical problems of a deeper sort will exist: even in the best of campaigns, voters may not be adequately informed and candidates and positions may be too vaguely specified to create any serious contract between the elected and the represented. After the election, the problems of information continue, as the complexity of government makes it difficult to claim that officials are accountable for any particular decision or even class of decisions. But one should also question seriously the automatic association of various negative norms with politics because, in my view, politicians often act against electoral self-interest, political majorities frequently show solicitude of minorities, and rationality trumps passion in most public debates.

Expertise and Science: Notwithstanding the pervasive paeans in administrative law court opinions and commentary, the objectivity and rationality of science is a hotly debated proposition, even when science is properly conducted, and even in the natural sciences.[121] In the policy sciences it is probably no longer respectable to dispute the claim that

120. This is more than a matter of misexecution. As the realists and now critical legal studies scholars have argued in criticizing rule-formalism, there is good reason to question the possibility—in an epistemological sense—of the kind of consistency and fairness at the core of the Rule of Law paradigm.

121. *See generally* Frug, *The Ideology of Bureaucracy in American Law,* 97 Harv. L. Rev. 1277, 1286–92, 1318–34 (1984).

the scope for discretion or subjectivity is inescapably enormous.[122] This is even an article of faith in the curricula of schools of public policy and management. With respect to the negative attributes, I know of no empirical literature suggesting that bureaucratic work life is any more or less alienated than any other form of work life; and if the rejoinder is that all of modern work life is (tragically) bureaucratic, then the universality of the condition is not a valid basis for prescription through the trichotomy. That is, there would be nothing undesirable about alienated bureaucratic decision making because any form of decision making would share the same alienated character.

But what are we to make of the pattern of empirical weaknesses in these associations, both positive and negative? The associations are almost too fundamental to our thinking to admit a serious possibility that they are descriptively untenable. And it is in the very nature of a paradigm that there will be exceptions and deviations, and hence the intellectual inclination to marginalize the counterexamples. We just cannot tell how broadly correct the critique of misspecification is. (This is especially true because our methods of case-by-case commentary make any effort to construct a global perspective subject to skepticism, if not derision, on grounds of being scattershot or anecdotal.) Yet the commonness of counterexamples to the normative attributions presents a fair challenge to the prescriptive coherence of the trichotomy's paradigms.[123] My conclusion is that these counterexamples go beyond mere instances of misexecution of the particular methodology. They go to the premises of each paradigm. We should reconsider whether the content of the trichotomy's paradigms are correctly specified: political decision making, for example, *may not mean what we commonly take it to mean.*[124]

This pitfall of misspecification, when combined with the reality of misexecution, makes a powerful argument indeed that the trichotomy is ill-suited for prescriptive tasks. Among those tasks is the implicit

122. *See generally* Reich, *Public Administration and Public Deliberation: An Interpretive Essay,* Yale L.J. 1617 (1985).

123. Shades of Talcott Parsons, worries a colleague. Not really. I am not claiming that conflict is ipso facto catastrophic, nor am I obsessed with tidiness. Indeed, our system's vitality and its engine of evolution would seem to be based on tension and competition. Nevertheless, my inquiry has, I think, little to do with functional sociology, and more to do with the history and evolution of ideas. Rather than Parsons, I think of Thomas Kuhn. How well do our familiar paradigms serve us in explaining and improving reality?

124. Then what does it mean? I offer small pieces of an answer in secs. 3.1 (the categorization problem, or difficulties in separating the paradigms) and 6.1 (varieties of politics, and the problem of judicial appraisal of its proper role in decision making).

work of role-definition entailed in scope of review analysis. And *that* is the very heart of administrative law.

2.5.6 Conclusions on the Descriptive Inadequacy of a Separation of Powers Ethos

What assurance does administrative law offer that systemic problems of governance are controlled? The procedures imposed by law *should* promote expertise, political accountability, and fairness; the rigors of substantive judicial review (under such verbal formulas as arbitrary and capricious, substantial evidence, abuse of discretion) *should* cause agencies to favor the legitimate methods of decision making identified by the trichotomy and to avoid arbitrariness and irrationality. But these approaches are quite indirect.

Efforts to make law more directly helpful in controlling the character of agency decision making processes run afoul of principles of deference based on the trichotomy. Areas of doctrine that demonstrate this include:

1. Judicially created limitations, as in the *Morgan IV* case, on the extent to which reviewing courts will "probe the mind" of the decision maker to ensure that the administrative record accurately reflects the decision making process, and to test the quality of the manner in which decision making methodologies (whether scientific, political, or fairness) are executed.[125]

2. Presumptions of "regularity," especially concerning the neutrality and expertise of the decision maker, which when combined with the preceding principle makes all but impossible the task of the party challenging the agency's decision making methodology.[126]

3. Deference to the agency's design of its decision making process, as in the *Vermont Yankee* case, with the consequent problem that courts are handicapped in identifying and prescribing procedural measures likely to improve the quality of administrative action.[127]

125. United States v. Morgan, 313 U.S. 409 (1941).
126. *See, e.g.*, Association of Nat'l Advertisers, Inc. v. FTC, 627 F.2d 1151 (D.C. Cir. 1979), *cert. denied*, 446 U.S. 921 (1980).
127. Vermont Yankee Nuclear Power Corp. v. NRDC, 435 U.S. 519 (1978). *See generally* Stewart, *Vermont Yankee and the Evolution of Administrative Procedure*, 91 Harv. L. Rev. 1805 (1978); Byse, *Vermont Yankee and the Evolution of Administrative Procedure: A Somewhat Different View*, 91 Harv. L. Rev. 1823 (1978); Nathanson, *The Vermont Yankee*

4. The unsatisfyingly pretermitted judicial effort to discipline off-the-record ex parte communications during informal proceedings, so promisingly launched in the *Home Box Office* case.[128]

Such fictions undermine the possibility of testing the genuine expertise of the agency in the matter at hand—at the time the decision was actually made, and by the person who actually made it, since the record on review can obviously be a post hoc or even irrelevant construction.[129] To the extent that the agency action is pursuant to a delegation requiring political choices as the agent of Congress, courts can do little to evaluate the quality of the political process employed to make the decision. Indeed, courts have done very little in administrative law to develop and enforce norms of effective political process.[130] And to the extent that the agency action is thought to deserve deference because it is courtlike, based on principles of the adjudicatory fairness paradigm, the leaded veil undermines the ability of judicial review to detect agency bias. Doctrine insists strongly on a presumption of regularity and fairness while denying effective means of policing the presumptions. I return to this theme in chapter 6.

Nuclear Power Opinion: A Masterpiece of Statutory Misinterpretation, 16 San Diego L. Rev. 183 (1979); Rodgers, Jr., *A Hard Look at Vermont Yankee: Environmental Law under Close Scrutiny*, 67 Geo. L.J. 699 (1979); Scalia, *Vermont Yankee: The APA, the D.C. Circuit, and the Supreme Court*, 1978 Sup. Ct. Rev. 345 (1978).

128. *Compare* Home Box Office, Inc., v. FCC, 567 F.2d 9 (D.C. Cir. 1977), *cert. denied*, 434 U.S. 829, *with* Action for Children's Television v. FCC, 564 F.2d 458 (D.C. Cir. 1977) (suggesting limitation of broadcasting rights or programming revenues), *and* Sierra Club v. Costle, 657 F.2d 298 (D.C. Cir. 1981) (relatively lax restrictions on interagency and congressional contacts).

129. This is true of both formal and informal action. No less than in court opinions, the reasons given may depart materially from the true grounds for the decision. In informal agency action the risks of this are obviously greater, inasmuch as the decision maker is not so strictly limited to a decision on the record. *See, e.g.,* Florida E. Coast Ry. v. United States, *supra* n. 4.

130. The expansion of standing, the growth of statutory and judicial requirements of disclosure, and the increasing popularity of regulatory negotiations are all aspects of what Richard Stewart first termed the interest group representation theory of administrative law (*see* sec. 5.6). These and other developments establish a protopolitical system of administrative decision making. The difficulty is the absence of sound norms for assessing the progress of this development in general and the soundness of its execution in particular cases. If judges will not or cannot reason and analyze about political decision making, then there can be no judicial review. If there can be no judicial review, then the Rule of Law approach to control of discretion is untenable. If the Rule of Law approach is untenable, then is the solution to ignore the familiar questions and choose some answerable ones or to find a substitute approach? *See* ch. 7, where I suggest the latter.

The point is not that legislatures, agencies, and courts are not really practicing politics, science, and adjudicatory fairness. I have meant here to demonstrate that understanding when, where, and how each paradigm is used is a deeply complicated exercise only poorly aided by the simplistic descriptions and norms reflected in administrative law doctrines and court opinions. The next stage of my argument, however, is that there are not only descriptive and normative weaknesses in the trichotomy but also fundamental conceptual problems with the categories.

CHAPTER 3

The Trichotomy's Conceptual Failings

The most immediate conceptual difficulty in using the trichotomy as a basis for scaling judicial deference is that the paradigms of politics, science, and adjudicatory fairness are difficult if not impossible to separate. Each entails elements of the other. So no particular problem or agency action can be fairly characterized as crucially dependent on any one method of decision making. Even highly technical matters of statistical methodology and scientific study, for example, almost *always* entail judgments quite plausibly termed "political" in nature. Yet most doctrinal analysis, at least as expressed in opinions, proceeds as though the paradigms were distinguishable in practice.[1] To the extent that judicial deference varies in relation to asserted but unsustainable differences in decision making methods, murkiness and confusion result. This is the central point of section 3.1, where I demonstrate the confu-

1. The media reported that, during district court oral argument on the constitutionality of the Gramm-Rudman-Hollings Deficit Reduction Act, Judge Scalia suggested that the "green eye shade" expertise of budget officials would effectively constrain discretion in forecasting deficits, thereby avoiding problems of excessive delegation of the congressional power of the purse. It is abundantly clear, however, that even short-term deficit projections are and have been tremendously influenced by politically based judgments about, for example: supply-side economics; the effectiveness of government programs intended to curb oil imports, control health care costs, solve engineering problems in development of defense systems; the future path of crop prices, farm incomes, and agriculture program costs; business and consumer confidence, which strongly affect the major macroeconomic variables, and so forth. Notwithstanding Judge Scalia's surmise, it was precisely the recognition of the discretionary nature of the forecasting task that led to so much congressional haggling over the respective roles of the Office of Management and Budget (OMB), the Congressional Budget Office, and the General Accounting Office (GAO).

sion and its sources by exploring examples from two seemingly unrelated regulatory contexts: control of occupational health hazards, and market deregulation in pipelines and radio broadcasting formats. In section 3.2, I return to the problem of attributive, or normative, duality described in my initial exposition of the trichotomy in chapter 2: Each paradigm has a set of positive and negative associations; the conceptual problem is that analyses based on these norms are unstable because there is no way to determine which attributes to emphasize and hence how deferential to be. As examples, I consider occupational health (in reprise) and aspects of procedural due process, or the design of fair procedures.

Chapter 4 is an extended example of how the trichotomy's conceptual shortcomings can account for confusion in doctrines of scope of judicial review. In scaling the rigor of that review, agency determinations are sorted into fact-law-policy categories, to which a verbal formula for the degree of judicial deference can be applied. Doctrine is unsuccessful at disciplining judicial discretion because (1) the categorical distinctions are unsustainable and (2) the verbal formulas (such as "arbitrary and capricious" or "substantial evidence") elude robust definition. Neither observation is novel. But explanations of the continuing difficulties in these areas usually amount to reminders that life is, after all, complicated.[2] The reminders are valid, but I urge that there are deeper difficulties, traceable to the two underlying conceptual failings of the trichotomy-based approach to scaling deference: (1) the unsustainable distinctions between the three paradigms, and (2) the uncertain, selective emphasis on opposing sides of the attributive duality.

Let me be clear about what I am *not* arguing. This is not an attack against the idle straw-man proposition that science, fairness, and politics are in some sense pure. Instead, I want to demonstrate that (1) too much doctrinal reasoning amounts to arbitrary selection and emphasis of one or another paradigm in order to scale judicial deference, and (2) this makes the resulting conclusions conceptually unstable. By this I mean that observers and self-conscious participants will find the process of scaling deference to be largely unguided. As a result, this scaling

2. *See, e.g.,* Universal Camera Corp. v. NLRB, 340 U.S. 474, 488–89 (1951) (Frankfurter, J.) ("A formula for judicial review of administrative action may afford grounds for certitude but cannot assure certainty of application. Some scope for judicial discretion can be avoided only by falsifying the actual process of judging or by using the formula as an instrument of futile casuistry"); *See also* Levin, *Federal Scope-of-Review Standards: A Preliminary Restatement,* 37 Admin. L. Rev. 95, 97 (1985) ("[R]eview standards inevitably call for subjective decisions by judges who employ them"); K. Davis, 5 Administrative Law Treatise § 29:1 (1984).

tends to degenerate from a subtle process of judgment into a coarse selection from a menu with only three options: at one end, independent or substituted judgment, an increasingly rare explicit choice; in the middle, a vast range, lumped together as "reasonableness"; and at the other end, extreme deference to the agency. The formlessness of the middle range is troubling enough, but the growing importance of extreme deference (including nonreviewability) is a crisis in administrative law: it portends an abdication of judicial responsibility for the quality of administrative government.

3.1 Collapsing Categories: Science, Fairness, and Politics; Fact, Law, and Policy

Each of the decision making methodologies—interest accommodation, science, and adjudicatory fairness—is an ideal type that never exists in pure form but in practice coexists with the others. So, for example, the balancing or accommodation of various interests is characteristic of political choice but will be affected by scientific information, as well as by fairness norms that the decision maker might develop and apply without regard to electoral consequences and personal preferences (at least over some range).

3.1.1 Example: OSHA and Carcinogens

Among its other missions, the Occupational Safety and Health Administration sets standards limiting the exposure of workers to substances believed to pose significant risks to health, such as asbestos, cotton dust, and benzene.[3] Judicial review of these regulations is especially difficult because each is a complex amalgam of scientific and political choices. Moreover, several elements of the adjudicatory fairness paradigm are implicit in the analyses of competing burdens and

3. See Occupational Safety and Health Act, 29 U.S.C. § 651, et seq. See generally R. Crandall & L. Lave, eds., The Scientific Basis of Health and Safety Regulation (1981). Among the key court decisions involving judicial review of OSHA actions are: Daniel Int'l Corp. v. OSHA, 683 F.2d 361 (11th Cir. 1982) (findings and conclusion upheld if supported by substantial evidence on the record considered as a whole); Boise Cascade Corp. v. OSHA, 694 F.2d 584 (9th Cir. 1982) ("feasibility" question is one of fact, subject to substantial evidence review); Donovan v. Anheuser-Busch, Inc., 666 F.2d 315 (8th Cir. 1981) (appropriate scope of review for questions of law); American Airlines, Inc. v. Secretary of Labor, 578 F.2d 38 (2d Cir. 1978) (court has power to ascertain whether agency applied correct legal standard); Electric Smith, Inc. v. Secretary of Labor, 666 F.2d 1267 (9th Cir. 1982) ("reasonable" administrative interpretations of statutory language must be upheld).

risks and in assigning burdens of production and persuasion in agency proceedings.

Clearly, selecting the appropriate ceiling on, say, cotton dust particulates in a textile mill, involves the scientific assessment of a dose-response curve relating levels of worker exposure to predictions of health consequences.[4] But that assessment is inevitably riddled with uncertainties because epidemiology, like virtually all sciences, involves uncertainties of prediction and measurement. Science alone, to the extent one can conceive of it, cannot determine what to do with those uncertainties. If, hypothetically, at an exposure of 500 micrograms per cubic meter per hour there is a 30 percent chance that a worker will contract secondary bysinosis (brown lung disease), and we are 80 percent confident that this estimate is correct within 10 percentage points . . . . There is obviously ample room for the play of values in deciding what to make of all the data and all the risk. And those uncertainties must be combined with uncertainties on the other side of the equation concerning the costs and effectiveness of control measures. The science is inseparable from the value choices which are the familiar grist of political decision making.

This problem of categorization is common outside the law. Consider the tremendous controversy concerning the disastrous explosion of the space shuttle *Challenger*. Apparently, most engineers at the company that constructed the solid fuel rocket boosters felt that the cold weather created uncertainty and hence added risk with respect to the performance of the O-ring seals. Managerial officials at the company and within NASA evaluated the importance of the uncertainty differently. Observers have speculated that nonscientific considerations, such as the already-delayed 1986 schedule of shuttle missions and the company management's strong desire to please NASA contracting officials, were given too much weight, with tragic consequences. The

4. *See* American Textile Mfrs. Inst., Inc. v. Donovan *(Cotton Dust)*, 452 U.S. 490 (1981). The dose-response curve shows what the consequences in health terms will be at each level of exposure, or doses, of the hazardous substance. The health effects may be measured in any of several ways, such as worker-years lost to illness, cost of treatment, or deaths. The dose-response curve is generally very difficult to construct. When examining human health effects, there are usually very few exposure levels at which one can measure the health effects. Those exposure levels may not be over the range of doses contemplated for the regulatory controls. Given a dosage, measuring the associated health effects is complicated, perhaps because of reporting problems, or because the effects take decades to develop, or because the interaction with other environmental factors (smoking, diet) can cause spurious data. Animal studies do not solve all of these problems. Obviously, there is a problem in extrapolating across species. Typically, the incidence rates are extremely low, so that many thousands of animals may be needed to do the testing on a single substance.

difficult conceptual and management problem is how to weight or blend the paradigms in making such choices. It is clearly wrong to ignore engineering advice, but it is also wrong to give the decision entirely to engineers—their professional perspective does not include certain practical constraints, and endless money and time might be devoted to risk-reduction.

The science is also inseparable from the concerns of consistency, precedent, neutrality, equity, and fidelity to established standards or law characteristic of adjudicatory decision making: the expert decision maker must bear all of these norms in mind as she sits in judgment about the selection of methodologies, the sequencing of experimental and research projects, the competing claims for priority for this or that group of workers, the principles used to regulate one industry as compared with another, the relevance of constraints of statutory purposes or settled agency policy, and so on. The scientist, or at least the scientist-manager, is judge as well as expert and interest accommodator.

As I develop below, the same sort of analysis can be repeated for the other two paradigms of the trichotomy. Thus, accommodation of interest group pressures in the regulation of occupational health hazards is certainly influenced by the methods and norms of science and adjudicatory fairness. And adjudicatory fairness—how much consistency, how much participation, how much freedom to fashion and impose new standards of conduct—can neither be assessed without attention to scientific learning nor divorced from concerns of political acceptability.

In short, the choice of a 500-microgram standard rather than 750, 250, or further research, can be made in any number of ways, including the spin of a roulette wheel. But choosing in a way that conforms to widely shared views about sound public policymaking requires the integration of scientific, political, and fairness elements, rather than reliance on any single method.

It should therefore come as no surprise that anomalous court decisions can occur as a result of a compartmentalized approach to methodological choices. In reviewing an OSHA rule limiting benzene exposures, for example, the Supreme Court was obviously troubled by the modest weight of evidence concerning risk at the exposure levels prohibited by the challenged rule.[5] Rather than directly challenging

5. Industrial Union Dep't, AFL-CIO v. American Petroleum Inst., 448 U.S. 607, 631 (1980) ("The evidence in the administrative record of adverse effects of benzene exposure at 10 ppm is sketchy at best"). For discussion of the case, *see, e.g.*, Bangser, *An Inherent Role for Cost-Benefit Analysis in Judicial Review of Agency Decisions: A New Perspective on OSHA Rulemaking*, 10 B.C. Envtl. Aff. L. Rev. 365 (1982); Rogers, *Judicial Review of Risk Assessments: The Role of Decision Theory in Unscrambling the Benzene Decision*, 11 Envtl. L.

and overruling the "expert" judgment of the agency on the merits of its estimate of the health threat, the Court was persuaded by the complaining industry to view the question as one of statutory interpretation. By approaching the dispute as a problem appropriate for traditional judicial law-finding, rather than scientific or political methods, the Court was able to avoid the logic of deference. Quite clearly, however, OSHA's regulatory action was the result of an amalgam of legal, scientific and policy judgments. The Court remanded, instructing that the statute requires a threshold determination of a "significant risk of harm" as predicate for regulation. Nothing in the Court's opinion suggests that the agency would not have been free—had it not been for the intervening change in administrations and regulatory philosophies[6]— to reach the identical result a second time, using the same mix of scientific and discretionary assessments of risks and competing concerns. In a hypothetical *Benzene II*, with no stronger evidentiary support but an agency "finding" of "significant risk," the Court would have faced precisely the same deference dilemma, but with a less plausible option of characterizing the challenge to the agency as a question of law; having rejected the agency position once, courts are unlikely to reject it again—and certainly not for the same reason.[7]

3.1.2 Example: Economics and Market Ideology

Pipelines: Another example, from a seemingly quite different regulatory field, is *Farmers Union Central Exchange v. FERC*, in which plaintiffs challenged the administrative deregulation of oil pipeline companies.[8] Reagan administration appointees, generally committed to a free market approach, concluded that after some seventy-five years of price controls, the forces of competition are now sufficient to assure that market forces would lead to "just and reasonable" rates—the stat-

---

301 (1981); Davis, *The "Shotgun Wedding" of Science and Law: Risk Assessment and Judicial Review,* 10 Colum. J. Env. L. 67, 78–82 (1985).

6. The decision was handed down in June 1980, and Carter administration officials indicated an intention to renew the rule making effort. After the election, however, newly appointed officials apparently put the benzene problem on the back burner. A court order remedied delay, and OSHA initiated another rule making to control benzene hazards. 50 Fed. Reg. 50512 (Dec. 10, 1985).

7. *Compare* Vermont Yankee Nuclear Power v. NRDC, 435 U.S. 519 (1978), *with* Baltimore Gas & Elec. Co. v. NRDC, 462 U.S. 87 (1983); Scenic Hudson Preservation Conf. v. FPC, 354 F.2d 608 (2d Cir. 1965), *with* Scenic Hudson Preservation Conf. v. FPC (II), 453 F.2d 463 (2d Cir. 1971), *rehearing en banc denied by an equally divided court,* 453 F.2d 494, *cert. denied,* 407 U.S. 926 (1972).

8. 734 F.2d 1486 (D.C. Cir. 1984).

utory standard. A Federal Energy Regulatory Commission (FERC) rule implemented this view by dismantling the traditional price regulation machinery and substituting a monitoring mechanism that would permit intervention only in cases of "gross overreaching and unconscionable gouging" by the unfettered pipeline companies.[9]

What is one to make of the FERC decision? Here again, it makes little sense to structure the analysis by assigning the decision (or even sub-elements of it) to categories of expertise, political choice, and adjudicatory fairness.

The D.C. Circuit Court of Appeals wrote an opinion focusing on the expertise dimension, and its "hard-look" review led to a reversal and remand, in essence because the proffered justification for the rule fell short of what the court considered an adequate demonstration of thorough expert consideration.[10] But by relying on trichotomy-based notions to dissect the agency action and conclude that expertise was the appropriate paradigm and the relevant normative framework, the court avoided confronting the difficult reality of the situation.

The thin evidentiary basis for FERC's conclusion that market forces would produce reasonable pipeline rates was perfectly appropriate in the minds of regulators who had an abiding faith in market economics and a strong inclination to err on the side of deregulation rather than government intervention. Moreover, they presumably calculated the economic costs and benefits—including considerations of equity and expectations—which led them to their policy conclusion.[11] One might well argue that the agency's judgment entailed an exercise of discretion no different from that which Congress delegated in the statutory command to assure "just and reasonable rates." It is misleading to evaluate the result in terms of the adequacy of the demonstrated expertise when a great deal of what is at stake are the largely political choices entailed in assessing risks, making predictions, and gauging what is just. The court faced, but did not directly address, the issue of *how much* political dis-

---

9. Williams Pipeline Co., 21 FERC (CCH) § 61,260 at 61,597 (Nov. 30, 1982), *quoted in* 734 F.2d at 1492. FERC did not explain at what point gouging becomes unconscionable. I use the term *rule* in its technical sense. Although the FERC decision was in form an individual rate proceeding, commonly referred to as an opinion or order, such actions are rule makings for APA purposes. *See* APA § 551. In the instant proceeding, for example, FERC sought to determine far-reaching quasi-legislative matters.

10. 734 F.2d at 1511 ("It is well established that an agency has a duty to consider responsible alternatives to its chosen policy and to give a reasoned explanation for its rejection of such alternatives. This responsibility becomes especially important when the agency admits its own choice is substantially flawed. We find that FERC failed to satisfy this duty" [footnotes and citations omitted]).

11. 21 FERC (CCH) at § 61,612.

cretion should be permitted, including the political discretion to decide what quantum of hard evidence should be required in order to support a major policy shift. The result happens to suit my own predilections, but as served up by the court it was an ill-conceived effort to separate politics and science.

Broadcasting: The court's approach in *Farmers Union* contrasts with that taken by the Supreme Court in *FCC v. WNCN Listeners Guild*.[12] In *WNCN*, the commission successfully appealed a D.C. Circuit decision rejecting administrative deregulation of radio format diversity—an area of FCC activity thrust on a reluctant agency ten years earlier in a D.C. Circuit interpretation of the "public interest" licensing standard in the Communications Act.[13] The agency's principal rationale for its decision was that market forces would lead to unregulated diversity in format as competing broadcasters interactively selected formats to appeal to various audiences. Rather than scientific proof of the effects of deregulation, or analysis of the obstacles to fluid adjustments in format by risk-averse broadcasters, the agency rested its decision on (1) arguments that format regulation is administratively difficult because of the nature of the judgments involved, (2) the (unproven) possibility that regulation would deter innovative programming, and (3) the absence of "proof" that format regulation is necessary to ensure diversity.[14]

The Supreme Court reasoned, first, that the need for format regulation was not a matter of interpreting the statutory "public interest" requirement—a question of law—as the D.C. Circuit had insisted for a decade.[15] Yet it is difficult to see why this need be so. Admittedly, the vagueness of the statutory public interest standard grants considerable discretion to the agency. But it argues too much to say, as the *WNCN* court did, that this discretion, if exercised rationally, must be free of constraints imposed by judicial construction of the statute. After all, the court of appeals was asserting not a strong judicial role in format review of individual broadcast licensees but only a rather modest requirement that the commission *consider* the diversity issue in order to ensure conformity with the statutory standard. Indeed, the court of appeals considered this requirement merely an effort to implement the general conclusion of law set forth in 1943 by the Supreme Court, in

12. 450 U.S. 582 (1981).

13. Citizens Committee to Save WEFM v. FCC, 506 F.2d 246, 268 (D.C. Cir. 1974) (en banc).

14. *WNCN*, 450 U.S. at 588.

15. *Id.* at 593–94. The court of appeals for the D.C. Circuit first articulated its format doctrine in Citizens Committee to Preserve the Voice of the Arts in Atlanta v. FCC, 436 F.2d 267 (D.C. Cir. 1970).

National Broadcasting Co. v. United States, that the goal of the act is "to secure the maximum benefits of radio to all the people." It is difficult to discern why this 1943 determination was one of law, appropriate for the court's paradigm of adjudicatory fairness, while the D.C. Circuit's format rule is a determination of policy inappropriate unless originated by the agency. Yes, the Supreme Court's conclusion on this point is reasonable enough. But so is the opposite conclusion, which would leave the commission free to apply the standard in particular cases and to develop substantial amounts of policy discretion concerning its application, much as the Labor Board enjoys in defining "employee" under the *Hearst* holding.[16]

Nevertheless, the Court went on to stress the importance of deference to the commission's expertise. But does not expertise require that facts be scientifically developed, and the decision based thereon? Not necessarily, the Court wrote, because "the Commission's decisions must sometimes rest on judgment and prediction rather than pure factual determinations. In such cases complete factual support for the Commission's ultimate conclusions is not required."[17] The Court then shifted to an emphasis on the "policy" character of the decision to deregulate format diversity, involving as it does the "accommodation" of conflicting objectives.

In terms of the trichotomy, this reasoning demonstrates the ready availability of the interest accommodation paradigm, by which conflicting policies are resolved, when a court for whatever reason concludes that it is inappropriate to insist on scientific rigor as the basis for agency choice. The Supreme Court did not require the FCC to *prove* its predictions of market forces and broadcaster responses or even demonstrate that proof was unobtainable. It instead simply ruled that the commissioners' faith in the market, combined with their denial of agency wisdom to regulate, was "reasonable." The contrast with *Farmers Union* is striking. Yet there is no particular reason to believe that economic predictions in the broadcasting sector are any more difficult than predictions in the energy sector. Indeed, the possibilities for experimentation in the former increase the plausibility of a scientific, or empirically driven, approach.

3.1.3 The General Boundary Problem: Recap and Conclusions

We can, therefore, revise figure 1, above, to reflect the notion that each methodology draws on the others. Consider figure 2, in which the characteristic methods of the paradigms are stated in shorthand.

16. *See* sec. 4.1 for a comparison of *Hearst* and *Packard* with *WNCN.* Policy and implementation discretion for the administrator do not disappear simply because the

FIGURE 2.

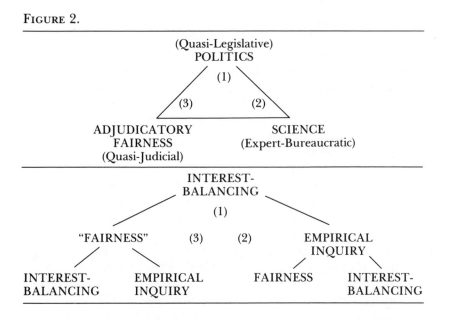

In the interest of concreteness, let me play out this interrelationship with respect to one characteristic of each paradigm. It may be helpful if the reader has a particular agency decision in mind, such as regulation of a workplace chemical hazard. The interests to be accommodated include those of exposed workers, unexposed workers concerned with job security, management, investors, and consumers. The technical issues include industry compliance costs, the wherewithal of differently situated companies to sustain those costs, the health risks and benefits associated with alternative levels of hazard control, and so forth. More particularly, these technical issues will require debatable judgments about: levels of statistical confidence deemed necessary to support administrative action (or forbearance from action); what kinds of studies to conduct and when; and choices in methodology, such as selecting among tools for economic forecasting, species of cost-benefit analysis, or not using cost benefit analysis at all.[18] With all this in mind:

1. BALANCING: To identify the interests implicated in a particular decision and measure their stakes, the putative pol must

court asserts power to construct some basic legal guidelines on that discretion. *See also Benzene, supra* n. 5 (interpreting broad grant of discretion to be limited by requirement, stated nowhere in the statute or legislative history, that OSHA may regulate only on finding a "significant risk").

17. *WNCN,* 450 U.S. at 594–95.

18. *See* S. Kelman, *Cost-Benefit Analysis: An Ethical Critique,* Regulation, Jan.–Feb. 1981, at 33–41.

rely on EMPIRICAL INQUIRY; go to *step 2*. But in judging how seriously to weigh the pros and cons as determined for each identified interest, the pol will consider matters of ADJUDICA-TORY FAIRNESS, such as the extent to which this decision will be consistent with the manner in which interests were balanced last time, or consistent with some pre-chosen set of policies, or *different* enough to justify inconsistency; the pol will be concerned with the political costs of the appearance of adjudicatory arbitrariness; go to *step 3*.

2. *EMPIRICAL:* To decide what data to collect, what levels of risk and uncertainty to tolerate in making scientific judgments, how much time and money to spend on research, and what problems to investigate and when, the putative expert must rely on INTEREST BALANCING; go to *step 1*. Moreover, in making judgments about methodology (such as how many studies to conduct, whether to insist on a small business impact statement, or whether to use industry or government cost projections) the expert will be concerned that judgments made in today's controversy be defensibly consistent with judgments made in controversies yesterday and tomorrow. And difficult judgment should not be made in splendid isolation but must be preceded by some fair opportunity for affected people to express their views. All of this being an inquiry into ADJUDICATORY FAIRNESS, we must go to *step 3*.

3. *FAIRNESS:* To decide whether the judgments at issue today are being handled in a manner consistent with previous and future judgments, the putative adjudicator must rely on EMPIRI-CAL INQUIRY to determine the extent to which the circumstances are comparable or similar to the circumstances upon which a prior decision rule (or law) was based; go to *step 2*. To decide whether the empirical dissimilarities in circumstances are important to the equities at stake, the decision maker must identify and weigh the interests affected, determining which are unsubstantially implicated and which must be accommodated. This, of course, requires the methods of INTEREST BALANCING; go to *step 1*.

The most important consequence of this conflation of the politics/adjudicatory fairness/science trichotomy is the instability and confusion it produces in applying those doctrines whose analytical robustness depends on these very distinctions. As long as courts decide the appropriate levels of deference based on unsustainable distinctions, their reasoning will often have an ad hoc appearance, if not reality—as in the examples above contrasting *Farmers Union Central Exchange* with *WNCN Listeners Guild*. Fuzziness is about the best we can hope for, but even that will usually be difficult to come by if one rigorously explores the interdependency and coincidence of the decision making paradigms. All of this would seem to be of some significance since, as shown in chapter 2, a great many legal doctrines rest to one degree or another on the trichotomy.[19] This is not to say there is absolutely no predictability to the application of doctrine. The issue is whether that modest predictability, such as it is, flows from an artificial truncation of possibilities induced by the pervasive separation of powers ethos.

3.2 The Attributive Duality Created by Positive and Negative Norms

The second conceptual difficulty with the separation of powers-based trichotomy of decision making paradigms is the doctrinal murkiness that results from the *attributive duality* of each paradigm. In chapter 4 I explore the significance of these difficulties in the particularly important context of scope of review doctrines. Recall that the trichotomy associates with each paradigm a rich set of positive and negative norms, reviewed in the margin.[20] I use the phrase *attributive duality* to refer to the analytical possibility of selectively emphasizing either negative or positive attributes, unchecked by thoroughgoing empirical inquiry. I could instead use the term *normative duality*. It depends on whether one is inclined to think, for example, that politics is both good and bad or

19. Outside of administrative law proper, a prominent example of the same unsatisfactory reliance on the trichotomy is equitable restraint in remedies against defendants in public law litigation, especially institutional reform cases. *See* Chayes, *Public Law Litigation and the Burger Court*, 96 Harv. L. Rev. 4 (1982); Fallon, *On Justiciability, Remedies, and Public Law Litigation: Notes on the Jurisprudence of Lyons*, 59 N.Y.U.L. Rev. 1, 59–74 (1984); D. Horowitz, The Courts and Social Policy (1977).

20. See sec. 2.2. This summarizes that discussion.

Associated with the paradigm of adjudicatory fairness are the normatively *positive* attributes of neutrality, consistency, adherence to precedent and, in a general sense, reasoned elaboration and Rule of Law; and the *negative* attributes of lack of accountability, proceduralism, and stultifying conservatism (in the sense of being past-focused).

Associated with the paradigm of science and technical expertise are the normatively *positive* attributes of objectivity, rationality and efficiency, including managerial efficiency; and the *negative* norms of being impersonal, alienating and elitist, objections familiar from critiques of bureaucracy and "technocracy."

Finally, associated with the paradigm of politics or interest accommodation are the normatively *positive* attributes of democratic control and participation; and the *negative* attributes of subjectivity, willfulness, and tyranny of the majority.

instead that politics has several attributes, some good and others bad. This selective weighting of pros and cons is merely the particular case of a problem common to the logical structure of many forms of reasoning, and in that sense I write loosely in counting it a failing of the trichotomy rather than an intrinsic property of categories and formality. Nevertheless, this familiar difficulty in reasoning deserves careful exploration in administrative law because it generates substantial uncertainty when trichotomy-based distinctions are used to scale judicial deference. This requires brief elaboration, after which I provide three doctrinal examples.

The Duality of Politics: On one hand, the court might feel that the political character of an agency's decision making process, with its associated positive attributes of accountability and participation, calls for substantial judicial deference. This is because (1) politics is not the method, and hence not the business, of courts, and (2) since the positive norms of politics afford protection against arbitrary, bad government, the court can safely distance itself from political choice and demonstrate comity. On the other hand, the court might look at the same matter and conclude that (1) the negative attributes of political decision making (majority tyranny, unaccountable subjectivity, unprincipled willfulness) present serious risks of arbitrary, bad government and hence (2) create an occasion for judicial intervention to impose other, more positive attributes. In the case of politics, that judicial intervention is rarely to impose the positive attributes of politics, such as improved representativeness.[21] Instead, the court will try to impose the positive attributes of one of the other paradigms—for example, the added objectivity and rationality of science[22] or the greater neutrality

21. John Ely's representation-reinforcing theory of judicial review provides some support for a stronger judicial role in this respect. *See* J. Ely, Democracy and Distrust (1980); *see also* Choper, *The Supreme Court and the Political Branches: Democratic Theory and Practice,* 122 U. Pa. L. Rev. 810 (1974). But the parallel is not perfect. There is a plausible argument that *sub*constitutional judicial decisions in administrative law are a far less appropriate context for these sorts of structural adjustments—at least explicitly. Nevertheless, I urge in chs. 6 and 7 a change in doctrine and practice that is consistent with Ely's thesis, though adding a more frankly substantive tone.

Judicially promoted intervention in agency proceedings, the expansion of reviewability, agency-sponsored public interest participation, and related developments have been interpreted by some commentators, notably Richard Stewart, as evidence of increasing attention to the role of politics in curbing administrative arbitrariness and promoting "public values." See my discussion of the interest group representation model in sec. 5.2.

22. *See, e.g.,* Motor Vehicle Mfrs. Ass'n v. State Farm Mut. Ins. Co., 463 U.S. 29 (1983) (agency cannot unreasonably narrow range of regulatory options to be thoroughly evaluated); Farmers Union Cent. Exch. v. FERC, 734 F.2d 1486 (D.C. Cir. 1984) (agency must supply evidence rather than market ideology to justify administrative

and regularity of Rule of Law formalities.[23] The imposition may be in the form of a court substituting its own judgment but is more commonly accomplished by remand, with accompanying instructions effectively commanding an adjustment in the agency's choice of decision making paradigm.[24]

The Duality of Science and Expertise: On one hand, the court might feel that the agency's expert determination of facts or integration of competing considerations deserves judicial deference because (1) such expert decision making methods are not the province of judges and (2) in light of the positive qualities of objectivity, professionalism, and rationality, expertness assures us of good government. On the other hand, the court might (1) focus on negative norms—the dangers that experts will be isolated, insensitive to external criticism from opposing scientists or others, and unresponsive to the legitimate claims of political accountability and responsiveness. In such circumstances, (2) the court will intervene to address the perceived deficiencies in the agency's execution of the expert methodology[25] or will elevate the importance of another of the trichotomy's paradigms in the decision making mix. This latter approach is characteristic of judicial rhetoric dismissing plaintiffs' demand that science rather than political or policy discre-

---

deregulation); Containerfreight Corp. v. United States, 752 F.2d 419, 424 (9th Cir. 1985) ("policy considerations alone cannot support a finding of public need").

23. *See, e.g.,* Hornsby v. Allen, 326 F.2d 605 (5th Cir. 1964) (due process required that municipality award liquor licenses through regularized application of standards rather than discretionary system of "aldermanic privilege"); Home Box Office, Inc. v. FCC, 567 F.2d 9 (D.C. Cir. 1977), *cert. denied,* 434 U.S. 829 (1977); Association of Nat'l Advertisers, Inc. v. FTC, 460 F. Supp. 996 (D.D.C. 1978) (disqualification of commissioner for bias in rule making, based on numerous impassioned speeches and writings), *reversed,* 627 F.2d 1151 (D.C. Cir. 1979), *cert. denied,* 447 U.S. 921 (1980) (disqualification for bias in hybrid rule making only if decision maker has "unalterably closed mind"); Cinderella Career and Finishing Schools, Inc. v. FTC, 425 F.2d 583 (D.C. Cir. 1970) (disqualification of commissioner in formal adjudication, based on apparent prejudgment of facts and law).

24. *See, e.g.,* Brennan v. Butler Lime & Cement Co., 520 F.2d 1011 (7th Cir. 1975) (remand where agency based its decision on a theory not developed at hearing without giving adverse party opportunity to respond); Duane Swelser Roofing Co. v. Marshall, 617 F.2d 448 (6th Cir. 1980) (remand with instructions to include statutorily required statement of reasons and findings); RMI Co. v. Secretary of Labor, 594 F.2d 566 (6th Cir. 1979) (remand with instructions to gather more factual evidence on issue of economic feasibility).

25. *See, e.g.,* Portland Cement Ass'n v. Ruckelshaus, 486 F.2d 375 (D.C. Cir. 1973), *cert. denied,* 417 U.S. 921 (1974) (agency can not isolate itself and must respond to significant scientific criticisms made in rule making comments); Nova Scotia Food Prod. Corp. v. United States, 568 F.2d 240 (2d Cir. 1977) (no secret science allowed—agency must subject its internal expertise to external scrutiny).

tion be the dominant decision making method. The court responds by accepting the nonscientific method adopted by the agency and emphasizing its positive norms.[26]

The Duality of Rule of Law-Adjudicatory Fairness: On one hand, (1) the court might stress the positive attributes of neutrality, fairness, and formal regularity, and defer to agency action that appears to implement these, on a theory that (2) these methods reliably prevent governmental abuses—as they are assumed to when employed by the courts. On the other hand, (1) the court may focus on the negative attributes of proceduralism (including constricted participation and narrowing of issues) and precedent-bound conservatism in concluding that agency reliance on the Rule of Law paradigm is inappropriate and threatens the objectives of good government. The result, although uncommon, will be (2) judicial intervention to temper agency adjudicatory methods with increased participation or even politicization, for example, broadened standing,[27] or requiring policymaking by rule rather than adjudication.[28] Similarly, the negative attributes may be the articulated basis for a court's refusal to impose on the agency such Rule of Law methods as consistency, neutrality, and formality.[29]

In the sections that follow I try to demonstrate the operation of this attributive duality in particular settings. Generally, I reexamine cases discussed earlier to convey the onionlike layering of reliance on the trichotomy and the interrelatedness of the conceptual difficulties created by that reliance.

26. This is also similar to opinions emphasizing the court's statutory construction as against the agency's attempt to rely on specialized knowledge to justify a rule or order. *See, e.g.,* Board of Governors of Fed. Reserve Bank v. Dimension Credit Corp., 106 S. Ct. 681 (1986) (rejecting the Fed's effort to broaden its regulatory reach in response to innovative banking practices); *contrast* Mourning v. Family Publications Serv., Inc., 411 U.S. 356 (1973) (approving the Fed's expansive regulatory definition of "consumer credit" despite seeming statutory obstacle).

27. *See generally* Chayes, *Public Law Litigation and the Burger Court,* 96 Harv. L. Rev. 4 (1982); Stewart, *The Reformation of American Administrative Law,* 88 Harv. L. Rev. 1667, 1723 (1976).

28. *See* Morton v. Ruiz, 415 U.S. 199 (1974); Ford Motor Co. v. FTC, 673 F.2d 1008 (9th Cir. 1981); NLRB v. Wyman-Gordon, 394 U.S. 759 (1969) (dissenting opinions of Justices Douglas and Harlan).

29. *See, e.g.,* Association of Nat'l Advertisers, Inc. v. FTC, 627 F.2d 1151 (D.C. Cir. 1979), *cert. denied,* 447 U.S. 921 (1980) (strict adjudicatory neutrality inappropriate for rule making because the policymaking paradigm is controlling); Heckler v. Campbell, 461 U.S. 458 (1983) (upholding SSA use of matrix promulgated by rule to determine availability of jobs for various combinations of disability and claimant characteristics; employability largely removed from adjudication).

3.2.1 Example: Reprise—OSHA

Review of OSHA regulations offers a good example of how the attributive duality of politics or policy discretion can trigger inconsistent analytical postures toward judicial review. In *Industrial Union Department, AFL-CIO v. Hodgson*,[30] the principal rationale for the court's deferential attitude toward the agency's asbestos standard was its conclusion that:

> Judicial review of . . . decisions of this sort is obviously an undertaking of different dimensions [from that involved in review of factual determinations] . . . . This choice . . . rests in the final analysis on an essentially legislative policy judgment, rather than a factual determination, concerning the relative risks of underprotection as compared to overprotection . . . . Congress normally makes [these decisions] itself, and by processes, as the courts have long recognized and accepted, peculiar to itself. A due respect for the boundaries between the legislative and judicial function dictates that we approach our reviewing task with a flexibility informed and shaped by sensitivity to the diverse origins of the determinations that enter into a legislative judgment.[31]

The court's repeated comparisons with the political process of the legislature underscore the judges' conception of these choices as matters of interest accommodation, subject to political accountability, rather than matters of scientific expertise or Rule of Law fairness.

Why discount the role of objective science? Would not an emphasis on scientific expertise support a strong claim for judicial deference? Yes, but only if accompanied by an emphasis on the positive attributes of expertise.[32] From a tactical viewpoint, the agency must be able to

---

30. 499 F.2d 467 (D.C. Cir. 1974) (McGowan, J., joined by Leventhal and MacKinnon, JJ.).

31. 499 F.2d at 475. Also: "[E]xplicit factual findings are not possible, and the act of decision is essentially a prediction based upon pure legislative judgment." *Id.* at 474.

32. The *Hodgson* court's invocations of deference to expertise are puzzling because they are logically inconsistent with Judge McGowan's insistence that expertise does not solve this regulatory problem. *Compare* 499 F.2d at 474. The only way to make these references material, I believe, is to say that the choice between the paradigms of science and of policy discretion (or politics) is a matter for the agency's expert determination in the first instance, subject to deferential review. *See, e.g., id.* at 474 n. 18 ("Where existing methodology . . . is deficient, the agency necessarily enjoys broad discretion to formulate a solution to the best of its ability"). Of course, this recapitulates the trichotomy. That is, why is this metaquestion of paradigm choice a matter for expert reasoning rather than

martial enough persuasive scientific evidence to withstand a reviewing court's probing inquiry as to whether the positive norms of objectivity and rationality really apply. That is, if the agency's asbestos regulation is to rest on a claim of deference to expertise, there is a risk (but not a certainty) that a reviewing court will employ hard-look review and ask for proof of expertise sufficient to withstand the hostile counterarguments made in rule making comments and litigation. If the comments are hard to deal with, the veil of objective, rational expertise may be pierced, and the reviewing court may pay more attention to the negative attributes of isolation, lack of participation, and so forth.[33] Relatedly, a judge or advocate writing in support of the agency can be expected to argue within the science paradigm only when it seems advantageous to do so.

In *Hodgson*, McGowan's analogies to legislative decision making are an implicit emphasis on the positive norms associated with interest accommodation, with parallel claims of legitimacy. Of course, judicial deference to the legislature is itself grounded in the normative framework (and the formalism) of separation of powers. But the attributive duality of politics should make us suspect that McGowan could instead have focused on the negative norms associated with politics: willfulness, tyranny of the majority, and so forth. How might he have done so?

Elsewhere in the *Hodgson* opinion is a passing reference to the need for "exacting scrutiny" to "negate the dangers of arbitrariness and irrationality,"[34] and thus a recognition that hand in hand with the virtues of political choice are the vices. On these grounds the court might have reversed, yet for some reason it did not. On intellectual grounds alone, the court need not have been so deferential. After all, even the empirical uncertainty involved in regulation of asbestos can be tightly disciplined with high-powered policy science—this exploits the boundary problem between discretion and fact. The court could have

---

law? Or why not insist on facts to justify the agency's decision to forgo scientific analysis in favor of discretionary policy choice? The agency might, for example, be required to demonstrate that further epidemiological studies would be infeasible or would not provide useful information.

33. Gerald Frug has analyzed this tension in terms of a subjective-objective dichotomy. Emphasizing the subjective quality of expertise causes a court to defer because the expert personally knows the truth and should be left alone. Emphasizing the objective quality causes a court to reason that if the matter is truly a question for science, then the agency expert should be able to withstand rigorous scrutiny by the external community of scientific colleagues. *See* Frug, *The Ideology of Bureaucracy in American Law*, 97 Harv. L. Rev. 1276, 1331–34 (1984).

34. 499 F.2d at 475 (quoting Automotive Parts and Accessories Ass'n v. Boyd, 407 F.2d 330, 338 (D.C. Cir. 1968) (McGowan, J.).

done more to control discretion without opening the door so wide to the negative attributes of political decision making (while simultaneously enhancing the role of scientific expertise). The court focused on the positive rather than negative attributes of political choice and, after a nod to the claims for exacting scrutiny, accorded substantial deference to the agency's action.

In contrast, the Supreme Court in the *Benzene* case noted the extraordinary complexity and discretion entailed in OSHA's regulatory policy choices and concluded that the delegation was so broad that the statute should be read to require, as a prerequisite to regulation, that the agency "find" that a particular substance poses a "significant risk."[35] As in *Hodgson,* one can discern in the *Benzene* opinions acknowledgment of the positive and negative attributes of policy choice—the virtue of interest accommodation and accountability in making such difficult judgments on the one hand, and the vice of zealous overregulation through a failure to exercise balanced judgment of the many decisional factors implicit in the organic statute.[36] Yet, unlike *Hodgson,* the Court in *Benzene* was more impressed with the threateningly negative attributes of the agency's decision making method and the potential for abuses created by the broad delegation. Indeed, Justice Rehnquist, concurring in the result, would have invalidated the statute on nondelegation doctrine grounds because the statutory guidance for so wide-ranging a policy judgment was simply too vague.[37] The dissenters decried the *Lochner*esque tone of the majority's insistence that the agency is not free to accommodate the competing interests of workers and employers in the way it sees fit.[38] This we might ascribe to their emphasis on the positive attributes of political discretionary choice. In my terms, however, the dissenters' argument is no better than that of the majority because it has no limiting principle—no sense of when the court should or should not defer to an agency's

35. Industrial Union Dep't, AFL-CIO v. American Petroleum Inst., 448 U.S. 607, 639–40 (1980).

36. *Compare id.* at 656–58, *with id.* at 645.

37. *Id.* 448 U.S. at 672 (Rehnquist, J., concurring in the result). The nondelegation doctrine, so called because it responds to a formalist prohibition on delegation of legislative power to the executive, requires that Congress make the fundamental policy judgment by including an "intelligible principle" in the statute to constrain agency discretion and make judicial review feasible. Only in the early New Deal cases of *Schechter Poultry* and *Panama Refining* has the Court ever declared a statute unconstitutional on nondelegation doctrine grounds. In several cases, however, concern over a vague, broad delegation has led a court to adopt a narrow statutory construction or to insist that the agency promulgate rules that narrow its discretion.

38. *Id.* 448 U.S. at 688, 723–24 (Marshall, J., dissenting, joined by Brennan, White, and Blackmun, JJ.).

political acts of interest accommodation. The easy answer is that the agency's discretion must be limited by the scope of the delegation and by the substantial evidence test. But, as I have attempted to show in analyzing the conceptual failings of the fact-law-policy trichotomy, that is no answer at all.

There is no compelling reason why the approaches in *Hodgson* and *Benzene* should be so different. True, the evidence of risk in *Benzene* was less clear, and in a qualitative sense the relation of benefits to costs appeared more problematic.[39] But no circumstances suggested that the general *Hodgson* principle of deference to policy judgments should not apply—as the dissenters pointedly argued.[40] It is also true that the *Hodgson* panel was considerably more "liberal" than the majority of the Supreme Court in *Benzene*,[41] but that is hardly the point. This crude realist observation, with its implicit assertion of result-oriented jurisprudence, is evidence of the descriptive insufficiency of the trichotomy's characterization of judicial and quasi-judicial decision making. Instead, I want to describe the conceptual mechanism that makes it possible to generate the two alternative approaches to essentially the same issue—in this instance, controversial OSHA regulations. In a sense, the observation that the politics of the panels differed helps

39. The Supreme Court avoided the thorny cost-benefit issue by grounding its decision solely in OSHA's failure to make the threshold determination of significant harm. *Id.* at 615. The court of appeals, however, had based its rejection of the rule in part on the agency's failure to provide an adequate cost-benefit analysis. According to the lower court, OSHA had sufficiently accounted for the costs of the new rule, but the agency's assertion that its benefits were "likely to be appreciable" lacked the support of substantial evidence necessary for a determination of the statutorily required reasonable relationship between costs and benefits. 581 F.2d 493, 504–5 (5th Cir. 1978). OSHA argued that "lack of knowledge concerning the effects of exposure to benzene at low levels [made] an estimate of benefits . . . impossible." But the court was not moved: Because Congress required OSHA decisions to be based on "the best available evidence," including "research, demonstration . . . and such other information as may be appropriate," as well as "experience gained under [OSHA] and other such health and safety laws," all regulations must be based on "knowledge rather than the unknown." *Id.* at 504.

40. 448 U.S. at 706. Indeed, the statutory language quoted by the D.C. Circuit to support its requiring substantial factual evidence of benefits could just as strongly support judicial deference to agency policy decisions. The panel recognized this conflict but chose not to resolve it: "We will not attempt to resolve our decision with the cases from other circuits which uphold other standards regulating exposure to carcinogens. *See* Industrial Union Dep't, AFL-CIO v. Hodgson (other citations omitted)." 581 F.2d at 505.

41. Justices Powell and Stewart and Chief Justice Burger joined in this aspect of Justice Stewart's plurality opinion in the *Benzene* case. 448 U.S. 607 (1980). Justice Rehnquist concurred in the judgment, 448 U.S. at 671, and Justices Blackmun, Brennan, and White joined in Justice Marshall's dissenting opinion. 448 U.S. at 688. By contrast, Judges McGowan, Leventhal, and MacKinnon formed the panel in Hodgson, 499 F.2d 467 (D.C. Cir. 1974).

prove my point: trichotomy-based analyses give courts and advocates the mechanism they need in order to rationalize the results they want to reach.

My earlier analysis of the science-politics-fairness categorization problem suggests that at least a part of the mechanism is the availability of alternative paradigm choices: the *Hodgson* panel saw the problem as a matter for discretionary policy choice, whereas the *Benzene* majority focused on statutory construction and Rule of Law constraints on agency discretion. But another conceptual problem available as a mechanism for generating different results is selective emphasis on one side of the attributive duality: in *Hodgson*, the emphasis was on the positive qualities of political choice at what were asserted to be the edges of science, coupled with a descriptively implausible denial of the applicability of the expertise model's constraint on discretion; in *Benzene* the emphasis was on the *negative* qualities of politics as demanding the constraints of rigorous judicial review, going so far as to impose a limiting statutory construction, coupled with a comparably implausible emphasis on the potential contribution of science.[42]

In short, the trichotomy becomes the basis for the calculation of deference, and the dual normative structure contributes to the instability of the result. Combining this point with my earlier one about the collapsing conceptual categories of politics, science, and fairness (or policy, fact, and law), the parallel structure of the two failings emerges. In a sense, the normative complication is the deeper of the two failings—*it is a great part of the reason why politics, science, and adjudicatory fairness are conceptually problematic categories.*

42. As for the descriptively inaccurate emphasis in *Benzene* on the potential contributions of science, the plurality does disclaim any effort to impose a rigidly mathematical cost-benefit test or specific risk threshold. 448 U.S. at 655. But the necessary result of the court's reasoning is that a higher standard of scientific evidence will be required to support OSHA health regulations. *See* Rogers, *Judicial Review of Risk Assessments: The Role of Decision Theory in Unscrambling the Benzene Decision*, 11 Envtl. L. Rev. 301, 305 (1981); Huber, *Safety and the Second Best: The Hazards of Public Risk Management in the Courts*, 85 Colum. L. Rev. 277, 326–35 (1985); Huber, *The Old-New Division in Risk Regulation*, 69 Va. L. Rev. 1025, 1049 (1983); Rabin, *Legitimacy, Discretion, and the Concept of Rights*, 92 Yale L.J. 1174, 1184–85 (1983); Note, *Occupationally Induced Cancer Susceptibility: Regulating the Risk*, 96 Harv. L. Rev. 697, 711 (1983). This restricts the agency's domain to problems capable of concrete, quantifiable risk assessment, when a plausible reading of the statute would have permitted deference to an agency determination to regulate even in the face of overwhelming uncertainty. For example, the *Benzene* opinion would probably make it impossible for a more regulation-oriented administration to adopt the "carcinogens policy" proposed but not implemented during the 1970s. That policy would have triggered virtually automatic regulation of substances on a very modest showing of cancer-causing potential. The purpose was to shorten the severe delays in substance-by-substance control of health hazards.

Does this mean that the doctrinal analysis is wholly without meaningful content? That claim is perhaps too sweeping, especially since the categories of the trichotomy, reflecting as they do a separation of powers ethos, continue to have intuitive appeal and thus both legitimating and prescriptive force. This, however, does not make the conceptual difficulties disappear.

3.2.2 Example: Proceduralism versus Discretion

The same mixing and matching of emphases on attributes is apparent in cases focusing on adjudicatory fairness and expert decision methods. Thus, cases that have "creatively" imposed elements of formality on agency processes have emphasized the positive attributes of Rule of Law methods, such as neutrality and confrontation.[43] Cases rejecting this interventionist approach always recite the negative attributes, such as costly proceduralization, or the fact that Rule of Law decision making would tend to exclude positive attributes of competing methods of decision making, such as expert problem solving, interest accommodation, and unalienated participation.

Specifically, this mixing and matching of emphases is evident in due process cases, such as *Goldberg v. Kelly,*[44] the path-breaking welfare "fair hearing" decision, and *Holmes v. New York City Housing Authority,* in which the Second Circuit required a chaotic, putatively expert agency to discipline itself by adopting procedures and standards.[45] Of course, such rulings are less frequent now than they were in the heyday of the Warren Court, but they still occur. A recent example is *Cleveland Board of Education v. Loudermill,* in which the Supreme Court found due process protections applicable to a security guard dismissed for falsely denying a felony conviction on his job application.[46] Justice Rehnquist argued somewhat bitterly in dissent that the only process due the plaintiff before he was deprived of his state-given property interest in employment was that process provided by the state in its civil service statute; the requirement by the courts of additional procedures takes the judiciary out of its institutional role of neutral law-applier and into

43. *See, e.g.,* EDF v. Ruckelshaus, 439 F.2d 584 (D.C. Cir. 1971) ("substantial" issues raised concerning DDT by environmental groups deserved more formal hearing).
44. 397 U.S. 254 (1970).
45. 398 F.2d 262, 265 (2d Cir. 1968).
46. 470 U.S. 532 (1985).

the business of "*ad hoc* weighing which depends to a great extent upon how the Court subjectively views the underlying interests at stake."[47]

It is striking how much the rhetoric of due process disputes takes on the norms and distinctions of the trichotomy, even though the question of "what process is due" is structured by the three-factor balancing inquiry of *Mathews v. Eldridge*. After all, those factors—the nature of the public and private interests at stake, and the risk of an erroneous determination—are not grounded in the trichotomy in the same strong sense that I developed in chapter 2 with respect to, for example, the rule making versus adjudication choice or the fact-law-policy distinction. But in a fundamental sense, due process review is just another question of when it is appropriate for a court to displace the agency's conclusion about proper procedure.

An interesting contrast is presented by *Heckler v. Campbell*, in which an unsuccessful applicant for disability benefits challenged the Social Security Administration's use of a "grid" or matrix of yes-no answers on the penultimate issue of employability, based on the claimant's characteristics: residual functional capacity, age, education, and work experience.[48] The grid reflected the SSA's judgment about whether some-

47. *Id.* at 562 (Rehnquist, J., dissenting). Rehnquist's argument for deference is based in part on his professed concern that the "lack of principled standards in this area means that these due process cases will recur time and again." *Id.* at 562–63. Yet, implicit in his positivist rhetoric, first developed in his Arnett v. Kennedy plurality decision, 416 U.S. 134, 151–52 (1974), is an equally strong interest in judicial deference to legislative choices. The positivism theme also animates Rehnquist's reasoning for the majority in Vermont Yankee Nuclear Power Corp. v. NRDC, 435 U.S. 519, 546 (1978) ("Congress intended that the discretion of the *agencies* and not that of the courts be exercised in determining when extra procedural devices should be employed" [emphasis in original]).

48. 461 U.S. 458 (1983). The challenged grid regulations appear at 20 C.F.R., part 404, subpt. P (1982). The Social Security Act, 42 U.S.C. § 401 *et seq.*, provides benefits to individuals who show that they are "disabled"—i.e., incapable of engaging in "any substantial gainful employment." *Id.* at § 423(d)(1)(A). Some impairments are per se disabling, 20 C.F.R. § 404.1525 (1981). For those that are not, the SSA has developed a two-stage analysis to determine eligibility. First, the claimant must show that she is prevented from working at the previous job. Second, the burden shifts to the agency to prove that the claimant is capable, "considering his age, education, and work experience, [of engaging] in any other kind of substantial gainful work which exists in the national economy." 42 U.S.C. § 423(d)(2)(A). This determination is made according to the Medical-Vocational Guidelines promulgated by the SSA and include the detailed grid system at issue in *Campbell*. 20 C.F.R. § 404 *et seq.* (1981). Under the grid regulations, an ALJ first ascertains which of three categories of "residual functional capacity" is appropriate for the claimant, based on findings as to her ability to lift a weight, sit, stand, push, and pull. For each such category there is a table which accounts for the statutory vocational factors of age, education, and work experience. The ALJ determines these three vocational

one with the attributes in a given cell of the grid should be able to find employment somewhere in the economy, which is the statutory test. Use of the grid essentially eliminated the need for the specific testimony of vocational experts in individual disability adjudications and focused the attention of the claims processors and administrative law judges (ALJs) on concrete, more readily ascertainable facts about the claimant. However, as the D.C. Circuit Court of Appeals observed in nullifying use of the grid, this also deprived claimants of an important opportunity to question effectively the claim that jobs appropriate for the claimant do in fact exist (neither the grid nor the supporting manual specify what jobs are really there), in violation of the organic statute's promise of a hearing and the constitutional due process protection.[49]

The Supreme Court reversed, stressing the positive aspects of expertise and the negative aspects of formal adjudication. Acknowledging that the act requires the secretary to determine eligibility on a case-by-case basis, the Court nonetheless concluded that "this does not bar the Secretary from relying on rule making to resolve certain classes of issues." Because the grids were thought to provide objective information regarding "an issue that is not unique to each claimant—the types and numbers of jobs that exist in the national economy," the Court thought it well within the agency's expertise to formulate the tables. Before the grid system, job availability was determined through a hearing that involved testimony by vocational experts and cross-examination by the claimant. The Court stated this approach was unnecessary and inefficient: "To require the Secretary to relitigate the existence of jobs in the national economy . . . would hinder needlessly an already over-burdened agency."[50]

Although many commentators have criticized the balancing approach to due process,[51] it seems an almost inevitable consequence of the attributive duality inherent in our conceptions of adjudication and the alternative paradigms. The difficulty of scaling due process is intellectually akin to the problem of scaling judicial deference to agency

---

factors and reads from the corresponding entry in the table the conclusion as to whether the claimant is disabled. Where the grid regulations apply (there are some "escape" clauses), the ALJ has *no discretion* in the determination of employability, and hence eligibility.

49. Campbell v. Secretary of HHS, 665 F.2d 48, 53 (2d Cir. 1981). The regulation itself was not attacked as arbitrary and capricious. *See* 461 U.S. at 470 n. 14.

50. *Id.* at 467, 468.

51. *See generally* J. Mashaw, Due Process and the Administrative State (1985); L. Tribe, American Constitutional Law, §§ 10–13 (1978).

choice, because the due process controversy is often a competition between the paradigms; the problems of description, conceptual categories, and attributive duality necessarily muddle the controversy.

3.2.3 Conclusions on Attributive Duality

Balancing may often be the sine qua non of rationality in our confused world; inescapable complexity demands due consideration of several factors. Indeed, cost-benefit analysis is just a special, scientistic case of balancing, and in many settings cost-benefit analysis is a crucial component of sound decision making. But much of the balancing in administrative law is constructed on the foundation of the trichotomy's distinctions in decision making paradigms. This invites unnecessary trouble, because the freedom to choose between positive and negative attributes is coupled with the empirical problems of discerning the actual circumstances and bases for agency action—especially the difficulty of appraising any one decision making methodology (for example, science) once we appreciate the indistinctness of the paradigms. There can be no effective disciplining of this selective emphasis on attributes if judges and advocates lack a firm fix on the realities of bureaucratic decision making and the intricacies of the problem at hand. (How much science is available? How participatory was the process? Did the legislators really consider this issue, or was a lowly staff member cranking out the committee report?) And the consequence of having no effective disciplining of legal argument is that judicial review becomes less stable, less predictable, and less legitimate.

CHAPTER 4

Scope of Judicial Review

Oddly, the law of scope of review is composed of two main ingredients that are in some degree at war with each other—the realities and the verbalisms.—Kenneth Culp Davis, 5 Administrative Law Treatise 333 (§ 29.1) (1984)

A great deal of administrative law boils down to the scope of review problem: defining what degree of deference a court will accord an agency's findings, conclusions, and choices, including choice of procedures.[1] It is misleading to speak of a "doctrine," or "the law," of scope of review. It is instead just a big problem, that is addressed piecemeal by a large collection of doctrines. Kenneth Culp Davis has offered a condensed summary of the subject: "Courts usually substitute [their own] judgment on the kind of questions of law that are within their special competence, but on other questions they limit themselves to deciding reasonableness; they do not clarify the meaning of reasonableness but retain full discretion in each case to stretch it in either direction."[2]

---

1. *See generally* K. Davis, 5 Administrative Law Treatise § 29 (1984); L. Jaffe, Judicial Control of Administrative Action ch. 14 (1965); S. Breyer & R. Stewart Administrative Law and Regulatory Policy ch. 4 (1985); W. Gellhorn, C. Byse, & P. Strauss Administrative Law 249–350 (1979).

Though every treatise and casebook contains sections on scope of review for facts and application of law to facts, other areas of doctrine are closely related. For example, official notice doctrine (see sec. 4.4.4) involves the question of appropriate deference to the *agency's* conclusions when they seem somewhat factlike but have been found through the agency's own expertise rather than through evidence on the record. Restrictions on ex parte communications can be viewed as a question of judicial review of agency procedures, the adequacy of the agency's record, and the reliability of the agency's claims of expertise and neutrality. Questions of statutory interpretation, including the agency's formulation of policy through rule making, are an aspect of scope of review. Issues of judicial deference also arise where a particular administrative action is said to be "committed to agency discretion."

2. Davis, 5 Treatise 332 (§ 29.1) (1984). After making the same point in another place, Davis writes: "But a treatise must consider the verbiage, because it is often the law,

This does not help much, however accurate it may be. Indeed, coming as it does from one of the preeminent figures in the field, the quoted confession that doctrine fails to impose any meaningful structure on the problems of deference and judicial discretion is striking. Nevertheless, Davis's view is that this gloss "may be more reliable than the many complexities and refinements that are constantly repeated in judicial opinions."[3] As I describe in the first two sections below, the variety of approaches and holdings is bewildering, and efforts to systematize are besieged by counterexamples. Davis's minimalism thus seems correct as a descriptive matter. But it is unacceptable as a conceptual matter.

But *must* it be that we can do no better than a reasonableness gloss? Much of this book is an effort to demonstrate that implicit reliance on the science-fairness-politics trichotomy must fail, on conceptual grounds, to constrain *judicial* discretion to scale the degree of deference to *agency* discretion. This seems true in two important respects. First, the fact-law-policy distinction (the focus of section 4.1) provides an unsure basis on which to sort the elements of complex agency decisions. And second, there is little robustness to the verbal formulas for judicial deference which courts apply to the sorted categories (the focus of section 4.2).

These trichotomy-related problems invite individual judges to strike whatever posture of deference or intervention they (somehow) deem appropriate. If this is not lawlessness, it is at least a degeneration in the scaling apparatus promised by administrative law. Tests of reasonableness, though straightforward, impose no consistent discipline on anyone. A still more troubling consequence of disillusion with any science of administrative law is that judges increasingly say: "We judges will not interfere; let Congress straighten the agency out; our hands are clean." This Pontius Pilate posture of great deference is abdication of any role in making the public sector successful.[4] And it is odd to justify abdicative deference by asserting that Congress will fix things: the broad delegations (and modern administrative law) arose because everyone conceded Congress's institutional inability to get involved in

---

even though it is often needlessly complex and even though it is both conflicting and confusing." *Id.* at 520 (1982 Supp.).

3. *Id.* at 332 (1984).

4. The doctrinal manifestations of this threat are increased judicial deference on questions of law, and a broadening of unreviewable agency action under APA § 701(a). *See, e.g.*, Chevron USA, Inc. v. NRDC, 467 U.S. 837 (1984); Heckler v. Chaney, 470 U.S. 821 (1985).

the details. Yet blind deference is just as mistaken as unchecked judicial supremacy.

Is the consequence of all this an admirable regime of careful judgment by intelligent courts or, instead, a regrettable regime of unconfessed and essentially unpoliced discretion? This is perhaps the crucial test for administrative law, so it is a problem worth worrying about.

So much for where I am going. Now I will try to get there.

4.1 The Conceptual Difficulty of Sorting into Fact-Law-Policy Categories

Let us review the separation of powers–related basis for using the law-fact-policy categories as the device for scaling deference, as I stated it in section 2.3. Earlier, my purpose was exposition of reliance on the trichotomy, but now we will focus on the doctrinal confusion created by the trichotomy's conceptual failings. (Bear in mind that this section concerns the problem of sorting, while the problem of giving content to the particular scope of review verbal formula is reserved for section 4.2.)

Questions of Law: Little deference is due the agency, because law finding is the business of courts, as it should be. The task is appropriate to the adjudicatory fairness methodology characteristic of judicial decision making.

The force of the separation of powers ethos has always been bound up in the sense that divided powers will promote the Rule of Law and thereby check arbitrariness and tyranny.[5] The source of persuasive force for this device has been in part the protection afforded by the *multiplicity* of divided sources of authority[6]—the consideration I emphasize in chapter 7—and in part the distinctness of the decision making methods to be employed by each branch. That is, Rule of Law is a valued liberal ideal because it suggests a method of decision making distinct from those employed by the political branches. The emphasis on distinctiveness is necessitated by attention to the normatively negative attributes of decision making within the political branches. Thus, Rule of Law "saves" us from tyranny of the majority and oppression at the hands of alienated bureaucrats.[7]

---

5. *See, e.g.,* F. Hayek, The Political Ideal of the Rule of Law 55–56 (1955).

6. The protection afforded by multiplicity of decision making forums is more commonly emphasized in explaining the importance of the vertical separation of powers accomplished through federalism. I argue, however, that it should also be crucial to our modern conception of horizontal separation of powers. *See* sec. 7.3.2.

7. *See also* J. Landis, The Administrative Process 152 (1938) (arguing that "question

Boundary problems make any flat statement of judicial authority problematic at best, however. As to the fact-law boundary, "mixed questions" abound, just as the intertwining of these categories is a classical puzzle in the common law.[8] The law-policy boundary is no more definite, whether or not policy discretion is expressly invited by the legislature. Here, courts too often follow either of two paths to nowhere. One path attempts to distinguish law applying, law finding, and lawmaking. This does nothing but restate the problem. The second path attempts to use statutory interpretation to provide some judicially enforceable delimitation of the range of discretion available to the administrator.

Louis Jaffe, for example, insisted that agencies and courts *share* law*making* responsibility and that the court's role is dominant only when a statutory purpose is clear.[9] On its face, this formulation seems to avoid the need to find a boundary between determinations of law on the one hand (the court's business) and determinations of fact or policy (the agency's business) on the other, because Jaffe willingly permitted agencies to "determine" what the law is, whether one calls the determination a question of law or a mixed question. But surely the inquiry into whether the statutory purpose is clear—and hence, for the judge to declare and enforce against wayward agency discretion—is an inquiry into whether there is law to be found respecting such constraints, and if so, what that law is. This is a distinction between law finding, lawmaking, and law applying, but carried on at perhaps slight remove from the principal decisional materials, the blood and guts, of the administrative matter at issue. The litigants and judges may argue about statutory interpretation in an effort to discern "clear purpose," but their argument will boil down to a judgment about the extent to which the question at hand will admit of some agency discretion or will require particular evidentiary support.

An example is the Supreme Court's decision in *Chevron USA, Inc. v. NRDC*,[10] upholding the EPA's "bubble" rule, which permitted pollution tradeoffs among sources within a plant. Justice Stevens reasoned

---

of law" is the crucial dividing line between judicial and agency authority and is the means by which Rule of Law is assured). Landis went on to argue that use of the fact-law distinction in scaling the scope of judicial review substitutes attention to "reality"—"an appreciation of the limitations and limitations and abilities of men, rather than . . . political dogma or righteous abstractions"—as the basis for judicial review. *Id.* at 153.

8. Thayer, A Preliminary Treatise on Evidence at the Common Law 228 (1898); O. Holmes, The Common Law 126 (1888); Jaffe, Treatise 546–55 (1965).

9. Jaffe, Treatise at 546, 569–75; *see also* ch. 5 for further discussion of the Jaffe approach and issues of statutory interpretation.

10. 467 U.S. 837 (1984).

that because there was no clear congressional intent with respect to the application of the term *stationary source* to the bubble concept, the agency had discretion to adopt the flexible definition rather than insist that each point source comply with pollution limits. But the inquiry into whether Congress had an intention (or even "purpose") relevant to the bubble proposal is obviously an inquiry into where the bounds are on the continuum of conceivable agency constructions of the statutory term, just as the Court in *Hearst Publications v. NLRB*[11] had to explore the limits on NLRB discretion in applying the term *employee*. In *Chevron*, as in *Hearst* forty years earlier, the Court's framework was to ask whether this definitional question was fairly answerable using the tools of judges and lawyers, or was it instead more suitable for the tools of agency officials charged with exercising policy discretion and staffed with bureaucratic resources to make specialized factual determinations. The statutory interpretation form of choice only recapitulates the law-fact-policy distinction, and thus the trichotomy with its separation of powers ethos.

Stated differently, one might argue that the agency may be due some deference in law *applying* because such matters are "administrative routine" amenable to expertise and experience and that the agency might enjoy deference in law*making* if its actions are pursuant to a statutory delegation of quasi-legislative authority. Plainly, however, this framework teaches us nothing about discerning when the statutory delegation is indeed "clear," what the limits of a delegation are, or when the agency's choice is "routine." We are ultimately left with the distinctions between law, policy, and fact.

Questions of Fact: There is more deference to agency factual determinations because such determinations are frequently the product of scientific or expert inquiry and judgment or because the determination is the result of an assimilation of detailed and varied evidence or experience for which the agency is particularly well qualified by virtue of its bureaucratic organization of resources. A corollary of this deference to factual findings is that the more the issue at hand looks amenable to technically expert bureaucratic decision making, the more likely the court is to conclude that it is a question of fact and that deference is due.

In *Radio Corporation of America v. United States*,[12] for example, the Supreme Court reviewed the FCC's decision to promulgate an engineering standard for color television broadcasting. The standard was incompatible with existing black-and-white televisions and required a gadget to permit black-and-white viewing of a color signal. The Court

11. 322 U.S. 111 (1944).
12. 341 U.S. 412 (1951).

rejected an argument that the statutory public interest standard should be read to require the FCC to await the allegedly imminent development (by RCA) of a compatible color technology. Justice Frankfurter expressed misgivings at the Court's highly deferential posture toward the FCC's decision, arguing that the technical issues were indeed accessible to the Court and that the crux of the decision was not at all bound up in highly discretionary matters uniquely appropriate to the commission, as the opinion for the Court stated. In a sense, the basis for the disagreement was Frankfurter's understanding of the problem as one of fact, whereas the majority's opinion viewed it as a largely discretionary policy judgment about how to accommodate the public's interest in the context of rapid technological change. The boundary between fact and policy was fairly disputable because this was, of course, both. In other circumstances, such as the familiar terrain of so-called mixed questions of fact and law, or application of law to facts, the most obvious boundary problem is between fact and law.[13]

But in many circumstances, it is readily apparent that *all* of the categories tend to merge, making it even more difficult to use them as the basis for scaling judicial deference. For example, OSHA has determined that the few studies available fail to provide an adequate evidentiary basis for regulating short-term exposures to ethylene oxide, a chemical used in sterilizing medical equipment that has been linked conclusively at some dosage levels to such maladies as spontaneous abortions, cancers, and birth defects. The agency considers regulation limited to longer-term exposures an adequate response to the risk.[14] Is OSHA's determination a factual and scientific one concerning epi-

13. *See generally* Davis, 5 Treatise § 29.9 *et seq.*: "The problem of scope of review that arises more frequently than any other is the choice between substitution of judgment [i.e., independent scope of review] and use of a reasonableness test when law is applied to undisputed or established facts. As of mid-1984, the Supreme Court during the 1980's has decided at least 34 cases involving this problem. One might expect that the 34 cases could be analyzed to discover what determines the Court's choice. But the Court substitutes judgment in some of the cases and it uses the reasonableness test in some of the cases, without disclosing any guiding principle.

"The question is a highly practical one and calls for a full treatment, even though conclusions are not very satisfying.

"The problem is: What motivates the Supreme Court to substitute judgment on some questions of applying law to facts and to refrain from substituting judgment on other such questions? Why is the Court inconsistent in its action? Why does the Court not explain what it does and why it does it?" *Id.* at 365–66. My view is that the explanation for the confusion lies in the conceptual instability of the trichotomy underlying scope of review analysis.

14. 29 C.F.R. § 1910.1047, 49 Fed. Reg. 25734–809 (June 22, 1984); 50 Fed. Reg. 64–77 (Jan. 2, 1985). *See* Public Citizen Health Research Group v. Rowland, 702 F.2d 1150 (D.C. Cir. 1983).

demiology? Is it a policy judgment concerning public policy toward scientific uncertainty, the evolution of regulatory programs over time, and the accommodation of worker and industry interests in the face of uncertainty? Or is it a legal judgment interpreting "substantial risk" or specifying the burden of proof for rule making? Even a seemingly technical judgment as to the methodological soundness of a research study implicates all three of the trichotomy's decision making paradigms. Thus, it makes little sense to reason in terms of boundaries, because the categories seem thoroughly indistinct.

Questions of Discretion and Policy: Policy choice inevitably and properly entails the accommodation of competing interests, the joining of value disputes, and political responsiveness. In the orthodox assignment of institutional roles, normatively rooted in the trichotomy, such decision making is decidedly not the province of judges, whose appointed decision making methods are quite otherwise. Hence, agency policy choices are entitled to deference.

By now my game is plain. First, the categories of policy discretion and fact are murkily indistinct. Once one admits that discretion must have *some* objective basis in fact, as the cases recite, one is immediately on the slippery slope debating "how much" of a basis.[15] At the top of the slope is the extreme claim that social preferences and political accountability provide a complete method of policy choice, and at the bottom is the determinist's assertion that if we only knew all the facts, there would be no cause for discretion because the best choice would be obvious.

The difficulty, however, is not just that the pragmatic line on the slippery slope is here-today-and-there-tomorrow, depending on factual subtleties or judicial personalities. Instead, the pragmatic line

15. *See, e.g.,* FCC v. National Citizens Comm. for Broadcasting, 436 U.S. 775, 814 (1978) ("[C]omplete factual support in the record for the Commission's judgment or prediction is not possible or required"); National Ass'n of Broadcasters v. FCC, 740 F.2d 1190, 1210–11 (D.C. Cir. 1984) (noting difficulty of drawing line as to how comprehensively an agency must consider all regulatory contingencies); Diver, *Policymaking Paradigms in Administrative Law,* 95 Harv. L. Rev. 393, 428 (1981) (requiring comprehensive rationality "makes ravenous demands on agencies' limited resources and cognitive faculties. Judged by [such] demanding standards, policymakers are virtually defenseless against reproof for falling short"). Of course, characterizing the quantum of required evidence as a "reasonable basis" is, without more, no help. Diver has explored the circumstances under which agencies (and presumably courts) might find it appropriate to require comprehensive or synoptic reasoning rather than incremental policy analysis. Strikingly, however, this sensible approach introduces factors that effectively recapitulate the problem of allocating judicial and agency authority (*see* ch. 5). In this sense they may not be helpful in structuring administrative law doctrine and yet may be sound guidelines for agencies seeking to optimize their allocation of policy analysis resources.

seems to be in several places at once: many good arguments are available, and no robust principles guide the choice among them.

Why so? The fancy answer to that surely lies somewhere in epistemology, or perhaps metaphysics. That is, this distinction between policy discretion and scientific fact-finding strikes me as similar to a chain of other distinctions often thought imponderably indeterminant: value, will, self, and mind versus fact, empiricism, other, and body.

For our purposes, perhaps it suffices to observe that so long as the legitimacy of bureaucratic action is thought to depend on a measure of objectivity, critics of such action will be free to insist on more objectivity (through grounding in science); and so long as bureaucratic efficacy is thought to depend on the administrator's freedom of judgment, defenders of such action will be moved to claim more of such freedom. The resolution of these competing claims is too big a problem for me, but I know it when I see it.

Second, apart from an undefinable policy-fact boundary, the categories of policy choice and *law* are necessarily murky. (I will state this in parallel to the policy-fact dilemma.) Once one admits that the exercise of discretion must be within the range permitted by the statutory delegation, as the cases recite, one must discern what that range is and whether the agency's policy choice falls within it. We are on a slippery slope of statutory interpretation, at the top of which is an interpretation allowing virtually unfettered agency discretion to set policy and make law, and at the bottom of which is a precise and unambiguous, judicially enforceable statutory command admitting of no administrative discretion. In the usual circumstance of merely human language, tea leaves of legislative history, and disorderly vectors of public policy, the process of drawing a line between these extremes bears almost no relation to science: the literature on statutory construction tells us so.[16] So long as the legitimacy of bureaucratic action is thought to require objective constraint accomplished through fidelity to the legislative delegation, critics of such action will be free to insist on judicial independence in specifying the terms of that delegation— arguing, for example, that the meaning of the statute is sufficiently "clear" or "plain" to be accessible to the judge; and so long as bureaucratic efficacy is thought to depend on the administrator's freedom of judgment pursuant to necessarily broad statutory grants of

16. *See, e.g.,* H. Hart & A. Sacks, Materials on the Legal Process 1218–25 (tent. ed. 1958); Abraham, *Statutory Interpretation and Literary Theory: Some Common Concerns of an Unlikely Pair,* 32 Rutgers L. Rev. 676 (1979). *See* sec. 5.1.

discretion, defenders of such action will be moved to claim more ambiguity in the statute and more freedom for the administrator. I see the big problem, again.

So, it is true that the degree of judicial deference depends on the clarity and scope of the statutory delegation of policymaking responsibility to the agency,[17] and it is true that a broad delegation of express substantive policymaking responsibility may trigger great deference indeed, especially under several more recent cases. But this principle of deference is never clearly controlling because there is the unavoidable possibility of reasonably characterizing the question at issue as one of law (what scope of delegation; what limits on discretion?) or fact (what evidentiary foundation for the policy choice?).

The traditional black letter statement scaling the scope of review, though it seems straightforward enough, presents great difficulties. Fact-law-policy distinctions are important in doctrine because of the underlying, pervasive role of separation of powers ethos and analysis based on the trichotomy of decision making paradigms. The doctrinal difficulties are therefore the inevitable consequence of conceptually problematic attempts to separate science, adjudicatory fairness, and politics. The categories are unsustainable.

Stated differently, agency decisions of any complexity (or interest) entail a mixture of all three decision making paradigms. Therefore, since the analytical framework for scope of review is based on separating the paradigms in order to assign institutional roles, that framework does not yield a unique or predictable way to parse the elements of decision in order to assign each element the appropriate scope of review. The response by commentators and judges to this muddle is often to retreat to such glosses as "reasonableness" and "due deference"—abandoning any convincing effort to discipline this central area of administrative law.

I do not mean that this is merely a conceptual problem amenable to pragmatic solution in practice. Quite the contrary. I offer the conceptual muddle as an *explanation* for the muddle evident in practice—indeed, evident in a number of seemingly unrelated doctrinal contexts.

If the foregoing has not been enough to kindle cynicism with respect to the sorting of decision making tasks, I offer further demon-

17. *Compare* Social Security Bd. v. Nierotko, 327 U.S. 358 (1946) (independent judicial review, overturning agency's exclusion of back pay awards from administrative construction of "wages"), *with* Schweiker v. Gray Panthers, 453 U.S. 34 (1981) (deferential judicial review, because Congress had expressly delegated rule making authority to define "available" income for purposes of medicaid eligibility).

stration in section 5.1.3. The deeper questions, however, are *why* so much has been based on the law-fact-policy distinctions and why this continues, long after the difficulty of separating the categories has been acknowledged.

The *reason* the distinctions have been critical in scope of review analysis is that the larger structure of doctrine is based on the trichotomy, *which itself suggests the distinction*: Scientists discover facts, politicians balance interests to determine policy, and Rule-of-Law adjudicators reach conclusions of law. Why continue to emphasize the fact-law-policy trichotomy? We cannot do otherwise, so long as the underlying trichotomy of decision making methods, inspired by separation of powers formalism, remains functional.

But the circularity is palpable. The trichotomy is functional within the traditional model of administrative law only insofar as analyses based on it are capable of disciplining judicial discretion. We can be confident of this discipline, however, only by ignoring the considerable evidence of fundamental conceptual failings and the consequent doctrinal murkiness. So, one interpretation of our continuing reliance on a seemingly unworkable framework is that we all insist on denying or ignoring its deficiencies. Although that is more than a little plausible, an alternative interpretation is that "functional" is a relative concept. There is no readily apparent alternative. Nor can there be one, consistent with the separation of powers ethos. I return to this in chapter 7. But before turning to more detailed examples, in section 4.3, let me explore the other major form of confusion in scope of review doctrine.

4.2 The Futile Search for Deference Formulas

4.2.1 Specifying the Scope of Review: Let a Zillion Flowers Bloom

The gloss that would collapse gradations in deference into an open-field "reasonableness" inquiry does achieve succinctness, but it blurs the conventional doctrines beyond recognition.

The most elementary black letter statement is that the scope of review of an agency determination is increasingly deferential as one moves from determinations of law, where the judicial posture is fairly independent, to those of law-fact mixture, fact, and finally discretionary policy.[18] Findings of fact in a formal proceeding will be upheld if

---

18. *See generally* Davis, 5 Treatise § 29; S. Breyer & R. Stewart, *supra* n. 1, ch. 4; Gellhorn, Byse, & Strauss, *supra* n. 1, ch. 3(4); Jaffe, Treatise chs. 14, 15.

supported by substantial evidence on the record as a whole; findings and reasoning in informal agency action must pass a more deferential test that they not be "arbitrary or capricious,"[19] although many courts and commentators use the term "reasonable." In mixed questions of law and fact, where the court reviews the agency's application of a statutory term to a set of specific facts, an oft-stated formula is that the agency should be upheld if its decision has "warrant in the record and a reasonable basis in law."[20] The placement of mixed law-fact problems on the scope of review spectrum depends on whether the court identifies particular components in the mix as undisputed. No separate category for discretionary policy choices as such exists in conventional formulations of scope of review. (Indeed, there is no mention of a "policy discretion" category in *Hearst, Gray v. Powell,* or the APA.) Policy questions are either treated as mixed questions or are disaggregated into a series of law, fact, and mixed determinations, with mixed decisions said to entail discretionary agency judgments entitled to deference if reasonable.

The courts initially developed this framework in the late nineteenth century.[21] Congress codified it in the scope of review provisions of the APA, which are as follows:

> § 706: To the extent necessary to decision and when presented, the reviewing court shall decide all relevant questions of law, interpret constitutional and statutory provisions, and determine the meaning or applicability of the terms of an agency action. The reviewing court shall—(1) compel agency action unlawfully withheld or unreasonably delayed; and (2) hold unlawful and set aside agency action, findings, and conclusions found to be—
>
> (A) arbitrary, capricious, and abuse of discretion, or not in accordance with law;
>
> (B) contrary to constitutional right, power, privilege, or immunity;
>
> (C) in excess of statutory jurisdiction, authority, or limitations, or short of statutory right;

19. Abbott Laboratories v. Gardner, 387 U.S. 136, 143 (1967). *See also* Industrial Union Dep't, AFL-CIO v. American Petroleum Inst., 448 U.S. 607, 705 (1980) (Marshall, J., dissenting, joined by Brennan, White, and Blackmun, JJ.).

20. NLRB v. Hearst, 322 U.S. 111 (1944). *See also* Gray v. Powell, 314 U.S. 402 (1941); Jaffe, Treatise ch. 14.

21. *See* Gaines v. Thompson, 7 Wall 347 (U.S. 1868), Noble v. Union R. Logging R.R., 147 U.S. 168 (1893). Jaffe points out that the American judiciary in "[t]he Eighties, and Nineties appears to have entertained considerable doubt, in the absence of statutory provision, as to the propriety of judicial control of 'executive' action." Jaffe, Treatise 337 (1965).

(D) without observance of procedure required by law;

(E) unsupported by substantial evidence in a case subject to sections 556 and 557 of this title [pertaining to formal rule making and formal adjudication] or otherwise reviewed on the record of an agency hearing provided by statute; or

(F) unwarranted by the facts to the extent that the facts are subject to trial de novo by the reviewing court.

In making the foregoing determinations, the court shall review the whole record or those parts of it cited by a party, and due account shall be taken of the rule of prejudicial error.

The APA thus contains several formulas. *First,* all agency action, if reviewable, can be reversed on any of several grounds: (1) arbitrary and capricious; (2) abuse of discretion; (3) unconstitutionality; and (4) three kinds of statutory violation: *(a)* substantively ultra vires (for example, the decision was based on a criterion not specified in the organic statute); *(b)* procedurally ultra vires (for example, the agency acted informally, but the organic statute required a formal hearing on the record); and *(c)* jurisdictionally ultra vires (for example, the agency sought to regulate a safety hazard in the exclusive jurisdiction of another agency). *Second,* and in addition, if the agency action was required by statute to be formal and "on the record" adjudication or rule making, then it must be supported by substantial evidence on the record as a whole. *Third,* and finally, in rare circumstances a reviewing court can consider some or all factual issues *de novo.*

The APA and common law approaches coexist in this compound structure, and it is far from simple. Any reasonably complicated agency decision has associated with it one or more brands of scope of review because, as we have seen, the decision is inevitably a knot of choices or determinations about facts, law, policy, and procedures. For each of these there is potentially an inquiry into the extent to which existing "law" (agency rules, the agency's organic statute, the APA, the Constitution, common law) constrains administrative determinations *and* how deferential the court should be when settled "law" is absolutely determinative—which is almost never.

For example, the scope of review for agency constructions of the statute is not always "independent" but depends on a host of factors, including whether the agency has been delegated substantive lawmaking powers and, if not, whether its construction is the product of respectable expertise and consistency.[22] And in countless cases one or another aspect of an agency decision, such as the application of a gen-

22. *See, e.g.,* Skidmore v. Swift & Co., 323 U.S. 134 (1944); Schweiker v. Gray Panthers, 453 U.S. 34 (1981); General Elec. v. Gilbert, 429 U.S. 125 (1976).

eral statutory term to particular facts, is subjected to a "reasonableness" scope of review *even though that word appears nowhere in the APA's scope of review provisions*. Courts have at times fashioned formulas for the scope of review that have no verbal foundation in the APA: in addition to "reasonable," "reasonable basis in law," and "warrant in the record," courts have tried "clearly erroneous," "clear error," and "clear error of judgment," among others.[23]

One might imagine that many if not most of these verbal formulas should be considered equivalent,[24] but for the canon of construction that we not interpret the legislature's terms so as to make any of them superfluous. After all, it would certainly be "unreasonable" to act "arbitrarily," and arbitrary to act unreasonably. And what other meaning could "abuse of discretion" have, except in terms of arbitrariness or unreasonableness? So, too, is it sensible for government to act on the basis of *in*substantial evidence?

The persistence of multiple gradations in the scope of review has been criticized along these lines, but the weight of such criticism should be limited to a complaint about the confused and confusing lack of discipline in the formulas rather than taken in broad terms as a compelling argument for a unitary reasonableness test. I see nothing wrong with a system of graduated burdens of proof, which I take to be the purpose of the APA and common law distinctions in scopes of review. No one seriously contends that the civil and criminal burdens of proof are identical or that the burden in a motion for preliminary relief is the same as the burden at the close of the trial. So, too, it seems worthwhile to distinguish those occasions when an agency may proceed with a somewhat looser reign from those when every *t* must be crossed and every *i* dotted. The difficulties have been (1) with the categories used to distinguish those occasions—the fact-law-policy conundrum explored in the preceding section—and (2) with the substantive content of the doctrinal tests of adequacy applied to agency choices.

Two other aspects of scope of review bear particular mention: review of an agency's choice of procedures (which some aggrieved party may have felt were somehow unfair), and those classes of agency action that Congress or courts have deemed *unreviewable*.

23. *See* Davis, 5 Treatise § 29.5–7 (1984); Jaffe, Treatise chs. 14, 15; Schwartz, Treatise 10.

24. *See, e.g.,* Association of Data Processing Serv. Org., Inc. v. Board of Governors of the Fed. Reserve Sys., 745 F.2d 677, 683 (D.C. Cir. 1984) (there is "no *substantive* difference" between the statutory phrases "arbitrary and capricious" and "unsupported by substantial evidence" as they apply to judicial review of factual support for agency decisions [emphasis in original]).

Seemingly procedural choices are not, as one might imagine, generally treated as questions of law for independent judicial redetermination. For example, when an agency has legal authority to formulate policy through either rule making or case-by-case adjudication, its choice between the two is, according to case law, subject to the highly deferential "abuse of discretion" scope of review. Ostensibly, the holding of *Vermont Yankee Nuclear Power Corporation v. NRDC* is that when the APA and the organic statute permit the agency to use informal procedures, a court may not impose more formal hybrid features, such as an oral hearing or a formal record, absent due process or other extraordinary concerns. Thus the agency's discretionary choice of hybrid procedures is almost unreviewable.[25]

An agency's denial of a petition for rule making—that is, an attempt to press the agency to act on some regulatory matter—may seem superficially like a procedural decision, but it frequently represents a substantive agency decision about the merits of the request for agency action. In the APA framework, the denial is usually considered informal adjudication subject to review on an arbitrary and capricious standard. In practice, the scope of review in such cases is highly deferential, even though other agency actions tested under the same verbal formula have been subject to "searching" scrutiny and a "hard look."[26]

Generally, procedural choices by an agency can be parsed into components of fact, law, and policy and the agency's choice thus analyzed using the same doctrinal tools as those applied to other agency choices. The *Vermont Yankee* holding is, in this interpretation, essentially a holding that Congress has, through the APA § 553 prescription of the procedural minimum for informal action, created the legal lower bound on the design of agency procedure; elaboration above that minimum is a matter of policy discretion subject to extremely deferential review. Justice Rehnquist's qualification to the ban on judicial interventionism, concerning extraordinary circumstances and constitutional considerations, is a way of saying that there are conceivable fact patterns under which the agency's broad discretion would indeed transgress legal constraints. Viewed this way, there is a strong parallel between *Vermont Yankee* and cases involving the deference to agency

25. Vermont Yankee Nuclear Power Corp. v. NRDC, 435 U.S. 519 (1978). *See also* SEC v. Chenery, 318 U.S. 80 (1943); NLRB v. Bell Aerospace Co., 416 U.S. 267 (1974); Ford Motor Co. v. FTC, 673 F.2d 1009 (10th Cir. 1981), *cert. denied*, 459 U.S. 999 (1982).

26. *See, e.g.*, NRDC v. SEC, 606 F.2d 1031 (D.C. Cir. 1979); National Org. for the Reform of Marijuana Laws v. Ingersoll, 497 F.2d 654 (D.C. Cir. 1974); Nader v. FAA, 440 F.2d 292 (D.C. Cir. 1971).

policy choices within a domain effectively assigned to them by Congress—cases such as *Hearst* (NLRB has broad discretion in specific application of statutory term *employee*) and *Chevron* (EPA has broad discretion to define pollution "source"). The import of the *Vermont Yankee* holding is that discretionary agency choices of *procedure* are put on much the same footing as discretionary agency choices of *policy,* thereby denying judges any license for heightened interventionism merely because the procedural appearance of the matter makes it seem more accessible to judges and rather less like the typical subjects of substantive agency expertise.

Some species of agency action are *unreviewable.* Agency actions are not subject to judicial review under the APA, as specified in APA section 701(a)(1) and (2), in two circumstances. First, the organic statute has expressly or by clear implication instructed the courts to keep out. Examples include veterans' benefits and certain medicare claimant disputes. (An example of preclusion by clear *implication* is *Block v. Community Nutrition Institute.*)[27] Second, the action may be "committed to agency discretion by law," which is essentially an invitation to judges to decline review of actions they for some reason find are not amenable to judicial oversight. In the *Overton Park* case this exception was read quite narrowly to apply only—as interpreted by most commentators and lower courts—when there is "no law to apply" to the agency's action, meaning that there were no judicially manageable standards with which to judge the agency's decision. More recently, the exception seems in danger of considerable expansion through judicial misadventure, and the extent of this class of unreviewable agency action is currently a matter of considerable confusion.[28]

A related concern is that doctrines often erect a strong barrier of presumptions to reinforce this nonreviewability, so that, for example, the plaintiff will have to make out a strong case in the pleadings in order to persuade most courts to consider on the merits a charge that nonreviewability must be dispensed with because of agency bias or prosecutorial misconduct.[29]

27. 464 U.S. 340 (1984).
28. *See* Heckler v. Chaney, 470 U.S. 821 (1985) (FDA, certain agency action unreviewable); Banzhaf v. Smith, 737 F.2d 1167 (D.C. Cir. 1984) (Ethics in Government Act). *See* Sunstein, *Reviewing Agency Inaction after Heckler v. Chaney,* 52 U. Chi. L. Rev. 653 (1985).
29. *See, e.g.,* Association of Nat'l Advertisers v. FTC 627 F.2d 1151, 1154 (D.C. Cir. 1979), *cert. denied,* 447 U.S. 921 (1980) (agency member can be disqualified only "when there is a clear convincing showing that he has an unalterably closed mind on matters critical to the disposition of the rulemaking"); United Steelworkers of America v. Marshall, 647 F.2d 1189, 1209 (D.C. Cir. 1980) (unalterably closed mind test is "an even

4.3 The Causes of Murky Deference Formulas

So, what about the content and application of the scope of review formulas? In attempting to define the degree of deference intended by "arbitrary and capricious" review, for example, Judge Breyer and Professor Stewart have written:

> In the thousands of federal court decisions annually reviewing federal administrative action, only a few invalidate agency action on this ground. Litigants attempting to persuade a reviewing court that the balance struck by an agency among relevant factors is "arbitrary and capricious" must be prepared to persuade the court that the agency's decision has no rational basis whatsoever. Given the artfulness of agency opinion writers, the skills of government lawyers, and the plausibility of agency claims of "expertise," this is a difficult burden to carry.[30]

Compare this with the picture of arbitrary and capricious review offered by the Supreme Court in *Overton Park*: "[T]he generally applicable standards of § 706 [of the APA] require the reviewing court to engage in a substantial inquiry. Certainly the Secretary's decision is entitled to a presumption of regularity . . . . [citations omitted] But that presumption is not to shield his action from a thorough, probing, in-depth review."[31]

Perhaps Breyer and Stewart are describing the realities, whereas the Supreme Court was simply spinning out verbalisms, to use Davis's distinction. But that *Overton Park* language, written in 1971, has not been repudiated. Lower courts continue to follow it in many cases[32] and cite it even when they do not seem to be following it.[33] What is one

---

higher barrier to claims of bias in a rulemaking proceeding . . . [than proving that a decision maker] had demonstrably made up her mind about important and specific factual questions and was impervious to contrary evidence").

30. S. Breyer & R. Stewart, *supra* n. 1, 336–37 (1985) (citations omitted).

31. 401 U.S. 402, 415 (1971).

32. *See, e.g.,* Citizen Advocates for Responsible Expansion, Inc. v. Dole, 770 F.2d 423, 441 (5th Cir. 1985) (enjoining highway construction approved by Department of Transportation); St. James Hospital v. Heckler, 760 F.2d 1460, 1465 (7th Cir. 1985) (vacating HHS regulation prescribing reimbursement formula for medicare providers); Stop H-3 Ass'n v. Dole 740 F.2d 1442, 1449 (9th Cir. 1984) (holding Department of Transportation's approval of proposed highway an abuse of discretion); Arka Exploration Co. v. Texas Oil & Gas Corp. 734 F.2d 347, 356 (8th Cir. 1984) (holding Department of Interior mileage rule arbitrary and unlawful).

33. *See, e.g.,* Baltimore Gas & Elec. Co. v. NRDC, 462 U.S. 87, 97–98 (1983) (sustaining rules for evaluating environmental impact of nuclear power plant's fuel cycles issued by NRC); FCC v. National Citizens Comm. for Broadcasting, 436 U.S. 775, 803 (1978) (sustaining FCC co-location common-ownership regulations and order mandating par-

to believe? Nor is it clear what the difference is, if any, between arbitrary and capricious review, and reasonableness review. In facing the problem of whether there might be a significant difference between the arbitrary and capricious standard and the substantial evidence standard, Judge Friendly on one occasion wrote that "the controversy is semantic in some degree, at least in the context of informal rulemaking . . . [and lacks] dispositional importance. . . . [T]he two criteria do tend to converge."[34] Similarly, when the D.C. Circuit in *Hodgson* reviewed the amalgam of fact, law, and policy issues underlying OSHA's asbestos standard, it concluded that it need not make the careful distinctions urged by the government between issues appropriate for arbitrary and capricious review and those suitable for substantial evidence review: "We do not believe [such an] approach would affect the rigorousness of our review to the extent the government seems to suppose, or that petitioners purport to fear."[35] Although lower courts occasionally acknowledge that these two standards of review tend to converge,[36] substantial authority remains to support the distinction.[37]

The confusion is at least as great with ultra vires review. The core, conventional understanding is that questions of law are reviewed independently—presumably whether the matter is jurisdictional, procedural, or substantive. Yet one line of cases suggests great deference

---

tial divestiture); Maryland Wild Life Fed'n v. Dole, 747 F.2d 229, 233–234 (4th Cir. 1984) (sustaining Department of Transportation's placement of a national freeway despite opposition by the Department of Interior and EPA).

34. Associated Indus. v. Department of Labor, 487 F.2d 342, 350 (2d Cir. 1973).

35. Industrial Union Dep't, AFL-CIO v. Hodgson, 499 F.2d 467, 473. The organic statute permitted informal rule making but prescribed substantial evidence review rather than the usual, less stringent, arbitrary and capricious standard. The government argued that its policy choices, as distinct from its factual ones, should be subject only to the weaker standard. Despite the quoted disclaimer, the *Hodgson* court went on to explain that a more deferential standard of review was appropriate for quasi-legislative policy judgments. *Id.* at 474.

36. *See* Association of Data Processing Serv. Org., Inc. v. Board of Governors of the Fed. Reserve Sys., 745 F.2d 677 (D.C. Cir. 1984). In reviewing both an informal rulemaking and formal adjudication, the court noted that the various APA scope of review provisions are cumulative; action supported by substantial evidence could still be arbitrary or capricious for other reasons. (As to this, *see also* Bowman Transp., Inc. v. Arkansas-Best Freight Sys., 419 U.S. 281, 284 (1974) (agency action satisfying substantial evidence test may nonetheless fail arbitrary and capricious test). However, when reviewing informal rulemaking, substantial evidence is not triggered, but in such cases arbitrary and capricious review "[t]akes up the slack . . . enabling the courts to strike down, as arbitrary, agency action that is devoid of needed factual support. When the arbitrary or capricious standard is performing that function of assuring factual support, there is no *substantive* difference between what it requires and what would be required by the substantial evidence test, since it is impossible to conceive of a 'non-arbitrary' factual judgment supported only by evidence that is not substantial in the APA sense. . . . [It is]

to the interpretive conclusion of the expert, politically informed agency, whereas another holds to the traditional understanding.[38]

This confusion in the content of verbal formulas is not unlike difficult close distinctions elsewhere in the law. Trial judges use standardized, cookbook jury instructions notwithstanding a general concern that even these do not guarantee that the trier truly understands. Probably only the custom of many decades, or even centuries, enables courts to agree regularly on the abstract content of verbal formulas specifying appropriate burdens for disposing of a civil suit on the pleadings, granting preliminary injunctive relief, appellate reversals of trial court findings, and so forth. Administrative law is, by comparison, in its infancy. Some lack of clarity is, if the reader will forgive the term, "reasonable."

Still, generations of very able judges and commentators have presumably tried to do better. Why so little success? Perhaps they did *not* in fact try carefully to refine scope of review standards because vagueness in the deference-intervention formulas is swamped by the vagueness entailed in actually applying those formulas to different circumstances. Doctrines distinguishing the material differences in issues—principally fact-law-policy—are so messy, that there is no reward for laboring to sharpen the content of scope of review labels. This was the underlying message of *Hodgson* when the court observed that the choice between the two standards of review made no real difference. It was plain that the fact-law-policy distinction could not possibly have enough robustness to make fine differences in scope of review worth worrying

---

the emerging consensus of the Courts of Appeals . . . that the distinction between the substantial evidence test and the arbitrary of capricious test is largely semantic." Data Processing, 745 F.2d at 683–684 (citations omitted; emphasis in original). *See also* Pacific Legal Found. v. Department of Transp., 593 F.2d 1338, 1343 n. 35 (D.C. Cir. 1979); Davis, 1 Treatise §§ 6–13 (2d ed. 1978) (extent of factual support required for rules probably no longer depends on whether the standard of review is arbitrary or capricious, or substantial evidence).

37. *See* Industrial Union Dep't, AFL-CIO v. American Petroleum Inst. 448 U.S. 607, 705 (1980) (dissenting opinion of Marshall, J., joined by Brennan, White, and Blackmun, JJ.) (arbitrary and capricious standard contemplates "searching inquiry into the facts," but substantial evidence is "comparatively more rigorous"); FCC v. National Citizens Comm. for Broadcasting, 436 U.S. 775, 803 (1978) (informal rule making subject only to arbitrary and capricious review, not substantial evidence); Bowman Transp., Inc. v. Arkansas Best-Freight Sys., Inc., 419 U.S. 281, 284 (1974) ("arbitrary and capricious standard contemplates a 'searching inquiry into the facts,'" but substantial evidence is "comparatively more rigorous"); Abbott Laboratories v. Gardner, 387 U.S. 136, 143 (1967) (substantial evidence affords "considerably more generous judicial review than the 'arbitrary and capricious' test available in the traditional [pre-APA] injunctive suit").

38. *See generally* Mayburg v. Secretary of HHS, 740 F.2d 100, 105 (1st Cir. 1984) (Breyer, J.) (collecting citations from each line of precedent).

about. This is also, perhaps, the underlying message in Davis's reasonableness gloss and his general advice that finer elaboration, however commonplace, is pointlessly confusing.

But there is a second and more general explanation for judicial difficulty in differentiating the content of scope of review labels. It, too, follows from the failings of the trichotomy. Such terms as *arbitrary, abuse of discretion,* and *substantial evidence* must be defined with reference to the decision making paradigm under examination; the definitions cannot be determinative if the paradigm is itself poorly discerned and inadequately specified.

This important point bears elaboration. I have stressed three sorts of failings in doctrinal efforts to rely implicitly on the trichotomy as a conceptual device for scaling judicial deference. These are failings of unsustainable categorization, descriptive accuracy, and normative (attribute) coherence.

These three failings make problematic both the distinctions between decision making paradigms and the clarity of our understanding of each paradigm in itself. For example:

> *Assertion:* It is neither arbitrary nor capricious for a politician legitimately employing the methods of interest accommodation to make a choice by splitting the difference between two opposing interests or by pledging to act in favor of interest *A* this time and in favor of *B* next time.
>
> *But Confusion 1:* If, however, we understand the choice between *A* and *B* to be a matter for scientific or adjudicatory fairness decision making, the identical reasoning and result may be branded arbitrary, abusive, or lacking substantial evidence. If we are unable to distinguish paradigms—my thesis in section 3.1—it follows that we will be unable confidently to label any particular decision making process arbitrary, abusive, or whatever. This is the trichotomy's problem of unsustainable categories, revisited.
>
> *And Confusion 2:* Suppose, in addition, that we are not *certain* that the political choice has in fact been based on a fair rather than biased split; or we fear that the log-rolling compact will not be honored; or we suspect that the apparent compromise between *A* and *B* was actually a calculated attempt at undisclosed favor for interests *C*. Then our empirical uncertainty may make it impossible to have firm judgments about arbitrariness, reasonableness, or whatever formula one might use.
>
> *And Confusion 3:* Finally, apart from problems of defensible

categorization and accurate description, the attributive duality of the paradigm creates problems—my thesis in section 3.2. Perhaps the interests of *A* and *B* have been taken into account. But is it arbitrary to have excluded the interests of *C* and *D*? Is it tyrannical if *C* is systemically excluded from log-rolling compacts because *A* and *B* are sufficient to create an electoral majority? The positive norms of participation and democracy suggest that a deal between *A* and *B* is reasonable; the negative norms of majority tyranny and subjectivity point the other way.

Precisely analogous assertions and confusions can be framed for the paradigms of adjudicatory fairness and scientific expertise.

This is more than a problem of distinguishing, say, politics from science or deciding when each of them is appropriate. A crucial consequence of the conceptual failings detailed earlier is that we are unsure of the core definition of each paradigm in and of itself. We will disagree when we try to detail what considerations and methods will be applied by the good scientist, the good politician, or the good Rule of Law-adjudicator. This inability to agree on a robust definition of the methodology of scientific expertise, for example, makes it difficult to spell out a robust definition of "arbitrary" or "substantial evidence." These problems—the categorization quagmire and the internal coherence issue—seem inescapable within the framework of the trichotomy, because within that separation of powers ethos we would deem it illegitimate for courts to undertake explicit prescription of what decision making processes and methods will be employed by administrators. In chapter 7 I speculate that we need not remain trapped in this problematic framework.

4.4 Examples: Case Law Confusion in Scope of Review Analyses

In this section I dissect specific case law examples to demonstrate the sweep and power of the analytical method developed thus far. (Some readers may wish to forego this demonstration and skip to the concluding section, 4.5.)

4.4.1 Example: The Classic Contrast of *Hearst* with *Packard*

In the seminal case of *NLRB v. Hearst Publications, Inc.*, the Court made implicit use of the trichotomy of decision making methods in order to parse the Labor Board's conclusion that newsboys were "employees" under the National Labor Relations Act (NLRA). The Court apparently felt it appropriate to use an independent scope of review—without so much as a nod at the board—in concluding that the statutory term should not be defined according to common law principles of independent contractor, which would probably have meant that the newsboys were not protected by the NLRA. On the other extreme, the Court was clear that basic evidentiary questions (wages, supervision practices) were for the board to decide so long as its findings had "support in the record." As to the delicate problem of actually developing and applying some definition of *employee* to the uncontested facts of the litigation, however, the Court chose a middle ground in deference to the board's expertise and practical experience in administering the statute: "[T]he Board's determination that specified persons are 'employees' under this Act is to be accepted [by reviewing courts] if it has 'warrant in the record' and a reasonable basis in law."[39]

The board's decision was simple in an ultimate sense: newsboys were "employees."[40] But the process of applying that broad term can be parsed in several ways, because fact-law-policy distinctions are subject to substantial dispute. Thus, Justice Roberts dissented in *Hearst*, agreeing with the court of appeals that "Congress did not delegate to the [NLRB] . . . the function of defining the relationship of employment . . . . The question who is an employee . . . is a question of the meaning of the Act, and therefore, is a judicial and not an administrative function."[41] This is a fair dispute over the boundaries suggested by the trichotomy. Alternatively, it could be argued that the board's ultimate decision is not a matter of policy discretion but instead requires as predicate explicit "factual" findings about worker-management relations, patterns of industrial strife facing newspapers, detailed comparisons with related occupations, and so forth.[42] Such disputes are invited and structured by reliance on the trichotomy but diverted the

39. 322 U.S. 111, 130, 131 (1944). *See also* Gray v. Powell, 314 U.S. 402, 411 (1941).

40. Congress reversed the specific outcomes of both *Hearst* and *Packard* in the Taft-Hartley Act, 61 Stat. 136, 137–38 (1947), 29 U.S.C. § 152.

41. 322 U.S. at 135–36.

42. The majority in *Hearst*, in holding inapposite the existing statutory and common law regarding independent contractors, reasoned that the NLRA definition of employee should be based on consideration of the purposes of that act—namely, quelling industrial strife. It is therefore arguable that in a given adjudicatory dispute, findings specific to that statutory purpose should be made and supported by substantial evidence. *Compare* Industrial Union Dep't, AFL-CIO v. American Petroleum Inst., 448 U.S. 607 (1980) (benzene regulation) (holding as matter of statutory construction that regulation is invalid without a specific finding of "significant risk" to health).

Court from examining the soundness of the board's process and result more directly. Neither the Supreme Court nor the court of appeals discussed the merits of the board's decision with respect to the policies of the statute and conditions in the newspaper industry; neither court examined the range of interests and ideas presented to the board through its adjudicatory process. (In chapter 7 I address the appropriateness of judicial analysis of the soundness of agency choices.)

By way of contrast, consider *Packard Motor Car Co. v. NLRB,* a case roughly contemporaneous with *Hearst,* in which the Court reviewed the board's determination that foremen as a class were protected "employees" under the act.[43] Justice Jackson wrote for the majority that there were "difficult questions of policy" involved in considering the status of foremen, and this, together with shifting membership on the board, explained the board's inconsistency over time in answering the general definitional question. In other words, he acknowledged the parts that expertise, politics, and policy had played in the agency's actions. But, he continued, "We are not at liberty to be governed by those policy considerations in deciding the naked question of law whether the Board is now, in this case, acting within the terms of the statute."[44] In both *Packard* and *Hearst* the Court upheld the board's definition of employee, but in *Hearst* the scope of review was highly deferential ("reasonable basis"), while in *Packard* the rhetoric of deference disappeared in favor of an independent judicial construction of the statute.

Can the difference be explained by the importance of particular facts to the newsboy controversy or the more accessible nature of the factual and policy disputes in *Packard?* This seems a doubtful basis on which to reconcile the results.[45] It finds absolutely no support in the broad language of the two opinions. Furthermore, it is highly debatable that the issues in *Hearst* are simpler than those in *Packard,* and in any event that proposition itself requires considerable expertise in the subject to evaluate. A more satisfying explanation for the differing analytical approaches lies in the conceptual failing of the trichotomy-based distinction between law, fact, and policy. In *Hearst,* a majority decided to treat the definition of employee as a matter for the reasonable policy discretion of the agency, while in *Packard* the majority and dissent treated it as a naked question of law, which they resolved by firing policy arguments at one another.

43. 330 U.S. 485 (1947).
44. *Id.* at 493.
45. *But see* Jaffe, Treatise at 561–62.

4.4.2 Example: Reprise—OSHA and Carcinogens

Returning to the OSHA example of section 3.1, conflation of the science, fairness, and politics paradigms is evident in the court opinions, which demonstrate unpredictability in the scope of judicial review fairly traceable to the fact-law-policy boundary problem.

In the *Benzene* case, the Supreme Court was plainly troubled by the inconclusiveness of the evidence supporting the rule, and the arguable disproportionality of costs and benefits.[46] Justice Stevens's plurality opinion, however, approached the problem as a question of law—did such statutory phrases as "most adequately assures . . . [no] material impairment" permit regulation of uncertain and unlikely cancer risks? The three-justice plurality argued as a matter of law that OSHA must find a "significant risk," supported by substantial evidence. Although the plurality acknowledged that scientific certainty was not necessary, they found that the secretary violated the statute by relying on a special agency policy with respect to carcinogens. That policy placed on industry the burden of proving the existence of a safe exposure level.[47] In sum, the plurality rejected characterizing the dispute as one of agency policy (OSHA wanted a rebuttable presumption that any exposure to a known carcinogen is subject to feasible regulation) or as a matter for expert routine (as the Court in *Hearst* had viewed application of the NLRA term *employee*). Justice Powell found his own question of law for independent judicial determination: he would require the agency to find a "reasonable relationship" between costs and benefits of the regulation.[48] But four dissenting justices characterized the question as one

46. Industrial Union Dep't, AFL-CIO v. American Petroleum Inst., 448 U.S. 607, 653 (1980).

47. 448 U.S. at 624–25, 635–36 (plurality opinion by Justice Stevens, with the Chief Justice and Justice Stewart joining). The relevant statutory provisions are: "The term 'occupational safety and health standard' means a standard which requires conditions, or the adoption or use of one or more practices, means, methods, operations, or processes, reasonably necessary or appropriate to provide safe or healthful employment and places of employment. . . . The Secretary, in promulgating standards dealing with toxic materials or harmful physical agents under this subsection, shall set the standard which most adequately assures, to the extent feasible, on the basis of the best available evidence, that no employee will suffer material impairment of health or functional capacity even if such employee has regular exposure to the hazard dealt with by such standard for the period of his working life." 29 U.S.C. §§ 652(8), 655(b)(5).

48. Justice Powell also argued that OSHA had not satisfied its substantial evidence burden with respect to the "reasonably necessary" language of the statute. Thus, although the gravamen of his opinion is his independent judgment of a question of law, he offered an alternative holding based on facts.

Justice Rehnquist found still another question of law: he noted the extreme range of policy discretion available to OSHA, disagreed that the statute could be interpreted to provide anything other than precatory qualifications to that discretion, and hence con-of fact and argued that OSHA had assembled substantial evidence of a definite, though unquantifiable, risk of cancer. Moreover, as to whether OSHA had relied on a special carcinogens policy, the dissenters insisted that it had not and that the agency's judgment concerning the substantiality of the risk and the need for regulatory action was a policy matter entitled to deference.[49]

There is no doubt that the difficulty of the substantive issues at stake in *Benzene*—complex science, substantial costs to industry, tremendous uncertainty, and the riveting image of cancer—all contributed to the sharp division on the Court. My argument is not that the split votes are the result of the trichotomy alone but rather that the trichotomy helps explain the split in analytical approaches taken by the justices.[50] The trichotomy is not the cause of the battle among judges and advocates, but it is the arsenal from which disputants arm themselves. Complex public policies are the battleground. Other cases reveal a similar, trichotomy-based rift in analysis.[51]

---

sidered the standardless delegation of quasi-legislative power unconstitutional. 448 U.S. at 672 (Rehnquist J., concurring in judgment). *See also* American Textile Mfrs. Inst. v. Donovan, 452 U.S. 490, 543 (1981) (Rehnquist, J., dissenting) (repeating his nondelegation doctrine argument from *Benzene*); Aranson, Gellhorn, & Robinson, *A Theory of Legislative Delegation*, 68 Cornell L. Rev. 1, 15–16 (1982) (discussing Justice Rehnquist's approach to nondelegation).

49. 448 U.S. at 688, 689, 695–96 (Marshall, J., dissenting, in which White, Brennan, and Blackmun, JJ., joined).

50. The trichotomy cannot account for all disagreements, obviously. Thus, both Powell and Stevens focus on a question of law, with Powell finding a requirement of cost-benefit correspondence and Stevens finding a requirement of "significant risk." Or, for example, all of the justices could have focused on the question of fact and simply split over whether the substantial evidence test had been satisfied. (Although even here, I would press to see whether differing judgments on the substantiality of the evidence reflected disagreement over the acceptable reach of unsubstantiated policy judgment. See the example of official notice doctrine, sec. 4.4.4.)

51. For example: (1) In American Textile Mfrs. Inst. v. Donovan, 452 U.S. 490 (1981), the Court upheld OSHA's regulation of cotton dust, which causes byssinosis, or brown lung disease. The principal holding in the case was that "cost-benefit analysis by OSHA is not required because feasibility analysis is," thereby rejecting the position taken by Justice Powell alone in *Benzene*. But for my present purposes, Justice Stewart's dissent in *Cotton Dust* is noteworthy. OSHA had asserted that various methodological errors in the study of industry compliance costs were approximately offsetting, but Stewart found no evidence for this position and concluded that the rule was not supported by "substantial evidence." *Id.* at 542 (Stewart, J., dissenting). The majority approved OSHA's reliance on the flawed study, relying on the statute and the implicit conferring of discretion in such matters on the agency: "The Secretary . . . shall set the standard . . . on the basis of the best available evidence." *Id.* at 528 (quoting OSHA act, 29 U.S.C. § 655(b)(5)). Thus, the boundary problems of the trichotomy are evident in the competing characterizations of the dispute over study methodology, with the majority viewing the issue as one

4.4.3 Example: Reprise—Market Ideology and Administrative
Deregulation

Several cases in recent years have shared the same difficulty: questions of law, fact, and policy dissolved in solution together, with the
ultimate court decision subject to dispute because another parsing of
the agency decision would change the deference and the result.

1. *Chevron USA, Inc. v. NRDC,*[52] the Supreme Court reviewed
the EPA's mildly deregulatory decision to permit economically
efficient pollution tradeoffs among various point sources within
a conceptual "bubble" at one site, rather than requiring that
every individual source meet pollution control standards. Environmental plaintiffs challenged the bubble concept. The D.C.
Circuit Court of Appeals decided the matter using an independent scope of review, treating it as a question of law calling for
the court's unique talent for statutory construction and, more
important, stare decisis. The Supreme Court held that the statute did not speak to the issue and that the agency had policy
discretion entitled to a deferential scope of review.[53] Neither
court chose to insist that the agency support its decision to adopt
a bubble concept with concrete scientific evidence that this regulatory innovation would promote the objectives of the statute,
although the emphasis on facts, as opposed to law or policy,
seems perfectly plausible and in many respects desirable.

---

of law and/or agency discretion and Justice Stewart insisting on more and better scientific
proof.

(2) In Industrial Union Dep't, AFL-CIO v. Hodgson, 499 F. 2d 467 (D.C. Cir. 1974)
(reviewing an OSHA standard for asbestos dust) discussed in sec. 4.2.1, the court struggled with the conceptual difficulty implicit in applying the act's substantial evidence test
in an instance of "essentially legislative type of decision making by the Secretary in the
performance of the broad delegation made to him by Congress." *Id.* at 488. Judge
McGowan, for the court, acknowledged that "at least some legislative judgments cannot
be anchored securely and solely in demonstrable fact." *Id.* at 476. Although the opinion
intelligently describes the conundrum—when is the agency obliged to make policy in the
face of uncertainty, and when should courts insist that facts are capable of being determined and must be?—it offers no solution. None is possible, in view of the trichotomy's
conceptual failings.

52. 467 U.S. 837 (1984).
53. *Chevron,* 467 U.S. at 845. For the decision below, see NRDC v. Gorsuch, 685 F.2d
718, 720 (D.C. Cir. 1982). In rejecting the EPA's bubble concept, the D.C. Circuit relied
on two of its earlier opinions in which it "determined the applicability *vel non* of the
bubble concept to distinct Clean Air Act programs" (discussing Alabama Power Co. v.
Costle, 636 F.2d 323 (D.C. Cir. 1979) and ASARCO, Inc. v. EPA, 578 F.2d 319 (D.C. Cir.
1978)).

2. In *Farmers Union Central Exchange v. FERC*,[54] another panel of the D.C. Circuit was more insistent on facts in rejecting FERC's attempt to deregulate oil pipeline prices, when it could easily have reached the same result by approaching the question as one of law; or it could have permitted FERC a range of policy discretion and made allowance for the inevitably "predictive" character of market analysis—as has been done in several other recent cases, involving, for example, the FCC, the ICC, and the Federal Reserve.[55] What explains the difference in emphasis between *Chevron* and *Farmers Union?* First, in *Chevron* the court of appeals panel was strongly influenced by prior appellate decisions evaluating the bubble concept in other settings, so that the allure of a Rule of Law decision-making method (analysis of precedents; stare decisis) was strong. Second, in *Farmers Union* there may have been a palpable partisan quality to the deregulatory decision, in contrast to the broader political support for the modest use of economic incentives in environmental regulation. And third, the panel in *Farmers Union* may have viewed general retreat from oil pipeline price regulation as a profound policy initiative requiring heightened scrutiny; the bubble concept as applied to one particular corner of environmental regulation is less dramatic. None of these considerations is expressed by the courts in their scaling of deference to agency action. They proceed, instead, by parsing the problem according to the categories of the trichotomy and deploying the appropriate verbal formula for scope of review.

3. In a very different setting, courts have for some time struggled with ICC decisions to award operating certificates. Judicial review is under the substantial evidence standard, but the ultimate statutory tests of public necessity, fitness to serve, and furtherance of the national transportation policy invite the ICC to develop and apply expert policy judgments rather than scientific proof. This has been particularly true after legislation in 1980 partially deregulated the trucking industry: the commission is charged with promoting competition but remains subject to substantial evidence review on the issue of public need. In an early case following enactment, the Fifth Circuit rejected the ICC's attempt to implement broad policies granting wide geographical authority in certificates, holding a presumptive de-

---

54. 734 F.2d 1486 (D.C. Cir. 1984); *see also* sec. 3.1.2.
55. *See, e.g.,* FCC v. WNCN Listeners Guild, 450 U.S. 582 (1981).

regulatory posture inconsistent with the continuing statutory requirement of evidentiary submissions by carrier-applicants and of substantial evidence to support the commission's awards of certificates.[56] The court understood the problem as a question of law rather than one of deference to agency policy judgment.

4. Similarly, in reviewing a recent ICC award with broad geographical authority, a Ninth Circuit panel explained: "The Commission relied on policy considerations and [its] general rule that '[b]road grants allow carriers to meet changing needs of shippers and receivers and the diverse demands of the market and the shipping public, and to take advantage of technological advances and changing industrial patterns' . . . . The Commission also found that two goals of the national transportation policy, the promotion of intermodal transportation and of service to small communities, would be served by the grant of authority."[57]

But then, after dutifully acknowledging that the commission has policy discretion as well as powers of official notice, the court ruled without elaboration that "policy considerations alone cannot support a finding of public need."[58] Read this flatly, the court's ruling seems to deprive the commission of discretion to conclude that particular awards will promote statutory policies, even though at best such conclusions are inevitably a matter of prediction and inference from such thin evidence as a handful of shippers' affidavits. Here again is the slippery slope between unfettered policy discretion and extremist scientific determinism. Where to draw the line? In the process of skirting this unresolvable confusion of fact-law-policy distinction, one court stated the difficulty this way:

> We need not rule on the exact quantum of evidence required to support the grant of authority to haul specific commodities in bulk. The Interstate Commerce Commission, not the federal judiciary, has expertise in trucking issues, and the Commission may in its discretion conclude that grants of bulk hauling certifi-

56. American Trucking Ass'ns, Inc. v. ICC, 659 F.2d 452 (5th Cir. 1981). See Motor Carrier Act of 1980, Pub. L. No. 96–296, 94 Stat. 793; Port Norris Express Co. v. ICC, 687 F.2d 803, 806 (3d Cir. 1982).

57. Containerfreight Corp. v. United States, 752 F.2d 419, 424 (9th Cir. 1985) (quoting Manlowe United, Inc., Common Carrier App. No. MC-153155 F (Feb. 14, 1983) ["Order"] at 6).

58. 752 F.2d at 424.

cates for certain commodities require less evidence than grants of similar certificates for other commodities. We only require that the certificates be supported by substantial evidence and that the issuance of the certificates not be arbitrary or capricious.[59]

4.4.4 Example: Official Notice

Still another example concerns official notice during formal proceedings, where cases draw a distinction between factual findings, which must have an evidentiary basis in the record, and policy or legal conclusions, which must only be explained in a manner consistent with the "facts" but need not be the subject of specific evidentiary submissions. For example, in *Market Street Railway Co. v. Railroad Commission of California,* the Supreme Court ruled that the agency could conclude that a fare reduction would generate a net increase in revenues without hearing expert testimony, because the prediction was a matter of "opinion," "inferences as to probable effect," and "argument."[60] In other words, this was a matter not of science and "fact" but of discretion and "policy." The difficulty, of course, is that nowadays everyone would agree that estimating the price elasticity of demand invites hordes of experts and endless days of hearings. This is not merely because the issue is disputable—in itself insufficient as a bar to officially noticing some matter—but because one may have the sense that there is a *knowable answer*. This evaluation of the matter, quite obviously, merely restates the conclusion that the answer is not discretionary. It is either law or fact. Although a policy choice is ultimately involved—if for no other reason than because one must weigh the uncertainties—that discretionary choice can be greatly informed by *evidence* which the Court in *Market Street Railway* did not require the agency to develop on the record, and therefore in effect did not require at all.[61]

The context of economic and scientific prediction is certainly not unique. The most recent Supreme Court statement on official notice was in *FCC v. National Citizens Committee for Broadcasting ("NCCB"),*[62] which repeated the theme that an agency's expertise may be sub-

---

59. Port Norris Express Co. v. ICC, 729 F.2d 204, 208 (3d Cir. 1984).

60. 324 U.S. 548, 560–61 (1945). *See also* FPC v. Transcontinental Gas Pipe Line Corp., 365 U.S. 1, 28–29 (1961); Davis, 3 Treatise 207–17 (1980).

61. *See also* Industrial Union Dep't, AFL-CIO v. Hodgson, 499 F.2d 467, 474 and n. 18 (D.C. Cir. 1974).

62. 436 U.S. 775, 813–14 (1978). *See* National Citizens Comm. for Broadcasting v. FCC, 555 F.2d 938, 961–62 (D.C. Cir. 1977).

stituted for "judgmental or predictive facts." In NCCB the lower court had overturned an FCC rule limiting joint ownership of broadcast and newspaper enterprises because of insufficient evidentiary support for the rule's exemption of most current combinations. Reversing, the Supreme Court emphasized that "[c]omplete factual support in the record for the Commission's judgment or prediction is not possible or required; 'a forecast of the direction in which future public interest lies necessarily involves deductions based on the expert knowledge of the agency.'"[63] Plainly, the prediction of business practices and programming at issue in NCCB can be pressed for evidentiary basis no less than the market forecasts at issue in *Market Street Railroad* and *Farmers Union*; or at least, experimentation and conditional policy choices could be imposed in the NCCB setting so that concrete evidence might be developed. But again, the difficulty of cleanly separating discretionary decision making from scientific decision making makes the courts' doctrinal categories unstable and the results confused. This is the inevitable result of scaling judicial deference by reference to the fact-law-policy trichotomy of agency decisions.[64]

The general descriptive and normative difficulties of the trichotomy also provide a way of understanding the conflict inherent in the doctrine of official notice, where the inclination to let the expert have an unfettered, efficient opportunity to just go ahead and make the "factual" finding is in tension with the desire to temper the cold rationality of expertise with participatory and fairness values.

My analysis suggests three characterizations of this tension. First, we may lack confidence that experts can decide accurately without broader participation—this is the descriptive insufficiency of the expertise model and is reflected in Davis's concept of "adjudicative facts," a defining characteristic of which is the individual's competence to make a substantive contribution to the agency's factually correct resolution of the dispute. Second, several cases reflect an assessment that the decision requires methods other than or in addition to expertise—the interest accommodation and participation of politics, or the confrontation, neutrality, and reasoned elaboration of adjudicatory fairness.[65] Such assessments reflect the conceptual confusion of the tricho-

---

63. 436 U.S. at 814 (quoting FPC v. Transcontinental Gas Pipeline Corp., 365 U.S. 1, 29 (1961)).

64. In an important sense, the doctrine of official notice is an adjunct of the substantial evidence standard of review problem: both concern the extent to which an agency conclusion requires a basis in the record. It is therefore not surprising that the trichotomy's category problems reappear in the official notice context.

65. *See, e.g.,* TRW-United Greenfield Div. v. NLRB, 716 F.2d 1535 (11th Cir. 1983) (administrative law judge properly refused to hear uncorroborated hearsay testimony);

tomy, which makes an argument about alternative appropriate methods available *all the time*. And, third, we may be inclined to emphasize the negative attributes of expertise—the distanced, alienating, impersonal character of bureaucratic action—over the positive attributes, as Justice Brandeis did in *Ohio Bell*. *That* is the problem of attributive duality.

4.5 Conclusions on Conceptual Failings of the Trichotomy and Scope of Review: Toward Judgment or Nihilism?

It is possible, at least as a matter of logic, that definition and application of the scope of judicial review involves a large but irreducible element of judicial discretion—there is some point at which we inevitably fail to capture in any controlling verbal formula the way in which we expect the judge to approach the deference-control problem. Justice Frankfurter, in *Universal Camera,* attempted to define the degree of deference intended by the substantial evidence test and concluded:

> A formula for judicial review of administrative action may afford grounds for certitude but cannot assure certainty of application. Some scope for judicial discretion in applying the formula can be avoided only by falsifying the actual process of judging or by using the formula as an instrument of futile casuistry. It cannot be too often repeated that judges are not automata. The ultimate reliance for the fair operation of any standard is a judiciary of high competence and character and the constant play of an informed professional critique upon its work. Since the precise way in which courts interfere with agency findings cannot be imprisoned within any form of words, new formulas attempting to rephrase the old are not likely to be

---

Johnson v. U.S. Dep't of Agriculture, 734 F.2d 774 (11th Cir. 1984) (fair hearing requires impartial arbiter); Texas v. United States, 756 F.2d 419 (5th Cir. 1985) (agency must provide adequate explanation for departure from previous policy); New York Council, Ass'n of Civilian Technicians v. FLRA, 757 F.2d 4502 (2d Cir. 1985) (same); Baltimore Gas & Elec. v. Heintz, 760 F.2d 1408 (4th Cir. 1985) (same); Seacoast Anti-Pollution League v. Costle, 572 F.2d 872 (1st Cir. 1978) (administrator not free to rely on undisclosed scientific evidence cited by staff in off-the-record internal deliberative process); Aqua Slide 'N Dive Corp. v. CPSC, 569 F.2d 831, 842–43 (5th Cir. 1978) (diminished confidence in agency determination where no opportunity to challenge given to opposing side); United States v. Nova Scotia, 568 F.2d 240, 251–52 (2d Cir. 1977) (same); Portland Cement Ass'n v. Ruckelshaus, 486 F.2d 375, 394 (D.C. Cir. 1974) (diminished confidence where agency failed adequately to consider opposing views).

more helpful than the old. *There are no talismanic words that can avoid the process of judgment.* The difficulty is that we cannot escape, in relation to this problem, the use of undefined defining terms.[66]

In this passage Justice Frankfurter frankly admits the limits of language and the irrepressibility of discretion, at least in this context. As though concerned, lest the reader be repelled by this revelation of raw judicial power, Frankfurter offers in the quoted passage what he takes to be some reassurance. But what is that reassurance? Only the informal checks of meritocratic appointment, professional colleagueship, and scrutiny through law reviews. This says more about Justice Frankfurter's view of the world than it does about the solution of a troubling problem of governance. What appears in law reviews about a particular matter can be of serious professional concern only to a law professor or a judge obsessively concerned with "ratings" by a minuscule audience. What proportion of colleagueship among judges is conviviality, and what part given to substantive criticism?[67] (I hope, but doubt, that they compare favorably with law faculties.) Finally, meritocratic appointments probably occur only by accident,[68] and article III tenure insulates the mistakes and allows merit (somehow defined) to fade. Frankfurter's argument cannot be "Don't worry, because there are adequate professional and other checks on judicial discretion." A more realistic message is that there is little point in worrying because nothing can be done about it.[69]

66. Universal Camera Corp. v. NLRB, 340 U.S. 474, 488–89 (1951) (emphasis added).

67. On the possible applications of small group psychology to decision making by courts, *see* Weiler, *Two Models of Judicial Decisionmaking,* 46 Can. B. Rev. 406, 452–53 (1968); Murphy, *Courts as Small Groups,* 79 Harv. L. Rev. 1565 (1966).

68. This claim reflects my harsh view engendered by experience as a White House and agency appointee in the Carter administration and as an alarmed observer of Reagan administration appointments.

69. In 1926, while a professor of administrative law at Harvard, Frankfurter professed a similar confidence in the constraining effect that legal professionalism could have over discretion within agencies. In a general introduction to a proposed Harvard study on administrative law he wrote: "Safeguards must . . . be institutionalized through machinery and processes. These safeguards largely depend on a highly professionalized civil service, an adequate technique of administrative application of legal standards, a flexible, appropriate and economical procedure . . . , easy access to public scrutiny, and a constant play of criticism by an informed and spirited bar." Frankfurter, *The Task of Administrative Law,* 75 U. Pa. L. Rev. 614, 618 (1926–27).

For a more recent example of this confidence in the profession to constrain judicial interpretive discretion, *see* Fiss, *Objectivity and Interpretation,* 34 Stan. L. Rev. 739 (1982). In an attempt to refute the deconstructionist claim of textual indeterminacy in the legal world, Fiss argues that the legal community, unlike the literary community, has an

So this is some support for Davis's inchoate nihilism. Frankfurter—sounding wise, candid, and reverential all at once—says doctrinal choice is ultimately "the process of judgment," while Davis says it is the judge's "stretching" of reasonableness. Two other prominent scholars, Ernest Gellhorn and Glen Robinson, have observed that the doctrines regulating scope of review "have no more substance at the core than a seedless grape," although they continue to command "endless attention."[70] And there are many judicial expressions of frustration with or disinterest in clarifying the distinctions among verbal formulas for the scope of review.[71]

This despair over standardlessness has the natural consequence of promoting one of two alternatives: virtually total deference, or a formless kind of reasonableness inquiry that must derive legitimacy from our broad agreement with Frankfurter that little else is possible and judges can be trusted to exercise judgment. But, symptomatic of broader trends in our political culture, the premise of trustworthiness has received mounting criticism in recent years. As a result, rather than exercise an essentially unguided power of reasonableness review, acknowledged to permit stretching almost at will, judges must feel under some pressure to forswear genuinely searching review and adopt the first alternative: a de facto practice of great deference, whatever the verbal formula employed.[72]

---

authoratative set of rules of interpretation (a grammar) that constrains interpretive discretion. This position relies on the same assumptions of community coherence made by Justice Frankfurter in *Universal Camera*. (We are all somewhat autobiographical. Fiss works in a happy New Haven community; I don't.) *See also* K. Llewellyn, The Bramble Bush 9 (2d ed. 1951) ("[T]he office of the institution of law as an instrument of conscious shaping [and] . . . work of that institution as a machinery of sometimes almost unconscious questing for the ideal").

70. Gellhorn & Robinson, *Perspectives on Administrative Law*, 75 Colum. L. Rev. 771, 780–81 (1975).

71. *See* Industrial Union Dep't, AFL-CIO v. Hodgson, 499 F.2d 467 (D.C. Cir. 1974); Automotive Parts and Accessories Ass'n v. Boyd, 407 F.2d 330 (D.C. Cir. 1968); Association of Data Processing Serv. Orgs., Inc. v. Board of Governors of the Fed. Reserve Sys., 745 F.2d 677, 683 (D.C. Cir. 1984). *See also* Allen, *Chairman's Message*, 35 Admin. L. Rev. iii (Spring 1983) (crying out in frustration and calling for legislative clarification).

72. More generally, the trichotomy and its failings offer a lens through which to view the history of administrative law. In the search for limiting and justifying norms, there has been an evolving, shifting, increasingly "layered" reliance on political accountability, then expertise, then judicial review, then political accountability. [*See* Frug, *The Ideology of Bureaucracy in American Law*, 97 Harv. L. Rev. 1276, 1377–80 (1985) (contemporary legal doctrine and theory combine or superimpose formalist, expertise, judicial review, and market/pluralist models of bureaucracy, but the result is no more coherent than any individual model).] In each phase, a contemporary and successful (in the short-

Commentators and courts state the law in many different ways. This seems especially true regarding the scope of review for questions of law. Yet courts function. They make decisions and they enjoy considerable legitimacy in the public eye, relative, at least, to the other major institutions of contemporary government and culture. How can this be? It is possible that the doctrinal failings described in chapters 3 and 4 actually help the courts function. Perhaps only the abler judges recognize the manipulability of doctrines and the consequent loose reign on their discretion, while less able judges are effectively confined by legal rules they mistakenly take to be clear.[73] This rosy formulation strikes me as unlikely. The gravamen of my critique is that the alternative avenues of analysis resulting from problems of description, attributive duality, and categorization are all too obvious. Judges and advocates are competent enough; in any case, one need not be a genius to fashion alternative arguments and be puzzled by administrative law. The plodding judge may stumble down any path, his choice poorly guided. The clever judge will choose cleverly, while perceiving even greater degrees of ambiguity in the doctrinal guidance. This does not amount to a happy state of affairs.

---

run) critique has stressed negative attributes of the decision making method at issue and pressed the positive attributes of a proposed alternative paradigm. Thus, even as the Founding Fathers proclaimed general faith in politics and participation, mediated by a written constitution, they had reservations about unfettered democratic control— qualms both about tyranny of the majority and about the passions (subjectivity) and irrationality of the masses. Those reservations are reflected in the constitutional compromise, which included republicanism, federalism, and such antidemocratic devices as the independent judiciary, the Bill of Rights, certain requirements of super majorities, restrictions on the franchise, and the perpetuation of slavery. *See* G. Wood, Creation of the American Republic, 469–564 (1969). Decades later, demands of expediency augmented these doubts about politics with the argument that competence and rational administration were at odds with politics. This was the debate over Jacksonian spoils, patronage, and civil service reform, setting the groundwork for the Progressives' construction of a nascent regulatory and welfare state. Then, arrayed against the positive claims for expertise and bureaucratic organization is the critique of alienation, impersonality, and distance from social experience—a critique with Jacksonian strands, realist strands challenging the existence of expertness, and more radical theoretical strands. Finally, judicial review has been criticized since before *Marbury* as an unaccountable threat to politics and (more recently) expertise. *See* Monaghan, *Marbury and the Administrative State*, 83 Colum. L. Rev. 1 (1983). This critique has emphasized the negative attributes of stultifying proceduralism and institutional limitations. *See* D. Horowitz, The Courts and Social Policy (1977); W. Crosskey, Politics and the Constitution 941 *et seq.* (1978) (popular response to early cases establishing judicial review of legislation); R. Berger, Congress v. the Supreme Court (1969); J. Goebel, ed., The Law Practice of Alexander Hamilton (1981).

73. Llewellyn, *supra* n. 68 at 68 (making this argument with respect to lines of precedent).

One response to all of this is to argue that a higher rationality explains judicial actions. If only we could as skillful lawyers discern that higher rationality, we could be very successful appellate litigators, both as persuaders and predictors. But a less hopeful view is that the ready availability of opposed arguments both empowers the advocate to present persuasive arguments for the desired scaling of judicial deference and untethers judges to decide cases however they please.

What is the possibility that such a higher rationality exists? To a great extent, of course, this is what law teachers do—provide *post hoc* rationality by reconciling seemingly inconsistent cases, offering considered interpretations, and flagging the irredeemably deviant case as inconsequentially aberrant. Indeed, discerning (or imposing) order on a conceptual jumble of holdings is taken to be the mark of a great scholar or judge.

But the creation of coherence should have some observable consequence over time: court decisions should be more predictable and more easily arrived at, doctrinal drift should be stemmed, and the din of realist charges of judicial willfulness should modulate in the face of convincingly reasoned elaboration. The absence of these developments, which I explore more fully in the next chapter, lends substantial support to the less hopeful view of things. Nor does the doctrinal muddle seem fairly attributable to a process of continually shifting frontiers, with rational litigators attacking there and settling their disputes elsewhere. The particular doctrines at stake in the muddle seem remarkably constant over the decades. This contrasts, for example, with the layer-upon-layer of wrinkles in search and seizure law or consumer protection.

Another response to the evident doctrinal disorder is that the verbal confusion does not reflect any deeper conceptual confusion but serves instead only to demonstrate an asynchrony between verbalisms and genuine judicial motivations. But if this is so, then my thesis is all the more defensible. For my argument is that the proper judicial motivation is sound governance and that sound governance should be the engine of judicial innovation and action.

Perhaps this is already so. But the language of analysis and explanation is the muddier, indirect rhetoric of the trichotomy—of separation of powers ethos. It is a sadly anachronistic tongue, rooted in an era of far more limited government and a far less evolved legal order. More to the point, the language of administrative law, and the apparent tokens of analysis, respond to yesterday's concerns about judicial legitimacy in imposing Rule of Law constraints on administrative and judicial discretion.

But today the crisis of legitimacy is with the quality of governance. It is not surprising that the deeper currents of doctrine might be so directed. They should be. The task, therefore, should be to make these currents more visible, so that reasoning based on concerns for good governance evolves under public and professional scrutiny rather than in subterranean fashion. This is the theme to which I return in chapters 6 and 7.

PART II

Rethinking Administrative Law

CHAPTER 5

Unsuccessful Remedies for the Futility
of Administrative Law

I have proposed the separation of powers ethos of the trichotomy to account for a raft of problems in the content and application of administrative law doctrines. As I explore in chapters 6 and 7, the structure of my critique can be used to generate ideas for doctrinal reform. Before turning from critique to construction, however, in this transition chapter I briefly survey some major strands of commentary to assess the extent to which established perspectives on the reform of administrative law have been able to address successfully the doctrinal difficulties explored in chapters 3 and 4.

At the risk of pressing elegant symmetry too far, we can group several commentators around each of three perspectives paralleling the decision making paradigms, plus a fourth anticonceptualist perspective that lays claim to pragmatism:

Rule of Law/Legal Process: This tradition, which includes the work of Hart and Sacks in the 1950s,[1] as well as most contemporary doctrinal analysis, emphasizes institutional roles, comparative institutional competence, and the role of courts in disciplining agency discretion through judicial review.[2] I will focus on the work of Professor Louis

---

1. H. Hart & A. Sacks, Materials on the Legal Process, 1–24, 212–25 (tent. ed. 1958).

2. *See, e.g.,* Garland, *Deregulation and Judicial Review*, 98 Harv. L. Rev. 505, 553–55 (1985). Garland identifies fidelity to statutory purpose as a necessary strategy for courts to contain agency discretion in administrative deregulation and notes that "hard-look" review is a "proxy" for "direct discovery of an agency's motives," including the decision maker's subjective fidelity to statutory purpose. Garland sees "direct discovery," however, as foreclosed by "considerations of comity and practicality."

Jaffe.[3] Because the process of statutory construction is invariably a critical element of this perspective, my presentation and critique will include a digression to appraise whether various notions of fidelity to legislative purpose can clarify the respective roles of judge and administrator.

Politics and Interest Accommodation: Some scholars, most notably Professor Richard Stewart, have explored the potential value of using the perspective of interest group, pluralist politics as both an explanatory and a normative tool for the development of doctrine.[4]

Expertise and Ideal Administration: Still others have focused on improving public administration, including the substantive soundness of the policy choices made by officials who exercise broad discretion. In this perspective, judicial review and interest group struggle are background factors (if not intrusive threats) to the process of bureaucratic reform and efficiency. Among the prominent contributors to this perspective are Judge Stephen Breyer and Professors Colin Diver and Jerry Mashaw.[5] I will focus on the latter.

Pragmatism and Reasonableness: Finally, the work of Professor Kenneth Culp Davis epitomizes a fourth perspective which, as he has described it, eschews conceptualism in favor of pragmatic analysis of trends and reforms in doctrine.[6]

The question is whether any of these perspectives is successful in escaping the descriptive and conceptual difficulties of the trichotomy.

3. L. Jaffe, Judicial Control of Administrative Action (1965) [hereinafter Jaffe, Treatise]; Jaffe, *The Illusion of Perfect Administration*, 86 Harv. L. Rev. 1183 (1973). For a contemporary restatement of the statutory interpretation method as expounded by Jaffe, *see* Diver, *Statutory Interpretation in the Administrative State*, 133 U. Penn. L. Rev. 549, 550 (1985) ("After a long period of relative neglect, the subject of statutory interpretation once again enjoys favor in the courts of academic discourse"). Diver concludes that the courts should allow a strong presumption of deference to agency interpretation, permitting the court to retain its role of review through a "reasonableness" constraint on agency action. For my views on this approach, *see* sec. 5.1.3.

4. *See* Stewart, *The Reformation of American Administrative Law*, 88 Harv. L. Rev. 1667, 1760–1802 (1975) (hereinafter Stewart, *Reformation*); Sunstein, *Participation, Public Law, and Venue Reform*, 49 U. Chi. L. Rev. 976, 986 (1982); Stewart, *The Development of Administrative and Quasi-Constitutional Law in Judicial Review of Environmental Decisionmaking: Lessons from the Clean Air Act*, 62 Iowa L. Rev. 713, 762–63 (1977); S. Breyer, Regulation and Its Reform 350–54 (1982); S. Breyer & R. Stewart, Administrative Law and Regulatory Policy ch. 10, 1014–58 (1979) (1985); W. Gellhorn, C. Byse, & P. Strauss, Administrative Law 634 (1979).

5. *See generally* Breyer, *supra* n. 4; J. Mashaw, Bureaucratic Justice (1983); Mashaw, *How Much of What Quality? A Comment on Conscientious Procedural Design*, 65 Com. L. Rev. 823 (1980); Diver, *The Optimal Precision of Administrative Rules*, 93 Yale L.J. 65 (1983).

6. *See* K. Davis, Administrative Law Treatise (2d ed. 1978–85).

5.1 The Perspective of Rule of Law/Legal Process Constraints

5.1.1 Exposition: Jaffe, Clear Purpose, and the Partnership of "Lawmaking"

> I am aware that an answer [to the scope of review question] in terms of statutory purpose will appear to be either a crashing platitude or a resounding rationalization for results otherwise determined. But . . . .[7]

The leading effort to bring some conceptual clarity to the subject is that of Louis Jaffe.[8] Jaffe begins the topic in his classic treatise by noting that "[t]he distinction between fact and law is vital to a correct appreciation of the respective roles of the administrative and the judiciary."[9] He goes on, however, seemingly to reject rigid formalisms that use the fact-law distinction to attempt sharp differentiation of roles and, derivatively, degrees of deference in the scope of review. His analysis rests on three points.

First, Jaffe notes the difficulty of distinguishing fact, law, and mixed questions, (others had made this point)[10] and argues that an emphasis on the processes of decision that characterize "law-concluding" and fact finding suggest that there are important elements of law-concluding in a great deal of what agencies do. On this much I agree, although, as I suggested in chapter 3, my view is that for all intents and purposes the categories collapse rather than merely mingle. In any nontrivial case the agency's fact-finding processes—ascertaining or predicting the ex-

---

7. Jaffe, Treatise at 572 (offering his view of when a court should impose its own statutory interpretation rather than assess the reasonableness of the agency's view).

8. L. Jaffe, Judicial Control of Administrative Action (1965). This volume is based on published articles. In particular, *see* Jaffe, *Judicial Review: Question of Law*, 69 Harv. L. Rev. 239 (1955); *Judicial Review, Question of Fact*, 69 Harv. L. Rev. 1020 (1956); and *The Judicial Enforcement of Administrative Orders*, 76 Harv. L. Rev. 865 (1963) (noteworthy for its rejection of formalistic roles for court and agency in the enforcement of administrative action).

9. Jaffe, Treatise at 546.

10. *See, e.g.*, Dickinson, Administrative Justice and the Supremacy of Law in the United States 55 (1927): "In truth, the distinction between 'questions of law' and 'questions of fact' really gives little help in determining how far the courts will review; and for the good reason that there is no fixed distinction. . . . Matters of law grow downward into roots of fact, and matters of fact reach upward, without a break, into matters of law." *See also* J. Thayer, A Preliminary Treatise on Evidence at the Common Law 228, 250 (1898); O. Holmes, The Common Law 126 (1881).

istence of something—contain an element of norm-making or norm-applying. Jaffe's own examples demonstrate this.[11] The central point in each example is that the fact-law distinction is a conceptually unsound basis on which to identify those occasions—questions of law—when the scope of review should be independent. He reaches this conclusion because in his vision the agency *should* have broad lawmaking authority. I reach the same conclusion because, owing to the collapse of the trichotomy's categories, I cannot imagine it otherwise.

But Jaffe's willingness to acknowledge the lawmaking content of much agency business—including what others might attempt to classify as mixed questions or application of a broad statutory term—does not lead him to subordinate agency decision making to an aggressively independent scope of judicial review. "[I]n my view . . . a law applying judgment is *presumptively* within the area of an agency's discretion and thus its conclusion should be sustained."[12]

This is because of his *second* point. Fact-finding is the exclusive domain of the agency—the reviewing court exercises only a veto power for inadequate evidentiary support, not affirmative fact-finding powers. *But the power to make law is shared in "partnership."*[13] By acknowledging the important capacity and authority of the agency to make law, Jaffe converts the scope of review inquiry from the crude, almost formalistic one suggested by the trichotomy's allocation of roles, into a subtler inquiry into when the court, as senior partner, should overrule the agency's conclusion of law—that is, in Jaffe's terms, the agency's *making* of law.

And the answer to that inquiry is in Jaffe's third and most important point, his "clear purpose rule." Jaffe's notion was that when Congress delegates a complex task to an administrative agency, there should be a rebuttable "presumption" that Congress intended for the agency to enjoy discretion consistent with the statutory purposes. It follows, for him, that the reviewing court should permit this discretion to be exercised "short of the point where the court is *convinced* that the purpose

11. *See, e.g.,* his hypothetical on the distribution of an estate, Treatise at 552, or his discussion of Dobson v. Commr., 320 U.S. 489 (1943), *id.* at 579.

12. *Id.* at 549.

13. *Id.* at 546. This concept of partnership has received support in modern case law, *see, e.g.,* NRDC v. SEC, 606 F.2d 1031, 1048 (D.C. Cir. 1979) ("[T]he partnership, if indeed that concept be at all apt, is thus an 'uneasy' one at best [cites omitted] as courts struggle to perform their congressionally-mandated task of judicial review without encroaching on territory which as judges they are ill-suited to enter"). *See also* Greater Boston Television Corp. v. FCC 444 F.2d 841 (D.C. Cir. 1970) *cert. denied,* 403 U.S. 923 (1971). What has made the partnership uneasy, of course, is the difficulty courts have in reviewing agency action effectively yet deferentially when the collapsing distinctions of the trichotomy are at play.

of the statute is contradicted." When the court's construction of the statute would permit more than one agency choice, the court's function is the far more deferential one of ensuring reasonableness.[14] It is important for Jaffe's theory, however, that the clear purpose rule not be subsumed by the reasonableness inquiry. The steps in the analysis are distinct; the agency's decision may well be reasonable, yet a reviewing court, convinced that the "clear purpose" of the statute is otherwise, is bound by Rule of Law notions to ignore the agency's reasonableness.

Jaffe uses the *Packard* case, which I discussed in section 4.3.1, as an illustration. There, the NLRB had decided that foremen were protected employees under the act and ordered the company to bargain. Both the majority and the dissent approached the question as a matter for independent judicial interpretation of the statute, the dissenters disagreeing with the board, and the majority reaching the same result as the board but without resting their conclusion on deference to the agency. The dissenters had reached a "reasonable" conclusion as to the application of the statute, but the majority was convinced that the clear purpose of the statute was consistent only with allowing foremen to organize, according to Jaffe.

For Jaffe, his clear purpose rule swallows up just about everything else as a basis for scaling judicial deference to agency choices of law and policy. Most important, deference to expertise is for him only a logical entailment of the inquiry brought about by the requirement that the reviewing court be *convinced* before it interferes;[15] if the subject matter or circumstances are such that the court considers the role of expertise crucial to reaching a sound conclusion about purpose, then perforce the court will be unable on its own to be convinced of any particular conclusion. Deference to the agency is unavoidable. I think Jaffe would have thought it immaterial in practice whether one characterizes this process of looking to agency expertise as deference to the agency or as independent review "informed" by expert agency instruction, but he would probably have preferred the "deference" formulation because it acknowledges the agency's legitimate lawmaking role.

5.1.2 Critique of the Thesis, through Failings of the Trichotomy

Now to the heart of the matter. Let me compare Jaffe's analysis with what I have said thus far about the role of the trichotomy in confusing judicial review. On its face, Jaffe's theory appears to eliminate reliance

14. *Id.* at 573; *see* Chevron USA, Inc. v. NRDC, 467 U.S. 837 (1984).
15. *Id.* at 576–77 (discussing Republic Aviation Corp. v. NLRB, 324 U.S. 793 (1945)).

on the trichotomy because, notwithstanding his opening emphasis on the fact-law distinction, his goal is to escape the formalism of assigning law-concluding to the judiciary through a rigid separation of fact and law and of judicial and administrative functions. He presses the partnership model of collaborative responsibility and launches us on a search for some basis of disciplining the relation between junior and senior partner other than fact versus law. Jaffe *seems* to construct an approach which all but obviates a fact-law distinction, in that the test becomes whether the agency's action is consistency with the statute, no matter whether the agency's choice is denominated fact or law. (Of course, a mere finding of "pure" fact, if such exists, is not susceptible to this test of statutory fidelity anyway.) And he seems to accomplish a similar service with respect to the trichotomy's parallel distinctions among decision making methods, by effectively collapsing the expertise and adjudicatory approaches: the court's adjudicatory law pronouncing is appropriate, under the clear purpose rule, only when the role of expertise is by the nature of the problem and circumstances immaterial to convincing the court about clear statutory purpose. Hence, there is no tension, for Jaffe, between the court's sense that it should decide questions of law independently and its sense that it should defer to agency expertise—the tension set up by the trichotomy's formalist prescriptions.

Or so it might seem. Jaffe's approach presents three substantial problems. His clear purpose rule puts decisive emphasis on the task of statutory interpretation, which he acknowledges to be an unruly, imprecise enterprise. But he dismisses this difficulty with a shrug, because statutory interpretation is always a messy business; his subtext is that it is a business familiar and appropriate to the courts.[16] There are at least three bits of separation-of-powers, trichotomy-related analysis at work in this: there is the assertion that this is the business of the courts (*must* they be senior partners over the entire realm Jaffe is willing to call lawmaking and law pronouncing?); there is the task of specifying the content of the "convincing" burden of proof in a given problem of interpretation; and there is the matter of how courts actually go about statutory interpretation. Each of these difficulties reintroduces the empirical and conceptual failings I have described in chapters 2, 3, and 4. This explains why his theory gives no more determinacy to case law than does the trichotomy. Even more troubling, we can discern in Jaffe's analysis the seeds of the contemporary malaise of judicial

16. *Id.* at 572, 576 (speaking of statutory construction as a method that "comports better with a confident and responsible judiciary").

review—the conceptual rationalization for the impoverishing of judicial review.

First, as regards the domain of the senior partner, this is nothing other than the fact-law dichotomy revisited. Jaffe would say, I think, that the distinction makes much less difference because he makes much less turn on it: categorizing a question as law triggers not independent review but only the clear purpose test. This is not completely accurate, however. In one sense, maximizing the fact-ness of the question pulls it toward the pole that Jaffe acknowledges (consistent with the trichotomy) to be the agency's exclusive preserve, subject only to veto based on inadequate factual support in the record.

Conversely, maximizing the policy-ness of the question invites inquiry as to whether there are controlling policy guidelines in the statute, discoverable and enforceable by the court. Jaffe has by no means avoided the fact-law dichotomy. Since virtually all exercises of discretion, including resolution of mixed questions, entail lawmaking, the very practical opportunity for a court to open the agency's discretion to the independent review of a senior partner is just as manipulable as it would be without Jaffe's two-pronged requirement of (1) pervasive law-ness plus (2) the clear purpose rule. The manipulability leaves undisturbed the opportunities for ad hoc judicial balancing of deference and control explored in chapters 3 and 4.

Unless, that is, Jaffe's clear purpose rule means that the senior partner is disciplined in a way the fact-law formalism could not manage. Jaffe defends his partnership/clear-purpose theory against the pragmatic attack of Davis and others by saying that basing judicial deference on the fact-ness of the problem is practical only because it provides an easy verbal subterfuge for the judge who wants to uphold the agency but prefers not to recognize (and accommodate) the agency's legitimate lawmaking function. But is the clear purpose test any less inviting of subterfuge? I think not.

This is because—my second criticism of his approach—Jaffe never gives content to the burden of proof contained in his "clear purpose" rule. How convinced must the majority of the court be in order to be convinced enough to make a determination independent of the agency's? As I have said, it is impossible to give truly precise content to a verbal formula such as "convincingly clear purpose," in whatever context. So my criticism is not that Jaffe quite understandably failed to do the impossible. The point is that his failure is at root the *same* failure as that of the fact-law distinction, and that failure is explained by the trichotomy.

How so? To figure out just how convinced the court must be in a given situation, we inevitably appeal however implicitly to norms about roles and a corresponding sorting of problems among institutions. That means the trichotomy. If one is inclined in the circumstances to defer to the agency, then clear purpose becomes a bit tougher to demonstrate, and conversely. But what are those circumstances? What principles or instincts press? As I showed in chapter 2, the cases indicate that what will matter to the judge is whether the question appears to be a matter for agency expertise; whether it calls for a political accommodation of interests; whether the circumstances require judicial intervention to cure a perceived problem of political or other "abuse"; whether there is call for the court's special competence (say in matters of common law); and so forth. And each of these judgments is made difficult by the empirical and conceptual problems I have detailed.

Jaffe's attempt to collapse expertise into the clear purpose rule illustrates my point. True, he decries robotic deference because the agency invokes a claim of expertise or because the problem is complicated. But, instead, he makes room for expertise by saying that it will be persuasive only if the court is not otherwise—that is, independently—*convinced* of the statutory policy. When will alleged expertise be persuasive? Answer: when the court decides to let it be persuasive, which will be when the court decides that the subject is an appropriate one for expert decision. Yet, we have said (in sections 3.1 and 4.2) that there is no neat way, or messy way, for that matter, to distinguish situations amenable to expertise from situations less so. Jaffe himself acknowledges that when expertise is appropriate is a debatable matter. Indeed, there is the meta-question of what deference to pay to the agency's claim that its expertise deserves deference—for example, that it as expert feels that the statutory term has a technical meaning as to which the agency's view should be controlling if reasonable.[17] By admitting an interaction between expertise and the rule of convincingly clear purpose, Jaffe necessarily readmits the problems of distinguishing ex-

17. This issue is raised in both NLRB v. Highland Park Mfg. Co., 341 U.S. 322 (1950) and NLRB v. Coca-Cola Bottling Co. of Louisville, Inc., 350 U.S. 264 (1955). In *Highland Park,* the Court, rather than defer to the NLRB's construction of the phrase "labor organization national or international in scope," assumed the judicial task of statutory interpretation and gave its own construction of the phrase. The board's presumed expertise is dismissed: "The Board is a *statutory* agency." 341 U.S. at 325. By contrast, in *Coca-Cola Bottling* the Court viewed the statutory term *officer* as having a "technical meaning . . . doubtless drawn by specialist[s] in labor relations . . . of course the Board's expertness comes into play." 350 U.S. at 269. Because the board's construction was not too "farfetched," the Court deferred. *Id.*

pertise, adjudication, and politics as alternative methods of decision making.

This contrasts with another point he makes. Noting that many considerations, such as expertise, give richness or complexity to application of his clear purpose rule, he mentions that "the importance of the question" may make it appropriate for judicial decision even though the court is not convinced of any particular clear purpose.[18] The example he gives is the *Packard* case, in which a sharply divided Court reached an independent conclusion of law that the Labor Act included foremen with the class of protected "employees."[19] Taking the dissent of four justices as evidence that there was no convincingly clear statutory purpose, Jaffe suggests that the Court nevertheless decided the matter because of its tremendous importance to the statutory scheme and because of the possibility that the public would view its basing the result on deference to the NLRB as capitulation to a self-aggrandizing, zealous agency. In my terms, the Court chose to deemphasize the normatively positive attributes of expertise, emphasize the negative attributes of agency politics, and take seriously the possibility that as a descriptive matter the agency's choice was not (or might not be perceived as) neutral and expert.

Jaffe suggests nothing that would discipline this series of judgments. The Court did not apply the *Packard* reasoning he supposes in the recent *Chevron* case, when it grandly deferred to the EPA's construction of "point source" to permit plantwide averaging of pollution;[20] nor did it proceed on the basis of an independent scope of review when evaluating a series of efforts by the FCC to deregulate format diversity.[21] There are several other counterexamples, some of which may seem like judicial substitution of policy judgments for those of the expert agency when there is no arguable claim that the core policies of the statute make the case so important that Jaffe's special rule against deference might apply.[22] It is, of course, tempting (and in a sense correct) to account for these varying approaches by reference to the personalities on the Court and the political moment in history.

18. Jaffe, Treatise at 576, 585.
19. *Id.* at 560 (discussing Packard Motor Car Co. v. NLRB, 330 U.S. 485 (1947)).
20. Chevron USA, Inc. v. NRDC, 467 U.S. 837 (1984). *See also* Heckler v. Chaney, 470 U.S. 821 (1985) (deference to FDA on interpretation of agency jurisdiction).
21. FCC v. WNCN Listeners Guild, 450 U.S. 582 (1981).
22. *See, e.g.,* Dirks v. SEC, 463 U.S. 646 (1983) (both majority and dissent reaching independent conclusion on whether insider trading prohibitions based on broad anti-fraud statute extend to one who has received a tip from an insider).

Such accounts reinforce my general point about the absence of doctrinal discipline.

Third, and finally, the process of divining statutory purpose triggers the trichotomy's concerns in ways apart from the manipulability of the burden of proof. There are a series of methodological questions implicit whenever a Court is asked to construe an agency's organic statute. The court must adopt views about: the relevance (if any) of the agency's expertise (if any) to the task of interpreting legislative purpose; the significance of interactions between legislators and the agency during and since enactment; the reliability of the legislative process and the legislative history materials, in terms of providing an accurate reflection of 535 individual wills and the accumulation of legislative expertise; and so forth. These questions cannot be answered without a theory of roles, and the theory of roles employed by courts and commentators is based on the separation of powers-related trichotomy.

In sum, with impressive elegance, Jaffe attempts to deflect significant conceptual troubles with the traditional fact-law-policy basis for scaling the scope of review. In part, he does this by taking a strong position on the legitimacy of agency lawmaking, which is fine so far as it goes.[23] It is perfectly possible for judges to translate the demonstrably flawed framework of fact-law-policy distinctions into the Jaffe framework of shared lawmaking and the clear purpose rule. But both the clear purpose test of statutory interpretation and the senior partner metaphor of context-sensitive deference reincorporate the demonstrable flaws of reliance on the trichotomy; Jaffe's approach does not avoid the familiar norms and distinctions.

5.1.3 The Futility of Interpretation-Based Role Theories, Generally

I do not think that any project of administrative law theory, or any strategy of doctrinal reform, can escape the pitfalls of the trichotomy's separation of powers ethos through appeals to interpretation of statutes. There is considerable turmoil at the moment concerning the scope of review of the agency's interpretation of its statute, a special problem within the general scope of review doctrine. The topic has received little effective scholarly attention[24] but deserves special note here because interpretation of law is so closely linked to the policy

23. Jaffe, Treatise at 554 (it is appropriate that in certain cases an agency should have *primary* responsibility for lawmaking, whether by rule or application of rule, and in those cases the court should accept the conclusion unless clearly erroneous).

24. *But see* Diver, *Statutory Interpretation in the Administrative State*, 133 U. Pa. L. Rev. 549 (1985).

making function and to politics and because administrative law's single greatest shortcoming, to my mind, is its inability over the decades to come to terms in a realistic and constructive manner with the role of politics in agency discretion. The posture of the courts toward the other vertex of the trichotomy, expertise, has also been inadequate. But there have appeared important glimmerings of helpful doctrinal approaches, such as hard-look review and heightened requirements of reasons, findings, and consistency. These doctrinal innovations do little to contribute directly to the accommodation of administrative law and politics.

This is not to say that the doctrinal confusion surrounding issues of lawmaking are attributable exclusively to the politics corner of the trichotomy: my general thesis, after all, is that such a monochromatic picture of government action is necessarily inaccurate and deceptive.

Review of agency interpretations is a pervasive problem for two reasons. First, the breadth of modern delegations is irremediable without a workable theory of roles, deference, and activism. Second, our legal culture eventually brings almost every arguable question before the courts. My focus, however, is on the complexity rather than the pervasiveness of administrative review. The complexity arises because judges face not only the general intellectual problems of interpretation—language, intention, purpose, evidence, manipulation of canons—but also the role allocation concerns special to administrative law.

One line of cases suggests that judicial review of questions of law is to be "independent," meaning that no deference should attach to the agency's view on the question.[25] This classic view also finds support in the text of the APA, which in section 706 instructs courts to "decide all relevant questions of law, interpret constitutional and statutory provisions," "set aside agency action in excess of statutory jurisdiction, authority, or limitations . . . or otherwise not in accordance with law." It is in some respects the legacy of the earlier, less trusting era when the independent review of legal questions was quite clearly associated with the legitimacy of the agency. Without such an independent check, the agency would have been lawless.

25. *See* Barlow v. Collins, 397 U.S. 159, 166 (1970) ("[S]ince the only or principal dispute relates to the meaning of [a] statutory term, the controversy must ultimately be resolved, not on the basis of matters within the special competence of the [agency], but by judicial application of canons of statutory construction"); *see also* NLRB v. Highland Park Mfg. Co., 341 U.S. 322 (1951); NLRB v. Marcus Trucking Co., 286 F.2d 583, 590–91 (2d Cir. 1961) (Friendly, J.); Morton v. Ruiz, 415 U.S. 199, 236 (1974) (holding that an agency's interpretation of a statutory term was invalid after a lengthy independent statutory construction by the Court); Zuber v. Allen, 369 U.S. 168, 192–94 (1969); Wilderness Soc'y v. Morton, 479 F.2d 842 (D.C. Cir. 1973) (Skelly Wright, J.).

Another strand of cases suggests substantial deference, including simply according weight to the agency's view, but also reducing the court's responsibility to a mere test of "reasonableness."[26]

What are we to make of these competing views? I have three points. First, several commentators and courts have argued for deference by emphasizing that Congress has delegated substantive rule making authority to the agency. But Congress has also, by statute, assigned judicial view duties to the courts. There are situations in which Congress has deliberately and clearly confined the scope of judicial review—indeed, in several instances actually foreclosing all but the barest constitutionally required minimum of judicial review.[27] When Congress has not so spoken, it is inappropriate for the Court to refrain from exercising its traditional responsibility to say "what the law is," as Chief Justice Marshall put it in the 1803 case of *Marbury v. Madison.* Yes, Congress is the ultimate authority on many of these matters. But Congress has (almost always) said several things, pushing in different directions, resulting in an unavoidable problem of interpretation and hence an unavoidable tension between judicial and agency roles.[28] Overstated claims of deference ignore the responsibility to contend with those tensions and certainly cannot claim to represent fidelity to any

26. *See* Skidmore v. Swift & Co., 323 U.S. 134, 140 ("The weight of such a judgment in a particular case will depend upon the thoroughness evident in its consideration, the validity of its reasoning, its consistency with earlier and later pronouncements and all the factors which give it power to persuade, if lacking power to control"); Udall v. Tallman, 380 U.S. 1, 16 (1965) ("When faced with a problem of statutory construction, this Court shows great deference to the interpretation given the statute by the officers or agency charged with its administration"); Chevron USA, Inc. v. NRDC, 467 U.S. 837, 846 (1984) ("If this choice represents a reasonable accommodation of conflicting policies that were committed to the agency's care by the statute, we should not disturb it unless it appears from the statute or its legislative history that the accommodation is not one the Congress would have sanctioned").

27. Veterans' benefits claims and certain medicare reimbursements are two noteworthy areas in which judicial review is precluded by statute. Note, *Congressional Preclusion of Judicial Review of Federal Benefit Disbursement: Reasserting Separation of Powers,* 97 Harv. L. Rev. 778 (1984).

28. One might argue that to the extent it is based on the general authority of the APA, judicial review is implicitly limited by quasi-legislative delegations in subsequent organic statutes. This argument has several weaknesses. First, most modern organic statutes provide expressly for judicial review. Second, we might just as well argue that in view of the background of judicial review and broad pattern of court intervention, Congress would assume the possibility of aggressive judicial oversight of delegated lawmaking, absent specific restrictions on courts. Third, the traditional premise of quasi-legislative delegations is that the essential or "intelligible" principles that guide agency discretion have been established by the legislature; a derivative premise is that these enacted principles provide a "legal" standard by which a reviewing court can set aside interstitial lawmaking by the agency.

discernible congressional purpose or to the principle of checks and balances.

Second, another common argument in favor of deference to agency interpretation of statutes is that agency officials are more knowledgeable of the legislative intent since they were direct or indirect participants in the legislative process.[29] This argument is an implicit appeal to the trichotomy's separation of political and judicial competence. But it can be met by exploiting empirical insufficiencies. Sometimes the assertions of agency participation and special access are true, sometimes not.[30] The agency may have been completely uninvolved, it may have offered a little testimony for or against the measure, or it may have been very heavily involved. Even if involved, the agency may well have been *opposed* to the enacted provision at issue. In any case, the agency personnel assigned to legislative matters are often far removed organizationally from the staff who eventually write the regulations or adjudicate orders, or the involved personnel may have left the agency. Even if the agency was actually a supporter of the provision, it is fair to worry that zealous interpretation and implementation might not do justice to a more balanced intent of the legislature, combining as it did the motivations and intentions of zealous proponents, zealous opponents, and everyone in between. The highway agency that won authorization for construction grants may, despite its involvement in the legislative process, give short shrift to that undesirable amendment requiring accommodation of environmental concerns.[31]

Third, apart from all these claims and counterclaims concerning deference, there is the fundamental difficulty: the collapsibility of the law-fact-policy distinction makes it possible to argue, in virtually any situation, that deference is appropriate because the seemingly "legal" questions are largely questions of "fact" and "policy" appropriate for the agency or the seemingly "factual" or "policy" questions are largely questions of "law" appropriate for the court. At the extreme, this parsing becomes reductionist, with all the business going to one or the other institution. Professor Monaghan, for example, has argued that the article III duty to say what the law is, first stated in *Marbury v. Madison*,

29. *See, e.g.*, Chevron USA, Inc. v. NRDC, 467 U.S. at 846 (1984) ("If this choice represents a reasonable accommodation of conflicting policies that we committed to the agency's care by the statute, we should not disturb it unless it appears from the statute or its legislative history that the accommodation is not one that Congress would have sanctioned").

30. Stever, *Deference to Administrative Agencies in Federal Environmental, Health, and Safety Litigation: Thoughts on Varying Judicial Application of the Rule*, 6 W. New Eng. L. Rev. 35, 59–67 (1983).

31. Citizens to Preserve Overton Park, Inc. v. Volpe, 401 U.S. 402 (1971).

can be discharged simply by the court's determination of what range of statutory authority has been conferred to the agency, including so little as the basic determination that Congress has delegated substantive rule making authority.[32]

Doubtless the sound view of all of this is that courts should discipline the agency lawmaking through a variety of more refined doctrinal means. Professor Monaghan puts it this way: "[R]esponsibility for meaning is shared between court and agency; the judicial role is to specify what the statute cannot mean, and some of what it must mean, but not all that it does mean."

So the court should discern, as a matter of independent law concluding, the limits on permissible interpretation of the statute: *employee* does not mean *A, B,* or *E;* but it would be reasonable and thus permissible for the agency to choose either *C* or *D*. This is one (of many) plausible reading(s) of *Overton Park*[33] and of the more recent case of *Federal Election Commission v. Democratic Senatorial Campaign Committee*.[34] But *why* should the *agency* have discretion to choose between interpretations *C* and *D,* once it is clear to the Court that *A, B,* and *E* are impermissible? The underlying question is whether the court or the agency should make the choice. On what basis should the authority be allocated?

Justice Stevens's opinion for the Court in *Chevron* emphasizes that if Congress has not given a clear signal of its meaning, either in the text or in traditional materials of legislative history, then choosing within the remaining (*C* or *D*) range entails policy making—that is, politics and expertise. This leads Stevens, all the while implicitly relying on the trichotomy's assignment of roles, to a stance of great deference, under the label of "reasonableness."[35]

---

32. Monaghan, *Marbury and the Administrative State,* 83 Colum. L. Rev. 1 (1983).

33. "The Court is first required to decide whether the Secretary acted within the scope of his authority. . . . This determination naturally begins with a delineation of the scope of his authority." 401 U.S. at 415–16; *see also* Jaffe, Treatise at 359 ("We may for our present purposes define discretion as a power to make a choice within a class of actions. Despite such discretion, normally a court will review an agency's choice in order to determine whether it is within the permissible class of actions").

34. 454 U.S. 27, 39 (1981). ("[T]he task for the Court of Appeals was not to interpret the statute as it thought best but rather the narrower inquiry into whether the Commission's construction was 'sufficiently reasonable' to be accepted by a reviewing court [citations omitted]. To satisfy this standard it is not necessary for a court to find that the agency's construction was the only reasonable one or even the reading the court would have reached if the question initially had arisen in a judicial proceeding." *Id.* at 39.) *See also* Diver, *supra* n. 3 at 560–61.

35. Chevron USA, Inc. v. NRDC, 467 U.S. 837, 851 (1984).

This is not a sustainable prescription of roles. In Justice Stevens's single chain of logic, we can see first his denial of separation of powers formalism (just because it is a question of law does not mean that only the court can decide it; besides, it can be both law and policy), followed by his assertion of a subtler kind of formalism (since it involves policy-making, it is best left to the agency rather than the court). This result in *Chevron* can be reversed by emphasizing the law-ness, rather than policy-ness, of the problem at hand, as was done in the court below and in several other recent cases.[36] The most that can be said for the method of fencing-off permissible agency choices is that it sets a mood for the scaling of deference—a mood fully subject to the confusions of the trichotomy.

5.2 The Perspective of Politics: Interest Group Representation Theory

5.2.1 Exposition: The Interest Group Representation Thesis

In an important article a decade ago, Professor Richard Stewart argued that many doctrinal developments, and much of the commentary on the administrative process, can be understood to reflect an emerging model of administrative law stressing the importance of "interest group representation" as an alternative to the traditional model's emphasis on judicial review to assure fidelity to the statutory delegation.[37] Stewart demonstrated this thesis by detailing certain doctrinal developments from 1960 into the late 1970s that expanded opportunities for participation via three important avenues: procedural due process, efforts to cause agencies to initiate action, and standing to seek judicial review.

36. NRDC v. Gorsuch, 685 F.2d 718 (D.C. Cir. 1982). *See, e.g.,* General Motors Corp. v. Ruckelshaus, 724 F.2d 979 (D.C. Cir. 1983) (holding that an EPA interpretation of the Clean Air Act is, despite persuasive policy arguments, not supportable, given the Court's review of the history and language of the act); ASARCO, Inc. v. EPA, 578 F.2d 319 (D.C. Cir. 1978); Lubrizol Corp. v. EPA, 562 F.2d 807 (1977).

37. Stewart, *Reformation* at 1669. *See also* Stewart, *The Development of Administrative and Quasi-Constitutional Law in Judicial Review of Environmental Decisionmaking: Lessons from the Clean Air Act,* 62 Iowa L. Rev. 713, 762–64 (1977); S. Breyer, *supra* n. 4 at 378; Sunstein, *Participation, Public Law, and Venue Reform,* 49 U. Chi. L. Rev. 976, 986 (1982); Diver, *Policymaking Paradigms in Administrative Law,* 95 Harv. L. Rev. 393, 423–24 (1981); Garland, *Judicial Review and Deregulation,* 98 Harv. L. Rev. 507, 575–85 (1985). Apart from his affirmative offering of the interest group representation model, Stewart's seminal article gave a comprehensive account of the nature and sources of discontent with the traditional model of administrative law.

A more subtle but equally important example given by Stewart is the evolution of a requirement that agencies give "adequate consideration" to all of the relevant interests in a policymaking controversy, more commonly referred to as the requirement that agencies give a "hard look" at all relevant issues and alternatives.[38] The apparent judicial objective in this doctrinal development is assurance of substantive soundness in agency policy choices, and perhaps fidelity to statutory purposes. Stewart, however, considers hard-look review to be evidence of attraction to the interest group representation model, because its import is that the relevant interest groups will have the right not only to participate and make their views known before the agency but also to have those views adequately considered. Participation without consideration would be meaningless.

Stewart ultimately doubted whether interest group representation and its implications would be fully embraced by the courts.[39] This was wise. Case law developments since his 1975 article show important judicial reluctance to accept the implications of the theory, though perhaps not outright rejection of it.

Thus, for example, with respect to the general possibility of judicial fashioning of extra-APA procedural requirements that might help to assure full and adequate representation of diverse interests in agency decision making, the Supreme Court's decision in *Vermont Yankee*[40] (holding that courts are not free to impose on agency informal rule-

<hr>

38. Stewart, *Reformation* at 1756–60, 1781–85. Stewart discusses two cases in detail: Scenic Hudson Preservation Conf. v. FPC, 354 F.2d 608 (2d Cir. 1965), *cert. denied,* 384 U.S. 941 (1966); Scenic Hudson Preservation Conf. v. FPC, 453 F.2d 463 (2d Cir. 1971), *cert. denied,* 407 U.S. 926 (1972); Hudson River Fisherman's Ass'n v. FPC, 498 F.2d 827 (2d Cir. 1974); Office of Communication of the United Church of Christ v. FCC, 359 F.2d 994 (D.C. Cir. 1966); Office of Communication of the United Church of Christ v. FCC, 425 F.2d 543 (D.C. Cir. 1969). *See also* Greater Boston Television Corp. v. FCC, 444 F.2d 841, 851 (D.C. Cir. 1970), *cert. denied,* 403 U.S. 923 (1971); Portland Cement Ass'n v. Train, 513 F.2d 506 (D.C. Cir.), *cert. denied,* 423 U.S. 1025 (1975). As with the other three key elements of his story, recent developments suggest that hard-look review faces an uncertain future at best. *See* the discussion immediately below.

39. Stewart, *Reformation* at 1802–5.

40. Vermont Yankee Nuclear Power Corp. v. NRDC, 435 U.S. 519 (1978). *See generally* Stewart, *Vermont Yankee and the Evolution of Administrative Procedure,* 91 Harv. L. Rev. 1805 (1978) (arguing that *Vermont Yankee* is a regression in the search for administrative procedures which will allow effective judicial review of agency discretion); Byse, *Vermont Yankee and the Evolution of Administrative Procedure: A Somewhat Different View,* 91 Harv. L. Rev. 1823 (1978) (arguing that the Court properly appraised its institutional role in prohibiting additional procedural requirements on the administrative agencies); Breyer, *Vermont Yankee and the Court's Role in the Nuclear Energy Controversy,* 91 Harv. L. Rev. 1833 (1978) (arguing that the Court should have accepted the NRC's initial decision, given the Court's institutional inability to assess the complex technical data).

making any procedural requirements beyond those established by Congress in the APA) represents a powerful if not conclusive obstacle. The possibility that lower courts could effectively circumvent the strictures of *Vermont Yankee* by stressing the *substantive* rather than *procedural* deficiencies of the agency's policy making process at first seemed real enough, as courts continued to exploit the hard-look review encouraged by the pre–*Vermont Yankee* decision in *Overton Park*.[41] While this substantively aggressive hard-look approach is far from dead, the growing pattern mirrors *Vermont Yankee* by emphasizing substantive deference to agency choices. The two best examples are (1) the declining independence of judicial review of agency questions of law, broadly defined,[42] and (2) the growing importance of the "unreviewable discretion" exceptions to judicial review in APA section 702 and certain organic statutes.[43] More particularly, there has been important and, I think, disheartening doctrinal retrenchment in the past decade in the areas Stewart emphasized in 1975: procedural due process,[44] initiation of agency action,[45] and standing.[46]

41. Citizens to Preserve Overton Park, Inc. v. Volpe, 401 U.S. 402 (1971) (searching scrutiny in review of informal agency action to assure careful agency consideration of all "relevant factors" and no extrastatutory factors).

42. See Chevron USA, Inc. v. NRDC, 467 U.S. 837 (1984) (deference to agency's construction of statutory term because congressional intent is not clear); Byse, *Scope of Judicial Review in Informal Rulemaking*, 33 Ad. L. Rev. 183 (1981) (advocating independent scope of review for questions of law).

43. See, e.g., Heckler v. Chaney, 470 U.S. 821 (1985), and cases cited therein.

44. Among the post-*Reformation* developments: Cleveland Bd. of Educ. v. Loudermill, 470 U.S. 532 (1985) (pretermination procedure for school security guard need only provide "reasonable grounds" test, rather than more definitive test, through evidentiary hearing of the propriety of discharge); Paul v. Davis, 424 U.S. 693 (1976) (stigmatizing "posting" of alleged shoplifter not subject to procedural due process scrutiny); Mathews v. Eldridge, 424 U.S. 319 (1976) (pretermination evidentiary hearing not required for social security disability benefits); Ingraham v. Wright, 430 U.S. 651 (1977) (no process required for paddling of students; *Goss* distinguished in part because tort action is presumably available for excessive paddling); Parratt v. Taylor, 451 U.S. 527 (1981) (officials only liable in tort for negligent deprivation of prisoner's property); O'Bannon v. Town Court Nursing Center, 447 U.S. 773 (medicare and medicaid decertification of nursing home, with consequent mandatory transfer of patients, does not require evidentiary hearing).

45. Post-*Reformation* cases suggesting far less judicial sympathy for expanded rights of initiation include: Heckler v. Chaney, 470 U.S. 821 (1985) (FDA decision not to take enforcement action against the unapproved use of drugs for lethal injections in capital punishment, held unreviewable); Banzhaf v. Smith, 737 F.2d 1167 (D.C. Cir. 1984) (holding unreviewable the attorney general's refusal to investigate allegations of 1980 campaign illegalities concerning the purloined "Carter briefing book"); United States v. Snell, 592 F.2d 1083 (9th Cir. 1979) (agency's alleged refusal to follow its own rules regarding enforcement policy held unreviewable); Investment Co. Inst. v. FDIC, 728 F.2d 518 (D.C. Cir. 1984) (upholding agency refusal to consider merits of petition that it

Stewart combined his caution in projecting doctrinal implementation of the then-emerging interest group model with his healthy skepticism as to whether the model can provide what he termed a "unifying theory" for administrative law. Interest group representation does not in itself provide answers to such crucial questions as *which* interests must be represented or *how* substantive differences in interest group positions are to be accommodated in a discretionary policy choice. As to the latter point, Stewart noted that procedure can go far toward assuring that the relevant interests and arguments are heard at the table, but procedure alone cannot determine the result's content, much less assure its soundness. In identifying and reconciling competing interests, Stewart noted that the interest group representation model still affords administrators and judges considerable, troubling discretion. Stewart also pointed to such practical problems as financing the effective participation of typically unrepresented interests through public interest organizations or attorney's fee measures and the like.[47]

I believe the attractiveness of the interest group representation thesis can be explained in terms of the trichotomy. But the trichotomy can also be used to explain why the thesis is, in the end, unsatisfactory. More specifically, the failings of the trichotomy provide a way of understanding why Stewart's two senses of caution (doctrinal acceptance and conceptual cogency) have proven so well-taken.

5.2.2 Relation to the Trichotomy

In terms of the trichotomy, the interest group representation model is, on its face, the result of viewing administrative law through the prism of politics: pluralist politics is both the critical characteristic of discretionary agency decision making and the putative prophylactic for arbitrary bureaucratic power, at least in aspiration. The model's important advance over the crude separation-of-powers assignment of institutional roles (chapter 2) is that the agency's expertise is no longer the beginning and end of the justification for administrative discretion

---

declare unlawful certain plans by savings banks to market mutual funds); UAW v. Donovan, 547 F. Supp. 398 (D.D.C. 1983) (finding unreviewable the secretary's decision not to bring civil action against employer and his attorney for failure to comply with LMRDA). *See also* sec. 6.1.1 (discussing agency inaction).

46. *See, e.g.*, Rizzo v. Goode, 423 U.S. 302 (1976); Los Angeles v. Lyons, 461 U.S. 95 (1983); Simon v. Eastern Ky. Welfare Rights Org. (EKWRO), 426 U.S. 26 (1976); Warth v. Seldin, 422 U.S. 490 (1975). *See generally* Chayes, *Public Law Litigation and the Burger Court*, 86 Harv. L. Rev. 4, 8–26 (1982); Shapiro, *Wrong Turns*, 98 Harv. L. Rev. 61 (1984).

47. Stewart, *Reformation* at 1802–11.

and judicial deference. Instead, interest group representation theory debunks the pretensions of expertise (objectivity and science) in light of contemporary allegations of agency capture and incompetence. More important, Stewart and others have argued that expertise is no longer a credible check on discretion. This is because contemporary regulatory tasks entail pervasive and broad delegations, often implicating irresolvable and sometimes unfamiliar value clashes: agency choice is now seen to be far from the pole of the merely ministerial, toward the opposite pole of highly discretionary policy choice in a context of competing interests, conflicting values, and irreducible empirical uncertainty.

In this view, expertise and politics are still distinct modes of decision making.[48] But, claims the theory, the tasks at hand are even less amenable to expertise alone than were the tasks of earlier days.[49]

Interest group representation, with its prism of pluralist politics, contains not only a critique of expertise but also a critique of adjudicatory fairness as a decision making method. The structure of the critique parallels that of expertise. First, the judgelike decision making is flawed on its own terms, with lapses in neutrality, effectiveness of representational capacity, and the rigidity of bipolar, adversarial methods. Second, the conflicts in the contemporary administrative state are not so amenable as in the past to judicial or quasi-judicial determination, since they call less for application of established norms and precedents (Rule of Law decision-making) and more for balancing of competing

48. One can distinguish two strains of interest group representation theory. The modest version is that politics is really important, even most important. The extreme version is that everything *is* politics, meaning other approaches to choice, including adjudicatory fairness, science, and market, are not merely infected by politics but are conceptually and practically indistinguishable from politics, even as ideal types. A response to the extreme formulation would take me too far afield. I think it is incorrect. In any event, the distinctions in decision making methods is so ingrained in our consciousness that practical reform of the way we think about problems of law and government must take them as the initial position.

49. This seems dubious. The early delegation doctrine cases involved subjects and contexts that left much room for administrative discretion, but the reviewing courts sought to portray that discretion as perhaps inconsequential in and of itself, and as being well and tightly bounded by statutory guidance and judicial review. None of this was generally true. The counterfactual judicial rhetoric may have reflected either (1) judicial creation and fidelity to a fiction of legal constraint on delimited discretion—a useful fiction, given the otherwise irreconcilable conflict between separation of powers orthodoxy and the practical demands of modern governments—or (2) a failure by judges to recognize what was really at stake in the exercising of the administrative powers at issue. Whether this misfit between the courts' language and the reality (as I see it) is attributable to a problem of admission or of recognition, it is explainable by the relative novelty of the administrative powers under review and their then rather limited presence on the governance landscape.

interests and values (politics). In this sense, the ascendancy of a loose "reasonableness" standard over more rigid rules (separation of powers orthodoxy) is part of the evolution of realism, displacing formalism. My speculation in chapter 7 concerning sound governance review is a similar evolutionary step.

Thus, the trichotomy offers a ready explanation for the appeal of interest group representation theory: (1) interest group theory notes the descriptive inaccuracy of the claims that either expertise or adjudicatory fairness provides effective control of arbitrary discretion; (2) it then emphasizes the positive attributes of politics, along with the negative attributes of expertise and adjudicatory fairness; and (3) exploiting the instability of the categories, it arrogates to politics matters that might otherwise be characterized as issues of science or fairness. Interest group representation analysis pushes a lot of important buttons.

Stewart's interpretation of hard-look review as an expression of interest group representation analysis is possible because of the difficulty of distinguishing politics, science, and fairness. More particularly, a dispute about the importance of a risk posed to Hudson River fish by construction of a power facility might be thought of as the subject for a political contest between environmental, consumer, and industry interests, as a scientific issue for careful study by biologists and cost-benefit analysts, or as an issue for adjudicatory law-finding methods, inasmuch as the legislature or administrative precedents suggest what weight should be accorded the various interests.[50]

5.2.3 Critique of the Thesis, through Failings of the Trichotomy

Even as the interest group representation model criticizes important components of the traditional model, it incorporates failings of the trichotomy and the traditional approach to administrative law. This is so in two fundamental respects.

First, interest group representation is at its core an assertion that the politics paradigm has a distinctiveness and importance that justifies an ambition to view administrative law and governance through that prism. But the premise that there is something to be gained by disaggregating the organic character of bureaucratic activity is a trap, although an analytically elegant and necessary demonstration respon-

---

50. *See* Scenic Hudson Preservation Conf. v. FPC, 453 F.2d 463 (2d Cir. 1971), *cert. denied*, 407 U.S. 926 (1972).

sive to those who deny the significance of politics. It is a trap because it risks distorting our understanding and reform of bureaucratic life. These risks result from the descriptive and conceptual failings of the trichotomy itself. The prism of politics cannot be a satisfactory lens.

Specifically, the deployment of politics as a method of decision can be subjected to a critique precisely paralleling the critique made by interest group representation theory itself of the expertise and adjudication paradigms. Following the dissection detailed in chapters 3 and 4, the critique of the interest group representation model includes (1) an attack on the descriptive or factual accuracy of a political construct and (2) an attack on the appropriateness of the subject to political resolution, as opposed to (3) resolution through expert or fairness methods.

Thus, (1) exploiting the trichotomy's *descriptive failings:* one will always be able to question the comprehensiveness or representativeness of those interests seated at the policy making table and, as a consequence, doubt the soundness of the agency's process and conclusion. It will be very difficult for a court to evaluate such arguments, absent an aggressive effort to discern the deeply varied circumstances of the agency action, which is unlikely, and absent a helpful basis upon which to judge representativeness and the like. And for the same reasons, the court's task is no easier when evaluating arguments that exploit the trichotomy's *normative failing;* one can always argue that in the given situation the risks associated with the negative attributes of politics (majority tyranny, subjective and arbitrary willfulness) are too threatening or that the positive attributes associated with the alternatives to politics (the neutrality and rationality of science and adjudication) are too attractive. So, the proper exposure standard to a workplace carcinogen might be thought to be a matter for resolution by health science professionals, economists, and other experts rather than by a warring conclave of worker and industry lobbyists: this might be one's view either as a matter of statutory interpretation of the organic law or as a matter of judgment about sound governance.[51] By contrast, exploiting the trichotomy's *boundary-drawing failing*, one will always be able to make a credible argument (whether or not successfully persuasive) that a problem or process suggestive of interest representation is instead science or adjudicatory fairness. So, a complex environmental

51. For discussion of the negotiated resolution of regulatory issues, *see* Harter, *Dispute Resolution and Administrative Law: The History, Needs and Future of a Complex Relationship*, 29 Vill. L. Rev. 1393 (1984); Harter, *Negotiating Regulation: A Cure for Malaise*, 71 Geo. L.J. 1 (1982); Note, *Rethinking Regulation: Negotiation as an Alternative to Traditional Rulemaking*, 94 Harv. L. Rev. 1871 (1981); and Stewart, *Reformation* at 1790–1802 (1975).

controversy concerning construction of a new power facility, such as that involved in the *Scenic Hudson* litigation discussed by Stewart, may be approached as the appropriate occasion for mediated decision making among environmental, industry, and consumer interests.[52] But there will always be an element of the problem, such as the impact on wildlife or the true power needs over the next thirty years, as to which one can argue (with risk) that expertise "rather than" politics is required, and similarly for adjudicatory fairness. To be sure, another consequence of the boundary problem is that measures that appear to be based on politics can be recast in other terms and vice-versa. Thus, Stewart is able to take the rather substance-focused doctrinal invention of "adequate consideration" of significant alternatives and contrary evidence and characterize it as a manifestation of judicial interest in representation of diverse interests. Conversely, one might take the imperative of neutrality in quasi-adjudication and translate it into interest group representation terms: the competing interest groups must have equal access to or claims on the sympathies of the decision maker, else their representation in the process has been a sham. The failings of the trichotomy create this possibility of recharacterizing many things as being related to interest group representation and help to make it an attractive candidate for an all-encompassing theory of doctrinal change in administrative law.

The second fundamental respect in which the interest group representation approach to a theory of administrative law recapitulates the problems of its predecessors is that the overall project remains the task of constraining administrative discretion and lending legitimacy to administrative government. Hence, the difficulty of using the prism of politics in any determinate way to tell judges how to act or administrators what procedures to employ becomes, due to the failings or ambiguities just cataloged above, more than a conceptual inconvenience. It means that the approach fails to address the problem at hand. (This could be remedied by abandoning the antidiscretion project, as I urge in chapter 7.)

These difficulties with the interest group representation model explain why it cannot be successful as an all-encompassing theory of administrative law. Indeed, the reasons Professor Stewart gives at the end of his article for questioning the prospects for interest group representation, both doctrinal and theoretical, are the predictable consequences of the failings of the trichotomy.[53]

52. *See* Stewart, *Reformation* at 1748–56.
53. *See id.* at 1802–5. For example, Stewart notes the difficulty of identifying the relevant interests and their appropriate representatives. This falls within my notion of

5.3 The Perspective of Expert, Ideal Administration

Another perspective on reform of bureaucracy and doctrine focuses on how law can promote agency expertise and how attention to expertise (including science and managerial efficiency) can advance the desired social goals. My example is Professor Mashaw's seminal work on problems of mass justice in the Social Security Administration.

5.3.1 Exposition: Justice from Bureaucracy

Jerry Mashaw has made important contributions to the study of bureaucracy and administrative law, with a focus on issues of due process and mass justice. In *Bureaucratic Justice,*[54] Mashaw uses a comprehensive case study of the social security disability insurance program as a vehicle for developing a sophisticated argument that in mass justice settings, and to an extent throughout administration, there should be heightened emphasis on a model of justice he terms "bureaucratic rationality," in contrast to paradigms of justice related to professional treatment or moral judgment. He extracts these paradigms from strands in the critical literature on disability and from interviews in which agency officials discussed their own views of the program and their jobs. Mashaw's most provocative conclusions are that judicial review of eligibility determinations is not only troublesome to program administration and ineffectual as a guarantor of sound decision making but also an inferior instrument of mass justice in comparison to organizational routines and management methods carefully designed to maximize the accuracy of disability determinations given

---

the descriptive difficulty of using categories like politics. Stewart observes that we will have a residual concern that nonpolitical modes of decision be protected in certain settings, such as those involving fundamental interests. This ambivalence reflects what I have termed the attributive duality of the trichotomy.

54. J. Mashaw, Bureaucratic Justice (1983) (hereinafter Mashaw, Bureaucratic Justice). *See also* Mashaw, *The Management Side of Due Process,* 59 Cornell L. Rev. 772 (1974); J. Mashaw, Social Security Hearings and Appeals (1978); Mashaw, *How Much of What Quality,* Cornell L. Rev. 823 (1980). I focus on *Bureaucratic Justice* because of its singular importance in the field. As Professors Lance Liebman and Richard Stewart write in their review of it: "His book sets the standard for a genre of scholarship—the intellectually ambitious case study—that is especially valuable in afield as variegated as administrative law. . . . At a time when large organizations have been widely discredited, *Bureaucratic Justice* is an important neo-Weberian endorsement of bureaucracy as the best hope for justice and rationality. . . . [H]is case study has given the argument for bureaucratic justice its most cogent and sophisticated presentation since James Landis' *Administrative Process.*" Liebman & Stewart, *Book Review,* 96 Harv. L. Rev. 1952, 1954, 1968 (1983) (citing J. Landis, Administrative Process (1938)).

resource constraints.[55] This extends his earlier work suggesting that self-consciously designed quality control procedures within an agency can provide an attractive and constitutional alternative to the adversarial hearings sometimes required by due process.[56]

I have three points: First, there is an obvious correspondence between Mashaw's paradigm of bureaucratic rationality and the trichotomy's paradigm of expertise and science. Second, Mashaw's critique of judicial review and proceduralism nicely fits the mechanisms of argument generated by the critique of the trichotomy offered in chapters 3 and 4.[57] Third, the perspective of ideal administration cannot provide a totalizing theory of administrative justice or law within bureaucracy, for reasons conceptually related to the limitations of the Rule of Law and interest group representation perspectives. Such monochromatic exercises develop our sensibilities in important ways, just as studying the music for solo violin is helpful preparation for full appreciation of a symphony. But in the very effort to focus on one element, the whole is distorted.

Mashaw defines bureaucratically rationality as follows:

> Given the democratically (legislatively) approved task—to pay disability benefits to eligible persons—the administrative goal in the ideal conception of bureaucratic rationality is to develop, at the least possible cost, a system for distinguishing between true and false claims. Adjudicating should be both accurate (the legislatively specified goal) and cost-effective. . . . A system focused on correctness defines the questions presented to it by implementing decisions in essentially factual and technocratic terms. Individual adjudicators must be concerned about the

55. Mashaw, Bureaucratic Justice at 4, 13–16, 185–93. Mashaw is blunt: "The courts, as they themselves often maintain, are truly incompetent to deal with the complexities and subleties of engineering and managing a large administrative decision process." *Id.* at 193.

56. Mashaw, *The Management Side of Due Process,* 59 Cornell L. Rev. 772 (1974). I have always wondered whether it might not be appropriate for courts to impose on police departments various quality control and disciplinary measures calculated to maximize observance of constitutional criminal procedure, especially warrant requirements. Following Mashaw's logic, this would be a more effective prophylactic against abuses than is the exclusionary rule; after all, the principle argument in support of the exclusionary rule speaks to systemic justice rather than individual fairness to the defendant. However, the Supreme Court's decisions in Rizzo v. Goode, 423 U.S. 362 (1973), and Los Angeles v. Lyons, 461 U.S. 95 (1983), have unfortunately foreclosed such developments by creating virtually insurmountable obstacles to remedial standing and to institutional reform remedies in such cases.

57. *See also* Liebman & Stewart, *supra* n. 54.

facts in the real world that relate to the truth or falsity of the claimed disability. At a managerial level the question becomes technocratic: What is the least-cost methodology for collecting and combing those facts . . . . To illustrate by contrast, this model would exclude questions of value or preference as obviously irrelevant to the administrative task, and it would view reliance on nonreplicable *judgment* or *intuition* as a singularly unattractive methodology for decision. The legislature should have previously decided the value questions . . . . From the perspective of bureaucratic rationality, administrative justice is accurate decisionmaking carried on through processes appropriately rationalized to take account of costs.[58]

Mashaw's paradigm is obviously quite close to what I have termed the paradigm of expertise, science, and managerial efficiency. His discussion is concerned generally with the implications of his paradigm distinctions for organizational behavior, whereas I have been concerned with differences in reasoning or analytic form. Mashaw's work is richly textured, so he acknowledges that pure bureaucratic rationality is not coming any time soon, at least not to the disability programs. A raft of problems interfere, from realistic limits on staff competence, to ambiguous statutory commands, to management shortcomings. And even in the role definitions offered by Social Security Administration personnel, Mashaw found that his competing models of professional treatment and moral judgment played "supporting roles." Nevertheless, Mashaw unhesitatingly selects bureaucratic rationality as the preferred model—the aspirational ideal for the system as a whole.

The mechanism of trichotomy-based reasoning is reflected in Mashaw's effort to contrast bureaucratic rationality with the moral judgment model and the professional treatment model, both of which are more attuned to individualized, highly contextual eligibility determinations. Their goals are "conflict resolution" and "client satisfaction" rather than "program implementation."[59] Mashaw's description of moral judgment explicitly analogizes to adjudication. As for professional treatment, Mashaw views the doctor-patient analogy as central, but he tries to distinguish this from science by emphasizing the intuitive judgment and interpersonal character of this "helping" framework for disability determinations. These are obviously ken to the value-laden subjectivity of the politics, interest accommodation paradigm. Much of *Bureaucratic Justice* is devoted to an effort to distinguish the paradigms

58. Mashaw, Bureaucratic Justice at 25.
59. *Id.* at 31.

and argue that bureaucratic rationality is superior—certainly in the disability context, and probably elsewhere, too. Although the book is not doctrinal analysis, the intellectual structure is familiar.

5.3.2 Critique of the Thesis, through Failings of the Trichotomy

It follows from my analysis in chapters 3 and 4 that we could cautiously appraise Mashaw's invocation of the expertise paradigm and his efforts to distinguish and elevate it. Recall that the failings of the trichotomy make arguments on behalf of expertise available in three forms: (1) descriptive assessments of the decision making methods, (2) manipulation of attributive duality, and (3) boundary and definition problems with respect to adjudicatory fairness and politics. And these same three areas should provide arguments with which to challenge Mashaw's thesis.

Mashaw does indeed follow this trail in his critique of the adjudicatory fairness paradigm as it has been stressed by judicial oversight of disability determinations and by many members of the ALJ corps.[60] As a descriptive matter, he questions the fidelity of adjudicators to the standards laid out in statute and rules, their fidelity to facts, and their neutrality in the face of claimants who are in some sense morally deserving.[61] He emphasizes the negative attributes of adjudicatory fairness, especially costly proceduralism.[62] At the same time, he emphasizes the positive attributes of expertise and has special hope (and considerable evidence) that techniques of bureaucratic quality control can yield cost-effective error rate reductions.[63] And throughout, he makes the claim (sometimes explicit and sometimes implicit) that bureaucratic rationality involves a form of decision making distinguish-

60. *See id.* at 41–44 (discussing the conflicts between senior SSA managers and independent-minded leaders of the ALJ organization); *see also* Nash v. Califano, 613 F.2d 10 (2d Cir. 1980).

61. Mashaw, Bureaucratic Justice at 41–44, 38–39, 190–92.

62. Mashaw has noted that there is more to procedural design than cost-benefit analysis and rational resource allocation, *id.* at 132–44, and he specifically cites Thurman Arnold on the symbolic function of procedure. *Id.* at 11. He doubts, however, whether satisfactory core content and limiting principles can be found to make noninstrumental, noneconomic, dignitary values a workable basis for discovering procedural justice. Mashaw, *Administrative Due Process: The Quest for a Dignitary Theory,* 61 Boston Univ. L. Rev. 885 (1981).

63. *See, e.g.,* Mashaw, Bureaucratic Justice at 25–26, 171–75, 214. Mashaw stresses that by adopting bureaucratic rationality as its dominant decisionmaking technique, the program has achieved "neutrality, expertise, and efficiency . . . [and at the examiner level] diligence, developmental comprehensiveness, expedition, and higher quality outputs." *Id.* at 214.

able from the other paradigms, and *these* problems are appropriate for the expert bureaucracy.[64]

The analysis of the trichotomy also provides an interesting way to assemble a response to Mashaw. For example, in their review of *Bureaucratic Justice,* Liebman and Stewart note that the disability program is currently marked by "administrative and legal turmoil" and is faced with trying external problems, such as a large case load and an organic statute whose standards make "elucidation and enforcement . . . an extremely difficult task."[65] Mashaw acknowledges this but assumes that management can bring about improvements. Here is a question of descriptive accuracy. Further empirical work might be indicated, but I think it is unlikely that definitive empirical work could be done on such questions as "How good is the SSA bureaucracy, given the constraints, and could it realistically be better?" Mashaw's work makes it abundantly clear that achieving good bureaucratic performance, indeed even conceiving of such a notion, is far more than a question of pure managerial science. There are manifold complications of external and internal politics, extrastatutory legal norms, and the usual list of implementation difficulties.

On another descriptive matter, Liebman and Stewart question whether Mashaw's proposals for lay advocacy and medical-vocational panels would in fact be a cost-effective substitute for adjudication.[66] Again, more study seems too easy an answer. Without gain saying the general value of empirical work, I suspect that more study will raise more questions, because the framework itself will prevent the deeper questions from going away.

Moving from issues of how descriptive inaccuracy clouds the critique and selection of paradigms, one may also take issue with Mashaw's emphases on positive and negative norms. Thus, Liebman and Stewart gently note that Mashaw "does not address" the question of whether managerial efficiency may work at cross purposes with client assistance.[67] Their argument emphasizes the negative attributes of alienation and impersonality associated with expertise, in contrast to the

64. *See id.* at 25–40, 214–27. In a section entitled "Comparison," Mashaw asserts that "each justice model is composed of distinctive goals, specific approaches to framing the questions for administrative determination, basic techniques for resolving those questions, and subsidiary decision processes and routines that functionally describe the model." *Id.* at 25. The chart that follows states that each model employs a different "cognitive technique" of decision making; Mashaw does concede, however, that the models may "shade one into another at the margins." *Id.*

65. Liebman & Stewart, *supra* n. 54 at 1953, 1956.

66. *Id.* at 1962.

67. *Id.* at 1963 n. 38.

individualized and participatory character of adjudicatory fairness and the subjective flexibility available in the balancing/accommodation paradigm of politics.

Finally, the basic claim that bureaucratic rationality is easily distinguishable from the other paradigms cannot be true if much that was said in chapters 3 and 4 is true. Mashaw emphasizes that bureaucratic rationality is concerned with facts, but determinations of disability and employability plainly tap levels upon levels of judgment and law interacting with the raw evidence about education, prior work history, and medical condition. It cannot be that such complex decisions can be made by means of a single paradigm. But Mashaw stresses the superiority and distinctiveness of bureaucratic rationality, and hence he urges that the disability program be protected from the intrusions of proceduralism, as well as from the profligacy and corruption of subjectivity and politics. (My language, and the superposition of my framework on his ideas.)

Bureaucratic rationality, as a species of expertise and an element of the trichotomy, *cannot* be distinct. On examination, Mashaw's own analysis reflects this and leads one to question the value of isolating the perspective of expert administration, at least for purposes other than analysis—especially prescription. Indeed, because the paradigms are so inescapably indistinct, as Mashaw fleshes out his prescription the other elements of the trichotomy reappear. Policy discretion will still exist, but in the form of more internal, hierarchical judgments about eligibility grids and various program requirements and in thinly reviewed case-by-case determinations.[68] Rather than being avoided, the balancing and subjectivity are in significant measure merely displaced to a prior moment of centralized judgment and a hierarchically superior level of bureaucratic authority.

This will, however, be an impoverished version of political and policy choice, because the interests and values figuring in the choice will be those of the technocracy. To what extent will this impoverishment be redeemed by the participation requirements of rule making, reinforced with substantive and quasi-procedural, hard-look judicial review? It is not clear why we would entertain firm judicial oversight of the bureaucracy at the level of policy generality if we are unwilling to entertain it at the level of individual justice. (The analysis of the trichotomy suggests, after all, that the court is in a stronger position in policing adjudicatory fairness than in policing rules expressing policy dis-

68. My own view is that the existence of judicial review inhibits reliance on unexpressed discretion as a sufficient basis for denial of a claim. Internal quality control might or might not function as well. And the element of discretion is unavoidable.

cretion.) And, in any event, judicial review of general rules will not suffice because there are levels of discretion subordinate to that expressed in rule making.

Similarly, bureaucratic rationality cannot be entirely divorced from adjudicatory fairness and proceduralism. As Davis might put it, the disability determination depends on adjudicative facts.[69] Mashaw does not successfully fend off all forms of proceduralism and individualization. Even as he proposes to curtail judicial review in disability cases, he is urging that there be internal rules and constraints on caseworker discretion, just as the adjudicatory fairness paradigm stresses fidelity to established rules. He also considers proposals for lay advocates and medical-vocational panels[70] to moderate the impersonality of bureaucratic action and the risk that cases would not be decided with sufficient attention to the individual circumstances—another prime characteristic of adjudicatory fairness. Of course, we are left to question, as did Stewart and Liebman, whether as a descriptive matter the elaborations offered by Mashaw would adequately express the concerns of adjudicatory fairness. The evident desirability of such "supplements"[71] in a "reformed" world without judicial review underscores that bureaucratic rationality alone is unsatisfying. But would these supplements do the job? In either practical or symbolic terms? Again, one is left uneasy by the impoverishment of the adjudicatory fairness element.

My point is not to appraise Mashaw's specific recommendations but rather to underscore the strong pull of the trichotomy as an implicit framework for analysis and its contribution to argument, and perhaps confusion.

Can the perspective of ideal administration be successful as a comprehensive theory of administrative justice or prescription for law within bureaucracies?

By attempting to distinguish bureaucratic rationality from the other elements of the trichotomy, one distorts and impoverishes the resulting portrait and prescription. But if, instead, one acknowledges that bureaucratic rationality must be accompanied by reasonable supplements from the other paradigms, thereby underscoring the essential interrelatedness of the paradigms, then the task of discovering the appropriate mix is prejudiced by the effort to elevate bureaucratic

69. *See* sec. 2.4 (discussing adjudicative versus legislative facts and the adjudication–rule making distinction).

70. Mashaw, Bureaucratic Justice at 198, 208.

71. See *infra* n. 77 (discussing Frug's use of "supplement," after Derrida).

rationality above the others. As appealing as the positive norms of expertise are, we find the subordination of the competing paradigms, with *their* positive norms, unappealing. No empirical work seems likely to dissolve this discomfort, because it reflects a deeper conceptual tension. Using the perspective of expertise (or bureaucratic rationality) as the touchstone will be unsuccessful as an all-encompassing strategy, for reasons conceptually related to the limitations of the politics and Rule of Law perspectives. In particular, the tremendous value of Mashaw's work is the complement it provides to the other, comparably partial perspectives.

5.4 The Allure of Pragmatism and Reasonableness

If the Court would make comparative qualifications the key factor in determining whether or not to substitute judgment in any particular case, and if it would develop a body of reliable precedents about how it applies the comparative qualifications idea to various problems, predictability would rise sharply and litigation of question about scope of review would drop sharply. The present system of virtually uncontrolled judicial discretion about scope of review can be turned into a system in which predictable law will largely govern.[72]

Another approach, with Kenneth Culp Davis its leading proponent, has criticized Jaffe's conceptualism and emphasized the practical assessment of what the courts actually seem to do and how their performance of the difficult task of judicial review might be marginally improved. It thus comes as no surprise that his framework does little to avoid the problems of implicit reliance on the trichotomy.

5.4.1 Exposition: Factors in Scaling "Reasonableness"

To begin with, Davis notes that the current state of the law is neither independent scope of review on questions of law nor reasonableness review: "[T]he law is that courts have discretionary power either to use a reasonableness test *or* to substitute judgment."[73] There is ample case law support for his somewhat discouraging proposition, since the Supreme Court sometimes uses the language of independence, sometimes the language of deference.[74] As a descriptive matter, Davis lists

---

72. Davis, 5 Treatise at 392–93.
73. *Id.* at 402 (emphasis added).
74. *Compare* the highly deferential scope of review in such question-of-law cases as United States v. Clark, 454 U.S. 555, 565 (1982); Board of Governors of the Fed. Reserve

the various factors courts tend to use in making their discretionary choice between these two standards: agency consistency over a long period of time; whether the subject is within the agency's area of special competence or within the special competence of the court; special concern for the agency's need to have unified control over interpretations of its organic statute; the nature of any agency participation in the legislative process; and, of course, the fact-law dichotomy.[75] Davis observes that these are all aspects of a general inquiry into the comparative competence of court and agency, and, moving from description to prescription, he proposes this as the key inquiry which, if the courts would only systematically undertake it, provides the best hope of disciplining what he now characterizes as essentially unguided judicial discretion.

5.4.2 Critique

Davis's reliance on the trichotomy is evident, and we can move quickly from the analysis in chapters 3 and 4 to predict how and why Davis's proposed emphasis on comparative competence would fail to accomplish what he promises. In his approach, it is fair to understand consistency over time as being material because of its presumed correlation with expertise.[76] Basing deference on the technical character

---

Sys. v. Investment Co. Inst., 450 U.S. 46, 56 (1981) ("the greatest deference"), and Ford Motor Credit Co. v. Milhollin, 444 U.S. 555, 565 (1980) (not "demonstrably irrational" standard); FEC v. Democratic Senatorial Campaign Comm., 454 U.S. 27, 39 (1981) ("sufficiently reasonable" test); *with* the highly independent review in such cases as NLRB v. Yeshiva Univ., 444 U.S. 672 (1980); Dirks v. SEC, 463 U.S. 646 (1983).

75. Davis, 5 Treatise at 391–94, 399–404. *See also* Hi-Craft Clothing Co. v. NLRB, 660 F.2d 910 (3d Cir. 1981) (listing factors to be considered in choosing the scope of review).

76. In some circumstances, consistency is an attribute of Rule of Law fairness. *See* sec. 2.2 (discussing norms associated with Rule of Law, adjudicatory fairness). In the rule making context, the emphasis is more likely to be on the relationship between consistency and rationality—that is, expertise. Consistency in rate making cases, such as *Arizona Grocery*, are a middle ground, as one would expect, due to the hybrid character of formal rule making in the economic context. As one might predict, no consideration points in the same direction all the time. Thus, the absence of agency consistency can be forgiven and deference still accorded, based on a theory of evolving expertise, which may lead to a changed agency position, which the court should accept. *See, e.g.,* Morrison-Knudson Construction Co. v. Director, 461 U.S. 624 (1983); Atchison, T. & S. F. Ry. v. Wichita Bd. of Trade, 412 U.S. 800 (1973) (need of agency to have flexibility to revise its views over time); Arizona Grocery Co. v. Atchison, T. & S. F. Ry., 284 U.S. 370 (1932) (same). At the extreme, the absence of agency consistency was cited by Justice Stevens in *Chevron* as support for the proposition that there was not a single appropriate interpretation of the statute, and therefore that the Court should defer to this, the latest agency interpretation.

of a matter or, in the opposite direction, on the subject's being outside the agency mission, are likewise examples of decisions about deference based on a distinction between the realm of expertise and the realm of Rule of Law judging.

Still another of Davis's factors, the attention to the agency's role in the legislative process, can be understood as tying the deference calculation either to some special agency expertise concerning the content of the legislature's political "deal," or to the political competence of the agency itself. There might be judicial deference to agency expertise if, for example, the agency ran the computer simulations that formed the basis for a legislative compromise on the formula for distributing grants, so that it would have special expertise on the definition of the vague variables in the statutory formula, or if the agency participated in the political choices—sitting at the table with the key legislators to "cut the deal" which the vague language was meant to capture. In these situations, the empirical and conceptual problems of expertise create uncertainty in judicial analysis. Empirically, the alleged expertise may not exist: perhaps the officials who participated in the legislative negotiations are long gone or have nothing to do with the officials who now propose the troubling statutory interpretation; or perhaps the definitions of the computer variables used as the basis for the legislative compromise were never disclosed to, or understood by, the legislators— who thought they were agreeing to something quite different (say, *family* defined as nuclear rather than extended). Even if the categorization as *expert* seems descriptively reasonable on its face, conceptual problems remain. That it is a technical matter suggests deference, but it also suggests that perhaps the agency's process should have been opened up for more criticism from and accommodation with outside experts. This is what I have termed attributive duality.[77] The expertise born of having been an actor in the legislative process may instead be perceived by the court as political decision making—that is, the expertise-politics transmutation—in which case the attributive duality of politics must be contended with. Davis's various ways of invoking expertise are not helpful as guides to judicial discretion, for all of the reasons I have described in chapters 3 and 4.

Alternatively, the court could focus on the political process of agency decision making itself, if the court perceives, as is sometimes the case, that the complex process of interest accommodation during agency rule making is just the continuation with a new venue of the political

77. *See* secs. 2.4, 4.4; Frug, *The Ideology of Bureaucracy in American Law,* 97 Harv. L. Rev. 1276, 1331–34 (1984) (objective-subjective distinction in judicial treatment of agency expertise).

process that occurred in the legislature: the parties are just sitting around another table. As my earlier discussion suggested, this political character of agency action may trigger deference, or it may not. The empirical and conceptual difficulties rooted in the trichotomy make either result quite possible. For example, in *Sierra Club v. Costle*,[78] the agency was implementing the new source performance standards for coal-fired electric utility plants. Judge Wald's analysis was clearly influenced by her perception of the agency's decision as part of a political process. In this view, White House involvement was to be expected, as was the involvement of Sen. Robert Byrd, given the interests of coal producers and mine workers in West Virginia. (The rule making involved not only environmental versus industry interests, but Western low-sulfur producers versus Eastern high-sulfur producers.) Judge Wald's political pragmatism contrasts with the majority approach in *Benzene*, where Justice Marshall in dissent criticized the majority sharply for overriding the agency's political choice. Indeed, the regulatory result in *Benzene* seemed too one-sided—as though the agency had not in fact engaged in the desirable kind of interest group accommodation. The agency's action was perceived as politically biased or unbalanced; rather than, like *Cotton Dust* and *Sierra Club*, accommodating and splitting the difference. Put in terms of my preceding analysis, one way of describing the cases stresses the availability to the court of a choice: insisting on the science paradigm versus accepting use of the politics paradigm. This choice is available because of the instability of the paradigm distinctions—that is, the boundary problem. A second characterization is that the court can choose to emphasize the positive attributes of political choice, such as participation and accountability, or the negative attributes, such as willfulness and majority tyranny (through imposition of unnecessary, uneconomic regulations in *Benzene*). Still a third approach exploits the descriptive difficulties. Perhaps the political roles of White House and Congress were benign in *Sierra Club*, perhaps they were not. Perhaps the science was indeed well executed in *Benzene*, perhaps not.

It is interesting to contrast the Jaffe and Davis approaches because each author is a giant presence in the field. Davis's criticism of Jaffe boils down to three points.[79] The first two are that Jaffe's conceptual framework is an inaccurate description of what the law is, meaning that it cannot be derived from the cases. Specifically, the courts do not agree with Jaffe's broad, Holmesian definition of *law* and instead treat as

78. 657 F.2d 298 (D.C. Cir. 1981).
79. *See* Davis, *Judicial Control of Administrative Action*, 66 Colum. L. Rev. 635, 636, 669–72 (1966).

findings of fact (conclusive if adequately supported in the record) many matters that Jaffe would term conclusions of law. Davis is certainly correct here, but I cannot see that it matters very much. I simply take Jaffe's analysis to be in a prescriptive vein. There is an important conceptual difference between fact and law, but drawing the line where the cases sometimes seem to is an intellectual error which leads to confused reasoning and excessive unpredictability; adopting a more expansive understanding of law, in combination with respect for agency lawmaking through the clear purpose rule, would convert the fact-law distinction into a useful analytical tool rather than a mere label deployed to explain "results otherwise determined," as he puts it.[80] Of course, as I have said, in the end Jaffe's framework is no solution either, because of its implicit reliance on the trichotomy of norms, methods of decisions, and institutions.

Second, Davis argues, rather than a unified "analytic" approach to the scope of review for questions of law, the cases comprise distinct lines of authority—that is Davis's point about the courts' highly discretionary choice between independent and reasonableness review. On this, I side with Jaffe. True, the decisions do not by and large use Jaffe's terms of reference, such as the convincingly clear purpose formula. (This may, as I discuss below, be changing. Justice Steven's emphasis in *Chevron* on statutory fidelity points in Jaffe's direction and unfortunately may take root.) But the case law *results* are reasonably consistent with Jaffe's terms of analysis, certainly no less than they are consistent with Davis's double gloss of multiple factors and reasonableness. Again, I see nothing wrong with interpreting Jaffe to be speaking prescriptively about a preferable way to analyze cases that is consistent with the spine of precedent and promises for the future more conceptual clarity and, hence, consistency of verbiage. Where I part company with Jaffe, however, is in my view that his framework would not in fact impose any greatly improved order on judicial decision making. Comparing the Jaffe and Davis approaches, Jaffe's framework fits the cases as well as it does because, though conceptually more elegant, it remains as subject to easy, inconsistent application.

Third, Davis implicitly argues that Jaffe's framework will not do as well at disciplining judicial discretion as that proposed by Davis. But I have already said enough on this point. In short, Jaffe's approach, for all its elegance, ultimately appeals to the trichotomy and thus fails. The shortcomings of Davis's approach are all the more evident—both at the

80. Jaffe, Treatise at 572.

first step of judicial selection of independent versus reasonableness review (based on a laundry list infected with the trichotomy) and at the second step of implementing the reasonableness test—which, apart from the intrinsic stretchability Davis himself acknowledges, will be just as influenced by the trichotomy as is the content of Jaffe's "convincingly clear purpose" standard. It is worth remembering that the reasonableness test to which Davis refers can be stretched virtually to abdication, and the considerations that would lead a court to stretch or contract are the familiar, unsatisfactory ones.

In short, the trichotomy makes the approaches of both Jaffe and Davis uncertain enough in application to be rendered consistent with most cases. Each can be made to replicate the confusion in the case law, and hence neither helps solve the problem of unreliable judicial discretion.

5.4.3 Conclusions on Conventional Doctrinal Solutions

There are other attempts to formulate the scope of review problem so as not to focus on this troubling fact-law-policy distinction, but none seem successful. For example, the authors of one leading casebook wrote:

> [T]wo basic threshold questions should be resolved in every case in which the scope of judicial review is at issue. The first question is, What precisely is the alleged error the complaining party contends the agency has committed? The second question is, What is the scope of power or discretion which the legislature has delegated to the agency? Only after these questions have been answered can the court intelligently determine what its scope of review shall be—or, in other words, what its responsibility is and what the agency's responsibility is. Courts have not customarily analyzed the problem in these terms.[81]

This is a useful start, but it leaves hugely difficult problems. Congress will not spell out the scope of judicial review for each relevant kind of agency action and choice, because creating those categories, mapping them onto the choices for scope of review, and applying those categories to the circumstances of the litigated dispute all involve the familiar problem of choice of roles. Without more, such choices clearly

81. Gellhorn, Byse, & Strauss, *supra* n. 4 at 250–52. The corresponding passage in a later edition is less formalistic but no less rooted in the trichotomy. *See* W. Gellhorn, C. Byse, P. Strauss, T. Rakoff, & R. Schotland, Administrative Law 352 (1987).

will be made with reference to the problematic distinctions and norms of the trichotomy.

Professor Ronald M. Levin made a particularly ambitious effort in a study of scope of review that he undertook on behalf of the Administrative Conference of the United States.[82] The form of "restatement" or recodification of the law of scope of review clearly will rely on the same separation of powers ethos in order to scale judicial deference toward agency decisions. Absent some new invention, unmoored from the trichotomy, the conceptual categories used will be law, fact, and policy. No mere reformulation can suffice if its method implicitly reflects separation of powers formalism.

82. Levin, *Federal Scope-of-Review Standards: A Preliminary Statement,* 37 Ad. L. Rev. 95 (1985).

CHAPTER 6

A Constructive Essay: "Harder-Look" Review

After devoting so much attention to the deep difficulties and present futility of administrative law, I feel obliged to offer something constructive and hopeful. In the next, final chapter I sketch an approach to administrative law—admittedly quite speculative—that tries to avoid reliance on the trichotomy and separation of powers approaches to constraining discretion.

Assume for the purposes of this chapter, however, that we are unwilling to embrace, or unable to conceive of, a fundamental alternative to the traditional understanding of the administrative law project and method. The lessons of the failed trichotomy nevertheless provide clues as to which sorts of incremental developments tend to make things worse and which tend to make things (marginally) better. Because such modest improvements do not remake the foundation of doctrine, they cannot remedy the pervasive difficulties of obscure judicial discretion.

The examples in this chapter, however, suggest that even a modest agenda can be worthwhile without being delusive. I will consider three areas in significant doctrinal flux. Each area presents a major obstacle to successful evolution of administrative law—that is, each poses puzzles that, if not solved, make it quite likely that law will increasingly be irrelevant to modern problems of governance. The three puzzles are:

1. What is the appropriate and coherent judicial posture toward politics as an ingredient of agency decision making?

2. How should courts grapple with the problem of disciplining

agency decision making under conditions of scientific uncertainty?

3. What is the judiciary's responsibility for the quality of the *procedural* choices made by an agency?

In each area, present doctrine often ignores or distorts the complexities of description, categorization, and attributive duality detailed in chapters 3 and 4. Instead, courts should intensify their methods of "hard-look" review to take explicit account of the necessary interplay of decision making paradigms. This entails an expanded set of mostly quasi-procedural initiatives, such as disclosure of political choices. Courts must take a "hard*er* look" at the agency's use of all three paradigms.

It bears repeating that because my purpose and method in this chapter are wholly within the framework of the trichotomy, the attentive reader will feel contradictions with my earlier critique of that framework. I expect, however, that some have found my critique interesting but not conclusively persuasive, whereas others will be persuaded as to the critique but not as to my speculative alternative (chapter 7). What can I usefully say to them?

6.1 The Accommodation of Politics and the Rule of Law: The Puzzle Described

As one should expect in light of the conceptual difficulties of characterizing administrative action within the trichotomy, politics is lurking in almost every agency decision and in every corner of administrative law. Yet, judicial opinions rarely include frank appraisals of the political forces at work in agency decision making. On judicial review, a court might conceivably ignore, reject, or accept the role of politics in an agency action:

First, the court could *ignore* the possibility of politics altogether and just assume that the other paradigmatic decision making methods were the exclusive means employed by the agency, or practically so. This may be accomplished either by blindness to politics or by using the conceptual failings of the trichotomy to push the boundary of politics so that a political method is recast by the agency and court as science or adjudicatory fairness.

Second, the court might *acknowledge but condemn* the politics, focusing its analysis on a combination of (1) the negative attributes associated with politics, (2) perhaps a descriptive assessment of the agency's political process as being flawed in its own terms (for example, unrepresentative), and (3) a resolution of the boundary ambiguities so as to justify rigidly categorizing the problem at hand as being one appropriate for resolution by scientific or adjudicatory methods.

Third, rather than ignore or recharacterize politics, the court might *acknowledge and accept* politics as playing a permissible or even helpful role in the agency's action. This approach typically entails a combination of (1) stressing the positive attributes associated with politics (accountability and representativeness as constraints on arbitrariness), (2) perhaps noting that as a descriptive matter the agency's political process was sound (for example, all appropriate interests represented), and (3) stressing the boundary ambiguities that make it undesirable to insist on rigid application of scientific or adjudicatory methods to the problem at hand.

Many areas of administrative law are plagued by the judicial ambivalence (actually, *doctrinal* ambivalence) suggested by this brief outline. Yet the evolution of the administrative state has made it increasingly important for law to come to terms with politics.[1] Failing to do so can only result in continued confusion and a resulting disservice to the conventional goal of disciplined discretion, as well as the more ambitious goal of sound governance. The four brief examples in the following sections suggest the broad significance of the politics puzzle: the constitution's structural constraints on the locus of discretion; political influence, bias, and ex parte communications; agency inaction; and agency policy shifts, especially deregulation.

---

1. Professor Cass Sunstein has made a related observation in the constitutional context, arguing that "[t]he requirement of equal protection turns out to be a requirement that representatives engage in a deliberative task, rather than responding mechanically to constituent pressures." Sunstein, *Madison and Constitutional Equality,* 9 Harv. J. L. & Pub. Pol. 11, 17 (1986); *see also* Sunstein, *Interest Groups in American Public Law,* 38 Stan. L. Rev. 29, 59–64 (1985). The significant difficulty with this, especially in light of the post hoc rationalization apparent in such cases as Pacific States Box & Basket Co. v. White, 296 U.S. 176 (1935), is that the stated test amounts to a mere requirement that the legislative result be *capable of characterization* as the product of deliberation, not that it truly be such. In administrative law, at least, this gap between imputation and performance is addressed by requirements of reasons and findings, together with the *Chenery I* prohibition of post hoc rationalizations. Sunstein means to contrast deliberation and rationality with subjective, irrational, willful politics—the jungle of passionate factions drawn from Hobbesian and Madisonian images—the negative attributes of politics familiar from trichotomy-based analyses. One of his purposes, however, is to promote a new republicanism by questioning such attributions and distinctions on both practical and intellectual grounds. 9 Harv. J. L. & Pub. Pol. at 18 (citing M. Fiorina, Congress: Keystone of the Washington Establishment [1981]). Only by happenstance does pluralist politics produce outcomes desirable in utilitarian terms. 38 Stan. L. Rev. at 30–31.

6.1.1 Politics and the Constitutional Locus of Discretion

The most fundamental example of judicial schizophrenia regarding politics can be found in recent cases applying structural constitutional principles to police statutory allocations of discretion between Congress and administrative agencies. Statutes containing legislative vetoes have been increasingly commonplace for fifty years, and most recently they have been especially important devices to strengthen the role of Congress vis-à-vis the executive branch with respect to foreign policy, as in the post-Vietnam War Powers Act, and with respect to controversial regulatory agencies, as with the Federal Trade Commission. In *Immigration and Naturalization Service v. Chadha,*[2] Chief Justice Burger's majority opinion struck down a provision of the Immigration and Naturalization Act that empowered a single house of Congress to "veto" certain discretionary decisions of the attorney general granting relief to otherwise deportable aliens. The Court held that separation of powers principles—the Constitution's requirements that statutes be passed by both chambers (bicameralism) and presented to the president for approval or veto (presentment)—make such a legislative veto provision invalid.

The Court's language in *Chadha* was sweeping, and subsequent cases extended the holding to a wide range of legislative veto provisions.[3] In dissent, however, Justice White defended the legislative veto device in part because the political realities of the relations among Congress, the president, and the agencies provide substantial assurance that the functional objectives of the Constitution's structural safeguards are in fact well served.[4] Every recent legislative veto provision, after all, has been the product of a delicate political deal between president and Congress—reauthorizing the FTC despite its controversial rule making activities, for example, with its sweeping delegation of quasi-legislative powers substantially intact, but with the president reluctantly accepting the legislative veto constraint. The majority reasoning in *Chadha* does little to explain why its mechanical application of two-hundred-year-old phrases is more compelling than a realistic and functional assessment of those innovations of the administrative state that disturb separation of powers convention.

Perhaps the majority rejected White's pragmatic functionalism be-

---

2. 462 U.S. 919 (1984).

3. *See generally* Leahy, *The Fate of the Legislative Veto after Chadha,* 53 Geo. Wash. L. Rev. 168, (1985); *see also* Muller Optical Co. v. EEOC, 743 F.2d 380, 385 n.5 (6th Cir. 1984) (collecting cases applying *Chadha* to other statutes).

4. 462 U.S. at 972, 994–95, 998–1001. *See also* Process Gas Consumers Group v. Consumer Energy Council of Am., 463 U.S. at 1217 (1983) (White, J., dissenting).

cause judges are *supposedly* ill-prepared to make context-specific assessments of interbranch political dynamics: the plausible availability of oversight devices other than the *Chadha*-type veto cannot be the essential basis for the holding. Alternatives to the *actually* legislated compromise are *always* conceivable but will by tautology be less satisfactory to one or both political branches. How is a court to judge whether such "political" assessments about comparative efficacy justify bending those old phrases to meet contemporary needs? *Chadha*'s result is easy, but its method potentially voracious. Perhaps the War Powers Act is invalid. Then why accept the convenience of the FTC? Or the General Accounting Office? Or flexible tariffs?

Indeed, two years after *Chadha*, in *Bowsher v. Synar*, the Court invalidated the comptroller general's role in the Gramm-Rudman budget reduction mechanism.[5] The irony in all this is that the balance and separation of powers was broadly debated during enactment of this extraordinary deficit-reduction measure—it was politics of the highest order. But the Court was unable to appreciate the structural protections evident in both the deliberative process and in the practical workings of the scheme. Justice Burger's majority opinion would permit a delegation of the automatic budget reduction calculations to an independent administrator subject to neither presidential nor congressional removal (short of impeachment). Burger's focus on the vestigial, forgotten, *politically impracticable* congressional power to remove the comptroller general was an exercise in extreme formalism.[6] The far more important problem with the Gramm-Rudman device was Congress's effort to avoid political accountability for painful budget choices. One would like to have had available some doctrine quite directly focusing on the problem of diluted accountability.

Use of all this rigid formalism to invalidate deals between the two political branches compares interestingly with the repose of pre–New Deal doctrine against delegation of legislative power. As I discussed in

5. 478 U.S. 714 (1986).

6. Justice Stevens, concurring and joined by Justice Marshall, placed much less reliance on the removal provision and instead made a general assessment of the comptroller general's functions to conclude that he is an agent of Congress. The statute was thus an unconstitutional effort by Congress to make binding policy through its agent without satisfying article I's requirements of bicamerality and presentment, as emphasized in *Chadha*. Burger's majority opinion reasoned that the comptroller general's tasks under the statute made him an executive officer but that congressional participation in the removal of an executive officer violated article II. Justice White dissented as he had in *Chadha*, stressing functional considerations. Justice Blackmun dissented, believing the more sensible course would be to cure the unconstitutionality of congressional "control" over the comptroller general by invalidating the removal provision of the 1921 statute that created the GAO, while preserving the more momentous Gramm-Rudman Act.

chapter 1, for almost one hundred years the Court has had little trouble approving sweeping grants of authority to administrative agencies, excepting only a few New Deal cases and a few more recent rumblings, principally from Chief Justice Rehnquist. Why the virtual abandonment of separation of powers principles in the delegation context, when formal bright lines are the order of the day regarding appointments and oversight?

The common thread is the Court's unwillingness to make close judgments about politics. No line can be drawn to determine which delegations are too vague (set reasonable rail rates) and which sufficiently narrow (assure the airworthiness of airplane designs) without developing criteria about political accountability and sophisticated insights concerning the institutional capacity of the political branches to anticipate and face hard choices. Practical demands of the modern administrative state make *some* delegations inevitable. With no easy line to be drawn, the judges must avoid the delicate task by permitting excessive statutory delegations and then trusting to the less lethal armaments of administrative law to seek out and destroy particular abuses of agency discretion. In contrast, *Chadha* and *Synar* offer formalistic, bright line tests that preserve the conventional separation of powers while avoiding judicial analysis of politics.

There is a related problem concerning agency adjudications, where the question is whether the article III assignment of "the judicial power" to federal judges with life tenure and salary protection is unconstitutionally compromised when Congress assigns adjudicatory tasks to administrative agencies. The Supreme Court had a recent and surprising flirtation with a rather formalistic emphasis on preserving the powers and prerogatives of the article III courts, in *Northern Pipeline Construction Co. v. Marathon Pipe Line Co.*,[7] invalidating a broad statutory delegation of common law adjudicatory powers to non–article III bankruptcy judges. A more moderate, functional balancing of several factors has emerged in later cases, under the leadership of Justice O'Connor.[8] The move away from the formalistic reasoning in *Northern Pipeline* is understandable in that reconciling the competing concerns of articles I (congressional powers) and III (judicial powers) is not as politically "hot" as reconciling articles I and II (executive powers), nor is it necessary for judges to immerse themselves in political controversies and unfamiliar analyses in order to take rare action invalidating statutory intrusions on their own core domain.

---

7. 458 U.S. 50 (1982).
8. Commodity Futures Trading Comm. v. Schor, 478 U.S. 833 (1986); Thomas v. Union Carbide Agricultural Products Co., 473 U.S. 568 (1985).

So, in certain contexts, especially delegation doctrine, constitutional doctrine seems to create and respond to an image of politics, whereas in other contexts politics is held just out of sight. The results have not been truly disastrous for governance. But the Court's opinions occasionally have an otherworldliness about them.

6.1.2 Political Influence, Bias, and Ex Parte Communications

Another cluster of examples involves the strong presumptions in doctrine that agency officials do and must act in a neutral or unbiased manner, notwithstanding the political currents that swirl around them. Thus, it takes a very strong showing of wrongdoing or bias to persuade a court to consider a claim of impermissible political influence,[9] prejudgment of a material issue,[10] or general bias.[11] The result is a series

9. Sierra Club v. Costle, 657 F.2d 298 (D.C. Cir. 1981) (Wald, J.). *See also* Power Auth. of N.Y. v. FERC, 743 F.2d 93, 109–10 (2d Cir. 1984) (letters from New York congressmen to commission severely criticizing an opinion while agency review was pending did not require disqualification of commission because letters contained no factual matters outside record); Gulf Oil Corp. v. FPC, 563 F.2d 588, 610–12 (3d Cir. 1977) (legislative interference by two House subcommittees regarding the commission's choice of procedures in pending adjudication did not require invalidation of resulting order). *Compare* Pillsbury Co. v. FTC, 354 F.2d 952 (5th Cir. 1966) (commissioners' participation in adjudication denied due process where they had been questioned by Senate subcommittee concerning "the mental decisional processes" of the commission regarding pending case). *Compare* APA § 557(d) (prohibition on ex parte contacts with interested persons applies only to formal agency action). *See* D.C. Fed'n of Civic Ass'n v. Volpe, 459 F.2d 1231, 1246 (D.C. Cir. 1971), *cert. denied*, 405 U.S. 1030 (1972) (vacating and remanding decision by secretary of Transportation approving construction of bridge through park land, where such decision may have been influenced by a congressman's threat to withhold funds for construction of D.C. subway system).

10. The leading case of Association of Nat'l Advertisers, Inc. v. FTC, 627 F.2d 1151 (D.C. Cir. 1979), *cert. denied*, 447 U.S. 921 (1980), set a virtually unsurmountable hurdle for parties seeking to challenge an agency member for bias in a rule making, even one subject to fairly formal procedural requirements. *But see* American Cyanamid Co. v. FTC, 363 F.2d 757, 763–68 (6th Cir. 1966) (commission's order vacated where one commissioner had previously served as chief counsel to a legislative subcommittee involved in investigating some of the same facts, issues, and parties subsequently involved in the administrative proceedings); Texaco, Inc. v. FTC, 336 F.2d 754, 759–60 (D.C. Cir. 1964) *vacated and remanded on other grounds*, 381 U.S. 739 (1965) (commissioner's participation in administrative adjudication was a denial of due process where a speech made while the matter was pending before the hearing examiner indicated he had already concluded that the parties were engaged in unlawful business practices). *Compare* APA § 556(b) (for formal proceedings "on the filing in good faith of a timely and sufficient affidavit of personal bias or other disqualification. . . . The agency shall determine the matter as part of the record and decision in the case").

11. *See* Withrow v. Larkin, 421 U.S. 35, 47 (1975) (procedures whereby state medical board both investigated and adjudicated code violations by doctors was not per se due

of doctrines that, for example: (1) make it difficult to review the propriety of interagency communications, notwithstanding the *fact* that agency contacts with White House and OMB staff regularly involve arm-twisting strongly linked to extrastatutory political and ideological considerations;[12] (2) create an essentially impossible burden of proof in allegations of substantive prejudgment in formal agency adjudications and rule makings, notwithstanding the *fact* that agency heads may be, say, anti-industry consumer advocates or anticonsumerist free mar-

---

process violation; the contention that such functional commingling "creates an unconstitutional risk of bias in administrative adjudication has a much more difficult burden of persuasion to carry . . . [than when] the adjudicator has a pecuniary interest in the outcome . . . [or when] he has been the target of personal abuse or criticism from the party before him"); Hortonville Joint School Dist. No. 1 v. Hortonville Educ. Ass'n, 426 U.S. 482, 497 (1976) (school board's adjudication and firing of striking teachers after contract negotiations between the two had failed to produce an agreement "not enough to overcome the presumption of honesty and integrity in policymakers with decision-making power"); United States v. Morgan, 313 U.S. 409, 421 (Morgan IV) (1941) (secretary of Agriculture's vigorous criticism of Supreme Court decision not grounds for disqualification on remand; "cabinet officers charged by Congress with adjudicatory functions . . . [as well as judges] are assumed to be men of conscience and intellectual discipline, capable of judging a particular controversy fairly on the basis of its own circumstances"); Ash Grove Cement Co. v. FTC, 577 F.2d 1368, 1376 (9th Cir. 1978) (commission's investigation of cement company leading to formulation of general enforcement policy, and subsequent complaint brought by commission against company based on same facts not violative of due process; "claims that an administrative agency is impermissibly biased because of its combination of investigative and adjudicative functions must overcome a presumption of honesty and integrity on the part of the decision-maker"). *Compare* APA § 554(d) (prohibition against combining investigative or prosecutorial functions with decision making function does not apply to rule making, initial licensing, rate making, or rate application or to the actual decision making members of an agency, commission, or board). *But see* Gibson v. Berryhill, 411 U.S. 564, 578–579 (1973) (district court correctly concluded that state board of optometrists, composed of independent optometrists, was "so biased by . . . pecuniary interest that it could not constitutionally conduct hearings looking toward the revocation of appellee's [corporate optometrists] licenses to practice optometry"); Arnett v. Kennedy, 416 U.S. 134, 196–99 (1974) (White, J., concurring in part and dissenting in part) (appearance and risk of bias too great where the hearing officer that discharged civil servant employee was the object of criticism and alleged slander that was itself "the basis for the employee's proposed discharge").

12. In *Sierra Club*, 657 F.2d 298 (D.C. Cir. 1981), the court reasoned that "[i]n a proceeding . . . of vital concern to so many interests—industry, environmental groups, as well as Congress and the Administration—it would be unrealistic to think there would not naturally be attempts on all sides to stay in contact with EPA right up to the final moment the rule is promulgated." *Id.* at 397. The court did note newspaper accounts of Senator Byrd engaging in "hard-ball arm twisting by reminding EPA and White House officials that his support was needed for other programs" but downplayed them as insubstantial evidence. *Id.* at 409 n. 539. Other mechanisms of legislative interference apart from arm-twisting include the "adversarial interrogation" of commissioners regarding the result and particular factors in the cost analysis of an agency order while its

keteers;[13] and (3) apply strong presumptions that politically motivated "management reforms" have not affected the neutrality of hearing officers in the Social Security Administration.[14]

The leading case of *Sierra Club v. Costle,* decided by now-Chief Judge Patricia Wald, involved several kinds of ex parte contacts and political influence. Generally, the court said, "Judges . . . must refrain from the easy temptation to look askance at all face-to-face lobbying efforts, regardless of the forum in which they occur, merely because we

---

rehearing was pending, American Pub. Gas Ass'n v. FPC, 567 F.2d 1016, 1067–70 (D.C. Cir. 1977), and "the implicit influence inherent in congressional control over tenure and salary," Pillsbury Co. v. FTC, 354 F.2d 952, 963 (5th Cir. 1966).

During the Reagan administration's heyday, the debate over political interference with agency decision making surrounded OMB and its implementation of Executive Order 12291, 46 Fed. Reg. 13193 (1981). The order dramatically increased the potential for executive influence over agency decision making by requiring that for all "major rules" (defined in sec. 1[b]), agencies prepare and transmit a report to OMB "at least 60 days *prior* to the publication of a notice of proposed rulemaking" (emphasis added). Executive Order 12291 at § 3(c)(2); 46 Fed. Reg. at 13194. The OMB can thus attempt to veto proposed regulations and policies before the notice and comment period begins, in effect insulating whatever pressure is brought to bear for judicial review. *See* Rosenberg, *Beyond the Limits of Executive Power: Presidential Control of Agency Rulemaking under Executive Order 12291,* 80 Mich. L. Rev. 193, 195 (1981) ("unrecorded and unreviewable communications [between the White House, presidential advisers, and the agencies] threaten to deprive individuals of due process and to distort the APA's provisions for judicial review and public participation").

OMB practices consequently attracted fire from the courts and Congress. In October 1985 a House subcommittee issued a report charging the OMB with an "unlawful abuse of power" in blocking proposed EPA asbestos regulations and proposed rules until *after* they have been published in the Federal Register. *See OMB Slowed Asbestos Regulation—Report,* L.A. Daily Journal, Oct. 8, 1985, at 5. Representative John Dingell (D-Mich.) is quoted as saying, "The report reveals how the OMB is engaging in a pervasive and unlawful scheme to displace agency rule making authority." *Id.* For coverage of pending litigation challenging OMB conduct, *see Judge Bars U.S. Plea for Secrecy in Suit over Budget Office Delay,* New York Times, Dec. 20, 1985, at A28, col. 3; *Suit Challenges Revision of Worker Safety Rule,* L.A. Daily Journal, Apr. 11, 1985, at 3, col. 2; Public Citizens' Health Research Group v. Rowland, 702 F.2d 1150 (D.C. Cir. 1983). For a positive view of the executive order, *see* Strauss & Sunstein, *Analysis of OMB Oversight Role Misunderstood,* Legal Times, May 27, 1985, at 13, col. 1 (letter).

13. A claim of bias or substantive prejudgment is more likely to succeed in the adjudicatory context. *National Advertisers* rejected the applicability of the lower standard for disqualification in an adjudication, as enunciated in Cinderella Career and Finishing Schools, Inc. v. FTC, 425 F.2d 583 (D.C. Cir. 1970), but presumably left its applicability to adjudication untouched. In *Cinderella* the court held that the standard for disqualification was "whether a disinterested observer may conclude that [the agency] has in some measure adjudged the facts as well as the law of a particular case in advance of hearing it." *Id.* at 591. *National Advertisers'* rationale for rejecting this test looked to the asserted difference between legislative and adjudicative facts, assumed that rules rely on legislative facts per se and orders on adjudicative facts, and concluded that "the *Cinderella* view of a neutral and detached adjudicator is simply an inapposite role model for an admin-

see them as inappropriate in the judicial context." Specifically, the court held that intra-executive branch meetings between the president and EPA officials during the post-comment period of an informal rule making, along with the agency's failure to docket the substance of such meetings, did not violate due process. And as to legislative influence, the court held it "entirely proper for congressional representatives vigorously to represent the interests of their constituents before administrative agencies engaged in general policy rulemaking, so long as individual congressmen do not frustrate the intent of Congress as a whole as expressed in statute, nor undermine applicable rules of procedure."[15] Judge Wald, it should be recalled, was a subcabinet appointee in the Carter administration.

---

istrator who must translate broad statutory commands into concrete social policies." 627 F.2d at 1168–69.

This reasoning suffers from two flaws. The assumption that rules involve only legislative facts and orders only adjudicative facts is not correct. Most obviously, legislative facts can play a major role in adjudication when the agency chooses to announce new policies through adjudication (see sec. 2.4.2); and rules can be founded on adjudicative facts. See United Airlines, Inc. v. CAB, 760 F.2d 1107 (7th Cir. 1985) (informal rule making used to promulgate antitrust regulation based on adjudicative facts); see generally K. Davis, 3 Administrative Law Treatise § 19.7, 399–403 (2d ed. 1980). Accordingly, in United Farm Workers of America v. Arizona Agricultural Employment Relations Bd., 727 F.2d 1475 (9th Cir. 1984), the court held that any distinction between rule making and adjudication "is not a proper basis for determining disqualification for bias." Id. at 1477. Moreover, the two-tiered approach ignores that agencies do not have one set of officials to promulgate rules and a second to issue orders and assumes that the "subjective partiality" officials are encouraged to exercise in rule making will somehow be miraculously shed when the officials participate in an adjudication. Judge Leventhal's concurring opinion in National Advertisers accepts this assumption without question. See 627 F.2d at 1176. Judge MacKinnon, in dissent, seemed to realize this, arguing that since both rule making and adjudication require "fair decisionmakers, no reason exists why the same rule should not be applied [to both]." Id. at 1195.

An example is the recent controversy over FTC Chairman William Miller's efforts to deregulate advertising that tends to deceive the "gullible consumer" and to restrict the commission's investigative activity, with an attendant decrease in the number enforcement actions. See, e.g., Seeking a Narrower Mandate, New York Times, Mar. 24, 1984, at A33, col. 1; Dingell Assails FTC Chairman for Policy Shift on Deceptive Ads, New York Times, Oct. 27, 1983, at B17, col. 1.

14. See NLRB v. Pittsburgh Steamship Co., 337 U.S. 656, 658–59 (1949) (ALJ's unvarying acceptance of all pro-union evidence and repudiation of all pro-employer evidence did not prove bias; "total rejection of an opposed view cannot of itself impugn the integrity or competence of a trier of fact").

In Ramspeck v. Federal Trial Examiners Conference, 345 U.S. 128 (1953), the court held that the position of hearing examiner had no constitutional protections, only statutory, sustained civil service commission regulations that established multiple salary grades for examiners within agencies, and gave agency officials limited discretion in deciding how vacancies in higher grade positions would be filled. Recently, however, some ALJs claimed that "the Reagan administration has launched an unprecedented assault on their

Similarly, in another leading case, *Association of National Advertisers, Inc. v. FTC,* the court held that disqualification was not required where the commission chairman had publicly advocated legal and factual theories and assumptions during speeches and press interviews which were later involved in a rule making concerning children's television advertising. The dissent quoted Chairman Michael Pertschuk's comments: "I have some serious doubts as to whether any television advertising should be directed at a . . . 3 or 4 or 5 year old. . . . [A]dvertisers *seize* on the child's trust and *exploit* it as a weakness for their gain . . . . *It is a major, serious problem.*"

The majority held that an agency member could be disqualified from a rule making only "when there is a clear and convincing showing that he has an *unalterably closed mind* on *matters critical* to the disposition

---

professional independence and integrity." Yore, *No Strings Attached,* California Lawyer, Jan. 1985, at 42, col. 1. Thus, ALJs have challenged agency conduct in the past few years. In Association of Admin. Law Judges, Inc. v. Heckler, 594 F. Supp. 1132 (D.D.C. 1984), the ALJs in the SSA alleged that several management policies, in combination, created improper pressure to reduce allowance rates and thus jeopardized their "rights . . . to decisional independence under the APA." *Id.* at 1133. Their primary concern was with the targeting of review by the SSA's Appeals Council at ALJs with high allowance rates, along with the threat of adverse personnel proceedings before the Merit Systems Protection Board. The court concluded that such targeting violated the "spirit" of the APA because it "could have tended to corrupt the ability of [ALJs] to exercise . . . independence . . . [In close cases] that pressure may have intruded upon the factfinding process and may have influenced some outcomes." *Id.* at 1142–43. For commentary on this very interesting clash of paradigms, *see ALJs Lose Bid against Quota System Pressure,* Nat'l L.J., Sept. 24, 1984, at 8, col. 1; *see also* Nash v. Califano, 613 F.2d 10 (2d Cir. 1980) (ALJ had standing to challenge various agency practices, such as "mandatory instructions [from superiors] concerning the proper length of hearings and opinions, the amount of evidence required in specific cases, and the proper use of expert witnesses," all outside the normal appellate process, an "arbitrary monthly production quota of which failure to meet could lead to incompetence charges [and] . . . attempts to control the number of decisions denying . . . benefits" through a "Quality Assurance Program"); Goodman v. Svahn, 614 F. Supp. 726, 727 n. 1 (D.D.C. 1985) (approving Merit Systems Protection Board holding that poor quantitative performance could serve as good cause to remove an ALJ).

In response to the perceived increase in pressures on ALJs, several bills have been introduced in Congress over the past few years seeking to further insulate hearing officers from agency control. *See generally* Yore, *supra* at 44–45. One, drafted by several ALJs and introduced by Senator Heflin (D-FL.) would create an independent "ALJ corps." Cong. Rec. S2970–73 (Mar. 14, 1985). According to Heflin, the bill "would ensure that administrative law judges will no longer be subject to the potential bias of a particular agency—bias which whether actual or perceived, nonetheless weakness the public's perception of administrative justice." *Id.* at S2970. For extensive commentary on the Heflin bill and other issues of agency influence over ALJs, *see Symposium: Administrative Law Judges,* 6 W. New Eng. L. Rev. 587–849 (1984).

15. 657 F.2d 298, 401, 408, 409 (D.C. Cir. 1981).

of the rulemaking."[16] In another case, one year later, the court elaborated that the "unalterably closed mind test" is "an even higher barrier to claims of bias in a rulemaking proceeding . . . [than proving that a decision maker] had demonstrably made up her mind about important and specific factual questions and was impervious to contrary evidence. . . . Subjective partiality [as to policy views] . . . does not invalidate a proceeding the agency conducts in good faith."[17] The insurmountability of such a rule is clear; it is scarcely a serious test, perhaps reflecting a judicial realization that politics, not science, was the decision making paradigm employed, along with judicial reluctance to review the politics paradigm for the soundness of its execution.

6.1.3 Agency Inaction

There is also considerable doctrinal turmoil at the moment concerning the problem of judicial review of agency inaction.[18] This issue arises in several contexts, from complete failure to implement a program,[19] to substantial inaction attributable to agency priorities,[20] to particular challenges to the agency's choice (or nonchoice) of regulatory, enforcement, or investigation targets.[21] In all of these areas poli-

16. 627 F.2d 1151, 1154, 1189–90 (D.C. Cir. 1979), *cert. denied*, 447 U.S. 921 (1980). Judge MacKinnon's dissent argued, in part, that Chairman Pertschuk's remarks demonstrated bias, even under the majority's standard.

17. United Steelworkers of Am. v. Marshall, 647 F.2d 1189, 1209 (D.C. Cir. 1980).

18. *See generally* Sunstein, *Reviewing Agency Inaction after Heckler v. Chaney*, 52 U. Chi. L. Rev. 653 (1985).

19. *See, e.g.,* Adams v. Richardson, 480 F.2d 1159, 1162–63 (D.C. Cir. 1973) (imposing enforcement obligations for Title VI of the 1964 Civil Rights Act); United States v. Markgraf, 736 F.2d 1179 (1984) (secretary must develop standards for administration of discretionary farm debt relief program); Allison v. Block, 723 F.2d 631 (1983) (same as *Markgraf*); Matzke v. Block, 732 F.2d 799 (1984) (secretary must develop standards for administration of discretionary farm debt relief program and must do so through rule making rather than adjudication).

20. *See* Heckler v. Day, 467 U.S. 104 (1984) (using statutory construction and trichotomy-based analysis to reverse, 5–4, lower court's imposition of deadlines in class action for unreasonable hearing delays in social security disability program); New York Racing Ass'n v. NLRB, 708 F.2d 46 (2d Cir. 1983) (board's refusal to assert jurisdiction over racing industry held unreviewable since some labor disputes may be too insignificant to warrant involvement); Sierra Club v. Ruckelshaus, 61 Ad. L. Rep. 2d (P&F) 65 (N.D. Cal., 12/11/1984) (EPA administrator held in contempt for regulatory inaction on radionuclides).

21. *See, e.g.,* Heckler v. Chaney, 470 U.S. 821 (1985) (denying review of FDA refusal to investigate unapproved lethal use of approved drug for capital punishment); Banzhaf v. Smith, 737 F.2d 1167 (D.C. Cir. 1984) (denying review of attorney general's refusal to initiate investigation under the Ethics in Government Act); *see also* Vaca v. Sipes, 368 U.S. 171, 182 (1967) (NLRB's refusal to initiate unfair labor practice complaint held unreviewable). *Compare* Carpet, Linoleum & Tile Layers Local 419 v. Brown, 656 F.2d 564

tics can and often does play an important role. Yet the tools and language of judicial review rarely come to terms with that role. Politics is either ignored or it is acknowledged as a reason to treat the agency's discretion as unreviewable, and hence immune to legal discipline.[22] Specific examples, cited in the footnotes, include the failure of the Department of Agriculture to implement a statute providing discretionary debt relief for farmers, the failure of OSHA and the EPA to regulate arguably hazardous substances or conditions, and the failure of the attorney general to investigate alleged violations of the Ethics in Government Act. This issue is particularly important now because, at the same time that shifts in government priorities and dramatically greater fiscal stringency will make agency inaction an increasingly prominent tool of policy administration, judicial opinions increasingly tend toward highly deferential judicial review—especially, one fears, in the Supreme Court.

6.1.4 Policy Shifts and Deregulation

When an agency changes an important policy, the reviewing court is presented with an especially difficult problem of scaling the degree of deference, because there is a sometimes extensive body of evidence and judgment developed earlier by the expert agency and pointing in another direction.[23] Often, the change in direction is most naturally

---

(10th Cir. 1981) (mandamus to require Defense Department enforcement of contractor compliance with Davis-Bacon Act wage floors); Dunlop v. Bachowski, 421 U.S. 560 (1975); FTC v. Universal-Rundle, 387 U.S. 244 (1967) (requiring explanation for Labor secretary's refusal to prosecute LMRDA complaint); Medical Comm. for Human Rights v. SEC, 432 F.2d 659 (D.C. Cir. 1970), *vacated as moot*, 404 U.S. 403 (1972); Sierra Club v. Ruckelshaus, 61 Ad. L. Rep. 2d (P&F) 65, 70 (N.D. Cal. Dec. 11, 1984) (EPA administrator in contempt for regulatory inaction on radionuclides).

22. *Chaney*, 470 U.S. at 832; Associated Builders, etc. v. Irving 610 F.2d 1221, 1224 (4th Cir. 1979) (NLRB general counsel's refusal to file complaint unreviewable). *See* secs. 3.2, 3.3, and 3.5.

23. *See, e.g.*, Motor Vehicle Mfrs. Ass'n v. State Farm Mut. Auto Ins. Co., 463 U.S. 29, 46 (1983) (pointing to original rule making record to demonstrate absence of support for agency's decision to rescind air bags rule); Public Citizen v. Steed, 733 F.2d 93, 100–102 (D.C. Cir. 1984) (pointing to agency's appraisal and judgment of evidence in the original rule making record, and judicial approval of that rule, to render agency's new and reversed appraisal of similar evidence arbitrary and capricious); Office of Communication v. FCC, 560 F.2d 529, 533–35 (2d Cir. 1977) (pointing to agency's judgment and analysis in the original rule and rule making proposal to demonstrate the irrational and unreasoned nature of its decision to rescind). *See generally* Edwards, *Judicial Review of Deregulation*, 11 N. Ky. L. Rev. 229, 249–53 (1984) (judicial review generally presumes validity of pre-existing regulatory policies); Garland, *Deregulation and Judicial Review*, 98 Harv. L. Rev. 505, 536–37 (1984) ("dual nature of record" in recision cases facilitates valuable substantive review); Sunstein, *Deregulation and the Hard Look Doctrine*, 1983 Sup. Ct. Rev. 177, 181–84 (1984).

accounted for by a politically based shift in personnel.[24] But this explanation is rarely offered by the agency, and rarely explored by the courts. The result is an extremely artificial and obscure assessment of the agency's action, as though legislative history or statistical methodology were the key evaluation for the court, when the heart of the problem is to accommodate politics with our notions of Rule of Law and scientific method. An important contemporary class of cases in this vein involves judicial review of administrative deregulation, especially in the wake of the 1980 presidential elections. But there are other instances as well, such as shifts in NLRB policies or in the implementation administration of social welfare programs.

In *Schweiker v. Gray Panthers,* for example, the Supreme Court reviewed a medicaid regulation under which income of the recipient's spouse was "deemed" to be "available" to the recipient in order to determine eligibility for income-tested health care, whether or not the income was *actually* available. The dissenters stressed the apparent willingness of the department to rethink its harsh deeming policy, which drove some elderly couples to divorce in order to gain nursing home medicaid coverage for nursing home care without impoverishing the healthy spouse. But the majority saw the agency's policy rethinking as a legally unreliable responsiveness to the earlier, unwarranted intrusiveness of the lower court.[25] A more plausible explanation, and one consistent with the dissenters' unwillingness to defer, is that late in the Carter administration key agency officials, including the secretary, *had changed.*

In *Motor Vehicle Manufacturers Association v. State Farm Mutual Insurance Co.,* the Supreme Court struck down the Reagan administration's rescission of a regulation that would have required automobile manufacturers to install passive passenger safety devices—either automatic seat belts or air bags. The agency had newly concluded that detachable automatic seat belts were an unsatisfactory safety measure, because of possible public objections to automatic seat belts and because the detachability might drastically reduce usage and hence the benefits of the regulation.[26] The majority held this to be arbitrary and capricious. Justice Rehnquist was joined by three other justices in a partial dissent:

> The agency's changed view of the [passenger safety] standard
> seems to be related to the election of a new President of a differ-

24. *See, e.g.,* Columbia Broadcasting Sys. v. FCC, 454 F.2d 1018, 1036 (D.C. Cir. 1971) (Tamm, J., concurring) (policy shift suggests partisan political motives).

25. *Compare* 453 U.S. 34 (1981) at 42 n. 12 (majority opinion) *with id.* at 53–56 (dissenting opinion).

26. An automatic seatbelt extends from the top of the door, across the chest, attaching between the driver and passenger seats; when the door is open, it is possible to slip

ent political party. It is readily apparent that the responsible
members of one administration may consider public resistance
and uncertainties to be more important than do their counterparts in a previous administration. *A change in administration
brought about by the people casting their votes is a perfectly reasonable
basis for an executive agency's reappraisal of the costs and benefits of its
programs and regulations.* As long as the agency remains within
the bounds established by Congress, it is entitled to assess administrative records and evaluate priorities in light of the philosophy of the administration.[27]

Justice Rehnquist's opinion in *State Farm* is striking for two reasons.
It is both a *descriptive* acknowledgment that politics was an ingredient of
the deregulatory decision at issue *and* a *normative* assertion that politics
has a legitimate place in sound agency decision making. These points
are all the more striking because they contrast sharply with the total
absence from Justice White's majority opinion of any mention of politics. White's opinion entails a conception of politics as distinguishable
from and in opposition to the required rationality of agency decision
making. President Reagan's electoral victory, which included a significant campaign emphasis on deregulation, was simply irrelevant to the
majority's construction of the arbitrary and capricious standard of review: There was a probing discussion of scientific studies and regulatory alternatives, but no mention of politics.

In contrast, implicit in Justice Rehnquist's observation is the notion
that the political reality which is often the explanation for a major
policy shift should not be ignored in the process of judicial review. To
the extent that politics and politically inspired choice are considered
rational, then the political story is just as important to understanding
the "reasons and findings" of the agency and the "basis and purpose"
of its action. Although we have no indication that Justice Rehnquist
would go so far as to remand an agency action that failed to incorporate
some consideration of politics (and it is surely unlikely), he is clear that
within the statutory range of permissible policy choices, political factors may be part of "reasonable"—that is, reasoned—choice.

The puzzle suggested here is by no means unique to *State Farm*.

---

underneath the belt into the seat. The seatbelt is "automatic" in the sense that it does not
require the active participation, by buckling, of the user. The detachable variety can be
disengaged between the seats and put out of the way. It therefore provides no protection
at all unless reattached. The rescission was challenged in part because the agency did not
document, i.e., quantify, the assumption of consumer hostility toward automatic seatbelts. Moreover, the agency seemed to overstate the problem of detachability by failing to
analyze the benefits that might be salvaged by people reattaching their belts.

27. *State Farm,* 463 U.S. 29 at 59 (1983) (emphasis added).

Unsettled notions of what politics is and what role it may properly play in agency decision making are evident in many contexts.

6.2 Two Conceptions: Politics-as-Preferences versus Politics-as-Market

Of the many and varied contexts in which the law's treatment of politics is lacking, I have discussed only a few—structural constraints, bias, inaction, and policy shifts. The case for doctrinal reform is strong. But how?

It is important to be clear about what Justice Rehnquist's partial dissent in *State Farm* does *not* say. His endorsement of politics can probably be most fairly read as a realistic embracing of the subjective, or value-laden, character of public policy choice: The preferences of the decision maker cannot be eliminated from agency choices,[28] and those preferences will be correlated with political affiliation and, hence, with electoral fortunes. Stated differently, this observation is simply that the boundaries among politics, science, and fairness are virtually unobservable in practice because any complicated problem will involve the integration of all three decision making paradigms; the administrator cannot avoid deploying subjective preferences, even while making a putatively "scientific" decision. Justice Rehnquist would have us acknowledge this. The alternative approach, evident in Justice White's *State Farm* majority opinion, as it is in almost all cases, is to ignore (descriptively) the insistent presence of politically linked preferences and even to require (normatively) that the alternative, nonpolitical decision making paradigms of science and fairness be the exclusive legitimate bases for agency choice—at least with respect to the overt presentation and analysis of the choice by agency and court.

However, tolerance for the *politics-as-preferences* perspective, such as that demonstrated in Justice Rehnquist's *State Farm* dissent, is only a "weak" version of how administrative law might recognize the demands of politics. A stronger version, at best only suggested by Justice Rehnquist's remarks, would recognize the process of interest group competition, balancing, and accommodation. We can term this *politics-*

---

28. Davis makes this point in regard to the Supreme Court itself in the *Benzene* case, Industrial Union Dep't v. American Petroleum Inst., 448 U.S. 607 (1980), asserting that although all the justices "were genuinely striving to avoid substitution of judgment on the ultimate policy question . . . all eight, perhaps because of intrinsic necessity, to some extent allowed their policy preferences to affect the result." Davis, 5 Treatise § 29.21 426 (1984).

as-market, with the currency being electoral reward. This is a distinction in kind, independent of the distinction between politics as a factor in the decision and politics as a controlling concern. So, for example, if politics is present only in the weak form of the decision maker's personal preferences, those preferences may or may not be controlling.

The contrast between the weak and strong versions of political influence is superficially striking and an appealing basis for separating permissible from impermissible. It is one thing to acknowledge that the individuality and subjectivity of the decision maker influence choice. One can do this easily enough within the framework of the trichotomy by continuing to emphasize expertise or fairness as the central, legitimating paradigm and accepting a small role for politics-as-preferences in a concession to the realities of human frailty. I have already discussed the conceptually analogous issue of marginalizing the allegations of judicial willfulness and bias. The central claims to neutrality and legitimacy are thought to be defended by continual resort to "core-periphery" distinctions or "supplements." Thus, politics (as preferences) is tolerable so long as it is kept within bounds defined in terms of evident distortion of the overall scientific or adjudicatory character of the decision making process.

Another way of putting this is that the *weak* version of politics, unthreateningly characterized as politically linked preferences, was acceptable to four partially dissenting justices in *State Farm* perhaps because the overall character of the process, in their view, was not so distorted as to *force* attention to the negative attributes of politics. Justice Rehnquist's opinion could have been written without mention of the 1980 election and still have been credible, certainly enough so as to avoid embarrassment. The shift in agency evaluation of the air bags evidence could have been deferred to as a "reasonable" difference in views over time, period. The "politics" basis for the deference could have been ignored because the result was both explainable and acceptable without it.

This sufficiency-of-the-(nonpolitical)-analysis thesis is deceptively complex. If one presses the question of *why* the *State Farm* dissenters were satisfied with NHTSA's analysis, given its apparent imperfections, three answers come to mind. First, they may simply have felt incompetent to second-guess the agency's view about the significance of the imperfections. But this suggests a rule of deference except for "clear error," which is decidedly not the APA or common law basis for administrative review. Moreover, intellectual incapacity is implausible on the facts of *State Farm.* Second, the dissenters may have concluded, substantively, that the imperfections in the agency analysis weren't too bad. Third, they may have imagined a narrow domain of questions as to which "expert analysis" was appropriate, and concluded that within that constricted domain NHTSA had done just fine. These second and third accounts require confidence in the categorization of political and scientific reasoning by the justices and by the secretary. Thus, the sufficiency-of-the-evidence approach is problematic in light of my earlier critique, though useful for the present incremental analysis.

On the other hand, had the agency made its decision using politics-as-market, we must wonder whether the four justices in the *State Farm* partial dissent would have been as descriptively and normatively accepting. If, for example, the rescission rule had been the obvious product of interest group pressure or political fealty, then a claim that expert analysis was the independent and sufficient basis for the decision would not have been plausible. What collection of circumstances would be taken as "proof" that political pressures had dominated the decision? This evidentiary problem merely recapitulates the basic descriptive and boundary problems of science and politics. A series of White House or congressional meetings may appear to some as evidence of impermissible politics while appearing to others as perfectly appropriate to the expert's eclectic consideration of all relevant factors and values.[29]

But there is a deeper point than the evidentiary one: Politics-as-preferences and politics-as-market are not conceptually distinct in any important way. The difference is between the administrator who conducts the bargaining among and weighting of interest group concerns *in his or her head,* versus the administrator who does precisely the same thing on the basis of a live drama played out around the conference table in the proverbial smoke-filled room. The decision making methods are cognitively identical. (Assume that the administrator does not abdicate power in the course of such a meeting, in which case the cognitive processes would be very different.) Indeed, the live drama is in some respects preferable because it is overt and because the actual—rather than imagined—participation of relevant interest representatives may improve the quality of the balancing and accommodating. *Thus the logic of accepting the weak version of politics suggests the need to accept the strong version as well: If raw ideological preferences are permissible, then so is an electoral marketplace, in principle. There remains only the question of degree.*

29. *See* Sierra Club v. Costle, 657 F.2d (D.C. Cir. 1981).

6.3 Incremental Lessons from the Trichotomy: Avoiding the Extremes

What are we to make of all of this within a mode of marginal doctrinal reform? I have analyzed some failings of the separation of powers foundations of administrative law. Can we profit from that analysis without altogether abandoning the foundation?

Keeping descriptive accuracy in mind, the cognitive identity of the weak and strong versions of politics in agency choice must matter. Arguments for and against the acceptability of one version must essentially apply to the other. To begin with, let us imagine a situation in which the decision maker has *relied* on the strong (market) version of politics, meaning that politics-as-market was at least necessary to the decision, though perhaps not alone sufficient. Then *by definition* it is implausible to claim that politics is immaterial to the agency's decision. If one believes, in accordance with the trichotomy, that politics, science, and fairness are distinct, then legal acceptance of strong politics means abandoning the requirement that the agency act exclusively as an expert in formulating rules or as a fair adjudicator in applying them. But this abandonment raises legitimacy concerns so long as the trichotomy's normative assignment of roles is accepted as a successful and necessary guard against arbitrary government. (This seems true except for a very limited set of problems, where there is every expectation that the agency action will be political. Trivial examples are the appointment of advisory committees and the location of branch offices.) Thus, in terms of marginal doctrinal reform, we must exclude the extreme of a complete embracing of politics-as-market, notwithstanding any tenuous reading to the contrary of Justice Rehnquist's opinion in *State Farm.* Justice Rehnquist is perfectly correct to note the role of politics in agency decision making and perfectly correct to argue that some role is "reasonable."

Yet to ignore or reject the role of politics—the usual judicial method—is problematic for three reasons:

First, ignoring politics may lead a court to misunderstand the agency's action, either because the court has the descriptively mistaken belief that, say, *science* was the method employed when *politics* was actually the dominant method; or because the court has the conceptually mistaken belief that in using *science* the agency has somehow *avoided* politics. Misperceiving the agency's action can create problems in assessing the action and in prescribing corrective measures. The court may believe, for example, that the agency's decision not to ban a pesticide is based on a scientifically mistaken failure to heed the results of a particular laboratory study and may remand accordingly—perhaps using the quasi-procedural device of a more elaborate requirement of reasons and findings with respect to the scientific evidence. In fact, however, the agency's decision may reflect the self-conscious though unconfessed political balancing of environmental and industrial considerations, or even an ideological predisposition against regulation. In these circumstances, the remand justified through a scientific lens merely invites a subterfuge in the parading of expertise. A more appropriate judicial response would be a remand that causes the political bases for the choice to become more explicit and, if appropriate, to be subjected to public scrutiny.

For example, in *EDF v. Ruckelshaus*, the court reversed the agency's refusal to begin proceedings to cancel the registration of DDT. Rejecting an argument that the agency's discretion to initiate a cancellation proceeding is unreviewable, the court reasoned that the decision to cancel involved a determination of the legal standard for initiating such a proceeding and then a factual inquiry to weigh the available evidence; believing that both determinations are amenable to judicial review for abuse or arbitrariness, the court exercised its powers of review and reversed on the merits.[30] If, however, the administrator's decision had been understood more in terms of a political or policy judgment—reflecting such things as a solicitude for the interests of farmers with no ready alternatives to DDT or a judgment that there were "enough" pending regulatory initiatives in the pro-environment vein—then the determination of reviewability and the court's picture of the agency's decision making process might have been very different. In particular, rather than a simple remand to initiate the cancellation proceeding, a court concerned with the nature of the policy and political judgments at stake might have opined on the legally permissible range of nonscientific concerns in registration decisions and might have signaled explicitly the sorts of reasons and findings the agency would be expected to prepare to defend the result reached by the cancellation proceeding.[31]

30. 439 F.2d 584, at 595 (D.C. Cir. 1971). *Compare* Nor-Am Agricultural Prod., Inc. v. Hardin, 435 F.2d 1151 (7th Cir. 1970 (en banc); Pax Co. v. United States, 454 F.2d 93 (10th Cir. 1972).

31. *See* R. Pierce, S. Shapiro, & P. Verkuil, Administrative Law and Process 187 (1985) (suggesting that judge may have been "outraged" by agency delay in the DDT case arguably resulting from the secretary's sympathy for "constituents in the agricultural community and among pesticide manufacturers," though there is no such indication in the opinion). Colin Diver has pointed out that "[c]omprehensive rationality [the "policy

Second, blindness to politics precludes focusing on the *positive* attributes of politics, especially the potential contribution of participation and accountability in curbing arbitrariness. As a result, courts may feel compelled to overemphasize the promises made by science and adjudicatory fairness as devices to control agency discretion. In *State Farm,* for example, one could argue that the majority demanded too fine a scientific explanation for what was inherently a largely political agency choice; Justice White was unwilling to acknowledge the role of politics in the choice and to accept the legitimacy of indirect electoral control of that choice. This contrasts well with the Justice Stevens's ringing endorsement of the agency's policy role in *Chevron,* the air pollution "bubble" case.

Third, blindness to politics precludes focusing on the *negative* attributes of politics: the potential problems of subjective willfulness and majority tyranny. Thus, in several cases delimiting judicial review of agricultural marketing orders, the courts give no attention to the possible dangers of agency "capture" by majority farming interests, resulting in biases against certain other commercial interests and against consumers.[32]

One might argue that ignoring or suppressing politics is good, however unrealistic, because it signals something or provides incentives of some sort. Fictions and myths, after all, can be useful. But it is difficult to perceive how this particular fiction is beneficial. It might be claimed that by ignoring politics the courts are able to escape the difficult problems of assessment and balancing that might be thrust on them were the veil lifted; and similarly, by requiring that agencies express the reasons and findings for their actions in nonpolitical terms, perhaps the agencies are somehow forced to eschew political decision making. Such claims seem profoundly counterfactual and, in light of the tri-

---

science" model of rule making] merely masks the decision maker's private biases under a legitimizing facade of objectivity and analytic rigor." Diver, *Policymaking Paradigms in Administrative Law,* 95 Harv. L. Rev. 393, 428–29 (1981).

32. *See, e.g.,* Block v. Community Nutrition Inst., 467 U.S. 340 (1984); Pescosolido v. Block, 765 F.2d 827 (9th Cir. 1985), and cases cited therein. *But see* Stark v. Wickard, 321 U.S. 288 (1944) (subsequently construed narrowly); Suntex Dairy v. Bergland, 591 F.2d 1063 (5th Cir. 1979). In Marketing Assistance Program, Inc. v. Bergland, 562 F.2d 1305 (D.C. Cir. 1977), agency negotiations before the notice of proposed rule making did not constitute impermissible ex parte communications, nor were they evidence of reversible bias. The ruling focuses on the difficult problem of how early in a policymaking exercise to impose APA procedural requirements. But in drawing the line, the court's opinion does not include an analysis of the practical political realities of early, undisclosed policy "deals."

chotomy's conceptual problems, completely implausible. The instability and confusion suggested in the first three points above are not outweighed by any benefits that result from reliance on fiction.

So, blindness is clearly not the appropriate doctrinal response to the political ingredient in agency decision making, any more than is the opposite extreme of uncritically accepting the strong version of politics. Between these two we must search for a reasonable (incrementalist) accommodation of politics with—and perhaps within—legal norms.

6.3.1 Some Reformist Suggestions

Needless to say, it is impossible to formulate the precise recipe for appropriate admixtures of politics, science, and fairness in agency decision making: our exploration of the descriptive and conceptual problems of the trichotomy teaches us that.[33] Nevertheless, one can identify some helpful incremental measures. Immediately below, I discuss the disclosure of otherwise secret politics, the mix of politics with the other paradigms, and the question of misexecution of politics. Then, in section 6.4, I elaborate further by considering these approaches in the context of deregulation. Finally, in chapter 7, I will experiment with some "recipes" in the context of sound governance reviews.

6.3.1.(a) Disclosure: No Secret Politics. Judicial analysis of agency action should uncover and address political and subjective factors in agency choice rather than be blind to them. This requires a judicial insistence that agencies frankly acknowledge the role of political, ideological, or subjective analyses in their reasons and findings rather than attempting to obscure those elements behind the filigree so readily generated by the scientific and adjudicatory fairness methods of decision making and explanation. An analogy here are those cases in which courts have rejected agency decisions that seems to be based on secret or undisclosed expert studies or reasoning. In those cases, courts have emphasized the importance of disclosure on the record and of consequent public scrutiny and feedback as a means to pursue even sounder expertise (through correction), attract and facilitate wider public participation, and provide adversarial fairness to the affected interests. (These three justifications for disclosure requirements track the trichotomy.)[34] The disclosure of the subjective, ideological, and electoral

33. Chevron USA, Inc. v. NRDC, 467 U.S. 837 (1984).
34. *See, e.g.,* Seacoast Anti-Pollution League v. Costle, 572 F.2d 872, 880–82 (1st Cir.), *cert. denied,* 439 U.S. 824 (1978); United States v. Nova Scotia Food Prod. Corp., 568 F.2d 240, 251–52 (2d Cir. 1977); Portland Cement Ass'n v. Ruckelshaus, 486 F.2d 375, 392–95 (D.C. Cir. 1973), *cert. denied,* 417 U.S. 921 (1974).

factors that influence the agency's decision is a crucial step toward disciplining them. The failure of courts to demand disclosure encourages secret politics, pretermitting the process of continuing, between-elections political accountability. More important, it invites a confusion of political and scientific justifications for the agency action.

In practice, disclosure might mean stating:

> The epidemiological studies indicate, with 80 percent confidence, that a fifty-microgram exposure to xynothalic creostate is no more dangerous than a twenty-microgram exposure. But our survey of the industry suggests that the expected compliance cost per prevented injury is $100,000 at the fifty-microgram level and almost twice that at the twenty-microgram level. Although some rule making comments argue that the added cost is a modest price for the added protection, we interpret the act as affording us discretion to strike a balance between industry costs and worker protection, and we are unwilling to impose the higher costs absent convincing evidence of added benefit.

This hypothetical agency statement is an abbreviated disclosure of certain values or even ideological predispositions. It includes an assertion that such preferences are within statutory bounds. In the same circumstances, another form of politics might be problematic. On the other hand, consider the following:

> The act does not specify criteria by which the secretary is to select the thirty-five demonstration sites for the experimental housing program. In addition to considering the various demographic and market factors detailed elsewhere, we have consulted widely in an effort to allow as many interested members of Congress as possible to feel some involvement in shaping the program, including through the participation of their constituents. We have also been mindful of the importance of building a broad base of interest and support within the Congress for programs of the department.

This statement confesses that there was more to the decision than a computer formula and implicitly claims that the statute permits the strong (electoral) version of politics. The importance and feasibility of required disclosure is underscored by the variety in forms of the paradigm.[35] Rather than a presumption rejecting all but the weakest, narrowly cabined expressions of politics, harder-look review avoids such

---

35. Each paradigm has several alternative manifestations. On the problem of deciding when one form rather than another is permissible, *see* secs. 3.1 and 3.2. On the problem of regulating "how much" politics, *see* sec. 6.3.1.(b).

extremes and permits agency and court a realistic and valuable flexibility.

Agencies should be more willing to disclose politics if a reviewing court is likely to credit politics as an acceptable and even desirable element of decision making. Such predictability in judicial response, of course, depends in turn on development of doctrine concerning paradigm mix and quality, as discussed in the next section. It also requires a substantial number of cases that squarely address the politics issues. Only leadership can overcome the chicken-and-egg problem. With such reform of judicial perspective, stretching a thin scientific or legal argument would become a less necessary risk. But what can a court do if the agency neither discloses politics nor stretches its expertise but instead claims that it was indifferent between two factually supportable, statutorily permissible alternatives? The ultimate test is to ask whether the agency would willingly be bound by a coin toss. Only in such a case is there a genuine absence of agency preference based on *something*.[36] Short of this, the court may analyze the claim of nonpolitical indifference as tantamount to an agency "finding" that reliable science can go no further and that positive sources of controlling values (statute, regulations, precedent) are in equipoise. The reviewing court must be persuaded. For its part, the agency's burden of persuasion on these matters is an important problem. That burden must not be so lax as to undermine the goal of harder-look review—that is, effective oversight of paradigm disclosure, mix, and quality.

6.3.1.(b) Paradigm Mix: How Much Politics? Disciplining political considerations, once disclosed, must not mean suppressing them altogether. Doctrine must try to identify when the agency's decision has involved too much,not enough, or flawed politics. Although a full answer to those questions must be sought outside the bounds of a marginal reform agenda, I can suggest some beginnings.

There is "too much" politics when the agency's choice is inconsistent with sound application of the nonpolitical methods. (Note that this is a distinctly marginalist formulation, because it assumes that the basic paradigm distinctions of the trichotomy are compelling.) Traditional hard-look review, as we have seen, includes requirements that agencies give detailed explanations, allow broad participation, explain departures from precedent, and give adequate consideration to key alterna-

36. My colleague Professor David Shapiro suggested this device, only partly in jest. Perhaps doctrine could require that agencies send their counsel to court with a fair coin? One might well argue, though, that random official choice should only in the rarest circumstances displace ratiocination. Complex policy judgments are always, by definition, amenable to further analysis.

tives. These can be largely interpreted as a judicial invention to calibrate the mix of paradigms, and especially the relation between pluralist politics and policy science. It is not, however, a successful invention: at one extreme, courts remain free to discover questions of law or external standards of expertise and adopt an interventionist posture; at the other extreme, courts are free to discover broad policy discretion deserving deference. The effect is to make hard-look review merely one option along a continuum of deference rather than a coherent approach to scope of review in its own right. The specific element of this shortcoming most important for the present discussion is the ambivalence toward politics, even within hard-look review. Thus, the citations accompanying my exposition (section 6.1) of the politics puzzle include many cases from the hard-look era.

It might be contended that within the hard-look model the proper role for politics is to fill gaps in the matrix of legislated values controlling agency discretion, and as to this gap-filling, the agency's preferences are controlling. The definition of the gap, however, is a question of law—of discerning the boundary for the agency's domain of policy discretion. I explored, in chapter 4, how categorization problems of the trichotomy make this approach a very weak form of doctrinal discipline, so that recent cases present a range of independent and deferential judicial approaches to questions of law. Indeed, the modus operandi of hard-look review is precisely to exploit the categorization problem by stressing questions of law and factual sufficiency in order to squeeze the less reviewable political, discretionary elements out of the problem. Hard-look review is largely designed to repress rather than accommodate politics. This view contrasts with commentators who have urged that hard-look review somewhat reflects the importance of interest group pluralism in that competing arguments must be seriously considered. To the extent that hard-look cases reflect both impulses— both repressing and effectuating pluralist politics—they do so as a result of the attributive duality discussed in chapter 2; this ambivalent treatment of politics underscores the importance of trichotomy-based reasoning at the core of hard-look doctrine. (Of course, the other important piece of the problem is that a court may or may not decide to invoke hard-look review. See section 4.2.)

The dominant theme of case law, however, is clearly that hard-look review provides a means of cabining political discretion and permitting judges, if so disposed, to impose arbitrarily stringent standards of comprehensive rationality. As Cass Sunstein has put it,

> What do the courts—and to some degree Congress and administrative agencies—hope to accomplish with these procedural

safeguards? . . . Reviewing courts are attempting to ensure that the agency has not merely responded to political pressure but that it is instead deliberating in order to identify and implement the public values that should control the controversy. A principal concern is that without the procedural and substantive requirements of the hard-look doctrine, the governing values may be subverted in the enforcement [implementation] process through the domination of powerful private groups.[37]

In contrast to this, the harder-look review sketched in this chapter does *not* mean that the agency action must be sustainable on the basis of nonpolitical decision making alone. Rather, the agency's application of politics and preferences to answer questions and fill gaps left open by the other paradigms should be explicit rather than assumed, and it should be accepted by the court (subject to policing the mix and quality of paradigms, as discussed below). Politics would not justify ignoring evidence contrary to the administrator's preferences. But politics should be permitted, for example, as the rational basis for choice among otherwise reasonable alternative constructions of the evidence or as the rational basis for a resource allocation decision concerning the desirability of further research. If the evidence and adjudicatory fairness support either X or Y, it would be too much politics to allow politics to dictate result Z. This is a principle designed to minimize the effects of the negative attributes of politics. It is a formula consistent with Justice Rehnquist's in *State Farm:* inasmuch as he accepts the scientific rationality of a choice in either direction with respect to detachable automatic seat belts, politics may tip the scale. The difficulty with this approach, however, is that Justice Rehnquist did not demand that the agency expressly disclose its reliance on politics, as my preceding point on disclosure would require.

Relatedly, the possibility of too little politics arises when other methods do not determine a choice between alternatives, so the agency might decide:

1. by casuist distortion of science to produce, by subterfuge, an "expert" answer;

2. by casuist distortion of the statute to pretend that the answer is provided by "law";

3. by flipping a coin;

4. or by deploying political (subjective) considerations.

---

37. Sunstein, *Interest Groups, supra* n. 1 at 63 (footnotes omitted). An excellent example of Congress's procedural activism is, e.g., 42 U.S.C. §§ 7401–7642 (1982) (Clean Air Act).

The first two approaches should be rejected when discerned, and there will be circumstances in which a coin toss is undesirable because the law seems to require the application of reasoned discretion[38] or because the coin toss implausibly presupposes an equipoise of evidence and values. We generally should prefer politics and accept it as a form of rationality. In contrast to a coin toss, political choice involves ratiocination, is subject to persuasion, and if disclosed can be made accountable. There is no point in arguing with dice, but arguing with government is often a positive good. Government should not be able to avoid responsibility for its choices by attributing them to rolls of the dice. This is a principle designed to maximize the positive attributes of politics.

The proposition that politics is preferable to a coin toss does not apply in all contexts. When fundamental interests are at stake, for example, we may prefer random to political selection (although randomness is itself a political choice to reject alternative ordering principles). The military draft is a good example. In many situations, including both the military draft and the allocation of scarce public housing (see Holmes v. New York City Housing Authority, 398 F.2d 262 [2d Cir. 1968]), we may insist that the role of politics and preferences be restricted to general rule-like policy choices rather than individual case decisions. This is another application of the rule making–adjudication distinction and of the trichotomy. In some circumstances randomness is a kind of standard or value. Few unsuccessful conscientious objectors or draft resisters during the Vietnam era would agree that local draft boards were apolitical—even, or perhaps especially, when those boards were relentlessly applying the lottery system.

A related issue is the introduction of market forces as an alternative to command and control regulation. Although not stochastic in the same sense as a series of coin tosses, incentive systems have the advantage of defusing controversy through a seeming dissociation of the governmental decision maker from the policy consequences.[39] There is, however, the severe drawback of impaired accountability.

Superficially, the likelihood of a direct harder-look holding that there has been too little politics seems limited to those rare instances when an agency asserts that its decision is a nonpolitical, indifferent one or is controlled by persuasively conclusive expertise or adjudica-

38. This is a special case of the broader question of when individualized decision making (typically adjudication) is required instead of application of general statements of policy (typically rule making). *See, e.g.*, Asimakopoulos v. INS, 445 F.2d 1362 (9th Cir. 1971) (reversible error for the board to apply a standard effectively precluding the use of individualized discretion contemplated by Congress).

39. *See* Stewart, *The Discontents of Legalism*, 1985 Wis. L. Rev. 655, 683–86.

tory fairness. But in combination with the requirements of disclosure and the threateningly stringent harder-look review of both expert and Rule of Law–fairness conclusions, an agency may be naturally inclined to give freer expression to at least the weak, preference-based form of politics—which the trichotomy's boundary problem tells us is virtually always present. Moreover, the hypothetical disclosure statements in section 6.3.1.(a) are modest and represent a starting point. Only case-by-case evolution will produce workable guidance on disclosure or, ultimately, on the occasions that require more politics. This is precisely the process through which courts continue to develop such quasi-procedural requirements as reasons and findings.

The incremental reform of pressing courts in certain respects to acknowledge politics, though worthwhile, is necessarily limited because it is still within the problematic framework of the trichotomy. Specifically, the possibility of satisfactorily regulating the mix of politics and other decision making methods is crucially complicated by the categorization problem—the tendency for law, politics, and science to become indistinct. "How much" is a strange question to ask, when there are such considerable problems of description and measurement.

Less troubling is the superficial similarity between this approach to paradigm mix and cases that accord great judicial deference to any reasonable agency choice, requiring that it be within a permissible range fenced in by the organic statute and the evidence. It differs in two significant respects. First, by providing a legitimate role for politics in both making and explaining a decision, the agency and court are relieved of pressure to distort the role of the science and fairness paradigms. This is analogous to Professor Jaffe's helpful insistence that agency and court share responsibility for deciding questions of law, so that the fact-law distinction need not bear the full weight of role allocation in every scope of review inquiry. In particular, this should reduce the considerable pressure to manipulate the permissible range analysis by shifting the boundaries of agency discretion through exploitation of the trichotomy's failings. Second, this modest reform begins to provide affirmative content to the test of reasonable agency discretion: politics is a presumptively appropriate method of decision. There remains the question of whether the method is well executed.

6.3.1.(c) Quality Control: Good Politics. Reformed doctrine must do more than force disclosure of politics and loosely regulate the mix of political and nonpolitical decision making paradigms, however tentatively. Because administrative government reaches everywhere and the paradigm is variegated, some political processes will be more likely than others to embody the positive attributes like representativeness and accountability that make us more willing to tolerate political methods of choice or even demand them. So doctrine should also undertake to distinguish successful and unsuccessful applications of the political paradigm.[40]

If an agency's policy analysis excludes consideration of a key scientific study, the reviewing court may reverse on either of two grounds. Using a quasi-procedural formula, the court may say the statement of reasons and findings was inadequate because it failed to explain the agency's reaction to an important issue. Alternatively, the court may say the agency's reasoning was substantively unsound under the arbitrary and capricious test. (The APA applies the "substantial evidence" test for judicial review of formal agency proceedings.) The ease of flipping between the two alternative grounds—inadequate explanation versus unsound reasoning—is just symptomatic of the boundary problem between procedure and substance.

A parallel analysis is possible with respect to the political paradigm of decision making. Doctrines of standing, which we might label quasi-procedural, play a limited and ultimately inadequate role in assuring some access to agency decisional processes for affected interests. The chief difficulties are that (1) access does not guarantee a genuine hearing, (2) access can be costly and impractical for many interests, and (3) it is sometimes unclear precisely which interests should indeed be involved.[41] This last problem, identifying the groups deserving of representation, is a key obstacle to elevating the procedural and substantive enforcement of good politics to an affirmative area of judicial attention. Yet courts have increasingly been willing to engage in the scientific analogue—evaluating the claims of affected interests that a particular alternative or scientific study was ignored or too lightly considered by the agency.[42] Earlier protests that such searching, substantive judicial review would prove unworkable[43] (even at the modest levels we

40. Again, this is from the reformist perspective. A more radical formulation would include thoroughgoing skepticism about the possibility of eliminating the negative attributes. The attributive duality, like the yin and yang of Chinese cosmology, is an inevitable feature of politics, so that *purely* "good" politics is impossible in an epistemological, not merely practical, sense. *See* sec. 3.2. *See also* sec. 3.2.3, on the proposition that this duality is simply a special case of the pro-and-con structure of many forms of reasoning.

41. *See* Stewart, *The Reformation of American Administrative Law*, 88 Harv. L. Rev. 1734–47, 1802–4 (1975).

42. *See generally* Garland, *Deregulation and Judicial Review*, 98 Harv. L. Rev. 525–42 (1985); Stewart, *supra* n. 41 at 1757–60. Stewart links the procedural analysis of participation with the substantive analysis of adequate consideration.

43. For example, Judge Bazelon, in exchanges with Judge Leventhal, argued against substantive judicial review, claiming that the court's emphasis belonged on agen-

see) have proven unwarranted, in my view.[44] So, too, judicial attention to the list of participants in the agency's political process is conceivable over a broad range of actions, if not everywhere.

Perhaps, for example, an agency implementing a new statute decides to meet with certain interest groups and sponsors of the legislation to ensure that implementation choices closely track their policy preferences. A court might welcome such a process as justifying substantial judicial deference to the resulting agency decisions. But a court could insist as the price for deference that the agency include in those discussions other legislators and interest groups whose views were part of the political stew that generated the statute. To the extent that deference is justified because the administrative process is a continuation of the politics of legislation, the court can act to assure some fidelity in the imitation. Linkage to a specific legislative saga would structure

---

cy procedures. In International Harvester Co. v. Ruckelshaus, 478 F.2d 615 (D.C. Cir. 1973), Bazelon concurred in the court's decision to vacate and remand an EPA decision denying a one-year suspension of Clean Air Act emissions standards but castigated the court for its substantive approach: "Socrates said that wisdom is the recognition of how much one does not know . . . . I recognize that I do not know enough about dynamometer extrapolations, deterioration factor adjustments and the like to decide whether or not the government's approach to these matters was statistically valid . . . . [I]n cases of great technological complexity, the best way for courts to guard against unreasonable or erroneous administrative decisions is not for the judges themselves to scrutinize the technical merits of each decision. Rather, it is to establish a decision-making process which assures a reasoned decision." *Id.* at 650–52 (footnote omitted). And in Ethyl Corp. v. EPA, 541 F.2d 1 (D.C. Cir. 1976) (en banc), Bazelon continued his criticism of substantive review, contending that "substantive review of mathematical and scientific evidence by technically illiterate judges is dangerously unreliable." *Id.* at 67.

According to Garland, at this time the Court's application of substantive review was "extremely narrow"; it upheld any not "wholly irrational" agency action. *Supra* n. 42 at 532. *But see* Citizens to Preserve Overton Park, Inc. v. Volpe, 401 U.S. 402 (1971). *See also* Allen, Panel IV, Judicial Review of Agency Action, 26 Admin. L. Rev. 545, 562–63 (1974) (warning that rigorous application of substantive arbitrary and capricious standard "may obscure the real nature of issues in some cases").

44. Though the Supreme Court limited judicially fashioned procedural inventions as a route to sound decision making in Vermont Yankee Nuclear Power Corp. v. NRDC, 435 U.S. 519 (1978), it endorsed and applied searching substantive review in State Farm, 463 U.S. 29 (1983), and American Textile Workers, 452 U.S. 490 (1981). Not only has substantive review proven to be workable, *see generally* Byse, *Judicial Review of Informal Rulemaking*, 33 Admin. L. Rev. 183 (1981); Cooke, *An Evolving Model for Judicial Review of Environmental, Safety and Health Rulemaking*, 33 Cath. U. L. Rev. 1027 (1984), it has proven *invaluable* to reviewing courts concerned with deregulation and fidelity to legislative purpose. But see my conceptual critique of scope of review principles based on legislative purpose in sec. 5.1. In fact, given Judge Bazelon's opinion in NRDC v. NRC, 685 F.2d 459 (D.C. Cir. 1982), *reversed*, 462 U.S. 89 (1983), even he may have come to accept substantive review. In dissent, Judge Wilkey accused Bazelon of "stepping boldly into the arena of nuclear regulation" and creating "a novel standard of *substantive* and procedural scrutiny of NRC activity which we as a court are . . . ill-equipped to manage." *Id.* at 517 (emphasis added).

judgments concerning the minimal participatory elements of agency politics, because official and unofficial history of the legislation would be adequate to permit reasoned decision as to which interests and arguments were of major concern to legislators.

As another example, if the judgments of a commission in certain matters are admittedly controversial and political, then a reviewing court might consider it a plus that the membership of the commission represents varying political perspectives or a minus that one party or one ideology has been able to dominate the decision without apparent concern for compromise. In this view, a sharply divided NLRB or FTC, though perhaps problematic for the agency's image of expertise, strengthens the impression of thorough efforts to consider competing interest group claims.

In short, failure to include key groups in a bargaining process should be considered a substantial and substantive flaw in the agency's political decision making, not merely a question of standing.[45] The agency's overall claim for deference is weakened to the extent that deference might have been based on the proper execution of the politics paradigm. The judgments underlying determinations of this sort are admittedly in major respects unfamiliar terrain for judicial discourse, and as a consequence evaluative guide posts are thinly scattered. It is perhaps reaching a bit to include this topic in a chapter on incrementalism. I will return to it later. In particular, as I sketch in chapter 7, assessing the quality of politics is at least implicit when judges decide issues of intervention and party structure in complex class actions, and especially in adding elements of participation to the remedial process in structural injunction and institutional reform litigation.

6.4 An Application: Harder-Look Review of Deregulation and Policy Shifts

6.4.1 Paradigm Disclosure, Mix, and Quality

I now return to the primary example of policy shifts and deregulation discussed in section 6.1.4 and suggest briefly how the reasoning in

---

45. The burden of demonstrating that the agency has involved all relevant interests could be placed on either party. There is a comparable puzzle regarding burden of proof when the question is whether the agency has considered all relevant alternatives. It appears that the petitioning party has a burden of production and must make a threshold prima facie case that the alternative is significant and was not well considered. Ultimately, however, the agency-proponent of a rule or order has to persuade the court that the policy satisfies the substantive test of soundness implied by the scope of review. APA § 556(d).

some typical decision might be altered as a result of marginal reforms that would increase judicial attentiveness to the disclosure, mix, and quality of politics in agency decision making.

Disclosure: In the context of administrative deregulation, it seems unarguable that disclosure of ideological or value premises will help explain the agency's approach to uncertainty: *Will* broadcasters be flexible in shifting format to respond to the preferences of a minority of listeners? *Will* oil pipeline companies feel intermodal competitive pressures sufficient to keep rates "reasonable"? *Is* the risk of exposure to ethylene oxide "significant"?[46] By inviting and pressing for disclosure of political preferences, courts would be more likely to discern the fair limits of scientific explanation on the one hand and policy judgment on the other. An OSHA statement that available evidence does not demonstrate a "significant risk" of harm may, by invoking apparent expertise, prevent a court from probing to test the scientific bases for the decision. But the same agency statement will also invite pointed contrary assertions of scientific "fact," and the reviewing court *might* (we have learned that one cannot be sure) use hard-look review and conclude that the expert basis for OSHA's choice is unpersuasive. Failure to disclose can misdirect the court's attention to assessment of a methodology that is not, and need not be, the principal basis for the agency decision. By contrast, disclosure of the agency's essentially political judgment about risks, uncertainty, and burdens of persuasion would, within the trichotomy, probably be approached by a court on a wholly different basis. The court would ask whether politics bulks too large in the decision relative to contributions from other paradigms. But having disclosed the role of politics, OSHA would also have the opportunity to defend the particular mix of methodologies it has used in interpreting and applying the "substantial risk" test, and litigants could disagree. The court would not be left entirely on its own to gauge the appropriate mix of politics, science, and adjudicatory fairness.

In particular, the court and parties would be drawn to the heart of the matter in such doctrinal areas as official notice and scope of review for predictive (legislative) facts: Is it reasonable under all of the circumstances to expect the agency to develop more scientific or other evidence to support its decision, or should the court acknowledge that enough groundwork has been done to permit the play of political

---

46. FCC v. WNCN Listeners Guild, 450 U.S. 582 (1981); Farmers Union Cent. Exch. v. FERC, 584 F.2d 408 (D.C. Cir. 1978); Public Citizen Health Research Group v. Auchter, 702 F.2d 1150 (D.C. Cir. 1983) (*reversing* 554 F. Supp. 242 (D.D.C.); Public Citizen Health Research Group v. Rowland, Industrial Union Dep't v. American Petroleum Inst. (*Benzene*), 448 U.S. 697 (1980).

preferences and judgments? And are those political preferences honestly consistent with the statutory delegation and with the evidence at hand? That is, the agency may express and defend a preference to avoid costly regulation absent compelling proof of risk. The court may then counter, concluding that the "compelling" test is too stringent in view of congressional intent[47] and that the agency is unreasonable to insist on more than four epidemiological studies. In this way, the court and agency are engaged in a dialogue about whether and how the political discretion to avoid costly regulation is constrained by law and science.

The advantages of this approach to administrative discretion result from fairer characterization of what is truly at stake. There must be some scope for the agency's political attitudes about costly regulation. It is both realistic and desirable to expect agencies, with judicial prodding if necessary, to put these attitudes on the table for public scrutiny and the resulting accountability rather than bury them in scientific jargon about experimental methodology. Judges can and should be reasonably respectful of revealed political attitudes no less than they are of fairly disclosed and adequately defended agency reliance on the paradigms of adjudicatory fairness and expertise. Indeed, judicial intervention to displace choices that the agency labels *law* or *science* may be less controversial than intervention to stem confessedly value-based policy shifts. Therefore, judicial respect for political choices may be more likely if the politics is disclosed.

The variegated character of politics is again relevant. If strong versions of politics, such as electoral pandering or legislative logrolling, are *inappropriately* commonplace in agency decision making, then agencies will be unlikely to readily confess their true bases for decision. There are three responses to this. First, disclosure of inappropriate politics is certainly no less likely under a regime of harder-look review than under current doctrine. Second, only through disclosure can the several institutions and the public begin the debate about what might be appropriate in different settings. Third, I do not believe, based on my experience and study, that highly questionable politics is as common in government as detractors might imagine. Problems of questionable expertise are far greater. Fourth, the realistic accommodation of many forms of politics under harder-look review

47. Of course, the usefulness of legislative history is limited. The point is not that such history will be determinative or that it will constrain judicial discretion. The congressional debate may, however, cast light on the problem of discretionary policy shifts in a way that, though not clear enough to be controlling, will educate the agency and court as to the relevant considerations so that the judgment will be more sound.

will serve as an invitation to decision makers to focus carefully on their use of politics paradigm and their integration of it with science and adjudicatory fairness. I have discussed categorization problems and attributive duality primarily from the perspective of judges. The same descriptive and conceptual issues operate at the level of senior agency officials reviewing the work of subordinates. Thus, many decision makers will be educated and engaged by a draft preamble to a regulation that confesses the subjective, value-laden character of a choice of scientific methodology which that lay official—like a judge exercising deferential review—might otherwise have thought off limits. So, within the bureaucracy, disclosure may improve decision making.[48]

Paradigm Mix: Much of what might be said concerning too much or too little politics has been covered immediately above and in the preceding section. Doctrinal attention to disclosure and mix would also serve well in addressing policy shifts traceable to new personnel, as when the NLRB or FTC changes course because of new members. There is, as above, the basic question of the legitimate scope for political preferences or attitudes in the agency policy at issue; there may be special questions concerning the need for policy stability[49] (in the contemplation of the statute) and the extent to which the particular policy is or reasonably should be grounded in factual determinations. Without any review of the disclosure and mix of politics underlying an NLRB flip-flop, for example, it is wrong for a court to defer on the basis of expertise or policy discretion; but it is also wrong to *intervene* on the basis of a hard-look review that unmasks deficient expertise and unfairly inconsistent policy discretion, since those may not have been the actual or appropriate methods of agency decision.

In these various settings, from review of NLRB reversals to economic deregulation, courts could develop a variety of specific tools to help assess the adequacy of political disclosure and mix. For example, the question of mix should rest in part on a comparison with the mixes of decision making paradigms employed in similar administrative settings, including that agency's prior decisions in the area. If prior regulatory concessions to industry compliance costs have always rested on at least two broad-based empirical studies, it would be sensible for the court to insist on an explanation as to why a comparably important role for empiricism is no longer appropriate. Conversely, if prior policy flip-flops have occurred because of partisan changes in commission

48. *See also* the discussion of bureaucratic rationality, at sec. 2.5.2.

49. This is a consideration also identified by Colin Diver as being relevant to the agency's choice between incremental and synoptic approaches to policy analysis. Diver, *supra* n. 31.

membership, that suggests that today's similarly explainable shift should be acceptable on the same basis.

Paradigm Quality: By analyzing analogous agency decisions and relevant legislative processes, courts would also be able to assemble information necessary to make some basic judgments about "good" politics. As the court monitors the agency's discretionary judgment to see whether an appropriately broad range of views have been heard, it can inventory the various interests involved in the enactment of the Occupational Safety and Health Act, the interests represented at oversight and appropriations hearings, and even the groups regularly involved in litigation with the agency. If policy shifts appear to have been deaf to objections—even nonscientific objections—then deference would be inappropriate. Specifically, in regulating ethylene oxide, the substance at issue in *Public Citizen Health Research Group v. Rowland,* the plaintiff's objections to OMB interference and to OSHA unwillingness to regulate short-term exposures to hospital workers should have increased weight because the rule making record indicates little direct involvement of worker representatives or scientists advocating those interests in the discretionary deliberations concerning methodology and risk assessment. The same can be said of the FTC shift in regulation of deceptive advertising: To the extent that the shift appears to be the result of a raw assertion of partisan power made possible by a tip in commission composition (which it does) rather than the product of broader dialogue and quasi-legislative efforts to develop consensus, the reviewing court should doubt the quality of the political process; deference would have to be based on some other rationale. Crucial to this conclusion, however, is a judgment about which of several forms of politics might be appropriate in the decision to remake the regulatory law of deceptive advertising. My own instincts are that partisan shifts, where there is no plausible claim of specific electoral mandate, are less legitimate in this arena than would be a quasi-legislative shift accomplished through the broad-based participatory mechanisms of informal rule making or regulatory negotiation. To accomplish the shift through case-by-case adjudication in which ideological preferences were undisclosed and thinly disguised as novel statutory interpretation makes matters even worse.

So, whether or not "the law" permits a given agency choice, and apart from questioning the methodological soundness of the underlying science, there is important room for agency, court, and public to consider the clarity of an electoral mandate or the inclusiveness of a bargaining process. And although appraising an electoral mandate would be crude (a big campaign issue, versus not so clearly a big issue), courts regularly attempt to decide whether the legislature considered a specific problem. One should not assume that the two sorts of inquiry are essentially different just because statutory interpretation has the trappings of formality provided by extremely incomplete official documents containing staged evidence of deliberation.

6.4.2 The Connection with Political Bias

None of this effort to police policy shifts should gainsay the inevitable injection of personal and partisan preferences. We must take as given both human nature and the particular institutional arrangements Congress has chosen for, say, the FTC.[50] The question is whether and how such political influences should and can be limited. In such cases as *Association of National Advertisers v. FTC*,[51] in which the industry alleged impermissible bias of Chairman Pertschuk, or in a hypothetical challenge to the commission's recently revised enforcement policy regarding misleading advertising, the court is faced squarely with the problem of accommodating politics with the other paradigms: as to adjudicatory fairness, one worries that personal preferences will interfere with neutrality in finding facts, with consistency in comparison to other cases, and with fidelity in interpreting the statute; as to expertise, one worries about objectivity in measuring and weighing consumer and industry impacts, and rationality in assessing uncertainties and risks. On reflection, however, this elaboration of why politics is worrisome suggests that each mechanism of corruption could be effectively policed by a rigorous "reasonableness" review. That necessary rigor will not be forthcoming if the court is blinded by trichotomy-based deference to agency interpretations and findings. One possibility for doctrinal reform, therefore, is to reduce judicial distrust of politics and potential bias while increasing the effectiveness of reasonableness review. Harder-look review makes political corruption of the other paradigms less worrisome, both because paradigm quality is rigorously reviewed and because confessed politics is granted a legitimate role in agency choice.

Other reforms come to mind, based on our study of the trichotomy. Case law now distinguishes between rule making proceedings predominantly directed toward the development of general principles of

50. *See* United Farm Workers of America v. Arizona Agric. Employment Relations Bd., 727 F.2d 1475 (9th Cir. 1984) (rejecting due process challenge to facial validity of statute mandating that state labor board be composed of two employer representatives, two employee representatives, and three general public representatives).

51. 627 F.2d 1151 (D.C. Cir. 1979), *cert. denied*, 447 U.S. 921 (1980).

law and policy and adjudicatory proceedings thought to be essentially exercises of law application and fact determination. In rule making, as the court indicated in the Pertschuk disqualification case, the play of personal and partisan preferences is allowed broader scope, the ultimate check being electoral.

There are several significant opportunities for incremental reform here. First, in view of the trichotomy-related problems arising in the distinction and choice between rule making and adjudication, courts should base their assessment of alleged bias not on the form of the agency action but on a functional appraisal of the issues at stake. Second, again, is disclosure of partisan and personal preferences. Disclosure will facilitate that appraisal.

Davis's distinction between adjudicative and legislative facts is relevant. Although his distinction is flawed because it relies on the trichotomy in much the same way as the distinction between rule making and adjudication as procedural forms,[52] it is an incremental improvement over the coarser rule making–adjudication categories because it invites courts to attempt some appraisal of the practical significance of the decision maker's prejudgment or predisposition. Tolerance for political motives should not be a function of the mere *form* of the agency procedure: the FTC and NLRB, for example, routinely attempt sweeping policy changes through adjudications; the EPA and ICC routinely exert focused control over one of a small number of affected interests through quasi-legislative rule makings. Present doctrine leaves the choice between rule making and adjudication to the virtually unfettered discretion of the agency. Although courts do occasionally intervene to overturn such choices, as when an agency uses adjudication to impose retroactively some wholly new duty and accompanying liabilities, thereby altering "preexisting legal relationships,"[53] a far

52. Davis, 3 Treatise §§ 15.2–5, 138–53 (1980). Several scholars have criticized the Davis formulation. *See, e.g.,* Nathanson, 70 Yale L.J. 1210–14 (1961) (book review of Davis, Treatise); Robinson, *The Making of Administrative Policy: Another Look at Rulemaking and Adjudication and Administrative Procedure Reform,* 118 U. Pa. L. Rev. 485, 503–6 (1970).

53. *See* First Bancorporation v. Board of Governors of the Fed. Reserve Sys., 728 F.2d 434, 438 (10th Cir. 1984) ("Board abused its discretion by improperly attempting to propose legislative policy by an adjudicative order" where its factual conclusions concerned policy objectives and not the parties before it); Ford Motor Co. v. FTC, 673 F.2d 1008, 1010 (9th Cir. 1982) ("agency must proceed by rulemaking if it seeks to change the law and establish rules of widespread application"); Ruangswang v. INS, 591 F.2d 39, 46 (9th Cir. 1978) (abuse to develop new policies concerning exemption from labor certification through adjudication); Sheet Metal Workers' Int'l Ass'n v. NLRB, 716 F.2d 1249, 1257–58 (accepting agency choice of adjudication and distinguishing cases that have rejected agency's choice). A related category of cases involves eligibility standards for benefit programs. *See* Morton v. Ruiz, 415 U.S. 199 (1974) (agency could not an-

more aggressive posture seems desirable in view of the opportunities for improper political motive in the selection of policymaking procedures.[54] This procedural discretion makes it all the more important not to base the dimensions of the bias inquiry on the rule making–adjudication distinction.

For example, in an FTC decision involving antitrust policy, such as the famous *Pillsbury* case,[55] political pressure and policy prejudgment are probably no more important than in a proceeding to develop advertising restrictions for children's television,[56] even though the former is adjudication and the latter rule making. If it ignored the form of agency action, the court could address directly the appropriate mix of paradigms and the character of the politics underlying the alleged bias or prejudgment.

Incremental reforms such as these do not attempt some definitive balance or delimitation of politics vis--vis alternative decision making methods. The earlier analysis of the trichotomy's failings showed that to unattainable. My more modest ambition is to promote forthright articulation of the true bases for agency choice, so as to deter misexecution and permit frank appraisal, by the public, of the quality and character of political processes and ideologies.

6.5 Two Other Puzzles: Accommodation of Scientific Uncertainty and the Construction of Procedural Norms

Having discussed incremental doctrinal reforms to promote the sound accommodation of politics with administrative law, for the sake of symmetry I briefly address the comparably pervasive puzzles suggested by

nounce policy for classification in distributing Snyder Act benefits to American Indians through adjudication); Matzke v. Block, 732 F.2d 799 (10th Cir. 1984) (requiring rule making to establish eligibility criteria for discretionary farm debt relief).

54. Perhaps, for example, the failure to promulgate eligibility regulations in the Farm Foreclosure Cases was the product of administration hostility toward the program rather than some more legitimate "expert" calculus comparing the efficiency of general versus case-by-case decision. *See* Matzke v. Block, *supra* n. 53.

55. Pillsbury Co. v. FTC, 354 F.2d 952 (5th Cir. 1966) (holding that congressional pressure was impermissible). *See also* D.C. Federation of Civil Ass'ns v. Volpe, 459 F.2d 1231 (D.C. Cir. 1971) (congressional pressure concerning construction of bridge held to have tainted informal adjudication awarding bridge funds). Of course, bias cases can also be decided by concluding that the agency used impermissible, extrastatutory factors. *Id.* at 1247–49. The availability of this alternative characterization seems related to the distinction between considerations (law) and their weights (preferences)—in short, the law-politics boundary problem.

56. *National Advertisers*, 627 F.2d at 1127.

the two other decision making paradigms: the accommodation of scientific uncertainty and the appropriate construction of methodological or procedural norms generally. I treat the two in tandem in an effort to emphasize the disutility of the distinction between substance and procedure.

6.5.1 The Puzzles Described

In earlier sections I have offered examples of scientific and social scientific uncertainty involving several agencies, including OSHA,[57] the FCC,[58] FERC,[59] and the EPA.[60] The straw man statement of deference to administrative and scientific expertise would be that the court must remain agnostic as to how "good" policy analysis and scientific analysis are performed and as to what decision making procedures—negotiation, trial-type hearings, ex parte investigations, and so on—are best suited to the task at hand. Although one can find judicial statements this flat, the core of doctrine is less extreme. The agency's methodological choices within the paradigm of scientific expertise are always at issue, at least implicitly, in judicial review under the hard-look, substantial evidence, and arbitrary-or-capricious formulations; how else could a court assess rationality? As for discretionary procedural choices (for example, the extent of oral hearings in formal rule making), we can consider these the analogue within an adjudicatory fairness paradigm of the choices of method and experiment protocol faced within the science paradigm.[61] Even the Supreme Court's broad

57. The cases I have discussed include regulation of asbestos in Industrial Union Dep't, AFL-CIO v. Hodgson, 499 F.2d 467 (D.C. Cir. 1974); benzene in Industrial Union Dep't v. American Petroleum Inst., 448 U.S. 607 (1980); cotton dust in American Textile Mfrs. Inst., Inc. v. Donovan, 452 U.S. 490 (1981); and ethylene oxide in Public Citizen Health Research Group v. Auchter, 702 F.2d 1150 (D.C. Cir. 1983).

58. The key examples have been prediction of broadcaster response to listener preferences, at issue in FCC v. WNCN Listeners Guild, 450 U.S. 582 (1981) and anticompetitive market forces at issue in the trucking cases in sec. 4.4.3.

59. Farmers Union Cent. Exch. v. FERC, 734 F.2d 1486 (D.C. Cir. 1984) (strength of competitive forces in assuring just and reasonable unregulated oil pipeline prices).

60. My examples have included DDT in EDF v. Ruckelshaus, 439 F.2d 584 (D.C. Cir. 1971), and Nor-Am Agric. Prod., Inc. v. Hardin, 435 F.2d 1151 (7th Cir. 1970 (en banc), and pollution from coal-fired utility plants in Sierra Club v. Costle, 657 F.2d 298 (D.C. Cir. 1981).

61. Recall that my reference to adjudicatory fairness has nothing to do with the matter of whether the agency action is rule making or adjudication. The paradigm is constructed of a set of decision making norms or attributes and characteristic methods: neutral decision maker; consistency over time and across similar cases; fidelity to established standards, rules, or statutes; reasoned elaboration; etc. *See* sec. 2.1.

injunction in *Vermont Yankee* against judicial interventionism in this sphere was tempered by qualifications relating to constitutional due process and "extraordinary circumstances."[62] More important, courts remain free to address their concerns about the adequacy of decision making procedures indirectly—one might call it subterfuge—using heightened forms of substantive and quasi-procedural review, especially requirements of express evaluation of policy alternatives and detailed reasons and findings.[63] But *Vermont Yankee* has left us with a *doctrinal* world in which deference to expertise inhibits a court from requiring that the agency employ some species of cost-benefit analysis or some particular statistical technique; and deference to the agency's autonomous construction of procedure inhibits a court from requiring that it use rule making rather than adjudication, or that it use cross-examination to force a confrontation between disagreeing scientific experts.

This state of affairs is as lamentable as judicial irresolution with respect to politics. Returning to the trichotomy, judicial failure to identify and evaluate the agency's methodological choices generates:

Descriptive problems of diagnosing misexecution of the decision making paradigm. In the *Cotton Dust* case, OSHA argued that methodological flaws in its study of industry compliance costs were balanced by other flaws in the agency analysis;[64] Justice Stewart dissented, saying that this was "unproven."[65] Maybe Stewart was right, maybe he wasn't; we cannot tell.[66] Without a judicial willingness to confront the problem and avoid excessive obeisance to expertise, agencies will not be forced to make such crucial decisions with defensible rigor.

Boundary problems of distinguishing the paradigms, leading especially to the problem of political discretion hiding under a cloak of expertise—as in OSHA's choice of a particular form of risk assessment

62. Vermont Yankee Nuclear Power Corp. v. NRDC, 435 U.S. 519, 543 (1978).

63. *State Farm*, 463 U.S. at 50–51 (*Vermont Yankee* does not preclude remand to consider relevant alternatives); *see also* Garland, *supra* n. 42 at 528–31.

64. *American Textile Mfrs.*, 452 U.S. at 522–30 (study adopted by agency predicted compliance costs based on less stringent standard than the one actually promulgated, yet agency asserted any underestimate was roughly equaled by four independent reasons that made the study an overestimate).

65. *Id.* at 542–43 ("[I]n a remarkable non-sequitur, the agency decided that because the . . . study was an over-estimate of the cost of a less stringent standard, it could be treated as a reliable estimate for the more costly final standard actually promulgated, never rationally explaining how it came to this happy conclusion. This is not substantial evidence. It is unsupported speculation").

66. One study of implementation costs after adoption of the cotton dust standard indicated that OSHA's cost estimates had, in fact, been quite generous from the industry perspective.

rather than some species of cost-benefit analysis; or NHTSA's concern with consumer resistance to passive restraints and its decisions about whether and how to use data from surveys and experiments.

Normative problems, especially in the failure to attend adequately to the negative attributes of expertise and the positive attributes of adjudicatory fairness, leading courts to undervalue the bad consequences of bad methodology and thus to be excessively deferential.

The dangers created by blindness to methodological dilemmas increase as the business of government grows more complicated and the putative claims by all forms of expertise become more grasping. Discretion of ever-increasing moment will be exercised beyond a bank of fog created by cautious judicial deference to the methodological and procedural autonomy of administrators. Our analysis of the trichotomy serves to warn that everything important in an administrative decision can be subsumed into presumptively immune choices of scientific method or public participation. So, the alternative to reforming this deference is, in significant respects, judicial abdication of even the most conventional of administrative law tasks.

6.5.2 Some Reformist Suggestions: Disclosure, Reasoned Choice, and Generalized Balancing

Without abandoning separation of powers ethos, incremental reforms nevertheless seem possible.

Disclosure and Reasoned Choice: Paralleling the analysis of politics, courts should treat methodological choices in much the same way that they now use hard-look review to expose substantive policy alternatives and to demand reasoned evaluation of those alternatives. Thus, an agency decision to reject risk assessment studies because of methodological flaws should not be blindly accepted by a court on the basis of deference to expertise.[67] The agency should be expected to explain why the flaw is so serious that the study should be dismissed altogether and how better data might reasonably be available. To put my analytical point in the extreme, a decision about additional research may be

---

67. This is what the Supreme Court did in accepting the study adopted by OSHA as substantial evidence in *American Textile Mfrs.:* "[T]he agency's candor in confessing its own inability to achieve a more precise estimate (of industry compliance costs) should not precipitate a judicial review that nonetheless demands what the congressionally-delegated *expert* says it cannot provide." 452 U.S. at 528 n. 52 (emphasis added). The Court did temper this statement, however, by reference to the wide margin of error apparent in every available study. *Id.*

amenable to cost-benefit analysis, as one means of reasoned choice. Similarly, an agency refusal to allow plaintiff's consultants to confront and debate agency experts, whether in the context of a trial-type hearing or in some less elaborate forum, should be explained and justified. The present unfortunate pattern is to accept unsubstantiated, unanalyzed agency invocations, often post hoc, of managerial efficiency; equally problematic are instances where agencies uncritically accept industry risk assessments or cost-benefit analyses.

My goal here is not simply to sacrifice more trees to the printing presses at the *Federal Register*. Even if courts, in this context of incremental reform, are reluctant to be bold in imposing procedural and methodological norms on administrative agencies (see below), disclosure has considerable value. As with the more conventionally "substantive" matters involved in administrative policy, courts frequently insist on explanation, even when the ultimate scope of review is deferential. There is some justified faith in the rationalizing force of reasoned elaboration, and additional faith in the constraining force of public scrutiny. The potential in these respects seems just as great in the netherworlds of methodology as in the more familiar realms of policy and doctrinal conflict.[68]

Generalizing Mathews v. Eldridge: Having pressed for disclosure, I think still more gain could be had by imposing some weak standards of rational choice. The agency should not pick procedures by mere habit or chance.[69] It is an important matter to be approached in a disciplined manner. What reasons and findings should a court expect from the agency regarding choices of scientific method and decision making procedure?

The most thoroughly developed judicial norms about methodological design are in the procedural due process field. In *Mathews v. Eldridge* the Supreme Court identified three factors to be used in eval-

68. This much at least is implicit in such cases as Batterton v. Marshall, 648 F.2d 694 (D.C. Cir. 1980), and its progeny, where the court requires notice and comment rule making for certain changes in agency methodology or procedure.

69. *Compare* my earlier suggestion that the agency should be required to explain a deviation from its established scientific methodology. My argument now that the agency's procedural habits be subjected to questioning is consistent in that my concern in both settings is with opening up subtle agency decisions to rational inquiry. This is not to say that the old adjudicatory procedure was necessarily bad and the old scientific procedure good. Some slight presumption for precedent is practical, fair, and understandable. But where a serious challenge is offered, where the soundness of past practice is put at issue, inquiry cannot be cut off merely by citing custom or by saying that the agency is somehow entitled to have its way, whether or not substantively defensible. In my earlier example, the challenge to custom was by the agency; in the present example it is by the party seeking more procedural protections. It makes no difference.

uating additional procedural formality: the nature and weight of the public and private interests at stake; the incremental change in risk of an erroneous decision; and the incremental costs of added formality.[70] With minor modification, a similar framework could serve as the structure for rational selection of agency methodologies more generally. If the question is whether the agency has arbitrarily insisted on more research before regulating, the court could look at the agency's reasons and see if they have an analytical structure that meets at least the minimal formal character suggested by *Mathews*. If the question is whether the agency was sensible in refusing the request for a public conference of health scientists who disagree with the agency's assessment of a particular chemical, the court could use the *Mathews* framework to evaluate the agency's reasoning process in denying the requested meeting, even though there is no claim that a due process right is at stake. Indeed, I would go so far as to urge a rule of presumptive desirability of quasi-adversarial processes, including staged battles of the experts. (I say this notwithstanding the serious and familiar arguments to the contrary—which take as their starting point the negative attributes of the adjudicatory fairness paradigm.) In other words, I would place a burden of persuasion on an agency unwilling to design ad hoc procedures of some sort to expose and resolve important disputes amenable to expert debate. The purpose, of course, is not only to test the quality of the agency's asserted expertise but also to discern the real limits on the usefulness of the expertise paradigm. The dispute between scientists could, if properly structured, identify those areas of disagreement, some of which would doubtless reach into areas we would think more appropriate for decision making based on politics or fairness.

This is not to say that the *Mathews* analysis is wholly satisfactory. Far from it. At best it is a modest step beyond free-form balancing and reasonableness, notwithstanding its pseudo-scientific trappings. It provides some structure for the analysis and, as a result, perhaps, some rigor. Nevertheless, in these areas comparatively foreign to judges, it is valuable to have a framework that at least suggests the questions to guide scrutiny of the agency record and briefs of counsel.

To some extent, this may be reconcilable with *Vermont Yankee*, since the primary thrust is in the nature of a quasi-procedural insistence that choices of methodology be disclosed and supported with reasoned elaboration. I do not deny, however, that the heart of the proposal is

70. 424 U.S. 319, 335 (1976). *See also* Cleveland Bd. of Educ. v. Loudermill, 470 U.S. 532, 543–46 (1985); Board of Regents v. Roth, 408 U.S. 564 (1972); Goldberg v. Kelly, 397 U.S. 254 (1970).

contrary to the spirit of *Vermont Yankee*, broadly read. I believe the reality is that in a world in which the separation of procedure and substance is often impossible, Justice Rehnquist's sweeping formulation in that case is untenable. The continuing possibility of resort to hard-look and other forms of review has made the *Vermont Yankee* prohibitions on judicial activism more of an encumbrance to useful interbranch dialogue than an effective constraint on judicial over-reaching. My incremental, reformist suggestions here seem eminently reasonable incursions on the spirit of *Vermont Yankee*, while decently respectful of its letter.

CHAPTER 7

A Speculative Essay: From Trichotomy to Trio—And Sound Governance Review

Modest changes in doctrine, such as those sketched in chapter 6, would strengthen administrative law. But our success will be severely limited if we retain conventional, trichotomy-based conceptions of role and methods of reasoning. Now, after so many pages, I have earned the right to speculate. I want to explore the consequences of pushing my thesis to its logical limits. What if everything were up for grabs? What if we were willing, if necessary, to *reinvent* courts, agencies, and judicial review? What would legal reasoning be like after a conscientious effort to dispel the separation of powers ethos? Would anything be familiar?

I pursue this speculation in three stages. First, assuming for the sake of argument that the separation of powers ethos were somehow dispelled, the project of administrative law could move away from its anachronistic focus on discretion and face directly the problems of sound governance; indirectness is not good enough. Second, in section 7.2, I try to suggest what "sound governance" might mean, especially the problem of making such norms accessible to our reinvented judges. The kernel of this thesis has three parts. Sound governance requires (1) the integration and able execution of all three decision making paradigms, (2) assured by judicial review. This requires an integrative perspective on science, politics, and adjudicatory fairness rather than the familiar efforts to separate and distort them, as described in chapter 2 and analyzed in chapters 3 and 4. Moreover, (3) the specific content of sound governance must be defined in an evolutionary process that involves all branches of government and the public. Finally, in section 7.3, the third stage of this speculation considers what the sources of judicial legitimacy might be once all the dust from reconstruction has settled.

My thread may be easier to follow with some additional foreshadowing. My conception of the judicial role resembles the partnership model occasionally mentioned in cases and commentary, in that partners are jointly responsible for the success of the enterprise—here, democratic government. But I do not accept the imagery of a coequal relationship, with each partner supreme in its domain, like a corporation's vice president for marketing and vice president for manufacturing, with essentially separate though occasionally overlapping fields of responsibility. Much of what I have written is meant to cast doubt on the possibility of such a neat division, at least by means of the conventional categories. But this does not mean that no distinctions are possible.

I prefer an admission that the court-agency relation *is* in important respects hierarchical. The court *does* oversee and reverse agency decisions that are "wrong"—that is, illegal, somehow defined and determined. Arguably, this is fairly implied by the statutory provisions for judicial review, since it is highly unlikely that the only kind of oversight members of Congress have in mind is very narrow review limited to technical issues of agency compliance with (rare) unambiguous legislative commands. Certainly the public expects broader judicial authority to correct agency errors: the walls of the nuclear reactor container vessel are too brittle; the contraceptive causes cancer; the costs of the safety standard bear no reasonable relation to the benefits, and so on. The public expects and deserves that official errors of this sort be caught and corrected by courts, given the unquestioned inability of Congress to do so.

Thus, the partnership image requires some adjustment, adding elements akin to the relationship between the corporation's chief executive officer and the vice president for marketing. Even though the CEO's training may be as a production engineer, we accept some form of hierarchy, and we would not attempt to police the CEO's discretion to overrule the vice president for marketing by means of the same sort of categories we would use to allocate responsibility between marketing and manufacturing. Some other scheme is required, that reflects accurately the personal and institutional competencies—both highly contingent on circumstances—as well as the shared sense of mission for the organization as a whole.

Yet the CEO-VP image is also deficient. Although the CEO's authority over the VP may be fairly absolute, we will properly insist that the court not have the very final word over the *legislature*, at least not on subconstitutional matters. (I do not explore the implications of my separation of powers critique for constitutional law.) Thus, even as we might encourage law and courts to develop norms of sound governance, we should take care that agencies and the legislature retain the *practical wherewithal to correct judicial errors,* lest the qualified hierarchical authority be misused or abused. A variety of formal and informal mechanisms of judicial interaction and accountability must substitute for the unworkable role restraints of present doctrine. But I am, perhaps, getting ahead of myself.

7.1 Redefining the Project of Administrative Law

7.1.1 The Antidiscretion Focus as Anachronism

Courts and scholars have for decades attempted to devise legal and verbal formulas to constrain administrative discretion.[1] I have argued that the doctrinal scheme developed to pursue this project is largely unsuccessful because its deep reliance on murky separation-of-powers constructs produces poor guidance for the discretion of the unelected judge, which is no great substitute for the poorly guided discretion of the unelected bureaucrat. I have intended the analysis of the trichotomy and its failings as a demonstration of the sources and manifestations of the difficulty encountered by law in scaling the degree of judicial deference or interventionism toward administrative action.

But I have also alluded to a problem in the definition of the project itself. Obsession with the project of constraining administrative discretion is symptomatic of the separation-of-powers ethos, in that the generative concern is the legitimacy of blurred institutional roles. The

---

1. *See, e.g.,* Minnesota ex rel. R.R. & Warehouse Comm'n v. Chicago, M. & St. P. Ry., 38 Minn. 281, 37 N.W. 782 (1888) (quasi-legislative delegation permissible because legislature establishes judicially enforceable bounds on agency discretion); United States v. Grimaud, 220 U.S. 506 (1911) (secretary of agriculture's rule making powers were merely as to administrative detail; discretion had to be exercised within bounds). *See* sec. 1.1.

Davis has commented on the contrast between legal rhetoric and legal reality in this regard: "When the federal courts retreated from their former asserted position that Congress could not delegate legislative power, they transformed the non-delegation doctrine into the position that Congress would not delegate without meaningful standards. Verbiage to that effect can be found in at least a hundred Supreme Court opinions. But in the entire history of the United States, the verbiage became holding in only two cases, both decided in 1935." Panama Refining Co. v. Ryan, 293 U.S. (1935); A.L.A. Schechter Poultry Corp. v. United States, 295 U.S. 495 (1935). K. Davis, 1 Administrative Law Treatise § 3.2, 151 (2d ed. 1978).

historical basis for the obsession is obvious and important, as is the continuing intellectual momentum of those eighteenth-century architectural innovations. Had the New Deal victory over separation of powers formalism been complete, the obsession of administrative law would today no longer be rooted in the separation of powers ethos. We would obsess about something else.

And indeed we should. The *contemporary* problem of administrative legitimacy is not the problem of blurred institutional roles.[2] Doctrine and scholarship repeat endlessly the battle to legitimate the administrative state, when fifty years have established beyond peradventure that big government is here to stay.[3] That battle is won. Americans are not troubled by the vagueness of statutory mandates or poorly guided administrative discretion. This era's crisis is the growing social and economic costs of government waste, foolishness, neglect, and appetite. People distrust governmental institutions not because of discretion or commingling of functions but because they perceive that government is not doing a good enough job—a common judgment, though with varying political spins. Today's mainstream political debate does occasionally address administrative hegemony, but in historical context the disagreements are marginal: Will the administrative state be gigantic or merely huge? The core critique of big government emphasizes pro-

---

2. This is not to say that separation of powers concerns are irrelevant to political discourse. There are recurring waves of concern with judicial activism: in 1933–37, New Dealers decried the conservative judicial activism that threatened the nation's reconstruction. *See* P. Freund, A. Sutherland, H. Howe, & E. Brown, Constitutional Law 260–61 (1977). In the Warren Court era, conservatives often attacked the liberal Court. Today the pendulum is swinging in the other direction once more. But these public concerns are directed at the legitimacy of the court, not administrative agencies. *See* sec. 7.3 concerning judicial legitimacy.

3. "[T]he old terms of debate with liberalism no longer reflect (if they ever did) our dominant public values and conceptions. The old principles are thus no longer the most relevant normative criteria by which to evaluate contemporary (or more precisely, pre–1981) regulation. . . . Today, regulation implies not a minor adjustment in liberal theory but a paradigm shift. Evaluating contemporary regulation in light of the pre–New Deal understanding of liberalism is like planning a sea voyage on the premise that the earth is flat." Schuck, *Regulation, Non-Market Values, and the Administrative State*, 92 Yale L.J. 1602, at 1602, 1604 (1983). Schuck's comments are directed at the substantive content of philosophical liberalism, which Stewart had described in terms of a limited state thoroughly solicitous of individualism, neutrality, and market autonomy. Stewart, *Regulation in a Liberal State: The Role of Non-Commodity Values*, 92 Yale L.J. 1537 (1983). *Compare* Frug, *Why Neutrality?*, 92 Yale L.J. 1591 (1983). But the imperative of the antidiscretion project is derived from this substantive content, the nexus being the necessity of limiting government and controlling incursions on private interests through the rule of law. *See, e.g.*, Stewart & Sunstein, *Public Programs and Private Rights*, 95 Harv. L. Rev. 1193, 1202 (1982) (describing the traditional role of administrative law in policing government incursions into the realm of protected rights).

grammatic failings, not institutional roles. The decades-old obsession of administrative law is remarkably anachronistic. It threatens to make the law irrelevant to the genuine problems of governance.[4]

7.1.2 Why Control of Discretion Is Unacceptable as an Indirect Means to Sound Government

But can a case be made that the antidiscretion project[5] is an acceptable indirect means of pursuing the end of sound government? In the sense that separation of powers notions (including fidelity to statute and to the Rule of Law) are instrumental, the answer must be yes, *if the instruments really work.*

Do they work? We always answer that crucial question with myths, fictions, and romantic historicism rather than with evidence. Some empirical work might prove valuable. At a conceptual level, however, I offer four considerations that cast doubt on the efficacy of the antidiscretion approach to sound government. First, constraining discretion may be counterproductive. It is true that, given the awesome complexity of public affairs, executive discretion is an unavoidable result of imperfect governmental processes and inherent ambiguities of language. But it is also quite likely that this complexity makes broad discretion essential for effective government action. Embracing discretion as a necessary and desirable part of public administration is a sharply different perspective from the dominant one in administrative law, which is to fear discretion, reluctantly accept its presence, and attempt to control it through doctrines that offer no reliable basis for determining when discretion is good or bad. Indeed, one might be concerned that if administrative law were successful at rooting out discretion,

---

4. One interesting piece of evidence is that the concerns so central to administrative law are all but ignored in the curricula of university programs in public policy and management. Likewise, when schools of business administration consider the role of government, they rarely consider the role of courts, administrative law, problems of discretion, and so forth as they might relate to the quality of public policy and administration.

5. Why "antidiscretion project," rather than "control of discretion project?" Insofar as the aim of administrative law has been to reduce agency decision making to the "transmission belt" function described by Stewart, *The Reformation in American Administrative Law*, 88 Harv. L. Rev. 1669, 1671–76 (1975), and insofar as even such recent doctrinal inventions as hard-look review are commonly deployed to minimize discretion, it is fair to say that "control" has meant maximum feasible elimination. Nor is it sufficiently descriptive to term this the Rule of Law project, as I did in ch. 1 because the sound governance project described in this chapter is no less an effort to develop principles by which judges and agencies will be bound (within the limits of formality—*see* Kennedy, *Legal Formality*, 2 J. Leg. Stud. 351 [1973]).

government itself would be programmatically unsuccessful. Superficially, this is a recapitulation of the pragmatic argument that dissolved separation of powers rigidities to allow delegation of quasi-legislative and quasi-adjudicative powers in the first place. It is more, however, because the result of that earlier rapprochement when law and government seemed in conflict was to allow delegated discretion so long as law could be employed to control it. Five and more decades ago the concern was that if courts attempted to forbid or repress discretion altogether, government would not work. Now, with still more complex governmental tasks, there should be attention to the possibility, discussed immediately below, that *highly discretionary judicial attempts to regulate discretion pose a more subtle threat.*

Second, it may be that constraining discretion is no longer desirable as a value in itself, independent of instrumental contribution to sound government. Using independent courts to constrain unelected bureaucrats might have independent process-value if we want to force the legislature to make more of the discretionary choices or if we want to refine the nonpolitical qualities of the bureaucracy by excluding the distracting, controversial subjects as to which bureaucracy's comparative advantage is doubtful.[6] Such an argument, however, incorporates an anachronistic image of the bureaucrat as technical implementer—Richard Stewart's metaphor was a transmission belt—rather than full partner in the lawmaking and policy-making activity of government.[7] Moreover, the argument that limited discretion is desirable in and of itself is at odds with the pragmatic focus of contemporary political debate (including debate on the legislative veto)[8] and from the actual practices of government.[9] This does not imply that discretion should

6. *See, e.g.,* Industrial Union Dep't, AFL-CIO v. American Petroleum Inst. *(Benzene),* 448 U.S. 607, 671 (1980) (Rehnquist, J. concurring); American Textile Mfrs. Inc. v. Donovan *(Cotton Dust),* 452 U.S. 490, 543 (1981) (Rehnquist, J., dissenting).

7. As Jaffe notes, "The administrative and the judiciary *share* the role of law pronouncing and law making. They are in partnership." L. Jaffe, Judicial Control of Administrative Action 546 (1985) (hereinafter Jaffe, Treatise) (emphasis in original). *See also* sec. 5.1.1 Jaffe and the fact-law distinction.

8. Congressional interest in the legislative veto device, which accelerated during the late 1970s but was blocked by the Supreme Court in INS v. Chadha, 462 U.S. 919 (1983), would have been stillborn but for substantive objections to the way in which certain agencies, notably the FTC, were exercising their discretion. There was an insistent rhetoric of process-values whereby the principal proponents of the legislative veto device insisted that elected representatives should assert power to block agency actions through means short of amendatory legislation, but congressional and other critics saw this as a transparent effort to accomplish indirectly what veto advocates lacked the political resources to effect straightforwardly, by statute.

9. Indeed, protracted public and congressional debate in autumn 1985 resulted in an unprecedented, sweeping, and fundamental delegation of the spending power to the

be *un*limited. The limits, however, should be instrumentally rooted in the direct pursuit of sound governance, as developed below.

Third, indirectness is dangerous because it is obscure. Many judges I consider outstanding do approach their responsibilities as though they understand their role to be a collaborative one with agencies and legislature, with each institution concerned that governmental choices be sensible and just.[10] Judges Bazelon and Leventhal come to mind because, interestingly, their famous dispute in the *Ethyl* case demonstrates that virtue comes in many forms.[11] But the doctrinal and rhetorical conventions almost always cause judges to cast their analyses in terms of discretion and trichotomy-related distinctions rather than to formulate and defend direct assertions about the substantive and procedural quality of agency action.

It is only human for sensible judges, wise in the ways of the world and educated by the adversarial presentations, to *have views* about whether the government has acted wisely. It is unrealistic to expect

---

president in an effort to break the political impasse over massive budget deficits. Under the Gramm-Rudman-Hollings deficit reduction statute, if the Congress fails to adopt budgets meeting certain deficit-reduction targets in each of the years 1986–91, the president is required to impose unilateral reductions, computed by statutory formula, in certain domestic and defense spending categories, the goal being a balanced budget in fiscal year 1991. During the legislative maneuvering, debate was dominated by highly partisan argument about the relative burden of spending cuts on domestic and defense programs. The process-value of congressional supremacy on legislative matters, which several Democrats articulated, seemed to me to play a minor role, and was indistinguishable from the substantive objections to what this Republican president would do if the delegation of budget-cutting authority carried with it too much discretion. Pub. L. 99–177, 99 Stat. 1037. *See generally* 43 Cong. Q. 2267–75, 2604–11 (describing the legislative battle over Gramm-Rudman-Hollings).

10. *See, e.g.,* Greater Boston Television Co. v. FCC, 444 F.2d 841, 851 (D.C. Cir. 1970) (Leventhal, J.), *cert. denied,* 403 U.S. 923 (1971) (describing the relation between agencies and courts as a "partnership" in furtherance of the "public interest," quoting Niagara Mohawk Power Corp. v. FPC, 379 F.2d 153, 160 n. 24 (1967)). *Compare* Jaffe, Treatise at 546.

11. In Ethyl Corp. v. EPA, 541 F.2d 1 (D.C. Cir.) (en banc), *cert. denied,* 426 U.S. 941 (1976), Judge Wright wrote the majority opinion upholding regulatory limits on lead additives in gasoline. Chief Judge Bazelon and Judge Leventhal exchanged concurring opinions. Bazelon argued that the proper judicial role with respect to highly technical agency actions is to "establish a decision-making process that assures a reasoned decision that can be held up to the scrutiny of the scientific community and the public." 541 F.2d at 66 (quoting International Harvester Co. v. Ruckelshaus, 478 F.2d 615, 652 [D.C. Cir. 1973] [Bazelon, C.J., concurring]). Judge Leventhal, in sharp contrast, argued that the searching nature of judicial scrutiny should not be "jettisoned" merely because the subject is technical; though the task of review may be more difficult, it is precisely the responsibility Congress has assigned to the courts. 541 F.2d at 68–69. Both jurists, in *Ethyl* and elsewhere, seem well disposed toward ensuring the quality of governmental decision making—as best they can judge it. (I examine the legitimacy issue in sec. 7.3.)

judges to ignore these views when they turn to the delicate, highly discretionary process of scaling judicial deference to a particular government action before them. Even if a judge refrains from imposing a personal "substantive" view of the better result (whether for reasons of role conception or for reasons of personal uncertainty over the specific result demanded), the judge's view of the merits will affect his or her willingness to adopt a procedural or quasi-procedural form of intervention,[12] such as a heightened requirement of reasoned elaboration. This is inevitable for all but the most self-denying of jurists, notwithstanding the volumes of judicial rhetoric stating that the court must uphold "reasonable" agency action even if the choice is not what the judge would have made had the responsibility been his or hers. The price of indirectness, therefore, is that this inevitable judicial discretion and subjectivity is obscured by doctrinal exegesis. This is often elegant, even pleasantly diverting, to those of us engaged in the enterprise. But the doctrine should frame and illuminate choices, not make them obscure. It would be far preferable were judicial attention to soundness more direct and more explicit. The inevitable discretion could then be held up to clear-sighted criticism and correction.[13] Accountability would be enhanced.

Fourth, and most important, the antidiscretion project cannot be accepted as an indirect means of pursuing sound government because it has been unsuccessful on its own terms; as I have argued, the underlying failings of the doctrinal framework do little more than amplify the discretion, render it obscure, and allocate it, rather inconsistently, between agency and courts.

12. I adopt Merrick Garland's definitions of procedural and quasi-procedural intervention: "Although the hard look requirements [of heightened scope of judicial review] do have a procedural tinge, they may be more properly be referred to as 'quasi-procedural' because they also have a substantive aspect. At bottom, they focus not on the kind of procedure that an agency must use to generate a record, but rather on the kind of decisionmaking record the agency must produce to survive judicial review; the method of generating the record is left to the agency itself. Their concern is not with the external process by which litigants present their arguments to the agency, but with the internal thought process by which an agency decisionmaker reaches a rational decision. Thus, these requirements can be said to flow not from the APA's procedural dictates, but from its substantive command that agency decision making not be 'arbitrary' or 'capricious.'" Garland, *Deregulation and Judicial Review*, 98 Harv. L. Rev. 505, 530 (1985) (citations omitted).

13. I have elided the distinction between an argument that judges are inevitably influenced (somewhat) by their views on the merits and an argument that such influences are (somewhat) desirable. I believe both propositions.

Instead of pursuing familiar but indirect and untrustworthy means, administrative law must take the problem of efficacious governance and move it to center stage. After abandoning the antidiscretion project, doctrine and judges should take more direct measures to assure, as far as law and courts can, sound governmental decision making. In the next section I consider what we might mean by "sound governance"; following that, I suggest what courts might be able to do if we abandoned the separation of powers ethos in favor of constructive realism.

7.2 Defining Sound Governance: The Trio of Decision Making Methodologies

Some legal scholars have been drawn to the formidable task of considering what should be the actual policy content and array of implementation strategies for the administrative state. In turning to such subjects as the desirability of quasi-market incentives to curb pollution, the role of regional authorities in the control of pollution, or, more ambitiously, the importance of "noncommodity values" in designing and interpreting regulatory regimes,[14] these scholars are implicitly acknowledging that direct attention to the content of public policy— whether and how a problem should be addressed by government—is a needed complement to, if not replacement for, traditional doctrinal analysis. The same implicit judgment is reflected in scholarship directed at improving the design of the public administration apparatus—for example, in Mashaw's work on efficient and fair adjudication of social security disability claims or Diver's work on the optimal precision of regulations and the choice between incremental and synoptic policy analysis.[15] Such scholarship has little application to the problems of the

14. On incentives, *see* S. Breyer, Regulation and Its Reform 271 (1982); Stewart, *The Discontents of Legalism: Interest Group Relations in Administrative Regulation,* 1985 Wis. L. Rev. 655. On regional authorities, *see* B. Ackerman, S. Rose-Ackerman, J. Sawyer, & D. Henderson, The Uncertain Search for Environmental Quality (1974). On values, *see* Stewart, *supra* n. 3 at 1357 (see esp. pt. 5 on aspiration, diversity, mutuality, and civic virtue as bases for regulation).

15. J. Mashaw, Bureaucratic Justice (1983); Mashaw, *How Much of What Quality? A Comment on Procedural Design,* 65 Cornell L. Rev. 823 (1980) (describing the costs and benefits of current procedures in the SSA's Office of Hearings and Appeals, including such considerations as the relative importance and frequency of different types of errors, public perceptions of administrative conduct, and distributive aspects of reform); Diver, *The Optimal Precision of Rules,* 93 Yale L.J. 65 (1983); Diver, *Policymaking Paradigms,* 95 Harv. L. Rev. 393 (1981).

scope of judicial review and administrative law doctrine.[16] In short, these works are primarily about how to make government better apart from (or even despite) the workings of administrative law. As such, they are part of a broader social science and public management literature that contains many worthwhile prescriptions. My question, instead, is whether *administrative law* can be directly harnessed to play a constructive role by advancing those worthwhile prescriptions.

I offer four pieces of an answer in the sections immediately following: (1) sound governmental decision making must blend rather than separate the trichotomy's three methods of reasoning; (2) judicial review must be based upon rigorous descriptive realism, notwithstanding the costs of intrusive means of discovering that reality; (3) as norms of sound governance combine procedural and substantive elements, so should judicial review and intervention; and (4) we can self-consciously design our institutions and doctrines to facilitate the revelation and evolution of norms of sound governance.

7.2.1 The Trio as Blend and Balance of Methods

Administrative law should understand sound governmental decision making to require a combination of all three decision making paradigms included in the trichotomy. That objective is disserved by efforts to separate those paradigms and distribute them among the branches of government. I have emphasized the conceptual drawbacks to the separation of powers–based trichotomy as a means of defining and enforcing institutional roles, especially as reflected in decisions about the degree of deference accorded particular types of agency action. But I do not deny that the three decision making paradigms have content. Indeed, their distinctiveness—like the distinctiveness of administration, legislation, and adjudication—is deep in our con-

---

16. Its more natural audience, but for the abstruseness, are those in the executive and legislative branches with direct responsibility for the content of regulatory law and the design of processes to execute that law. This is not to say that judicial review is entirely unrelated to this scholarship. For example, surely Judge Breyer's book, by presenting the policy backdrop for the choice among alternative tools of regulatory intervention, is providing a context with which well-informed judges can better assess the rationality of agency choices; Mashaw's work on disability has not only direct relevance to the statutory design of judicial review (which he notes) but application to judicial design of procedural due process requirements. On the whole, however, work in this genre seems directed toward sound government rather than doctrinal reform. I am enthusiastically sympathetic with the sound government focus, but I want that focus integrated explicitly into doctrinal evolution.

sciousness no matter how difficult the boundary problems may be in practice.

Moreover, this consciousness is reinforced by the fact that *all three methods are crucial ingredients in sound decision making*. This crucial inter-relationship arises from and explains the conceptual boundary problem I detailed in chapter 3. The three paradigms must be viewed as an integrated trio rather than as a trichotomy. Analysis that fails to include a balanced portion of each method should strike us as faulty in an almost aesthetic way. Some analogies (helpful, though perhaps a bit cute) come to mind:

- The yin and yang of classical Chinese cosmology are sepa-rately describable yet always combined in nature. The com-bination must be balanced if harmony and order are to pre-vail. So, too, with the trichotomy of decision making methods.

- The salt and oregano in a good marinara sauce have separate tastes, but a sauce concocted with one to the exclusion of the other just wouldn't work. Selective emphasis on one decision making method will distort the process, and the quality of the result will suffer.

- Accurate interpretation of experience requires access to a full range of sounds and palate of colors. Someone deaf to high pitches and blind to red hues can "hear" a Beethoven sym-phony and "see" Vermont foliage in October, but for many purposes we would not consider their experience a reliable basis for evaluation or prescription ("Don't buy the record"; "Go in August, when it's easier to get a hotel room"). Sound governance requires access to the full palate of decision mak-ing paradigms.

Three things follow from this:

1. *Characterizing the question.* It is a mistake to pigeonhole a particular problem or issue as "appropriate" for solution through the substan-tially exclusive application of one decision making method. Yet, as I have argued, this is the practical effect of most doctrinal reasoning, in which the implicit matching of problem with paradigm is the backdrop for the court's assessment of the agency's choice and execution of method and the degree of deference owed. When OSHA regulates a workplace hazard, "good" answers to the problem will reflect explicit, integrated consideration of *(a)* expert scientific analysis, *(b)* accommo-dation of competing interests, and *(c)* such Rule of Law methods as

consistency and individual fairness. It would be unsound for political officials, say at OMB, to discard the considered views of epidemiologists in formulating a health standard, but it would also be unsound to suppose that political and even ideological choices should not play a significant part in the decision.

2. *Characterizing the agency's method.* It is a mistake to scale judicial review based on the agency's use (or avoidance) of only one decision making methodology—say, use of interest accommodation methods in highly discretionary policy choices. The majority in *State Farm* (the air bags case), for example, was mistaken to evaluate the "rationality" and hence acceptability of the agency's rescission of the passive restraints regulation solely in terms of the adequacy of the policy analysis, when political considerations were an (appropriately) important ingredient of the decision; the clearer flaw with the agency's action, from my perspective, was its failure to disclose the nature and weight of the political and social values it was applying to complement its scientific analysis.[17]

3. *Judicial rhetoric.* Because the nature of the agency's problem, the character of the agency's analysis, and the decision making processes of the judge all combine the three elements of the trichotomy, the court should explain itself in terms of all three methodologies, to the extent practicable. Thus, the court's opinion in a case such as *Association of National Advertisers* should explicitly consider the likely effects of Chairman Pertschuk's strongly held policy views on the three-dimensional soundness of the FTC's rule making on children's advertising: the district court analyzed the matter almost exclusively in the language of adjudicatory fairness, emphasizing neutrality; the court of appeals used the language of discretionary policy judgment, emphasizing the legitimate role for preferences in quasi-legislation.[18] As a practical matter this requires an opportunity for counsel to build an appropriate record and make arguments based on it. And it requires a particularized and realistic judicial appraisal of the mix of paradigms rather

17. Motor Vehicle Mfrs. Ass'n v. State Farm Mut. Ins. Co., 463 U.S. 29 (1983). *See* sec. 6.1.2; *see also* sec. 6.1.5 (importance of disclosing political preferences for public scrutiny).

18. Association of Nat'l Advertisers v. FTC, 627 F.2d 1151, 1168–69 (D.C. Cir. 1979), *cert. denied,* 447 U.S. 921 (1980) ("The Cinderella [Cinderella Career Finishing Schools, Inc. v. FTC, 435 F.2d 583 (C.A.D.C. 1970)] view of neutral and detached adjudicator is simply an inapposite role model for an administrator who must translate broad statutory commands into concrete social policies" [citations omitted]); 460 F. Supp. 996 (D.D.C. 1978) (decision below).

than the glossy categorizations based on the form of procedure—such as a rule that bias is more tolerable in rule making than in adjudication.

In short, the reviewing court that is exercising its partnership responsibility for sound governance should concern itself with the balanced use of all three methodologies, not with parsing a problem or action into decisional elements "deserving" neatly distinguishable degrees of deference.

Would this approach provide more certainty than do current doctrine and attitudes? In one sense, the question mixes apples and oranges. If certainty means constrained discretion, the answer is an unembarrassed no: constraining discretion was the sine qua non of the conventional project of administrative law. We are speculating about an alternative project. Indeed, this approach substitutes a different form of judicial and administrative discretion—discretion tied to the end we really care about. And with respect to the pursuit of that end, the alternative approach may provide more certainty.

But if this is the modus operandi of law's sound governance project, then there are some unavoidable implications for a reformulated judicial role. I have already sketched, in chapter 6, the minimalist outlines of this enterprise in the context of incremental doctrinal reform, especially regarding judicial postures toward politics. Now I broaden the thesis: Doctrine must be concerned with both the balance of the trio of decision making methods and the quality of the agency's effort in each of the three respects. This in turn entails two important subordinate enterprises: realism in describing the workings of the bureaucracy and a fuller recognition of the interplay of substance and procedure.

7.2.2 Descriptive Realism

Courts must ruthlessly dissolve descriptive myths, and their doctrinal props, which serve to obscure judicial perception and appraisal of the agency action. I discussed the nature of these descriptive inaccuracies in chapter 3, and I have argued that doctrinal impediments to clearer vision, and indeed the deeper judicial reluctance to dismantle these myths and impediments, are attributable to trichotomy-based separation of powers concerns. These inaccuracies would be even more problematic in a reformulated administrative law that emphasized frank appraisal of paradigm mix and quality. In particular, the program of disclosure I suggested in chapter 6 as an incremental doctrinal reform would be essential. Disclosure could be augmented by a more accommodating judicial posture toward plaintiffs' efforts to use discovery and evidentiary hearings to get a more accurate fix on just what has occurred in the agency.[19]

Of course, in a trichotomy-based administrative law, it is just as well for judges to avoid a realistic look: they would see things that would require doctrine to face thorny problems it is ill prepared to address, such as the appropriate role of political motives in agency decision making or the weight to be accorded the view of private and public interest parties that have better data and better scientists than the expert agency.[20]

7.2.3 Procedure and Substance

A second enterprise that would aid judicial assessment of the balance of decision making methods is a flexible and complex approach to both the substance-procedure distinction and the court's involvement in the evolution and enforcement of procedural, quasi-procedural, and substantive standards.

Having seen the agency's action for what it is, the court must still decide whether what it sees is good or bad, sound or unsound, in terms of whatever norms of legality and good sense are accessible to and articulable by the judge. In evaluating each decision making paradigm there is a procedure-substance dichotomy reminiscent of the famous Bazelon-Leventhal debate in the *Ethyl* case discussed in section 7.1.2.

19. The Freedom of Information Act's exemption for many internal and interagency documents is too broad. *See* 5 U.S.C. § 552(b)(5); EPA v. Mink, 410 U.S. 73 (1974) (test is "injurious to consultative process"); Schlefer v. U.S., 702 F.2d 233 (D.C. Cir. 1983) (using trichotomy-related distinction between matters of "law" and "deliberation"); Hoover v. Department of Interior, 611 F.2d 1132 (11th Cir. 1980) (needs of individual litigant are not relevant to disclosure issue). Considerable indeterminacy is added, as we would expect from ch. 3, by the countless cases reciting that the FOIA's purpose is disclosure and the exemptions are therefore to be narrowly construed. A good example of obscured and largely unreviewable interplay of paradigms is the White House/OMB role in President Reagan's regulatory reforms. *See* sec. 7.3.3.(b).

To control the potential disruption of such interventionism, courts would need to develop (perhaps aided by legislation) a middle ground between flat presumptions of agency regularity and the broad permissiveness characteristic of discovery in private civil litigation. Before ordering deposition of senior officials, for example, a court could require various showings of likely materiality, essentiality, and focus. Of course, to the extent that the agency has already explained the role of each paradigm in the decision and plausibly described their balanced integration, a reviewing court would have little cause to order discovery. For instance, judicial unease may have been alleviated had Pertschuk provided for the record (when the rule making began) a thorough explanation of his prejudices concerning children's advertising, with an explanation of how those prejudices did or did not play a role at various stages of the FTC proceedings.

20. *See* ch. 2 (discussing the poverty of evaluative standards).

The court can try to assure sound agency action by focusing either on the procedural and methodological character of the action or on the substance. But here is a boundary problem, alas, every bit as troubling as those of the trichotomy.

Suppose, for example, the court is concerned that the political process of agency choice was flawed because not all of the "key" groups were included in the negotiations that led to the consensus environmental standard adopted by the administrator. Is the court's concern, and any judicial intervention to address it, a procedural or a substantive matter?

I believe *this is the wrong question.* Certainly there is a sense in which the court stands on firmer ground when its objection to agency action is procedural rather than substantive, owing to our general, comparative confidence in the sophistication of a generalist judge's sensibilities. (If this inclination to trust the procedural instincts of the judge is based on a sense that procedural norms are legal rather than personal, then the limits of that trust are being defined with reference to the trichotomy's distinctions among law, politics, and fact.) Nevertheless, and unfortunately, the Supreme Court in *Vermont Yankee* sought to curb judicial activism by instructing courts not to impose on agencies any procedural requirements, such as an adversarial oral hearing in an informal rule making, beyond those specified in the Administrative Procedure Act.[21] But substance and procedure go hand-in-hand, in that the adequacy of one cannot be judged without consideration of the other. One reason we have confidence in a substantive result is that we have confidence in the procedure used to derive it; one reason we have confidence in the adequacy of any procedure is that it seems to have produced a substantively reasonable conclusion, or seems likely to. Bazelon and Leventhal were talking about two sides of the same coin, that coin being judicial activism motivated by a concern for sound governance.

As a special instance of the general means-ends dyad, the transmutability of substance and procedure is thoroughly familiar in law and beyond. Its potential to confuse is perhaps heightened in administrative law for two reasons. First, the reliance of doctrine on paradigm-driven distinctions appears, at a gross level, to be a method-focused analysis, while, by contrast, the deeply animating project of the law is an outcome-focused quality concern, albeit conventionally suppressed and confined to indirection. This tension between the naturally proceduralist spin of doctrinal analysis and the naturally substan-

21. Vermont Yankee Nuclear Power Corp. v. NRDC, 435 U.S. 519 (1978).

tive spin of our motivations encourages conflation of procedure and substance. Second, however, if one examines more closely the construction of each paradigm, especially the pattern of attributes, the apparent method-focus is clearly only part of the picture. Normatively potent attributes such as neutrality or representativeness directly implicate substantive values. These combine with the plumbing-like procedural specifications of the paradigms in order to give us a potentially rich, dyadic "aesthetic" about good politics, good science, and good adjudication. So, the conflation of substance and procedure is a designed-in feature of the paradigms.

Because substance and procedure can be transmuted so readily, the effect of *Vermont Yankee* is simply to make a court that is inclined toward interventionism express its concerns and its remand instructions in quasi-procedural language that has a substantive resonance: explore more alternatives, give a more detailed explanation, disclose considerations and staff information, demonstrate adequate consideration of statutory factors, and so on. The risk is that the reviewing court may use modes of rhetoric and intervention that miscommunicate the source and nature of its dissatisfaction with the administrative action—all because in any particular circumstance, the court is concerned that its legitimate purview is somehow delimited by the substance-procedure categorization. This approach is misleading and self-defeating, in view of both the boundary problem in these two categories and the related and more fundamental point that proper evaluation of agency action requires an eye to both procedure and substance.

Let me return to the example of the negotiated environmental standard. The question is whether the court should act on its sense that a key group was excluded from the political process—a seemingly procedural issue. A second way to frame the issue is to ask whether the court's conclusion that certain groups (or their arguments) were omitted amounts to a substitution of the judge's political analysis for that of the administrator. (Because of the politics-science boundary or categorization failing, this can also be cast as a matter of hard-look ["adequate consideration"] review of the agency's substantive expertise.) Put this way, we intuitively feel that such a substitution is undesirable. That intuition is in part a matter of separation of powers ethos. Entirely apart from ideology, however, we might fear that the judge will not be as substantively competent a political analyst, or mediator of interests, as the administrator, and we might want to be certain that the administrator's *public accountability for the results* of the regulatory action is not short-circuited by judicial intervention.

In this post-trichotomy world, however, we want the judge to do what clearly seems important to do in order to secure a sound decision (to be defined); short of that clarity, we want the administrator to feel the political costs and benefits of her decisions about which interests to include in the balancing process of policy formulation. We do *not* want to restrict the judge's a priori sense of domain or competence by reference to abstract role constructs if those constructs are not directly related to pragmatic concerns of sound governmental outcomes.

This suggests a core-penumbra analysis of deference, rather than an on-off approach based on roles or on the related procedure-substance dichotomy. It is not very helpful to ask whether the judge is substituting her political analysis (or scientific analysis, or adjudicatory fairness analysis) for that of the administrator. Any judicial intervention, wherever it falls along a spectrum from procedural to quasi-procedural to substantive, is in some respects a substitution of judgment. Instead, we can try to distinguish a core analysis or judgment which is presumptively the administrator's domain and a penumbra of judgments as to which the court should be assertive if the path to sounder governance seems to her discernible. My analysis here parallels that of Jaffe's concerning the occasions when a judge should displace the agency's conclusions of law.

I think, for example, that a decision about who is involved in a regulatory negotiation process is further from the core of the administrator's role than is the assigning of weights to the various interest group voices participating in the process. Within the decision on participation, it is tempting to distinguish between inclusion decisions the administrator makes in order to tilt the substantive outcome and inclusion choices made through some fairness calculation. This distinction, however, runs some risk of recapitulating the trichotomy's distinction between fairness and policy discretion and thus should not be pushed. Suffice it to say that acceptable decisions concerning membership or participation should not be agnostic with respect to adjudicatory fairness, politics, or expertise: a decision to exclude a party should be reversed if it seems starkly at odds with any of these three perspectives. A "rule" such as that just stated is precisely what might be generated and fleshed out by an evolutionary effort to establish new norms of sound governance review.

On the other hand, the specification of participants in the negotiation is closer to the core than is the specification of which participants' comments must be summarized on the record or who should be granted participation through standing to seek judicial review. This is one sort of proposition that should be stated and subjected to criticism, reasoned elaboration, and amendment.

How does this differ from conventional, trichotomy-based scaling of judicial deference? In this important respect: The judge must not be confined by separation of powers ethos in her self-conscious effort to determine whether there is a "clear" problem in the agency's action. The construction of what is in the core and what is in the periphery depends on the judge's determination that norms with which to appraise three-dimensional agency behavior are personally and institutionally accessible.

But that determination should be highly contingent and contextual, dependent on a rich set of features of the problem at hand, the nature of the arguments made by counsel in educating the judge, the training and capacity of the judge, and so forth. This list of features is a sharp break with any implicit separation of powers orthodoxy. At most, the familiar assignment of roles—that is, the parsing and sorting of agency action into decision making paradigms and institutional assignments—retains a merely cautionary function of instilling humility.

These features also introduce new contingencies, raising again the issue of certainty or determinacy. In this ends-focused context, determinacy has a different significance: indeed, we should applaud inconsistency generated by particular efforts to advance sound governance subject to overbearing uncertainty costs created by what might appear to be, at least initially, free-form scope of review. More generally, however, recognizing that the effort is so contextually dependent suggests a concerted program to reform both who judges administrative action and the institutional characteristics of the court. I take up these matters in section 7.4.2.

7.2.4 Revelation and Evolution of Norms of Sound Governance

Imagine a court reviewing an OSHA decision that regulates a hazardous chemical in the workplace. The court is concerned that within the mix of decision making methods used by the agency a problem exists with identifying and aggregating costs and benefits. A union makes a plausible claim that the agency has erred in omitting protections for workers in one subindustry; industry makes a plausible claim that the overall financial burdens of the regulatory standard are not justified by the meager benefits conferred. The court can do many things, including: remand for a fuller explanation and justification of the agency's judgments about which evidence to rely on;[22] remand and

---

22. *See generally* Byse, *Requirement of Findings and Reasons in Administrative Law,* 26 Am. J. Comp. L. 393 (1978).

require the agency to apply certain methodologies—say, some version of cost-benefit analysis, or a certain kind of statistical analysis, or a certain kind of laboratory test or epidemiological study; remand and require more procedures, such as further cross-examination of witnesses;[23] and so on. In rare circumstances a judge may even mandamus a particular administrative action. What should the court do?

With sound governance in mind, the court should communicate the reasons why the administrative record fails to instill confidence and provide clear guidance as to how the agency can assure the court that the administrative action is sound. The court's sense may be that participatory and political methods were inadequate, that the scientific evidence was too confused, that similar workers or industries were unfairly treated dissimilarly, or that the agency has broken with the precedents of previous policy. But whatever the court's perceptions, these qualms must be communicated—be they substantive, procedural, or somewhere in between. What might be the source for such implicit tests in our speculative, post-trichotomy world?

I would not object to a court requiring the agency to evaluate regulatory alternatives using cost-benefit analysis or the Ames test for bacterial mutagenicity[24] or to do so in terms of impact on each of several classes of affected individuals or firms. These matters seem substantive and certainly inappropriate for courts steeped in separation of powers ethos. But if a judge is persuaded that action without such analysis might well be unsound, the court should require it: When an accessible norm of sound decision making exists, or when the court can attempt to formulate one without prejudice to the power of agency or legislature to correct a judicial misconception, a conscientious judge should act on personal conviction.

There is little reason to consider that such a judicial command invades an essential core of agency prerogative (the prerogative to act with doubtful rationality?). And it is likely that in a given litigation context, many judges would understand the problem sufficiently to have a clear view of what should be required in order to make sound public policy. If an individual judge has such a view, she should press the agency explicitly, perhaps inviting supplementary briefing or argument. If still clearly of another view, she should act on it forthrightly rather than couching the objection and remanding in some indirect language that masks her discretion. As I have suggested, it seems altogether likely that such judicial willfulness is already commonplace.

23. *But see Vermont Yankee*, 435 U.S. 519.
24. The Ames test entails subjecting a particular strain of bacteria to a suspected carcinogen and watching for mutations.

This scheme requires three crucial lemmas, or subsidiary propositions. First, the judge's full, direct appraisal of the agency's mix and
quality of decision making methods would yield great benefits. Second,
over time, judges could evolve a reasonably valid set of guidelines or
standards (procedural, quasi-procedural, substantive) with which to
make such appraisals in an increasingly consistent and helpful way.
Third, when judges make mistakes in the development or application
of those standards, the revelation will permit a form of interaction with
agencies, other courts, *and Congress*, producing corrections.

*It is important for this mechanism, therefore, that the form of judicial inter-
vention be self-consciously designed to promote fluidity and feedback with respect
to the norms of sound government.* It would be unfortunate for a court to
require an agency to use cost-benefit analysis or the Ames mutagenicity
test as a matter of constitutional law, because the other branches of
government would have too much difficulty overturning that action.
Interpreting an organic statute to require cost-benefit analysis would
be less problematic because Congress could overrule the court, but it
would still have the drawback of restricting any continuing role for the
agency in developing the "meaning" of "sound government" under
that statute. Less intrusive, in the sense of leaving more room for
continuing dialogue and evolution, would be remands requiring the
agency to perform cost-benefit analysis for a certain class of hazardous
substances, for a particular substance, or even for a particular issue
among many issues raised by the standard-setting effort. At the far end
toward deference would be a requirement that the agency explain its
refusal to use cost-benefit analysis, perhaps even in court rather than
under the terms of a remand. There is no single cost-benefit methodology, and even within one brand there are many subtle methodological
choices to be made. Thus, even a judicial requirement that the agency
employ a certain type of analysis, substantive as it is, leaves enormous
room for agency discretion in the details of the analysis. A useful comparison is the rule making negotiation in the preceding example. Specifying cost-benefit analysis is analogous to saying "negotiate with the
interest groups." Several important matters are left to be resolved, not
the least of which is the actual result.

Thus, a court can engage in a partnership with the agency to develop norms of sound governance in many ways. The forcefulness of the
court's role should depend on the clarity with which the court sees the
demands of sound government in the case at hand and on the need to
allow all three branches to continue the collaboration.

What about the conservative judge reviewing a liberal agency's action he or she considers wrong-headed? Does sound governance re-

view invite wholesale nullification of executive actions with which willful judges disagree?

First, there is willfulness today. To the extent that the analysis of
chapters 3 and 4 is persuasive, judicial certitude is a mask for willfulness. Less harshly, it is at least true that the ability of judges to generate
powerful, acceptable arguments—by exploiting the problems of description, categorization, and attributive duality—provides cover for
willful decision making, if the judge is so inclined. (Just as manipulability of the trichotomy empowers litigators to fashion plausible
doctrinal arguments.) *That many judges will be thus inclined to willfulness is
a consequence of their humanness and their recognition that role constraints are
indefinite and instrumental, often capable of accommodating fidelity to a higher
social duty such as justice or sound governance.*

Second, harder-look and sound governance review would increase
the chances that such willfulness, by judges or by administrators, would
be visible rather than shrouded in doctrinal indirection. With clearer
expression of the basis for decision, there would be a clearer basis for
appellate review, for congressional and public scrutiny, and for agency
assessment of how to change its behavior. Rather than submerging the
judge's appreciation and application of the trichotomy's categories and
normatively opposed attributes, sound governance review would invite
both judges and administrators to bare their premises and prevail on
the basis of their persuasiveness. Why would an individual judge or
administrator choose revelation and the resulting criticism rather than
indirection and hope for blind deference? Suspicion of undisclosed
reasoning could be grounds for remand by the appellate or reviewing
court. An equally important consideration, however, would be the individual's understanding that such efforts at revelation and continuing, interactive criticism are an essential contribution to the evolution
of sounder governance. In a post-trichotomy world there would be
more emphasis on the personal virtue of self-revelation and less faith in
the possibility *or institutional virtue* of self-restraint defined with reference to the separation of powers ethos.

The third response to the problem of the willful judge is that the
diversity and the independence provided by life tenure and tradition
make it likely that the pluralism of political and social life generally will
be reflected in the wills of judges. The conservative judge has life
tenure and opportunity for willfulness, but so does the liberal judge,
thus reducing the risk that the judicial branch as a whole will steal the
entire process of governance. Understanding the issues of willfulness
and politics in these terms, moreover, underscores the importance of
the Senate confirmation process. As Lawrence Tribe has noted, the

stakes are too great to treat the constitutional "advice and consent" requirement as a rubber stamp or mere screen for incompetence.[25] Indeed, the analysis in chapters 3 and 4 of the trichotomy's failings, especially in distinguishing law from politics, in my view makes Tribe's proposition indisputable. *Who* the judges are not only shapes the law but also profoundly affects the quality of governance.

Judicial review in a post-trichotomy world undeniably brings judges into a new realm of norms and procedures. At present, judges and lawyers are comfortable with the methodological elements of adjudicatory fairness—neutrality, reasoned elaboration, adversarial argument, and so on. The other two decision making paradigms, politics and science, have their own methodologies and procedures. Those methods may seem unruly and perhaps mysterious to those trained only in the law, just as civil procedure and administrative law are bizarre to nonlawyers. By urging that we take seriously the indistinctness of the fairness-science-politics categories and that the project of administrative law be sound governance, I am also urging that judges and lawyers recognize that public policy and management cannot be analyzed or modeled solely with reference to the procedures and norms familiar to the law. It follows that judges cannot be fully competent partners unless they accept a responsibility to understand (at some minimal level of competence) all three sets of decision making methods.

The existence of substantive judicial review, whether rooted in common law or in congressional enactment, should be taken to mean *neither* that judges redetermine the agency's choices de novo *nor* that judges evaluate the agency solely with reference to a Rule of Law methodology—propositions clearly at odds with any credible definition of the tests of "reasonableness," "arbitrary and capricious," and so forth.

Judge Leventhal observed in *Ethyl* that although generalist judges may not be up to the task of substantive hard-look review, Congress has assigned them that responsibility. I would add the thought that society will take that responsibility away if judges prove inadequate to the task. Meanwhile, judges must do the best they can and not abdicate their duties of partnership.

7.3 Legitimating the Role of Courts: Multiple Forums and Institutional Competence

I have tried to suggest what judicial review might look like in a conception radically removed from separation of powers concerns and focus-

---

25. L. Tribe, God Save This Honorable Court (1985).

ing on sound governance rather than on control of administrative discretion. What would be the source of judicial legitimacy in such a world?

7.3.1 Sound Governance as a Source of Judicial Legitimacy

The role I have described for courts necessarily involves judges in deciding when agencies seem to be making decisions badly and when they do not. I must respond further to those who see this as illegitimate judicial usurpation of legislative and executive powers. That objection is based largely on perceptions that it would take judges out of the business of law and into the business of politics and policy, and we would see judicial aggrandizement at the expense of expert agencies.

But such perceptions are invocations of separation-of-powers role restrictions. These restrictions are subtly implemented, with the underlying formalism muted, through use of the trichotomy. The broad attack on a remodeled judicial role amounts to an argument that if courts do not conform to the trichotomy's doctrinal emanations, they sacrifice its cloak of legitimacy. I have argued at length, however, that those distinctions are too flawed to serve as a basis for doctrine and role definition. In this speculative essay, therefore, I eschew them and whatever undeserved legitimacy they would provide.

But just because I am speculating does not mean I am unconcerned with legitimacy. Where else might we look?

The generative element of legitimacy is that courts must be perceived to be contributing to sound government. This is a concrete source of public acceptance. The other two branches rely on it for their legitimacy, so it should suffice for the judiciary as well. Moreover, this test provides a good incentive for judges to see that their doctrines and actions in fact serve the desired end and are perceived to do so. As Judge Wright has put it, "The ultimate test of the Justices' work, I suggest, must be goodness."[26] Bad doctrine is not just an unfortunate wart on the corpus of Justice. It is potentially as tragic for governance as any grotesque error by one of the other branches. Lawyers and the public ought to treat it as such, but generally they do not.

Sound governance as a theme of legitimacy requires elaboration in two respects. First, the importance of the judiciary derives not from its unique trichotomy-related method of decision making but from its institutional position as an alternative forum for decision making. Second, legitimation through attention to sound governance requires in-

26. J. Skelly Wright, *Professor Bickel, The Scholarly Tradition, and the Supreme Court*, 84 Harv. L. Rev. 769, 797 (1971).

stitutional competence, which means that judges and courts will have to change (and, to an extent, they already are). I take these points up in turn.

7.3.2 Legitimacy through Multiple Forums and Indistinct Roles

In a post-trichotomy world, legitimacy could not depend on a claim that the judge's decision making methods and competence are sharply distinct from those of the administrator. The boundary problems of the trichotomy would make such a claim untenable, except perhaps as to core matters of a generally trivial sort.

Yet we would still insist on a separate judiciary. Judicial review of agency action provides the reassurance of multiple, separated forums of authoritative decision. The genius of the separation of powers is less in the unique character or role of each branch than in the multiplicity of forums provided the individual who seeks to influence or avoid government action. The familiar constitutional checks and balances are only the overt, mechanical aspect of this theme. One aspect of the multiple forums principle is that people with different talents and perspectives may be drawn to service in different branches, if for no other reason than the differences in processes of appointment/election. This diversity benefit would diminish, but not disappear, in a post-trichotomy world eschewing rigid professional role definitions.

This point about multiplicity of forums buttresses my earlier point concerning continuing dialogue among the branches in the evolution of norms of sound governance. The danger to separation of powers principles, properly conceived, is in choking off the interactive, dynamic process of governance. Sharp restrictions on judicial review are inherently dangerous. Broad areas of unreviewable discretion are inherently dangerous. Judicially imposed, rigid requirements of administrative procedure or substance, when chiseled in doctrinal or constitutional granite, are inherently dangerous.

There is good reason to emphasize the importance of multiple forums. With the exploding complexity of public policy and management concerns, the institutional capacity of each branch of government is stretched to the limits. The first to show serious signs of distress was the legislature, and its incapacity to deal with the plethora of lawmaking and political tasks was the proximate cause of the rise in broad delegations. It was not long, however, before the volume and difficulty of the work made it impossible for the particular official to whom responsibility was delegated to take personal responsibility for developing expertise and understanding the matter at hand, even while that

official retained the formal authority for agency decision or promulga-
tion. This problem of diffuse institutional responsibility for agency
decision making has its advantages in terms of the large-scale bureaucratic mobilization of skills and efforts, but it has costs in terms of
centralized, coherent policymaking, application of broader public values, and accountability. The Supreme Court faced these tensions in the
Morgan cases, and the conceptual crisis, implicit in the contrast between
personal and bureaucratic rationality, was finessed in a pragmatic concession to complex administration.[27] The result, however, is that teams
of specialists may work to produce pieces of a complex agency decision,
and middle-level supervisors may stitch the pieces together into a
broad rule or order, and the administrator may look over the product
to make sure that it is the proper size and shape. But it may be that no
one in the agency has the time, competence, and responsibility to ensure that the result is more like Michelangelo's *David* than Franken-
stein's brute. Indeed, one respected commentator has observed that
judicial review may provide the first integrated hard look at the agency's analysis and conclusions.[28]

Judicial review, however, has its own limitations. Surely courts
alone cannot be counted on to define and pursue sound governance.
Wholly apart from our democratic concerns about so charging them,
the institutional limitations of courts and the personal limitations of
judges have been well cataloged by others. I may be unusually sanguine
in my sense that federal appellate judges are more capable in more
senses, both presently and potentially, than critics maintain.

The opportunity to test the detailed formulation and application of
public policy in multiple forums thus becomes key, because we should
doubt that any one institution will today be adequate to the task. Lawyers and law firms increasingly recognize this. The traditional lawyerly
roles in advising and litigation are now complemented by legislative
and agency representation. Lawyers are increasingly prominent in direct political activity on behalf of clients' interests, such as fund raising
and organizing political action groups. Indeed, as if to complete the
conflation of the trichotomy, a few firms and lawyers offer to provide
or procure technical consulting in economics, financial and project
management, or engineering. Far more typically, lawyer-lobbyists regularly function as expert policy advocates, requiring a reach of compe-

27. Morgan v. United States [Morgan I], 298 U.S. 468 (1936); Morgan v. United
States [Morgan II], 304 U.S. 1 (1938); United States v. Morgan [Morgan IV], 313 U.S.
409 (1941). See discussion of bureaucratic rationality, sec. 2.5.

28. Pedersen, *Formal Records and Informal Rulemaking*, 85 Yale L.J. 38 (1975).
William Pedersen served as a career deputy general counsel in the EPA.

tence exceeding even that of the wide-ranging litigator. This system of integrated roles, while creating some risks that the influence industry will distort public processes, may on balance increase the likelihood of sound results by offering the public several opportunities to influence government decision making.

Of course, this is only my surmise, and it is a judgment about the net impact of lawyers and lobbyists, including good and bad effects. My faith on this point is perhaps at odds with the common criticism of lobbyists, political action committees, and the influence industry. Moreover, there is the general sentiment that lawyers tend to "muck things up" and are overpaid to do so. The contrary argument is based on no more than my personal experience and a general inclination to think that a reasonably free marketplace of ideas, information, and access will in general and over time lead decision makers to sound results. There are numerous imperfections in this pseudo-market of policy formation, but the influence industry could not possibly be abolished, and important possibilities exist for addressing the most serious market imperfections. Campaign finance laws and the Ethics in Government Act are limited examples. The point is that lobbying and other forms of representation usually involve developing and providing information and then persuading. These functions are valuable to policymakers. In this imperfect system, my sense is that effective representation, widely available, is a plus for both the interested private party and for the general quality of governmental decision making.

7.3.3 Legitimacy through Institutional and Personal Competence: The Future of Institutions

If sound governance is to be the explicit focus, then judicial review should be entrusted to judges broadly competent for that task. Their central concern with governmental legality cannot be pursued without considerable attention to the less familiar corners of the law-policy-science trichotomy, and hence considerable familiarity with the less familiar methods of the interest accommodation and science paradigms. Lawyers cannot be expected to become as familiar with the technical subtleties of statistical hypothesis testing as they are with the techniques of cross-examination and the subtleties of witness credibility. But they can and routinely do develop rudimentary familiarity with extralegal matters when necessary for the case at hand. Judges regularly called on for service in reviewing agency action should develop the necessary array of personal skills, and their courts should devise the requisite systems of intellectual and logistical support, including perhaps staff experts, broader libraries, resort to expert amici, consultants, and so forth, as I develop below.

I stress the contingency in all this. A court's ability to engage in sound governance review is seriously constrained by the competence of judges to see *clearly* how the agency's decision making can be improved. This capacity necessarily varies from person to person and is an instance of the general question of correspondence between the true personal competence of the individual and the competence of the institution. Judicial review in administrative law is not unique in this respect; no one would suggest that all judges are equally competent to try a mass accident tort suit or a large antitrust action, but we proceed without too much explicit attention to that question. Restricting my attention to administrative law, these assessments of institutional capacity should not be made in a flat, absolute fashion. The competence of judges is variable and can be enhanced through direct management and public policy measures. Continuing legal education programs for judges, including special programs in economics, are but one example. The role conceptions we employ should be based on reality and on the genuine possibilities for changing present circumstances. A related point concerns the need to appraise frankly the institutional competence of agencies (administrators) and legislatures. In a post-trichotomy world, the mythologies about institutional competence and methods can be stripped away so that the operation of the separation of powers partnership can be based on clearer perceptions. I would wager that few judges have a sophisticated understanding of House and Senate rules, committee and staff structure, procedures affecting floor debate, and how all of this should bear on statutory interpretation of legislative intent; or a sophisticated understanding of the roles of the White House, the OMB, and various arms of the particular agency in agency rule making (*see generally* section 2.5).

Below, I briefly consider four models for institutional redesign. These are (1) the French Conseil d'état; (2) increased and reformed centralized agency review in the executive branch; (3) specialized article I or article III courts; and (4) various incremental reforms within the general institutional framework we now have, such as expanded use of masters, ancillary consulting services, and techniques of docket management and case assignment. Then, in section 7.3.3.(d), I quickly consider comparisons with the remedial discretion and judicial creativity characteristic of institutional reform litigation, such as suits concerning school desegregation and prison conditions.

7.3.3.(a) The Conseil d'Etat.   In France, the Conseil d'état (Section du contentieux)[29] sits atop the system of administrative courts,[30] while the Cour de cassation is supreme over the ordinary civil and criminal courts.[31] These two supreme courts, whose jurisdiction is primarily by appeal and by petition, are not hierarchically related, so it would be incorrect to analogize the conseil to agency tribunals in the United States or even to the federal Court of Appeals for the District of Columbia Circuit.

29. In this discussion I draw on the translated materials and cases collected in A. Von Mehren & J. Gordley, The Civil Law System 97–126, 215–45, 307–24, 351–63, 456–91, 503–10 (2d ed. 1977) (hereinafter Von Mehren & Gordley), and L. Brown & J. Gardner, French Administrative Law (3d ed. 1983) (hereinafter Brown & Gardner). *See also* L. Hurwitz, The State As Defendant 66–77 (1981) (hereinafter Hurwitz) (a comparative study of the legal structures of various countries governed by law when the sovereign is sued by the citizen, containing a succinct description of the Conseil d'état); Bermann, *The Scope of Judicial Review in French Administrative Law,* 16 Colum. J. Transnat'l L. 195 (1977) (hereinafter Bermann) (describing the scope of the review the French judiciary uses for administrative action and including an exhaustive bibliography at p. 196, n. 4); Brown, *De Gaulle's Republic and the Rule of Law: Judicial Review and the Conseil d'Etat,* 46 B.U.L. Rev. 462 (1966) (tracing the growth in authority and reforms of the Conseil d'Etat during the Debaille Republic); Cake, *The French Conseil d'Etat: An Essay on Administrative Jurisprudence,* 24 Ad. L. Rev. 315 (1972) (advocating the adoption of some principles of French administrative law into American administrative law/jurisprudence); Ducamin, *The Role of the Conseil d'Etat in Drafting Legislation,* 30 Int'l Comp. L.Q. 882 (1981) (hereinafter Ducamin) (describing the Conseil d'état's role in drafting legislation and advising the legislature on measures under consideration); Neuborne, *Judicial Review and Separation of Powers in France and the United States,* 57 N.Y.U. L. Rev. 363 (1982) (analyzing the force of separation of powers analysis in French constitutional law, discussing primarily the Conseil constitutionnel); Note, *Judicial Review in the French Administrative Courts: Dame David (Conseil d'état 1974) (1977),* 16 Colum. J. Transnat'l L. 174 (1977) (illustrating French judicial review of administrative acts through the *Dame David* case); Riesenfeld, *The French System of Administrative Justice: A Model for American Law?,* 18 B.U.L. Rev. 48 (1938) (an early work comparing the French administrative/judicial relationship with the American and suggesting some similarities).

30. Von Mehren & Gordley at 108–10. The most important administrative courts of first instance are the Tribunaux administratifs, which are organized geographically. The Conseil d'état also reviews, by way of *cassation* (petition), decisions of certain special purpose courts, such as the Conseil suprieur des confiscations des profits illicites, and various special purpose tribunals, such as the Commission centrale d'aide sociale, which play an adjudicative role comparable to agency adjudications in the United States.

31. "In strict French constitutional theory there is only one judicial hierarchy, that for civil and criminal law matters, which is headed by the Cour de cassation. However, if the expression, *judicial,* is taken functionally rather than in a strict separation-of-powers sense, the administrative courts, headed by the Conseil d'état, also [comprise] a 'judicial' hierarchy. A special body—the Tribunal des conflits—exists to resolve jurisdictional disputes between these two hierarchies. Standing apart both institutionally and functionally from the regular- and administrative-court hierarchies is the Conseil Constitutionnel." *Id.* at 97. The Conseil constitutionnel has a limited function involving constitutional review of acts of the national assembly, and its judicial character is somewhat incomplete. *Id.* at 121, 324–40.

The Conseil d'état is an elite civil service organization in which entrance and promotion are competitive and prestigious, as in the Quay d'Orsay or the United States Foreign Service. Tenure, however, is guaranteed by tradition rather than statute.[32] The higher echelons are staffed largely from within, with only one-quarter of the middle grades and one-third of the highest grades filled by experienced government officials initially drawn from outside the Conseil d'état itself.[33]

Adjudication is generally conducted in panels whose members typically are a mix from the junior, intermediate, and senior ranks. To assure consistency among sections, there is a limited further appeal in certain special situations that, for present purposes, might be thought of as an en banc mechanism.[34] The deliberations of a panel are importantly influenced by a *commissaire du gouvernement*, a sort of institutionalized amicus, opinion-drafter, and public interest advocate combined.[35] The commissaires du gouvernement are drawn from the middle ranks of the Conseil d'état civil service and later return to service in its adjudicative and/or administrative sections.[36]

The Conseil d'état has several interesting institutional features apart from its status as an elite civil service. The bulk of its members are graduates of the prestigious Ecole nationale d'administration.[37] Most—*but not all*—of those serving in the adjudicatory section have also studied law. In addition to adjudication, the organization serves important advisory and even administrative functions, chief among them advising the executive departments on draft legislation and regulations.[38] And although the judicial and administrative sections are

32. Brown, *supra* n. 29 at 471; Von Mehren & Gordley at 117–19.

33. Brown & Gardner at 50–56; Ducamin at 896 n. 11; Von Mehren & Gordley at 117, 118.

34. Brown & Gardner at 48–49; Von Mehren & Gordley at 119.

35. The commissaire's functions include summarizing and analyzing the case, relating the proposed result to the corpus of case law, and predicting the future development of case law in light of the proposed result. He or she also has the general goal of recommending a result that is just for the parties and the public interest. The commissaire does not, however, represent the administration as a party in the case. The importance of the commissaire's role is suggested by the fact that official reports of important cases often include the presentation by the commissaire du gouvernement in addition to the brief opinion by the conseil's panel. Brown & Gardner at 64–65; Bermann at 223 n. 117; Von Mehren & Gordley at 147.

36. Von Mehren & Gordley at 117.

37. Hurwitz at 73.

38. *See generally* Ducamin; Von Mehren & Gordley at 119–20. In some instances the advisory participation of the conseil is required by statute; often the agency requests involvement. I note this in part because "legislative" or article I courts in the United States *could* play a comparably flexible role in offering advisory opinions and screening of agency actions in a context other than formal adversarial litigation.

essentially separate, officers in the judicial section usually spend part of their careers in the administrative sections, and a few of those in the administrative sections participate on the adjudicatory panels of the conseil. And not uncommonly, junior, intermediate, and even senior officials are detached for tours of duty in executive agencies.[39] On the whole, therefore, members of the judicial section develop considerable subject matter expertise along with an appreciation for the routines of administration.[40] This undoubtedly lends legitimacy to decisions of the conseil in the perception of administration officials.

Finally, since the late nineteenth century,[41] the French high courts have been instrumental in devising extrastatutory doctrines of quasi-constitutional administrative law *(principes généraux du droit)*— including principles of procedural due process, agency consistency, and requirements of reasons and findings—quite analogous to doctrinal developments in United States administrative law.[42] This is all the more remarkable because, in keeping with France's traditions as a civil law jurisdiction, the ordinary courts have generally not strayed beyond the usual sources of positive law.[43]

From the perspective of United States administrative law, therefore, the Conseil d'état is indeed a strange creature. From origins in the ancien régime as a creature of the sovereign, it has amassed an impressive stature of relative independence from the executive.[44] Yet the

39. Bermann at 197–98.

40. Von Mehren & Gordley at 119.

41. *See also The Blanco Decision*, Tribunal des conflits, 8 Feb. 1873, D. 1873. III. 17, 20 (note), S. 1873. II. 153 (note) (Von Mehren & Gordley at 351).

42. *See, e.g.,* Bermann at 219 n. 105 (general principle of nonretroactivity of administrative acts); Société Maison Genestal, [1968] Rec. Cons. d'Et. 62, [1969] D. Jur. 456, [1968] Jurisclasseur Priodique [J.C.P.] A.J.D.A. 102 (excerpted in Von Mehren & Gordley at 509; cited and quoted in Bermann at 210 n. 54) (denial of discretionary tax relief was explained in impermissibly general terms); Von Mehren & Gordley at 458–73 (discussing the principles of equality of treatment under the law and freedom of commerce and industry; discussing also the "procedural" principles of (1) notice, (2) minimum periods of time for preparation before appearance, (3) the right of defense, and (4) a right to a hearing).

43. Also: "The activity becomes more problematical, at least in the French view, when the court does not rely on a rule or norm set out, to take the most usual case, in a legislative enactment but depends instead on a judicial articulation of general ideas of justice or legality widely held by the society." Von Mehren & Gordley at 459.

44. On history of the conseil, *see* Von Mehren & Gordley at 110–17; Brown & Gardner at 27–40. True indicators of independence are, of course, difficult to state and measure. At a formal level, the president of the Republic appoints the minister of justice, who also acts as president of the conseil and plays a role in selecting the career vice presidents and section heads. In practice there is no pattern of executive control over the conseil. The conseil is, in a sense, a creature of classical French separation of powers

conseil's close relation to the executive provided the jurisprudential and political legitimacy for its substantially extrastatutory evolution of legal rules intended to constrain official discretion. Complainants can take comfort in the independent and judicial demeanor of the conseil's judicial section, while agencies consider that the conseil sits fairly close to the executive and is, structurally, part of the *"administration."* What, then, of the separation of powers?

In searching for institutional vehicles for our post-trichotomy, reconstructed administrative law, the Conseil d'état has several attractive features. For example, the mix of legal and nonlegal professional skills, and the leavening provided by tours of administrative service, promise greater personal and institutional capacity than in the American judiciary to appreciate the workings of all three decision making paradigms. Indeed, we might expect to see in the conseil something akin to sound governance review, as experienced conseilleurs developed a "common law" of sound governance and pressed agencies to improve the quality of scientific and political exercises.[45] We might also expect a jurisprudence of aggressive intervention and creative remedies, as the elite of the conseil sought to magnify their public service by exerting more control over bureaucratic action.

On the other hand, the mix of professional skills may tend to deflate the lawyerly inclination to find legal and judicial solutions for every ill. And professional exposure to the inner workings of executive agencies, through tours of duty, may instill a respect for the agency's autonomy and comparative advantage as strong as any trichotomy-based verbal formula about deference to expertise could ever manage. The absence of constitutional or statutory guarantees of tenure raises questions about independence, but an elite career bureaucracy can be obstinately independent; indeed, one would worry that careerist forces and "company-think" might produce gray spirits and intellects, as critics have sometimes said of career foreign service and military officers in the United States. How do these factors balance in France, and how would they balance in the United States?

I began examining French cases with the hypothesis that the Con-

---

theory. That theory emphasized problems of infringement rather than checks and balances, making supervision of the administration by traditional courts problematic.

45. Bermann finds a recent trend consistent with this hypothesis. The conseil, he argues, has begun to exercise "full review" over disputes involving legal characterization of fact in areas previously considered too delicate for judicial investigation. Bermann at 250–52, *citing* Société des Ciments Lafarge [1974] Rec. Cons. d'Et. 628 [1975] A.J.D.A. 237 (whether the minister of agriculture properly denied a deforestation permit allegedly necessary for a region's ecological equilibrium).

seil d'état would employ a more interventionist brand of review than we typically see in article III courts of general jurisdiction. I assumed that the significant institutional differences would yield a strikingly different jurisprudence. Interestingly, however, French public law includes many of the themes of deference to expertise, fact-law-policy distinctions, and so forth that are so prominent in United States law.[46] These shared themes are evident in spite of the considerably smaller separation of roles between the conseil and the French executive as compared with the distance between, say, the D.C. Court of Appeals and the EPA. For whatever reasons, an American administrative lawyer finds much that is familiar in the decisions of the conseil.

But does the similarity in themes necessarily mean that in the decisions of the Conseil d'état the overall scaling of deference and constraint is like that in American administrative law? It is difficult, of course, to form a reliable impression concerning this comparative point. That would require an ambitious research effort, carefully designed and quite beyond the scope of this book. Consider how one would reliably demonstrate a comparably sweeping characterization of American administrative law: "How deferential are the courts?" Does the questioner have in mind the D.C. Circuit, circa 1975, or Judge Friendly, Judge Harry Edwards, or Justice Antonin Scalia? Review of SEC actions, or the vastly more numerous cases concerning the SSA? Even without broaching the conceptual complexity (if not disarray) I have described in this work, a fair summation is no simple task.

As an amateur comparativist I can report only that no unambiguous conclusion emerges. On the whole, however, I doubt that one could establish that review by the Conseil d'état is markedly more interventionist than hard-look review,[47] when that approach is taken by

46. *See, e.g.,* Bermann at 198 (noting distinction between *legalité,* the conformity of administrative action to law, and *opportunité,* the wisdom and advisability of that action); Von Mehren & Gordley at 485 (in those cases in which findings require expertness, the scope of review is "manifest error"; relatively few administrative decisions, perhaps three or four, are reversed on this ground).

47. Bermann writes that "those who have examined the question conclude unanimously that, on balance, French administrative law judges are more demanding of the government than their counterparts in the [French] judicial courts on the occasions in which administrative law disputes come before [judicial courts]." Bermann at 208 (citations omitted). Those occasions, however, are infrequent. Moreover, the same is probably true in comparing American judges and courts, and hence the traditional leadership role of the D.C. Circuit in most areas of administrative law. The French-American comparison is rather elusive. *See, e.g.,* Gomel [1914], Rec. Cons. d'Et. 487, [1917] S. Jur. III 25 (Von Mehren & Gordley at 478). According to Bermann, *Gomel* is often cited for the proposition that "administrative courts scrutinize the application of law to facts as closely as they review the findings of fact themselves." Bermann at 211 (citing a treatise by a distinguished former president of the conseil). Even without considering the possibility that the particular statutory grant of reviewing powers gave the conseil authority to

American courts. Indeed, my impression is that the leading decisions of the conseil that might be cited as examples of interventionist review are easily understandable within the conventional framework of American administrative law, encompassing such cases as *NLRB v. Hearst, Benzene,* and *State Farm.*

It may be that the Conseil d'état has taken the course it has because even in the French brand of separation of powers, and even with the androgynous institutional character of the conseil, the conceptual models for agency and adjudicator have been essentially the same as those in the United States, and the project of administrative law has been the same: control of illegal and abusive discretion.

It is disappointing that the two bodies of law seem to be so similar at the fundamental level under examination here. Perhaps even radical restructuring of American institutions would leave us with the conceptual difficulties rooted in a separation of powers ethos. I take two more hopeful lessons, however. First, the evident importance of separation of powers themes in French public law simply underscores that those fundamental currents tend to direct the flow of doctrine no matter what institutional vessels we launch, so that the thorough reconstruction of conceptual categories is necessary, while institutional reform alone is not sufficient. Second, institutional reform alone can be sweeping without wreaking havoc. Transplanting the conseil to American soil sounds radical enough. But it might not change much about the way the environment is protected or the electromagnetic spectrum allocated.

Nevertheless, the Conseil d'état bears investigation and consideration as an alternative institutional vessel for judicially directed quality control. Its professionalism, though not its jurisprudence, fits the spirit of this chapter strikingly. Perhaps we should classify it as a hybrid of the D.C. Circuit Court of Appeals and OMB?[48]

---

substitute judgment on the question of whether a proposed building site would interfere with a "monumental perspective," the *Gomel* decision has many American analogues. Most obviously, thousands of district court decisions each year involve social security disability disputes comparable to the mixed law-fact question in *Gomel.* Finally, in characterizing the practical realities of scope of review, notwithstanding some doctrinal verbiage suggesting careful scaling and areas of interventionism, Bermann at 252 n. 282, quotes two members of the Conseil d'état: "[T]he doctrine of *erreur manifeste* 'has a solid basis in the psychology of the administrative judge, who tends to think, even in cases where his review theoretically is total, that he should not substitute his judgment for the governments, unless the latter is plainly enough in error'" (quoting Galabert & Gentot, *Chronique générale de jurisprudence administrative française* [1962], A.J.D.A. 552, 553).

48. In the following section I draw on my experience in the Carter administration on the White House staff and in the Immediate Office of the Secretary of Health, Education, and Welfare.

7.3.3.(b) The OMB Model. The Office of Management and Budget now has a centralized screening function for major regulations developed by the executive agencies.[49] To what extent can such a centralized form of nonjudicial review fulfill the objectives of the harder-look review described in chapter 6 or of still more ambitious sound governance review sketched in this chapter? Can centralized executive review obviate a recasting of the role of judges or the creation of new judicial institutions?[50]

Although only the very top tiers are appointed officials rather than career civil servants, OMB is first and foremost an agent of the president rather than a source of thoroughly independent review: its central mission is to assist the president in implementing his program, and that mission guides its oversight and coordination of agency budgets, regulatory activity, legislative proposals, congressional testimony by agency officials, procurement policy, and management practices. From the perspective of the president and his close advisers, the professionalism and high caliber of OMB civil servants are both blessing and curse, in that the staff provides able assistance but can also create obstacles when their experience and values lead them to resist administration initiatives. On balance, however, the influence of OMB has grown over the past twenty years with only brief interruptions, evidencing the cumulative judgment of chief executives that OMB generally serves them well.

Thus, although White House and OMB review of regulations includes attention to all three of the trichotomy's decision making paradigms and is a species of sound governance review in my sense, the guiding principle for that review is effective prosecution of the president's program, not sound governance.

The difficulty with conceiving of this OMB model as a substitute for genuine sound governance review is not simply that OMB is not part of the judiciary. Whatever institution is to police the appropriate mix of decision making paradigms must itself be constituted so as to promise

49. *See* Executive Order 12291, 46 Fed. Reg. 13193 (1981). The order requires that for any "major" rule, agencies prepare and transmit a Regulatory Impact Analysis to OMB at least 60 days prior to the publication in the Federal Register of the Notice of Proposed Rulemaking. Substantively, rules must be cost-effective. Pre-publication screening affords OMB the opportunity to reshape proposed regulations that conflict with the administration's political goals. States are also experimenting with regulatory reforms, including the creation of centralized administrative oversight. *See, e.g.,* A.B.1111, 1979 Cal. Stat. 567; Cohen, *Regulatory Reform: Assessing the California Plan,* 1983 Duke L.J. 231 (1983).

50. *See* Mashaw, Bureaucratic Justice, *supra* n. 15 at 226–27; *cf.* Stewart & Liebman, *Book Review,* 96 Harv. L. Rev. 1952, 1967–68 (1983).

an appropriate mix of those paradigms. OMB is inevitably deficient with respect to the adjudicatory fairness paradigm, because we reasonably anticipate that its institutional position will cause it to assess soundness in accordance with the president's perspective—*as it should.*[51] As a mere echo, it would thus defeat the notion of multiplicity of forums I have suggested as the core, continuing element of separation of powers protections.

7.3.3.(c) Specialized or Reformed Courts. In light of these questions about the shortcomings of the Conseil d'état and the OMB models, a more promising approach for implementation of sound governance review may be the more familiar notion of specialized courts. These include both article I courts and judges, such as the Tax Court and bankruptcy judges,[52] and article III courts with special jurisdictional or venue provisions.[53] The Court of Appeals for the Federal Circuit, for example, hears appeals from specialized tribunals, including patent and copyright matters.[54] Congress has established temporary dedicated courts, such as those responsible for litigation arising from price controls and railroad reorganizations. Special jurisdictional or venue provisions have been used to aid implementation of complex statutes, like the Clean Air Act, as to which Congress thought both timely consideration and nationwide uniformity were especially important.[55]

51. Even if we were more sanguine about creating an integrative perspective within OMB than within the judiciary, it makes no sense to do so, because presidents would reinvent an OMB to serve loyally its present, essential functions.

52. *See* 26 U.S.C. §§ 7441 *et seq.* (1983) (U.S. Tax Court); 28 U.S.C. §§ 151 *et seq.* (1983) (U.S. Bankruptcy Court). *See also* 28 U.S.C. §§ 171 *et seq.* (1983) (U.S. Claims Court); 10 U.S.C. §§ 86 *et seq.* (1983) (Court of Military Appeals); 7 U.S.C. §§ 136 *et seq.* (1983) (F.I.F.R.A. Compensation arbitrators). *See generally* M. Redish, Federal Jurisdiction: Tensions in the Allocation of Judicial Power (1980); C. Wright, A. Miller, & E. Cooper, 16 Federal Practice and Procedure §§ 4101–4 (1978); L. Tribe, American Constitutional Law §§ 3–5 at 40–47 (1978); Redish, *Legislative Courts, Administrative Agencies, and the Northern Pipeline Decision,* 1983 Duke L.J. 197 (1983).

53. *See* 28 U.S.C. §§ 251 *et seq.,* §§ 1581 *et seq.* (1983) (article III Court of International Trade, with jurisdiction over tariff, duty, and related trade matters); 42 U.S.C. § 1973 (1983) (D.C. District Court has exclusive jurisdiction to hear states' petitions for 1965 Voting Rights Act Exemptions); 28 U.S.C. §§ 2342, 2343 (1983) (D.C. Circuit has jurisdiction and venue to review all final orders of the secretary of agriculture, FMC, NRC, and FCC).

54. 28 U.S.C. § 1295 (1983). The court also hears appeals from the U.S. Claims Court, the Merit Systems Protection Board, and the U.S. Court of International Trade. It was created in 1982 by the merger of the Court of Claims and Court of Customs and Patent Appeals. *See* Federal Courts Improvement Act of 1982, Pub. L. 97–164, § 127(a), 96 Stat. 25, 37–38 (1982).

55. *See, e.g.,* 45 U.S.C. § 719(b) (1983) (Special Railroad Reorganization Courts); 12 U.S.C. § 1904 note (1983) and U.S.C. § 717 note (1983) (Temporary Emergency Court of

The purpose and results of such specialization are: greater subject matter competence of those judges and their supporting staffs; libraries can change; judicial clerks can be recruited with special reference to the mix of skills useful in appraising the issues at bar; and advocates can explore nuances and lines of argument that might not be accessible to ordinary judges.[56] And though there are a great many parallels between the work of such courts and the work of agency tribunals, there remain important differences.[57] The most salient difference, however, is that an agency tribunal is identified by the public generally and by the parties before it as part of the agency. It is implausible to claim that a social security administrative law judge or even the Social Security Appeals Council is functionally equivalent to a federal district or appellate court; even those who propose to curtail sharply the availability of judicial review of mass bureaucratic justice do not claim that the nature of the decision making undertaken by an adjudicator *within* the agency is—however insulated—equivalent to that of a judge outside of it. Indeed, initiatives to curb or eviscerate judicial review are usually based on a judgment that such external review *is* different and that this difference is to little good effect, at least in net terms.

A specialized court poses problems, of course. First, it is argued that generalist judges will be more disposed to the democratic tasks of integrating the development of law with the general cultural fabric. This is a sort of Jacksonian argument that judges should be "common" enough to truly have the interests of the people at heart, or that generalists will have a broader sense of the public welfare. A fine argument, so far as it goes. Its faults are the implications that specialized knowledge necessarily breeds elitists (if not oligarchs) and that generalists are immune to those diseases. It can hardly be argued, however, that

Appeals hears cases arising under Emergency Natural Gas Act of 1977); Lockerty v. Phillips, 319 U.S. 182 (1943) (sustaining exclusive jurisdiction of Emergency Court of Appeals to hear challenges to Emergency Price Control Act). *See generally* Wright, Miller, & Cooper, *supra* n. 52 at §§ 3508–28 (1984), §§ 4105, 4106 (1978).

56. Agreement that specialized judicial tribunals are a good idea, however, is far from unanimous. *See* Posner, *Will the Federal Courts of Appeals Survive until 1984? An Essay on Delegation and Specialization of the Judicial Function*, 56 S. Cal. L. Rev. 761, 775–89 (1983); *Report of the Study Group on the Caseload of the Supreme Court*, 57 F.R.D. 573, 585 (1972). For a more neutral presentation, *see* Jordan, *Specialized Courts: A Choice?*, 76 Nw. U.L. Rev. 745 (1981). Even Richard Posner, however, has agreed that the European system may have some merit: "In Europe, the judiciary is much more specialized than it is in this country; and I am not prepared to assert that is a bad thing, given the very different structure of the continental system." 56 S. Cal. L. Rev. at 778 (1983).

57. *See* Redish, *supra* n. 52 at 197 (reviewing the distinctions between article III courts, article I courts, and agency tribunals, in the wake of the *Northern Pipeline* decision invalidating broad grants of power to non-article III bankruptcy judges).

today's federal bench is a cross-section of America. Legal education and professional achievement—the prerequisites for appointment—together with life tenure, force a special reinterpretation of this Jacksonian imperative. I cannot envision, even in this essay, a markedly different political and social system for selection of federal article III judges.[58] Hence, by and large, judges would continue to be as representative (or not) as they are now.

Second, it can be argued that generalist judges are appropriate because courts should decide questions of law, by hypothesis accessible to generalist lawyers. The corollary of this is that by keeping judges as generalists and insisting that they restrict their attention to matters within their personal competence, one keeps the judiciary out of the realms of politics and expert policymaking. But this argument is quite evidently no more than a subtle restatement of the trichotomy-based theory of roles that it has been my purpose to challenge. Since I have abandoned the fairness-politics-science categories for purposes of this chapter, this second objection to enhanced judicial competence has no force. In particular, the analysis in chapters 3 and 4 of the trichotomy's conceptual failings teaches us that any such separation of roles will fail in practice, with the resulting doctrine subject to fair criticism that it is an elaborate mask for judicial discretion and an inefficacious means of improving government.

A related argument is that specialists will be controversial nominees, likely to further politicize the appointment process. We already have novel ideological screens and growing unease in the Senate. As yet, the confirmation process has focused usually on general qualifications and occasionally on judicial philosophy. Would substantive and ideological tests become more particular for specialized article III administrative judges? On the one hand, appointees to independent regulatory agencies and article I courts are carefully screened by the administration, and the Senate almost always defers. Life tenure raises the stakes for both ends of Pennsylvania Avenue; this is one reason why article III courts may not be appropriate for sound governance review. On the other hand, there is the old saw that judicial robes can work wondrous surprises. I do believe that assiduous judicial screening can be generally effective. The bottom line, however, is that politics (but far

58. Of course, the very purpose of establishing a science court or a conseil d'état would be to alter the selection process as well as the institutional character. In addition to the extensive participation of nonlawyers in the adjudicatory work of the conseil, distinguished officials from agencies and from the private sector, such as union officials, serve temporary terms as administrative judges. *See* Bermann at 197 n. 10; Brown & Gardner at 39–40.

short of a litmus test on a particular matter) is relevant to sound governance review. Some more deliberate "bilateral" review of a nominee's views is appropriate for the new tasks of administrative law.

A third reason to question specialized post-trichotomy courts is that the new brand of judge would play a partnership role in the evolution of norms of sound governance. Yet that evolutionary process is unproven. It probably could cloak itself in either the legitimating, protective garb of science[59] and managerial efficiency, as administrators do, or in the garb of priestly legal science and reasoned elaboration familiar to common law judges and courts generally.[60]

What circumstances would assure us that the special court would appropriately embody the combination of methodological sensibilities we want, rather than become a headless OMB or a more aggressive, but no more accountable, version of the D.C. Circuit?

Several considerations are reassuring. Professional exposure akin to that of officials in the Conseil d'état would moderate tendencies toward excessive interventions likely to disable administration. An article I tribunal might also be more appropriate than an article III court, so that terms of office and patterns of appointment would provide a balance of independence and accountability. There are, after all, many examples from which to choose. Even among the independent agencies, the status of the Federal Reserve Board is quite different from that of the Federal Trade Commission,[61] which is more closely identified as

59. Over the years, various proposals have been made for the creation of a pseudojudicial "science court" of scientists to pass on critical disputes, such as nuclear safety or whether cloroflourocarbons threaten the ozone layer. *See* Martin, *The Proposed "Science Court,"* 75 Mich. L. Rev. 1058 (1977); Kantrowitz, *Controlling Technology Democratically,* 63 American Scientist 505 (Sept.–Oct. 1975); Callan, *The Science Court,* 193 Science 950–51 (1976); Ackerman et al., The Uncertain Search for Environmental Quality 147–61 (1974). One could also imagine such tribunals operating as adjuncts or masters within the judiciary. I am quite skeptical of the notion of an independent science court, however, because I am persuaded by the analysis of ch. 3 that such a court could never disentangle pure science issues from their political and legal context. Efforts to do so would distort the ultimate decision.

60. Posner, *supra* n. 56 at 761, 780. "A person who does only one job may [do] better than an abler person who divides his time among several jobs. . . . But I wonder how transferable this insight is from the industrial, technical, and academic fields where it is conventionally articulated to appellate judging."

61. Governors of the FRB are appointed for fourteen-year terms by the president, with Senate confirmation; his choice is to have "due regard" for a "fair representation of the financial, agricultural, industrial and commercial interests, and geographical divisions of the country." 12 U.S.C. § 241 (1983). Federal Trade commissioners, by contrast, are appointed for seven-year terms by the president, with the advice and consent of the Senate; the only qualification on composition mandates that no more than three of the five commissioners can be members of the same political party. The president may

a creature of administration policy. Still further toward the pole of political accountability is the National Labor Relations Board.[62] And ultimately, of course, Congress would retain its powers to regulate the jurisdiction and even reconsider the existence of the administrative law tribunal.

Short of creating new courts, there are ways to develop and take advantage of greater sensibilities on the part of judges to the expert and policy issues before the courts. One can imagine far wider use of special masters, court-appointed experts, and court-appointed amici. Such consulting services would be expensive, but so are the costs of erroneous judicial action, including regulatory delays caused by quasi-procedural remands. On an individual level, we already see a wide-spread effort to expose federal judges to economic analysis, not only in the professional literature but in various training programs. It seems appropriate also to teach judges about particular policy fields: the environment, the energy sector, the transportation sector, disability and employment, food and drug quality, and so forth.[63]

The difficulty is that, under present practices, no judge can be certain enough that her caseload will present food and drug issues, for example, frequently enough to justify a human capital investment in that particular field.[64] If judges happen to have the expertise already, then they may be more likely to have a case assigned to them for trial or,

---

designate which commissioner will serve as chair. 15 U.S.C. § 41 (1983). Presidents not uncommonly are frustrated in their desire to dictate what economic policies the FRB will pursue. Such clashes over general FTC policy (as distinguished from a particular cease and desist adjudication) are unusual.

62. Members of the NLRB are appointed for five-year terms, with Senate confirmation; there are no restrictions on the composition of the board's membership. 29 U.S.C. § 153(a) (1982). The policy reversals that occur when a new party gains control of the executive is proof of the political accountability such an appointments scheme yields; yet the failings of the trichotomy discussed in chs. 3 and 4 make it possible for judges and advocates to characterize these flip-flops as misexecution of expertise or of adjudicatory fairness.

63. The University of Virginia Law School began a graduate program for judges in 1980. About one-half of the course work involves interdisciplinary studies, including law and economics, courts and the social sciences, and law and medicine. The program's premise, however, is that judges are and will be legal generalists. *See generally* Meador, *The Graduate Degree Program for Judges at the University of Virginia*, 22 Judges J. 19–22 (Spring 1983).

64. In rejecting the idea of specialized tribunals, Posner takes "as given the existing structure of the American legal system . . . [and assumes] that the methods of educating lawyers, appointing judges, and conducting trials will remain fundamentally the same." Posner, *supra* n. 56 at 777. He goes on to concede, however, that "[i]t is possible to conceive of the creation of a specialized judiciary as part of a more far-reaching reorganization of the American Legal System." *Id.* at 777–78.

at the appellate level, they may be more likely to be assigned the opinion for a panel.

But these informal mechanisms are very uncertain, and they are inadequate to the ambitious objectives of sound governance review. More explicit provisions for specialization seem both desirable and feasible. Docket management by court clerks and chief judges could accomplish much of this, as could an expanded subject matter–based process of allowing judges to sit for cases by designation. Venue transfers designed to place complex cases before judges with acknowledged subject matter competence would elevate harder look and sound governance above the objective of forum convenience, which seems desirable.

I have meant this sketch of some possible institutional arrangements to suggest how my general themes of (1) sound governance, (2) alternative bases for judicial legitimacy, (3) integration of all three paradigms, and (4) contingent competence and role-definition, might, with further study, be pressed toward concreteness.

7.3.3.(d) Lessons from the Structural Injunction in Institutional Reform Litigation. The judicial tasks contemplated in this and the preceding chapter have instructive parallels in institutional reform cases—that is, the subset of public law litigation in which the trial court is called on to implement a structural injunction.[65] The most prominent subject areas of this type are apportionment, school desegregation, prisons,[66] and mental hospital conditions.[67] The Supreme Court was reluctant to sail

65. The term *public law litigation* was coined by Chayes. Chayes, *The Role of the Judge in Public Law Litigation*, 89 Harv. L. Rev. 1281 (1976). On the term *structural injunction, see* O. Fiss, The Civil Rights Injunction 7 (1978), *and* Fiss, *The Supreme Court 1978 Term—Foreword: The Forms of Justice,* 93 Harv. L. Rev. 1, 2 (1979) ("structural reform").

66. *See, e.g.,* Ruiz v. Estelle, 503 F. Supp. 1265 (S.D. Tex. 1980) (unconstitutional conditions in Texas prisons), *motion to stay granted in part and denied in part,* 650 F.2d 555 (5th Cir. Unit A) *(per curiam), additional motion to stay granted in part and denied in part,* 666 F.2d 555 (5th Cir. 1982).

67. *See, e.g.,* Wyatt v. Stickney, 325 F. Supp. 781 (M.D. Ala. 1972), *aff'd in part sub nom.* Wyatt v. Aderholt, 503 F.2d 1305 (5th Cir. 1974). Other areas of litigation can take on important elements of the institutional reform case. *See, e.g.,* Rizzo v. Goode, 423 U.S. 362 (1976) (comprehensive injunctive relief for police misconduct overturned); Boston Chapter, NAACP v. Beecher, 749 F.2d 102 (1984) (and related cases cited therein) (Boston police and fire employment discrimination remedy required comprehensive prospective relief and repeated judicial supervision); United States v. Metropolitan Dist. Comm'n, slip op. Feb. 7, 1986, Dec. 23, 1985, and Sept. 5, 1985 (Nos. 85–0489-MA and 83–1614-MA, and related state and federal court orders cited therein) (D.-Mass.) (environmental pollution of Boston Harbor involving several parties, court-appointed expert and master, and several years of oversight). *See generally* Special Project, *The Remedial Process in Institutional Reform Litigation,* 78 Colum. L. Rev. 784 (1978).

into these waters, invoking both justiciability concerns[68] and restrictive interpretations of the "substantive" positive law rights at stake.[69] And once the course was set, there was resistance both within the judiciary[70] and among commentators.[71] Moreover, the course is by no means steady, because the Supreme Court has trimmed sails in every area—perhaps rejecting the earlier premises and promises or perhaps merely restraining lower courts and plaintiffs who prefer to go farther.[72]

In questioning the sweep of structural injunctions, appellate courts and commentators repeatedly lodge four conceptual complaints. These track the trichotomy and, in significant respects, parallel the predictable critique of sound governance review. This is not surprising, in that structural injunctions present the dual challenges familiar from chapter 1: Can one formulate criteria with which to control the public agency defendant while ensuring that those criteria are judicially manageable—that they constrain the remedial discretion of the courts?

Complaint 1. Nonlegal Issues and Polycentric Structure: The liability and remedy phases raise "nonlegal" issues. A judge in institutional reform cases must decide how much mixing of the races is necessary to establish a

68. *See, e.g.,* Colegrove v. Green, 328 U.S. 549 (1946) (political question doctrine prevents adjudicating malapportionment controversy).

69. *See, e.g.,* Sweatt v. Painter, 339 U.S. 629 (1950) (enforcing separate-but-equal doctrine to require admission of blacks to a state's white law school where the alternative black school was clearly inferior); San Antonio Indep. School Dist. v. Rodriguez, 411 U.S. 1 (1973) (rejecting equal protection claim against state's school financing system; minimum rationality review appropriate because of courts' inexperience and need to defer to legislative judgment).

70. *See, e.g.,* Baker v. Carr, 369 U.S. 186, 266–330 (Frankfurter, J., dissenting); Bickel, *The Decade of School Desegregation,* 64 Colum. L. Rev. 193, 209 ("opposition judges" in the district courts); Fletcher, *The Discretionary Constitution: Institutional Remedies and Judicial Legitimacy,* 91 Yale L.J. 635, 681 (1982) (noting resistance).

71. *See, e.g.,* A. Bickel, The Supreme Court and the Idea of Progress 151–73 (1970 ed.); Diver, *The Judge as Political Powerbroker: Superintending Structural Change in Public Institutions,* 65 Va. L. Rev. 43, 103–6 (1979).

72. *See, e.g.,* Mobile v. Bolden, 446 U.S. 55 (1980) (requiring proof of discriminatory intent in certain voting rights cases; subsequently reversed by statute); Rhodes v. Chapman, 452 U.S. 337 (1981) (overruling lower court order prohibiting double-celling in prison populated far beyond rated capacity); Pasadena City Bd. of Educ. v. Spangler, 427 U.S. 424 (1976) (district court exceeded its authority by requiring board to adjust attendance zones to reflect demographic shifts); Pennhurst State School and Hosp. v. Halderman, 451 U.S. 1 (1981) (overruling lower court to hold that there is no right to treatment under federal law for confined mental health patients). *See also* Rizzo v. Goode, 423 U.S. 362 (1976); Los Angeles v. Lyons, 461 U.S. 95, 101–13 (1983) (effectively curtailing vindication of substantive right by creating a requirement of remedial standing).

The voting rights struggle illustrates this interplay between the search for judicially workable "legal" standards in an area involving unfamiliar norms and social forces. The

multiracial "unitary" school district, how much departure from strict population equality is permissible in apportionment plans for jurisdictions with a history of discrimination, how large a prison cell must be for two human beings, or how quickly a public authority must stop dumping inadequately treated sewage into the ocean. In the administrative law context, sound governance review would thrust judges into the business of evaluating both the quality and the mix of unfamiliar paradigms, and without familiar legal constraints on their discretion to do so. One potential difficulty is thought to be that stating substantive tests for sound science or politics would require unfamiliar knowledge and language (see the counts of the indictment, below). A second is that there are few positive sources, legal or historical, for those standards. And a third is that the controversies are "polycentric" rather than bipolar[73] and thus not readily adaptable to traditional adversarial adjudication. Obviously, each of these difficulties has significance only in relation to our static assumptions about paradigm boundaries and comparative institutional competence. My earlier discussion of alternative institutional models was intended to illustrate the contingency of those assumptions.

 Complaint 2. Political Interference: The remedy will interfere with the

---

advantage of the "one man, one vote" formula in Reynolds v. Simms, 377 U.S. 533 (1964), was its apparent simplicity—a substantive constitutional right was announced, and in a form that appeared to limit remedial discretion. *See* the discussion in Fletcher, *supra* n. 42 at 668. The expectation that this formula might finesse the difficulty of judging the quality of political representativeness in inherently complex contexts was somewhat misplaced, however. *See, e.g.,* Gaffney v. Cummings, 412 U.S. 735 (1973) (divided court considering what deviations from strict proportionality might be tolerated in partisan redistricting scheme); *cf.* Kirkpatrick v. Preisler, 394 U.S. 526 (1969) (seemingly more stringent standard). Moreover, the Voting Rights Act of 1965, 42 U.S.C. § 1973c (1976), thrust the courts into a broader struggle as the volume of litigation swelled. Unease with the standardlessness of the inquiry pressed on judges by voting rights plaintiffs may help to explain the retrenchment of the Burger Court. In Mobile v. Bolden, 446 U.S. 55 (1980), a plurality of the Court sought to limit the substantive right by requiring proof of discriminatory intent under both the Fourteenth and Fifteenth amendments and under the Voting Rights Act, as the Court had already done with respect to employment and housing policy claims under the Fourteenth Amendment. Arlington Heights v. Metropolitan Housing Dev. Corp., 429 U.S. 252 (1977) (town excluded low-income housing); Washington v. Davis, 426 U.S. 229 (1976) (employment discrimination).

 73. *See generally* Eisenberg, *Participation, Responsiveness, and the Consultative Process: An Essay for Lon Fuller,* 92 Harv. L. Rev. 410 (1978); Chayes, *supra* n. 65 at 1282; Weiler, *Two Models of Judicial Decisionmaking,* 46 Can. B. Rev. 406, 420–26 (1968). The classic treatment of polycentric disputes is M. Polyani, The Logic of Liberty (1951). Polyani's work is consistent with trichotomy-based assumptions about institutional roles and competence.

political processes of the defendant public entity. This is both a concern about comparative competence and an independent claim about comity. Although strongest in the intergovernmental context when federalism is at play, it does have some significance when the defendant is a federal entity. But, in the administrative context, to the extent that judicial interventions are subconstitutional—perhaps even requiring no more than further agency analysis and explanation—the comity concerns would seem slight. Again, my contention is that the demonstrable link to a sound governance goal is available as a powerful legitimating force for court action.

Complaint 3. Expertise/Management Encroachment: The remedy will displace the expert administrators and interfere with managerial efficiency. For example, in *Rhodes v. Chapman,* the Supreme Court reversed the trial court order prohibiting double celling in a prison filled far beyond its rated capacity, saying: "[C]ourts cannot assume that state legislatures and prison officials are insensitive to the requirements of the Constitution or to the perplexing sociological problems of how best to achieve the goals of the penal function in the criminal justice system."[74] And in *Bell v. Wolfish,* the Court wrote:

> The deplorable conditions and Draconian restrictions of some of our Nation's prisons are too well known to require recounting here, and the federal courts rightly have condemned these sordid aspects of our prison systems. But many of these same courts have, in the name of the Constitution, become increasingly enmeshed in the minutiae of prison operations. Judges, after all, are human. They, no less than others in our society, have a natural tendency to believe that their individual solution to often intractable problems are better and more workable than those of the persons who are actually charged with and trained in the running of the particular institution under examination. But under the Constitution, the first question to be answered is not whose plan is best, but in what branch of the Government is lodged the authority to initially devise the plan. This does not mean that constitutional rights are not to be scrupulously observed. It does mean, however, that the inquiry of federal courts into prison management must be limited to the issue of whether a particular system violates any prohibition of the Constitution or, in the case of a federal prison, a statute. The wide range of "judgment calls" that meet constitutional and statutory require-

74. 452 U.S. at 352 (1981).

ments are confided to officials outside of the Judicial Branch of Government.[75]

This reads precisely like an administrative law case, invoking trichotomy-based notions of role and scope of review, except that administrative law is subconstitutional.

Complaint 4. Institutional Competence/Legitimacy: Because of the forgoing points, the courts lack competence to engage in institutional reform and in so doing put their legitimacy at risk. Notwithstanding the force of this traditionalist challenge and the recent pattern of retrenchment in many areas of institutional reform litigation, the parallels with administrative law suggest grounds for hope. Here are five particulars:

First, several general problematic factors are not present in the administrative law context. Institutional reform cases often involve federalism tensions, because a state or local institutional defendant has been sued in federal court and under federal law.[76] Most structural injunctions require several years of continuing oversight by a trial judge, whereas the overwhelming majority of administrative law controversies, even under sound governance review, would be handled with traditional tools of final disposition, such as the vacate-and-remand-with-guidance order. Complex, polycentric, institutional reform cases can involve many intervenors or amici, who are not only "heard" through paper filings but may participate in the conduct of a trial, the negotiation of a remedial order, and the continuing process of implementation.[77] By contrast, in the administrative law context the principal contribution of extra parties will be to inform the court. Because of the readily available remand device, only in rare circumstances would a court find it necessary to become the political, legislative, or scientific forum, as happens in, for example, school desegregation cases where the public body has defaulted in its role.[78] Even in the

75. 441 U.S. 520, 562 (1979). Earlier, however, in Hutto v. Finney, 437 U.S. 678 (1978), the Court had approved a very detailed remedial order, including financial penalties against the recalcitrant state agency analogous to civil contempt.

76. *See, e.g.*, Rizzo v. Goode, 423 U.S. 362, 378–79 (1976): "Where, as here, the exercise of authority by state officials is attacked, federal courts must be constantly mindful of the 'special delicacy of the adjustment to be preserved between federal equitable power and state administration of its own law.' . . . [A]ppropriate consideration must be given to principles of federalism in determining the availability and scope of equitable relief" (quoting Stefanelli v. Minard, 342 U.S. 117, 120 (1951)).

77. *See* L. Fuller, Anatomy of the Law 104 (1968) ("A judicial hearing may take on . . . something of the nature of a legislative hearing. The analogy to such a hearing becomes even stronger when the brief *amicus curiae* is employed"); Chayes, *supra* n. 65.

78. *See, e.g.*, Smith, *Two Centuries and Twenty-Four Months: A Chronicle of the Struggle to Desegregate the Boston Public Schools, in* H. Kalodner & J. Fishman, eds., Limits of Justice 34–43 (1978).

most difficult of remedial problems, agency inaction, the complexity of the court's supervisory role would be vastly less burdensome, intrusive, and complex than in typical institutional reform suits. For example, the noted case of *Adams v. Richardson* involved a pattern of virtual nonfeasance by the HEW Office of Civil Rights in administrative enforcement of the antidiscrimination requirement in education grant-in-aid programs.[79] The several years of court involvement, including substantial interference with traditional management prerogatives, simply bear no comparison with Judge Johnson's superintendency of the prisons and mental hospitals of Alabama[80] or Judge Garrity's struggle to desegregate Boston's schools.[81]

A second key point in salvaging hope from the experience with institutional reform litigation is that such judicial activity has received bad press, including broad attacks by the Reagan administration and conservative senators on the bugbear of judicial activism. Recent rhetoric in this vein was provided during debate on the nominations of Chief Justice Rehnquist, Justice Scalia, and Judge Robert Bork. Some balance is needed. Although a thorough review of the relevant literature is beyond the scope of this work, I believe a strong case can be made that structural injunctions have produced broad and significant benefits, however exceptional the strains on traditional roles. The literature is vast. The complex task of evaluating the sociological and educational effects of school desegregation, for example, is a cottage industry. And while 20–20 hindsight may identify better remedies in particular circumstances, the general course of the struggle since *Brown* has been a net positive. It may be that prison condition suits have not accomplished a thorough reform of penal institutions nationwide. But I think it plain that, in addition to general consciousness-raising, such suits have been ultimately successful, when carried to the remedial phase, in addressing the most obscene practices of public defendants. Controversial suits have also created public debate and focused official attention on buried problems. The Southern Governors Con-

79. Adams v. Richardson, 480 F.2d 1159 (D.C. Cir. 1973) (en banc) (per curiam), *affirming* 356 F.2d 92 (1973). Court supervision of the department continues. Recent developments are canvassed in the majority and dissenting opinions in Adams v. Bell, 711 F.2d 161 (1983) (en banc). *See also* Women's Equity Action League v. Bell, 743 F.2d 42 (D.C. Cir. 1984).

80. *See, e.g.*, Robbins and Buser, *Punitive Conditions of Prison Confinement: An Analysis of Pugh v. Locke and Federal Supervision of State Penal Administration under the Fifth Amendment*, 29 Stan. L. Rev. 893 (1977); Johnson, *The Role of the Federal Courts in Institutional Litigation*, 32 Ala. L. Rev. 271 (1981).

81. Morgan v. McDonough, 540 F.2d 527 (1st Cir. 1976); 456 F. Supp. 1113 (D. Mass. 1978) (ending receivership of South Boston H.S.); Roberts, *The Extent of Federal Judicial Equitable Power: Receivership of South Boston High School*, 12 New Eng. L. Rev. 55 (1976).

ference, for example, made prison reform a major agenda item in direct response to the rash of structural injunctions and accompanying media coverage. Could legislators and administrators have done better than federal judges? Certainly. But for too long they chose not to, and were successfully sued as a result. It is meaningless to compare real, human judges with hypothetical, ideal officials.

This raises the third point. The courts have often heeded the moral imperative of social reconstruction while political processes defaulted and civic leadership fiddled. It is the default of normal processes of governing that creates both the occasion and the need for judicial intervention. This is the insight of note 4 in *Carolene Products*, as John Hart Ely has elaborated.[82]

Fourth, judges in institutional reform litigation have engaged in reasoning and problem-solving akin to that required in sound governance review, and with some success. That success would be greater in the administrative context, especially with the reformation of roles, conceptual categories, and doctrinal ambitions sketched here. The courts are called on to assess and design *political processes*. This includes both formal processes, such as electoral systems or school board membership, and less formal procedures, such as participation of plaintiff subclasses and nonparty interests in negotiating the remedy. Even the court's decisions about class structure, representative plaintiffs, and intervenors are in important respects judgments about representation, participation, and balance.[83] Although the body of principles and precedents to guide such decisions resemble standard legal doctrine only faintly, judges have been able to function.[84] Who knows how much more coherent that body of principles might be if the politics-judging character were more frankly acknowledged and accepted as a necessary and proper subject for lawmaking? When courts have felt need of extraordinary *expertise*, including managerial expertise, they have been creative in using masters, receivers, expert witnesses, consultants, amici, interveners, and the parties themselves. In just the way that a lay

82. United States v. Carolene Prod. Co., 304 U.S. 144, 152 n. 4 (1938). The obvious analogy is with theories of market failure as the crucial premise for government intervention in the economy; Ely, Democracy and Distrust 101 (1981) ("representation reinforcing" theory of judicial review).

83. Of course, such decisions about participation can determine the substantive framework used by the court, and indeed the development of law more broadly. *See* Bell, *Serving Two Masters: Integration Ideals and Client Interests in School Desegregation Litigation,* 85 Yale L.J. 470 (1976).

84. An impressive example is the work of Judge Lord in the *Reserve Mining* case, before the court of appeals remanded the case to a different judge. *See, e.g.,* the impressive discussion of scientific matters and the description of the complex party structure in 380 F. Supp. 11 (D. Minn. 1974); *see also* 514 F.2d 492 (8th Cir. 1975) (affirming basic remedial injunction).

administrator assembles and manages the technical resources necessary for a regulatory decision, able judges discern the limits of their competence and develop appropriate aids.

Fifth, much institutional reform litigation has been grounded in the Constitution. This tends to promote public acceptance of the court interventions that override legislative judgments of federal or local officials. Yet a remedy packaged as a constitutional norm can impose undesirable rigidity when a more interactive and evolutionary exchange is called for among all parties, all branches of government, and the public. (This echoes my emphasis, in sections 7.3.2 and 7.2.4, on multiple forums and the interactive evolution of sound governance norms.)

In *Rhodes v. Chapman,* the Supreme Court raised this problem expressly,[85] notwithstanding the sound policy reasons to avoid double-celling of the sort at issue. In contrast, if the problem had been one of sound governance judicial review of a federal regulation permitting similar double-celling, the possibilities for thoughtful probing, testing, and exchange would be considerable. If a court were persuaded that the regulation was defective (with respect to the trio of decision making paradigms, including the fidelity to statutory constraints required by adjudicatory fairness), the agency and the Congress would have available several avenues of response, short of amending the Constitution (or changing the Supreme Court!).

The legitimacy of institutional reform litigation has certainly not been beyond challenge. Its ultimate justification, like the justification for sound governance review, must be found in necessity and success. Necessity is born of default—either the failure of politics or the errors of experts or both. Success must be measured not in narrow terms of conformity with well-mannered legal process or reassuringly mechanical judicial choice but in terms of worldly results and broader social ends. Both necessity and success are highly contextual inquiries, but there are undoubtedly general insights to be gleaned. Thorough study of the limits and potential of institutional reform litigation would provide important lessons for a new administrative law.

7.4 Conclusion: The Future Role of Law and Doctrine

In a shift to the sound governance project, the occasion and motive for judicial intervention would change somewhat, even if the tools of intervention remained much the same. There could be circumstances in

85. 452 U.S. 337, 351 (1981).

which the *conventional* vision would lead a court to defer because a trichotomy-based conception of roles would tilt away from intervention, offering plausible but unpersuasive avenues of attack on the agency's discretion;[86] in the *new vision*, however, the court might nevertheless intervene because it sees a possibility that through some form of intervention it can improve the governmental outcome.[87] Or, the conventional approach may have produced intervention but the new approach suggests a different form of intervention—a different remedy, or remand instruction, or explanation. The new approach also offers additional bases for deference, as when the agency's action is on balance supportable through grounding in three paradigms, even though focus on one alone might invite intervention. The discussion in section 6.3.1 concerning required disclosure of political values and decision making illustrates the contrast with some aspects of current doctrine:

- *Vermont Yankee*'s proscription of procedural innovations[88] seriously limits the ability of courts to appraise and reform agency decision making with candor and accuracy; judges easily circumvent the noninterventionist thrust of the decision by focusing on substantive and quasi-procedural weaknesses in the agency's case, but their message can be too obscure and the possibility that the court's misjudgment will be corrected from other quarters is thereby reduced. In a post-trichotomy vision, the emphasis would be on methods to develop judicial and administrative skill in fashioning administrative procedures appropriate to the task. So, the Administrative Procedure Act

---

86. Recall that my thesis is not that the descriptive and conceptual failings of the trichotomy create unqualified doctrinal indeterminacy. We experience considerable predictability in court decisions. (I find the trichotomy's deficiencies so striking that I would guess that administrative law rates as one of the least predictable fields.) My thesis is that the predictability is the result not of doctrinal discipline so much as of the application of shared subjective conceptions of judicial role and institutional competence—conceptions out of touch with the demands of reality or logic, and hence inviting manipulation. Judging a given judicial review problem fairly, one is hard put to offer a principled basis for preferring the analytical path chosen from those not even considered.

87. How much of a possibility must there be? Quantification is impossible, and one must perhaps resort to such indeterminate phrases as "reasonable possibility" or "clear possibility" to convey a sense of the hierarchy or presumptions operating as between the judge's views and those of the agency. It seems useful to distinguish between the burden an agency might have to persuade the reviewing court (and the public) that its decisional methods are sound and the judge's burden if he or she is inclined to impose an alternative method. The judge might feel unpersuaded as to the soundness of the agency's method but uncommitted to a particular alternative. The remand might be for more explanation or express consideration of alternatives.

88. *See* sec. 7.2.3.

might be read to authorize judicial review of agency procedural designs under the *Chenery II* abuse of discretion standard rather than making hybrid procedures a matter of essentially unreviewable discretion, per *Vermont Yankee*.

- *Chevron USA, Inc. v. NRDC*,[89] the "emissions bubble" case, is similarly troubling in its unrealistic emphasis on the process of reading congressional tea leaves and its willingness to read discretionary agency choices as matters of politics rather than as reviewable science and fairness. In a post-trichotomy approach, courts would more carefully audit the completeness of the political considerations that enter the agency's decision making, examine the reasonableness of the agency's decision not to require additional scientific support for its position, and insist on evaluation efforts over time to assure the public and the agency that the course chosen does fulfill the claims made for it. In short, the emphasis would be on sound governance rather than on questions of deference or the allocation of discretion.

- In *Sierra Club v. Costle* the inclination to assume a benign role for White House, OMB, and congressional staff would be replaced by more candid attention to the nature of the arguments and pressures brought to bear on agency action. Courts should both encourage more disclosure and, in partnership with the other branches, evolve standards concerning the appropriate limits and documentation of such pressures.[90] If the EPA tilted the regulations at issue in *Sierra Club* to favor eastern coal interests because President Carter could not afford to antagonize Senate Majority Leader Robert Byrd (D-W.Va.), whose support the president needed for ratification of the SALT II nuclear arms treaty, present doctrine would probably not discover that pressure and, if it did, would have only blunt tools with which to appraise its legality. Blindness to the dangers of improper influence is no substitute for a genuine effort to distinguish good and bad influences on governance.[91]

89. 467 U.S. 837 (1984).

90. Executive Orders and some statutory provisions are already going in this direction. The 1980 amendments to the Federal Trade Commission Act, like the Clean Air amendments at issue in *Sierra Club v. Costle*, expressly address such procedural issues, although the treatment is incomplete.

91. In referring to good and bad influences I do not reincorporate the trichotomy's conceptual failing related to the attributive duality of the trio of decision making meth-

The kernel of a very different administrative law is contained in the seemingly incremental reforms I sketched in chapter 6. The implications are clearer now. This is a pleasing continuity, to be sure, but what else might the future hold?

Doctrine—subject to evolution in the manner of common law, with instruction by litigants and correction by statute—would also speak to the range of newly explicit inquiries undertaken by courts. For example:

- Which interests, and which representatives, must participate in explicitly political bargaining in the course of agency policymaking? Though it may be rare that judges will feel competent to specify participation in detail, greater familiarity with the workings of the politics paradigm (as now revealed) should lead to greater competence. And though participation choices of this sort will never be as familiar to judges as say, decisions about standing to intervene, or certification of class actions and class representatives, judges might well participate quite forcefully in requiring agencies to make participation decisions in the first instance in a defensibly thorough and rational manner.

- What methods of analysis, and what administrative procedures, should be used to decide putatively scientific disputes, such as the reliability of a particular study or the desirability of further research? Courts now have only modest handles on such issues, yet the quality of policy choices is highly affected by them. What is more troubling, ample evidence casts doubt on the rigor with which agency decision makers approach these questions. There is every reason to hope that courts, with some institutional restructuring and differences in personnel, could participate with agencies in the evolution of norms and doctrine in this area. When is cost-benefit analysis required in order to make sound policy judgments? When

---

ods. That failing, as discussed in sec. 2.5, is the result of judicial unwillingness or inability to test the normative assertions of the trichotomy against an accurate description of agency decision making, combined with the effort to use these poorly informed, prescriptive attributions as the basis for scaling judicial deference. With a shift in attention away from deference, the normative attributes of the trichotomy's paradigms no longer serve as a set of untestable premises prejudicing judicial review. Instead, our recognition of attributive duality now provides the agenda for investigation and quality-control, telling us where to search for flaws in the agency action. As to when and whether the role of politics is benign, *see* sec. 6.1.

is experimentation desirable, rather than flat and permanent rules? None of these matters is intrinsically unmanageable by judges, given appropriate individual training, institutional support, and purposefully structured litigation; we do not consider them unmanageable for generalist administrators.

- How should courts weigh informal evidence of legislative intent, from press interviews to authoritative journalism? In multiplying the channels of information available to them, judges will increase the data but also the "noise." Patterns of reliable screening and testing would be needed to separate accurate from spurious messages, an effort rarely and imperfectly undertaken with conventional materials of legislative history.

As these points suggest, a modernist court would be directly involved in the problem of improving the quality of the administrative decision making process. In the mode of harder-look review, presented in chapter 6, judicial forays would initially be largely quasi-procedural, stressing disclosure and explanation. In the full development of sound governance review, the procedure-substance distinction would recede in importance, with contingent competence more determinative of a court's capacity to discern the occasions and means of intervention. The tools of review and supervision might be somewhat different, in that courts would more readily pose pointed substantive questions for the agency to answer, require the agency to promulgate rules detailing its methods or substantive views, and press for disclosure of internal deliberations. But the importance of the shift in administrative law, and indeed the reason to be hopeful about it, is that the courts would far more certainly be the ally of the agency in pursuit of a common goal. This is much less clear when the posture of administrative law is defined in terms of suspicion and control.

A truly modernist vision of administrative law strikes a different posture and holds out a different kind of promise. Not the tight control of agency and judicial discretion, because that is impossible: the post-trichotomy model of law would transmute the deathless discretion permitted and generated by the present doctrinal structure into a different form of discretion, centered on the evolution and application of norms directly tied to a modernist objective.

The promise is not unqualified, however. The substitution of "sound governance" for "control of discretion" is simultaneously a shift in focus and adoption of an overarching principle. Principles turn into rules. There is every reason to expect that sound governance review, when fully elaborated and functioning, would be subject to my own critique of descriptive accuracy, categorization failures, and attributive duality. Such may be the destiny of ideas that strain to be guides.[92] My defense of this essay is mere hope, not proof: As we grope to define sound governance and re-form institutional arrangements, we will inevitably learn a great deal. Eventually, the new doctrine will become calcified, loose touch with reality, and become increasingly irrelevant to the issues of that future day. Old categories will become delicate deceits, and old problems will seem boringly futile to younger generations. My speculative image of administrative law is certainly not the final vision. It has, like many ideas about law, both the limitation and the virtue of being an evolutionary response to simmering needs.

The central aspect of this evolutionary image is partnership. The court joins the agency and the legislature to confront directly the problem of governance in a complicated and uncertain world. Administrative law, far from an inappropriate charter for that partnership, is peculiarly called to the task. We want a government of laws not simply because that notion suggests order. Law should also nurture the development of society's collective vision of a just and prosperous order, to the extent one can discern it. Implementing such an inchoate, gossamer vision is an undertaking so difficult that every social institution must be harnessed.

92. *See* Kennedy, *Form and Substance in Private Law Adjudication*, 89 Harv. L. Rev. 1685 (1976).

Index